Walter Benjamin and Theology

John D. Caputo, *series editor*

PERSPECTIVES IN
CONTINENTAL
PHILOSOPHY

COLBY DICKINSON
and STÉPHANE SYMONS

EDITORS

Walter Benjamin and Theology

FORDHAM UNIVERSITY PRESS
New York ■ 2016

Library of Congress Cataloging-in-Publication Data

Names: Dickinson, Colby, editor.
Title: Walter Benjamin and theology / edited by Colby Dickinson and Stéphane Symons.
Description: First edition. | New York, NY : Fordham University Press, 2016. | Series: Perspectives in Continental philosophy | Includes bibliographical references and index.
Identifiers: LCCN 2015034640 | ISBN 9780823270170 (cloth : alk. paper) | ISBN 9780823270187 (pbk. : alk. paper)
Subjects: LCSH: Benjamin, Walter, 1892–1940. | Religion.
Classification: LCC B3209.B584 W339 2016 | DDC 193—dc23
LC record available at http://lccn.loc.gov/2015034640

Printed in the United States of America

18 17 16   5 4 3 2 1

First edition

Contents

Introduction

COLBY DICKINSON
AND STÉPHANE SYMONS

In a famous letter written to Max Horkheimer in March 1937, Walter Benjamin describes his philosophy as "something that forbids us to conceive of history as fundamentally atheological, little as it may be granted to us to try to write it with immediately theological concepts."[1] In *The Arcades Project*, he writes: "[My work is] related to theology as blotting pad is related to ink. It is saturated with it. Were one to go by the blotter, however, nothing of what is written would remain."[2] For a thinker so decisive to critical literary, cultural, political, and aesthetic writings over the past half century, Benjamin's relationship to theological matters has received far less attention than it should have, perhaps due to the many obscure allusions and contradictions that surrounded his taking up this theme throughout his own lifetime. Numerous scholars of Benjamin's work agree, however, that the time has come to reassess what stake the theological has within his writings, even and especially if such a reassessment prompts us to reconsider what the nature of the theological might even be in the first place.

Connecting the Dots

From the 1970s onward, the writings of Benjamin have known a success that is, in its intensity and diversity, comparable to almost no other postwar philosopher. The number of articles and books that have been published concerning his work has increased steadily for forty years to the point where it has become almost impossible for anyone working in the continental philosophical tradition to keep up with all relevant secondary literature. Characteristic of this situation is also the fact that Benjamin's texts have found a readership both within and outside of academia, and thus have had an impact on scholars with the most diverse backgrounds. What is more, almost all the major thinkers of our day have been profoundly influenced by the many facets of Benjamin's philosophical oeuvre. Philosophers as diverse as Jacques Derrida, Judith Butler, Giorgio Agamben, Slavoj Žižek, Antonio Negri, Jacques Rancière, Philippe Lacoue-Labarthe, George Steiner, and Samuel Weber have picked up threads that Benjamin had left unfinished, thereby granting him a continuous but oftentimes silent voice within the majority of contemporary debates within continental thought.

However, turning to Benjamin's thoughts on the theological at this precise moment in history is fruitful for reasons other than the number of scholars who have taken an interest in his work. There has been something of a shift within contemporary continental thought itself—often paraded as a substantial "return to religion"—that beckons us to consider theological motifs anew. From the steady phenomenological gaze toward the religious—as witnessed in the work of Jean-Luc Marion, Michel Henry, and Jean-Yves Lacoste, among others—to John Caputo and Gianni Vattimo's championing of "weak thought" in relation to both theological and philosophical sources, to Mark C. Taylor's efforts to develop a postmodern "a/theology," to Jacques Derrida's and Jean-Luc Nancy's various "deconstructions" of Christianity and religious identity in general, to Alain Badiou, Giorgio Agamben, Stanislas Breton and Slavoj Žižek and their interests in in Saint Paul's writings, there have been many reasons indeed for taking a closer look at philosophical readings of theology.[3] Although a good share of these contemporary critical efforts have maintained a more or less direct link to theological themes and writings, several of them have consciously built upon Benjamin's more indirect engagements with theology, a coupling of voices that has no doubt produced intriguing intermixtures, but may also produce some further dissonance over time.

In a period spanning but a mere couple of recent decades much has been said about this relationship between Benjamin's overall philosophical thought (including his political and materialist views) and theological issues, although it also seems that scholars can agree on little more than the idea that a *direct* link between the two is not tenable. Thus, in his theses "On the Concept of History" (also known as the "Theses on the Philosophy of History")—which, after "The Work of Art in the Age of Its Technological Reproducibility," is arguably the essay for which he is most known—Benjamin famously likens theology to "a hunchbacked dwarf" who has to be simultaneously "enlisted" and yet also "kept out of sight."[4] Focusing on the ways in which a "weak messianic power" could be said to aid in redeeming the past, to foster "remembrance, not resurrection,"[5] Benjamin's work cannot simply be a form of secularized messianism, as one might find conveniently assembled in a Marxist idiom.[6] Rather, something else is at work in his a/theological reflections, even if indirectly so. Trying to assess just what *is* at work in his thoughts and writings, as well as the impact that such formulations might have upon future theoretical interventions, is precisely why an engagement with Benjamin's more theologically minded writings is overdue.

It is precisely on account of his indirect connection with theology that Benjamin's views remain astutely relevant for today's world, although in a way that still needs to be further discerned. In the more or less forty-year-old discipline that is Benjamin studies, there have been a variety of attempts to illuminate the theological elements latent within his eclectic and occasional writings, often as a means of uniting their disparate focal points. This has often led scholars to take up certain religious themes as a central symbolic feature of his writing.[7] Yet such engagements, although undeniably crucial to comprehending his thought, remain in need of deeper systematic analysis. This book is but a series of gestures that point in a general direction for further explorations.

One of the reasons for this theological lacuna in contemporary research on Benjamin is the extraordinary complexity of the relationship between the theological and the philosophical in his work, and the reality that he wrote neither a clear elaboration on the theological elements at play in his theoretical views, nor practiced any religion in a sustained manner—the latter being a point that was often a source of tension between Benjamin and Gershom Scholem. Benjamin had once mentioned in a letter to Martin Buber that Judaism "was one of the most important and persistent objects of [his] thinking";[8] and yet, as he grew older, "the terms of his balance between Jewish identity and work on German traditions shifted: he did not abandon his idealist commitments, but he began to mobilize his Jewish identity in the process of recasting them."[9] The complexity of such a "recasting," as John McCole puts it, is precisely what makes this conjunction so extraordinarily relevant, and it sharply increases the urgency of the demand for a volume of essays that highlights this topic. As Sigrid Weigel reminds us in her book-length study of Benjamin's various theologically themed writings, Benjamin's thought "can in no way be called *theological*"; yet, she stresses a moment later, "it also cannot be described as *secular*" either.[10] What Weigel illustrates through such a juxtaposition is a more than problematic tension—it is in some ways *the* problematic tension manifest in his work and, for this very reason, it is doubly difficult to isolate within Benjamin's oeuvre.

Even though this book focuses on the relationship between Benjamin's philosophy and its possible connections to the theological, this does not mean that it establishes him as a theological thinker in the traditional sense of the word. As Andrew Benjamin, one of the more astute and prolific Benjamin scholars to comment on such themes over the past two decades, puts it: Benjamin's engagement with theological topics and concepts "is not straightforward Judeo-Christian theology, but rather a theology of the missed or distorted—hunchbacked—possibilities, a theology of missed, distorted or hunchbacked time."[11] For this reason, the philosophical stakes of this book are high, and yet its interpretative perspective must inevitably remain somewhat broad.

This book, therefore, aims for nothing less than a novel intervention into a field of inquiry. It is not a mere addition to the debates that started decades ago; rather it seeks to establish a new site from which to address not just the issue of Benjamin's relationship with theology but also all the crucial aspects that Benjamin himself grappled with when addressing the field and methodology of theological inquiry. In bringing together some of the most renowned experts from both sides of the Atlantic, this book aims to ring in a new phase in Anglophone Benjamin scholarship. Whereas scholars like Richard Wolin, Susan Buck-Morss, Irvin Wohlfarth, Beatrice Hanssen, and Andrew Benjamin have produced groundbreaking work on various key questions raised in Benjamin's work, this book takes a broader perspective by focusing on the topic of theology within Benjamin's oeuvre in its entirety.

One could argue that the theological elements of his thinking have remained to a certain extent ignored throughout all those years (in a 1934 letter to Benjamin, Adorno termed their type of thinking an "inverse theology"[12]), because they have influenced and impregnated his philosophical, political, literary, and aesthetic views in ways that were—however irreducible and profound they may be—oftentimes kept in the dark by Benjamin himself. However, Benjamin certainly seeks to provide a helpful corrective to those forms of mythology that continue to distort the modern world, and he does so in ways similar to Adorno and Horkheimer's counternarrative to the mythological as taken up in their *Dialectic of Enlightenment*.[13] Indeed, he was concerned with developing a counternarrative that was not yet afraid to cross the boundaries between the theological and the atheological, subverting and distorting the more traditional forms of religious belief and practice that saturated the Western world. What is clear from all of this is that, as Howard Eiland and Michael W. Jennings describe, "the profound theological interest that animated his writing from the beginning, moving deeper and deeper underground as he grew older, was at odds with all organized religion."[14]

It is not hard to imagine then why Benjamin sought to keep a certain distance from religious and theological ideas. And yet the question remains: Why did Benjamin find it so conducive to engage with theological concepts? What is it about being "at odds" with religious tradition that is also, somehow, a part of "being religious"? There is undoubtedly a certain *theological* impetus within his work that stands in permanent contrast to *religion* and that opens up new avenues of thought that are full of radical potential.[15] The "weak messianic forces" he spoke of toward the end of his life would seem to signal a clear movement in this direction, as they work from *within* a given history in order to, in turn, undo it. As such, we might suggest, following Andrew Benjamin, that indeed "theology becomes the theological-political as a result of having effected a constitutive separation from religion."[16] A certain form of a/theology, in this manner, becomes that which provides the best possible critique of religious doctrines and structures, cultures, and peoples. As McCole describes the appeal of theological language in this regard, "messianic language provided him with a resistant and resilient idiom rather than an inventory of fixed concepts."[17] Benjamin's focus, as such, is not on doctrine or dogma per se, but rather on learning to see the world entirely anew. It is little surprise that there has subsequently developed a certain resonance, although also at times a (confessional-theological) divergence, with several key theological thinkers of the past century who had sought to critique traditional religious concepts from within a theological context, most notably including Jürgen Moltmann, Johann Baptist Metz, and even Karl Barth, as Michael Jennings has argued.[18] It is precisely when "exporting" Benjamin's most salient thoughts that we begin to see just how massive his impact has been upon reshaping the more traditional landscapes of disciplinary thought.

In this vein of inquiry, it has been somewhat remarkable that perceptive readers of Benjamin's work—from philosophers eager to develop his theoretical insights, to political and cultural theorists looking to expand upon his social analysis—have steadily increased the visibility of the a/theological within his oeuvre, especially when the author at hand is trying to reconceive the discipline within which they situate themselves. Take, for example, Slavoj Žižek and his use of Benjamin in *The Puppet and the Dwarf,* a work that contains an implicit homage to Benjamin even as it tries to somewhat "reverse" his terms.[19] Moreover, Benjamin continuously resurfaces in Žižek's voluminous corpus at key junctures, featuring prominently at those times when Žižek's efforts are aimed at reviving the liberatory potential of the Judeo-Christian heritage.[20] Likewise, we might look at Eric Santner's creative rereadings of Benjamin, wherein one encounters the "radical otherness" of what lies wholly within the "natural," that which is found among the ruins of history and which, as Santner describes it, both "demands and resists symbolization."[21] Somewhat akin to Santner, Matthias Fritsch reads Benjamin as demonstrating how this "radical otherness" within history, and as it functions in the "fight for the oppressed past," may sometimes result in "no final day of redemption," but rather a complete redefining of time itself, a notion permeated with theological implications.[22] Peter Fenves's study on the concept of time within Benjamin's oeuvre similarly advances a detailed examination of such possibilities, concluding with the claim that "messianic time is not another time; it is just time—time and nothing but 'plastic' time."[23] This points us toward what Fenves further calls the "messianic resolution" of the tension between history and time when history essentially forms itself more in accord with "natural" time.[24]

The stakes latent within such thoughts for the complete reformulation of theology are highly significant, and what, in many ways, Giorgio Agamben has had in mind throughout his own long engagement with Benjamin's often fragmentary, albeit highly intriguing, career. As the Italian editor of Benjamin's writings, and as the individual who discovered a good deal of previously unseen Benjamin work in the Bibliothèque nationale de France, Agamben's profound interpretation of Benjamin in his *The Time That Remains*—that Benjamin is a "secret" interpreter of Pauline thought and is therefore utilized through his use of the messianic as an autodeconstructive force as a highly significant counterpoint to institutionalized religious forms—not only confirms Benjamin's presence within disciplinary boundaries as the great "deconstructor" of normative claims; it also provides justification for the demand that Benjamin's work be read more closely in conjunction with the remnants of the a/theological that are strewn across our modern world.[25] Indeed, the theological, in Agamben's eyes, is one of Benjamin's "secret indexes" that permeate the strategic use of concepts in the modern era.[26]

Another way we might determine the weight of those theological ideas that underlie Benjamin's philosophy is by starting with their relevance for issues related to violence, justice, and state politics. In this manner, Judith Butler's recent discussion of Benjamin's work in her book *Parting Ways* can be understood as having prepared the way for this new intervention into Anglophone scholarship. Butler engages with the most urgent political layer of Benjamin's philosophy and understands that this political commitment can never be disentangled from his preoccupations with religion. One of the key questions that consequently arises from her work, as well as from the present volume, is whether Benjamin's own dealings with Judaism do not grant us the most urgently needed tools to counter current forms of political religion, warning us against the detrimental dynamic behind identity politics and the political exploitation of teleological thinking. Moreover, the volume brings out the necessary subtleties and ambivalences of Benjamin's relationship with theological debates since it makes palpable why, for Benjamin, nihilism is an appealing philosophical stance, while also not denying that, from his perspective, Judaism and Christianity might not seem so alien to each other after all.

Benjamin's final focus on a "weak messianic force" moving through history, and in contrast to a mythical conception of fate that towers over it—one of the most significant contrasts taken up in his work—prompts him to envision the messianic as a "state of emergency" in contrast to the otherwise sovereign or even totalitarian states of the world.[27] This translation of a religious concept into a secularized one amounts to an interesting reversal of the "state of emergency" that has been, and continues to be, invoked by political systems in a move to overstep their legitimate powers: rather than portray it as the justification for sovereign power, it dislocates such a form of power by *suspending the suspension itself.* Agamben describes this process as the fundamental Pauline maneuver (the "division of division itself") and it pertains, in Agamben's reading, to that part of Benjamin's philosophy that is most theologically inspired.[28]

As has already been hinted at, Benjamin's implicit "double reference" to both profane and religious resonances of modern concepts presently in use—specifically regarding his rereadings of the "holy" and secularization alike—contains deep political implications, perhaps nowhere more discernable than in his early essay on the nature of violence.[29] His "Critique of Violence" points us toward comprehending a form of "divine violence" that "can never completely escape the contamination from the dialectic . . . of the mythological foundation of right and its historical conservation."[30] And yet it does serve to "interrupt" its narrativizing of history and the mythological foundations it grants to society and law. Such are the dynamics at work as well in his later theses on history. As is evident in that context, and as Eli Friedlander has considered it elsewhere, "destruction viewed as divine force that obliterates the traces of misdeeds can be seen as redeeming life for humanity as a whole even in the face of human violence in history."[31] This "storm" moving throughout history, as Benjamin would render it, is subsequently "always something related to the divine or the absolute," and is, as such, what the messianic force moving through history is all about.[32]

Benjamin's understanding of a "nonteleological" divine violence, that eradicates all mythology from our world, allows us to reconceive of the divine as "the name for what opposes myth," as Judith Butler phrases it.[33] Rather than read this particular essay as "too Heideggerian, too messianico-Marxist or archeo-eschatological," as Jacques Derrida has already famously done,[34] what we are left with in Butler's reading—one more fruitful for an a/theological interpretation—is "*not* a vengeful God but a God who is seeking to destroy vengeance itself. And, if it is a God, it is in war against another, one that opposes the lightning bolts of divine wrath, one that precedes it, sweeping away the marks of misdeeds and so foiling plots of revenge."[35] It is in this sense that we might read Benjamin's views on divine violence side by side with his ideas on "pure means" (the noncoercive apprehension of human action) and look toward something like Johann Baptist Metz's Benjamin-influenced attempt to redefine religion solely as "interruption."[36] Here, again, something of the "theological" which is also not quite "theological" is exposed as the very force that can critique the institutionalized religious as well the mythical. It is for this reason that Butler's use of Benjamin in the context of political representation is so significant, for "Benjamin's messianic politics," if read alongside the work of Hannah Arendt, as Butler proceeds to do, is the very thing which opens us up to concepts such as diaspora, plurality, and cohabitation.[37] As the history of religion in the West attests, these concepts are as central to theological thought as they have been to our shared political realities, although we must continue to discern exactly what their meaning may be for both present and future generations.

An Overview of the Volume

Creative readings that open us toward the a/theological as a new way to think through the political theological resonances that lie deep within a modern Western consciousness are very much what the present collection of essays is about and where its strength is to be found. From the outset, this volume turns directly to the theological elements resonant in Benjamin's thinking and explores them on their own terms, hoping to provide new insights into Benjamin's work if perceived in interaction with its uniquely theological elements. The essays provided by Annika Thiem and Peter Fenves, for example, analyze the "metaphysics of transience" that is deployed in his quintessential "Theological-Political Fragment" (1921), a short and enigmatic text that will resurface in many different contexts throughout this volume. Sigrid Weigel and Michael Jennings examine the twofold background behind Benjamin's philosophical account of life and the recurrence, in different disguises, of the concept of an "apokatastatic will" throughout his writings. The sharpest expression of such a "metaphysics of transience" resonating with apokatastatic elements can be encountered in a notoriously complex line from the "Theological-Political Fragment": "Nature is messianic by reason of its eternal and total passing away."[38] This statement, however puzzling it may be, casts light on at least one of the most fundamental insights underlying Benjamin's theological views. As Thiem describes in her contribution, for Benjamin, "the issue of transience is always . . . related to the possibility of redemption."

It is crucial to stress the lack of immediacy of the connection between transience and redemption (nihilism and happiness) since, as Benjamin makes plain from his *The Origin of German Tragic Drama* onward, there is nothing messianic about nature *as such*. In *The Origin of German Tragic Drama*, Benjamin addresses the topic of the "physiognomy of the nature-history" as the "form of the ruin." The German tragic drama (*Trauerspiel*) authors are set apart from the Renaissance authors in that they reduce the historical to the merely natural ("nature-history") and nature itself to "the over-ripeness and decay of her creations . . . [in which] they saw eternal transience." This "saturnine vision" that "piles up fragments ceaselessly" is the "polar opposite to the idea of transfigured nature": "The Baroque work of art wants only to endure, and clings with all its senses to the eternal."[39] These same dystopic views on a merely natural temporality of eternal recurrence form the background of Benjamin's criticism of the "dogma" of the sacredness of life,[40] and of "a conception of history that considers only shallow, causal forms";[41] they are also behind his reflections on "Modernity as Hell" (Auguste Blanqui's *Eternity by the Stars*, fashion's repetitive infatuation with novelty) as well as his famous interpretation of Paul Klee's "Angelus Novus" (which Benjamin cast as the "Angel of History") who "sees one single catastrophe, which keeps piling wreckage upon wreckage and hurls it at his feet."[42] There is, in short, nothing redemptive about the movement of life as such and no form of transcendence can be thought to spontaneously arise from within the merely natural. Thiem's essay puts such insights into stark relief against the backdrop of a complete reconsideration of history as we typically construct and utilize it. And Fenves's contribution is very illuminating in this regard, since it lays bare how Benjamin's understanding of the possibility of life's *Vollendung* ("completion" or "consummation") entails a fundamental criticism of the *Lebensphilosophie* of some of his colleagues: life can only express a state of completion to the extent that it makes visible a "fullness" that cannot be reduced to it.

Starting from the same complex issues, while also branching out to new ground, Sigrid Weigel's article further analyzes this realm that is irreducible to natural or mere life. In her essay, the concept of fidelity is read as "the logos of the supernatural duration of love," indicating as such the temporality of a *decision* that is capable of securing a space for transcendence. Although it may not appear at times as if she deals expressly with the theme of the a/theological in her essay, its very premise circulates and redefines our approach to the question of what constitutes the theological in Benjamin's work in the first place. It is also, for this reason, a fitting complement to her book-length study of Benjamin's writings on the "supernatural" and the "holy."

The four essays that make up the first part of the present volume—Thiem, Fenves, Weigel and Jennings—all revolve around an awareness that what Benjamin calls "messianic" in his work is necessarily intertwined with a form of disparity: the experience of transcendence does not indicate the ambiguous and, to a certain extent even pernicious, merging of the profane and the absolute, but it marks off what Weigel has called the "double reference" of those two realms, presenting them *alongside* each other.[43] From the outset, it should be obvious that Benjamin's "weak messianic force" could never be accompanied by anything but a "weak messianic theology," one perhaps wholly unrecognizable to theology proper as a disciplinary endeavor, especially since only a "profane illumination" will go beyond the "religious" to shed a light upon things.[44] The concept of "weakness" emphasizes the finite and contingent character of the messianic force and reading the "theological" *in* or *out of*, *through* or *beyond* Benjamin's work has therefore been a perplexing but also necessary exercise for many throughout the years since his death.[45]

As Benjamin himself has shown, the actuality of a given form of thought does not merely depend on any recognized resemblances with another form of thought, however obvious these parallels may be. The utmost relevance of a given historical event can in his mind only become present in and through a *critical* moment that understands itself simultaneously as *different* from that event.[46] For this reason, the argument about the contemporary relevance of Benjamin's relation with theology cannot be based solely on an awareness of the continuities that exist between his philosophy and that of some of today's most influential scholars. Such a stance needs to go hand-in-hand with a full-fledged and systematic understanding of the *particularities* that color his work and the intellectual climate in which he was active, a point that Jennings's essay drives home with particular clarity.

As Peter E. Gordon puts it in a recent essay that draws an encompassing portrait of the field of theology during the Weimar era—and which is Jennings's most direct subject matter in his contribution to this volume—

the majority of its most well-known proponents revolved around a form of "crisis theology." In this manner, the possibility of an encounter with the divine is in various ways connected with forms of irrationalism and even Gnostic thought, escaping all doctrinal categorization and affirming the chasm between the transcendent and the profane.[47] Similarly, Benjamin's own theological views need to be situated, in the formula of Anson Rabinbach, "between Enlightenment and Apocalypse," a theme to which Jennings's essay is direly attentive. For an understanding of the stakes of Benjamin's relationship with theology, the impact of World War I and the shadow that was cast by the rise of fascism can hardly be exaggerated. We are even tempted to make the same claim about Benjamin's perpetually nascent theology as the one made by Peter Osborne to qualify Benjamin's cultural theories: "it is the first world war which provides [its] traumatic background . . . , fascism its ultimate context."[48]

The second part of the book seeks to identify and understand the various religious and philosophical connections that have helped shape the most important theological strands within Benjamin's thinking by addressing the larger historical and intellectual network of Benjamin's dealings with theology. Howard Eiland's essay, for example, renders a substantial analysis of the deep Jewish backdrop that is interwoven with Benjamin's philosophy and, through such a study, allows his thought to surface in a much fuller complexity. In many ways motivated by the same philosophical and historical interests as Jennings, Eiland's Judaic account of Benjamin is expanded through essays that determine the broader intellectual influences that cannot be overlooked in assessing the theological substructure of Benjamin's ideas. Howard Caygill's essay on Benjamin's "natural theology"—which explores new relationships between the divine and humanity via Benjamin's "negative natural theology of an uncreated cosmos"—is published alongside an essay by and the lecture notes of Jacob Taubes, thus making palpable the fact that one needs to look as far back as Friedrich Nietzsche, Arthur Stanley Eddington, or Gnosticism in order to fully comprehend the theological genealogy behind Benjamin's philosophy. In Caygill's view, Benjamin understood both the theological significance of the modern relation to the cosmos and the redemptive significance of the "paroxysm of genuine cosmic experience." This is a form of redemption that, according to Caygill, refers to a natural rather than messianic theology, that is to say, to the conjuncture of contemporary cosmology and mystic theology that Benjamin sees at work in Eddington and Kafka.

There is no doubt that Benjamin's theologized conceptualization of history and of the *Jetztzeit* ("now-time") had a significant impact upon Taubes's formulations of Western eschatology, something that scholars are only now coming to recognize.[49] Having lain almost dormant for quite some time before scholars noticed the significance of his provocative commentary, Taubes's reading of Benjamin opens up an alleged path of Pauline influence—a point that Agamben declares more forthrightly in his own commentary on Paul's letter to the Romans;[50] it also demonstrates the resonances between Benjamin and Karl Barth noted by Jennings.[51] The two essays by Taubes—which appear here for the first time in English translation—are central pieces in Benjamin scholarship that have not been accessed as much as they should have been since their original publication. Perhaps it was Benjamin's desire, like Barth before him, Taubes suggests, to rid theological thinking of its philosophical presuppositions—a claim made in his, now highly influential, lectures on the political theology of Paul.[52] Yet, despite labeling Benjamin as a modern-day Marcionite, Taubes in some sense also sought to embody the task of the "messianic historian" that Benjamin had outlined in his own work, a fact that makes these essays that much more noteworthy.[53] Such insights into Benjamin's legacy with regard to the theological make Taubes an absolutely necessary conversation partner in this volume.

The essays in the third part explore how important theological intuitions surface in contexts that are seemingly unrelated to them, but which, in many ways, undergird the strain of the a/theological throughout Benjamin's oeuvre. Giorgio Agamben's important introduction to Benjamin's book on Baudelaire—published here for the first time in English—is a crucial text in this regard, since it outlines the deep connection between Benjamin's views on theological issues and his views on Marxism and modernity. In highlighting this precise connection, the volume follows the example of Michael Löwy who has explored the "elective affinity, mutual attraction and reciprocal reinforcement of the two approaches," thus looking for the unity within Benjamin's work and distancing itself from the so-called materialist school (Brecht), theological school (Scholem), and the school of contradiction (Habermas, Tiedemann).[54] Agamben's preface to Benjamin's study draws deeply upon those final phases of Benjamin's own scholarship wherein Baudelaire's writings proved so important in the sketching of his *Arcades Project* and his late reflections on history. Although the essay may not take as direct a route toward the theological as Agamben has done elsewhere throughout his oeuvre, it is nonetheless essential for situating Benjamin's work on Baudelaire within his late-phase emphasis on specific theological elements within his writing.

Eli Friedlander, Astrid Deuber-Mankowsky, and Judith Butler turn to Benjamin's political views and his early essay on violence in order to assess the proper nature of what he has famously termed "divine violence."

Friedlander focuses on the *redemptive* logic that Benjamin discovers in specific forms of dissolution and annihilation and clarifies why and how this needs to be differentiated from what he has called "mythical violence." Concepts like guilt, fate, justice, and forgiveness prove to be indispensable for a further elucidation of the stakes of Benjamin's philosophy of violence and, in Friedlander's contribution, this discussion is broached by referring to Benjamin's philosophy of language and, ultimately, through an exploration of the complex issue of meaning and its actualization. Friedlander, moreover, brings to the surface how Benjamin's concept of "pure means" (instrumentality without ends) should not be confused with "means for pure ends," thereby marking off the difference between actions that can, at most, dissolve a conflict on the one hand and true morality or justice on the other.

Deuber-Mankowsky and Butler elaborate further on the idea that justice depends on the destruction of the mythic manifestation of violence and thereby address the political, legal, and economic layers of Benjamin's essay. They explain how Benjamin's conceptual vocabulary has drawn inspiration from other Jewish thinkers such as Hermann Cohen, but they also focus on his analysis of the connection between capitalism and religion. In a short but important text, "Capitalism as Religion" (1921), Benjamin considers capitalism not, as Weber thought, a "formation conditioned by religion" but as a "purely cultic religion";[55] capitalism is "the first instance of a cult that creates guilt [*Schuld*] not atonement."[56]

The book concludes by engaging Benjamin's thought directly in dialogue with more recent developments within theology. Hille Haker's contribution responds to almost all of the other essays in the book but not without complementing some of the claims made by other authors. Haker's piece focuses on the manner in which Benjamin's dealings with theology open up possibilities of a new theology within a Catholic or Christian context. By zooming in on the work of Johann Baptist Metz's political theology, Haker explores the possible connections between a philosophy that is confronted with its own limits, thus pointing toward a theology that, as she puts it, "takes serious the political dimension of its own tradition." Both Benjamin and Metz, despite some fundamental differences between their perspectives, share a concern with the connection between justice, forgiveness, and remembrance. Not merely a political-philosophical concept, justice is for both men an ethical concept that presupposes the possibility of a completion in forgiveness and a redemption of the past that can, at most, be expected. Hoping that a more sustained discussion of Benjamin's work in relation to theology will continue to emerge over time, Haker takes a look at the manner in which Benjamin's thought has been received by the discipline of theology proper, as well as what kind of a legacy Benjamin might continue to have within theology in the near future.

Notes

1. Walter Benjamin, *The Arcades Project* (Cambridge, MA: Harvard University Press, 2004), 471.

2. Ibid.

3. For an overview of these movements within a French setting, for example, see Enda McCaffrey, *The Return of Religion in France: From Democratisation to Postmetaphysics* (London: Palgrave-Macmillan, 2009).

4. Walter Benjamin, "On the Concept of History," in *Selected Writings*, 4 vols., ed. Michael W. Jennings et al. (Cambridge, MA: Harvard University Press, 1996–2003), 4:389.

5. John D. Caputo, *The Weakness of God: A Theology of the Event* (Bloomington: Indiana University Press, 2006), 95.

6. See Matthias Fritsch, *The Promise of Memory: History and Politics in Marx, Benjamin, and Derrida* (Albany: State University of New York Press, 2005), 47.

7. From Richard Wolin's *Walter Benjamin: An Aesthetic of Redemption* (Berkeley: University of California Press, 1994) to James R. Martel's *Divine Violence: Walter Benjamin and the Eschatology of Sovereignty* (London: Routledge, 2012), theological themes continue to dominate a good deal of Benjamin scholarship, even though what exactly his relationship to the theological is continues to be a subject of much debate. See also, Beatrice Hanssen, *Walter Benjamin's Other History: Of Stones, Animals, Human Beings, and Angels* (Berkeley: University of California Press, 2000), and Alison Ross, *Walter Benjamin's Concept of the Image* (London: Routledge, 2014).

8. Walter Benjamin, *The Correspondence of Walter Benjamin, 1910–1940*, ed. Gershom Scholem and Theodor W. Adorno, trans. Manfred R. Jacobson and Evelyn M. Jacobson (Chicago: University of Chicago Press, 1994), 79.

9. John McCole, *Walter Benjamin and the Antinomies of Tradition* (Ithaca, NY: Cornell University Press, 1993), 66.

10. Sigrid Weigel, *Walter Benjamin: Images, the Creaturely, and the Holy*, trans. Chadwick Truscott Smith (Stanford, CA: Stanford University Press, 2013), xxii.

11. Werner Hamacher, "'Now': Walter Benjamin and Historical Time," in *Walter Benjamin and History*, ed. Andrew Benjamin (London: Continuum, 2005), 40–41; see also, Michael G. Levine, *A Weak Messianic Power: Figures of a Time to Come in Benjamin, Derrida, and Celan* (New York: Fordham University Press, 2014), 3.

12. Walter Benjamin and Theodor Adorno, *The Complete Correspondence, 1928–1940* (Cambridge, MA: Harvard University Press, 2003), 67.

13. See Eli Friedlander, *Walter Benjamin: A Philosophical Portrait* (Cambridge, MA: Harvard University Press, 2012), 112–131. See also Max

Horkheimer and Theodor W. Adorno, *Dialectic of Enlightenment: Philosophical Fragments*, ed. Gunzelin Schmid Noerr, trans. Edmund Jephcott (Stanford, CA: Stanford University Press, 2007).

14. Howard Eiland and Michael W. Jennings, *Walter Benjamin: A Critical Life* (Cambridge, MA: Harvard University Press, 2014), 46.

15. Andrew Benjamin, *Working with Walter Benjamin: Recovering a Political Philosophy* (Edinburgh: Edinburgh University Press, 2013), 7.

16. Ibid., 165.

17. McCole, *Walter Benjamin*, 67.

18. See Kornel Zathureczky, *The Messianic Disruption of Trinitarian Theology* (Lanham, MD: Lexington, 2009); Michael W. Jennings, "Towards Eschatology: The Development of Benjamin's Theological Politics in the Early 1920's," in *Walter Benjamins Anthropologisches Denken*, ed. Carolin Duttinger, Ben Morgan, and Anthony Phelan (Freiburg: Rombach Verlag, 2012), 41–58. See also Eiland and Jennings, *Walter Benjamin*, 129; and Giorgio Agamben, *The Kingdom and the Glory: For a Theological Genealogy of Economy and Government* (Homo Sacer II, 2), trans. Lorenzo Chiesa (Stanford, CA: Stanford University Press, 2011), 8, where he contrasts Benjamin and Moltmann on the grounds of messianism and eschatology.

19. Slavoj Žižek, *The Puppet and the Dwarf: The Perverse Core of Christianity* (Cambridge, MA: MIT Press, 2003), 3.

20. See Slavoj Žižek, *The Fragile Absolute: Or, Why Is the Christian Legacy Worth Fighting For?* (London: Verso, 2000), 89.

21. Eric L. Santner, *On Creaturely Life: Rilke, Benjamin, Sebald* (Chicago: University of Chicago Press, 2006), xv.

22. Fritsch, *Promise of Memory*, 188.

23. Peter Fenves, *The Messianic Reduction: Walter Benjamin and the Shape of Time* (Stanford, CA: Stanford University Press, 2010), 244.

24. Ibid., 16.

25. Giorgio Agamben, *The Time That Remains: A Commentary on the Letter to the Romans*, trans. Patricia Dailey (Stanford, CA: Stanford University Press, 2005).

26. Agamben has sought to develop such "secret indexes" as the lasting "signature" of a concept that moves throughout history despite the apparent surpassing of any given concept, such as is the case with secularization/sacrality. See Agamben, *Kingdom and the Glory*, 4.

27. Ibid., 94.

28. Agamben, *Time That Remains*, 49.

29. Weigel, *Walter Benjamin*, 29. As Weigel describes the intermixture of elements: "Benjamin rather inscribes the central terms in the contemporary debate on revolutionary violence in terms of their mythic and religious-historical foundations, which remain embedded within them and are thereby used in mediated ways" (xxviii).

30. Hent de Vries, *Religion and Violence: Philosophical Perspectives from Kant to Derrida* (Baltimore, MD: Johns Hopkins University Press, 2002), 282.

31. Friedlander, *Walter Benjamin*, 204.

32. Ibid., 205.

33. Butler, *Parting Ways*, 80.

34. Jacques Derrida, "Force of Law: The "Mystical Foundation of Authority," in *Acts of Religion*, ed. Gil Anidjar, trans. Mary Quaintance (London: Routledge, 2002), 298.

35. Butler, *Parting Ways*, 96.

36. Johann Baptist Metz, *Faith in History and Society: Toward a Practical Fundamental Theology*, trans. J. Matthew Ashley (New York: Crossroad, 2007).

37. See Butler, *Parting Ways*, 99–113.

38. Walter Benjamin, "Theological-Political Fragment," in *Selected Writings*, 3:306.

39. Walter Benjamin, *The Origin of German Tragic Drama*, trans. John Osborne (London: Verso, 1998), 178–181.

40. In the "Critique of Violence" the concept of an inherently sacred life is read as "the last mistaken attempt of the weakened Western tradition to seek the saint it has lost" (*Selected Writings*, 1:251).

41. Walter Benjamin, "Über den Begriff der Geschichte," in *Gesammelte Schriften*, vol. 1.2, ed. Rolf Tiedemann and Hermann Schweppenhäuser (Frankfurt am Main: Suhrkamp Verlag, 1991), 697; translation ours.

42. Benjamin, *Selected Writings*, 4:392. For an interpretation of this concept of repetition, see, for example, Beatrice Hanssen, "The Turn to Natural History," in *Walter Benjamin's Other History*, 49–65; and Peter Osborne, "Small-Scale Histories, Large-Scale Defeats," in *Walter Benjamin's Philosophy: Destruction and Experience*, ed. Peter Osborne and Andrew Benjamin (London: Routledge, 1994), 82–85. For Benjamin's criticism of historicism see Beatrice Hanssen, "Philosophy at Its Origin: Walter Benjamin's Prologue to the *Ursprung des deutschen Trauerspiels*," *MLN* 110, no. 4 (1995): 786–816, and her "The Epistemo-Critical Prologue Reconsidered," in *Walter Benjamin's Other History*, 24–48. For its relevance for Benjamin's reading of "Modernity as Hell," see Susan Buck-Morss, *The Dialectics of Seeing: Walter Benjamin and the Arcades Project* (Cambridge, MA: MIT Press, 1991), 96–109. See also Sigrid Weigel's ideas on the theme of a "secularization of the historical" in Benjamin's work in her *Walter Benjamin*, 11–14.

43. See Weigel, *Walter Benjamin*, 29.

44. See, for example, Eric Jacobson, *Metaphysics of the Profane: The Political Theology of Walter Benjamin and Gershom Scholem* (New York: Columbia University Press, 2003), as well as Margaret Cohen, *Profane Illumination: Walter Benjamin and the Paris of Surrealist Revolution* (Berkeley: University of California Press, 1993).

45. See Benjamin, *Working with Walter Benjamin*, 168. See also Margarete Kohlenbach, *Walter Benjamin: Self-Reference and Religiosity* (New York: Palgrave Macmillan, 2002); S. Brent Plate, *Walter Benjamin, Religion, and Aesthetics: Rethinking Religion Through the Arts* (London: Routledge, 2005);

Zathureczky, *Messianic Disruption*; and Marc Goldschmit, *L'écriture du messianique: La philosophie secrète de Walter Benjamin* (Paris: Hermann, 2010).

46. In this regard, see also Sigrid Weigel, "Benjamin's 'World of Universal and Integral Actuality,'" in *Body- and Image-Space: Re-reading Walter Benjamin*, trans. Georgina Paul with Rachel McNicholl and Jeremy Gaines (London and New York: Routledge, 1996), 3–15.

47. Peter E. Gordon, "Weimar Theology: From Historicism to Crisis," in *Weimar Thought: A Contested Legacy*, ed. Peter E. Gordon and John P. McCormick (Princeton and Oxford: Princeton University Press, 2013), 150–178.

48. Peter Osborne, *The Politics of Time: Modernity and the Avant-Garde* (London: Verso, 1995), 227.

49. See David Ratmoko's introduction to Jacob Taubes, *Occidental Eschatology*, trans. David Ratmoko (Stanford, CA: Stanford University Press, 2009), xviii.

50. Agamben, *Time That Remains*, 138–145.

51. Jacob Taubes, *The Political Theology of Paul*, trans. Dana Hollander (Stanford, CA: Stanford University Press, 2003), 72–76.

52. See Hent de Vries, "Inverse Versus Dialectical Theology: Two Faces of Negativity and the Miracle of Faith," in *Paul and the Philosophers*, ed. Ward Blanton and Hent de Vries (New York: Fordham University Press, 2013), 479.

53. See Larry L. Welborn, "Jacob Taubes—Paulinist, Messianist," in *Paul in the Grip of the Philosophers*, ed. Peter Frick (Minneapolis, MN: Fortress Press, 2013), 69–89. Following Taubes's suggestion, it is possible to read both Agamben and Alain Badiou, as Simon Critchley has done in *The Faith of the Faithless: Experiments in Political Theology* (London: Verso, 2012), as "crypto-Marcionites" who foster a radical antinomian impulse that tries to "break the connection between law and faith" (15).

54. Michael Löwy, *Fire Alarm: Reading Walter Benjamin's "On the Concept of History"* (New York and London: Verso, 2005), 68.

55. Benjamin, *Selected Writings*, 1:288.

56. Ibid.

Metaphysics of Transience, Natural and Supernatural Life, and Apokatastasis

Benjamin's Messianic Metaphysics of Transience

ANNIKA THIEM

While religious and theological questions have seen a renewed interest within critical theory, metaphysics still remains under suspicion when it is not, as is so often the case in contemporary critical theory, considered a matter of little consequence. Similarly, Walter Benjamin's drawing upon theological tropes as the conceptual framework for theorizing history and life is no longer met with criticism but rather is widely embraced and harnessed as a theoretical resource for political and ethical thought. However, as obvious as it is that Benjamin's work is shot through with theological tropes and concepts, it proves more difficult to reflect systematically on *why* Benjamin turns to theological concepts in particular as a philosophical register to reflect critically on history and life and on how to attend to the theological specificity of this register.[1] Consequently, Axel Honneth, for instance, can read Benjamin's theological references, especially in "On the Concept of History" (1940), as poetic metaphors that refer to moral rights and to an ethical practice of restitution of full membership to the moral community to those who were previously excluded.[2] Differing from such a reading, Eric Jacobson's *Metaphysics of the Profane* provides an attentive study of the early political theology in Benjamin's and Gershom Scholem's thought and elaborates on the theological and the specifically Jewish dimension in Benjamin. At the same time, Jacobson cautions against overemphasizing Benjamin's involvement with Judaism and explains that his own method and goal will be "not [to] seek to apply Judaism to Benjamin, but rather Benjamin to Judaism."[3] In *Der frühe Walter Benjamin und*

Hermann Cohen, Astrid Deuber-Mankowsky elaborates on how Benjamin's interest in Jewish thought connects his epistemological critique and cultural critique, especially his critique of Zionism. By examining the philosophical relationship of Benjamin's work to the work of the neo-Kantian Jewish philosopher Hermann Cohen, Deuber-Mankowsky analyzes systematically how the Jewish context animates Cohen's and Benjamin's conceptions of epistemological critique as an ethical imperative and demonstrates how Benjamin's emphasis on contingency and transience originates out of his critical engagement with Cohen's philosophy. Taking up the attention to transience in Benjamin, while differing from Jacobson's and Deuber-Mankowsky's explorations of the Jewish specificity, I argue for reading the theological register in Benjamin as a historical metaphysics of transient experience, which understands theological concepts as sites where truth and affect converge.

The theological significance of Benjamin's approach lies in his insistence on understanding transience in reference to redemption—transient experience as in need of and as an occasion for redemption. The epistemic and, by implication, practical difficulty with reading Benjamin's understanding of theology on its own terms lies in the fact that for him the divine or theological can manifest itself in the profane only as a form of undoing or destruction, which does not necessarily appear as distinct from profane phenomena.[4]

Benjamin introduces his unique metaphysical interpretation of theology in philosophical essays written before 1920 and continues to work with the concept throughout his projects, much to the frequent displeasure of his Marxist friends and later leftist commentators.[5] In a letter from May 25, 1935, to Werner Kraft, Benjamin explains that joining experience and theology remains crucial to his work, in this case the *Arcades Project*. Benjamin comments on the need for a "total revolution" of his terminology to save the "immediately metaphysical, indeed, theological thinking" out of which his terminology had come, so that he could work with these ideas throughout the *Arcades Project*.[6] In *Dialectics of Seeing*, Susan Buck-Morss suggests that for Benjamin theology is a hermeneutic that invests objects and experiences with a metaphysical dimension that carries both ethical and political meaning.[7] In *Metaphysics of the Profane*, Jacobson suggests it is important to understand Benjamin's metaphysics as "a highly speculative philosophy of fundamental questions regarding politics and theology."[8] Throughout his work, Benjamin positions theology as a discourse and a tradition of knowledge that forms and transmits the underlying conceptions of life and history that shape our experience.[9] Taking up this metaphysical perspective on

Benjamin's work, I will argue that the theological concepts in Benjamin, on the one hand, provide an immanent critique of theologically informed conceptions shaping our experience in history and, on the other hand, elaborate an affective register to transform those ideas that orient our experience.[10]

To develop this interpretation, I begin by focusing on Benjamin's early essay "On the Program of the Coming Philosophy" (1918) in order to explain Benjamin's unique recuperation of a metaphysics of transient experience against the Kantian and neo-Kantian antinomial limitation of experience.[11] Understanding theology as a theory of experience means to disarticulate theology from being primarily conceived as a set of transcendent ideas or personal beliefs. Benjamin's approach does not locate theology beyond history, but rather considers theology as a historical, nonsubjective elaboration of the experience of existence, of the experience of transience.[12] Benjamin's approach offers an implicit critique of how the concepts of theology and religion in European modernity have become narrowly defined through reference to individuality and interiority. Within Protestantism in particular, religion becomes primarily a matter of individual faith. Benjamin's work offers an inroad to consider how the experiences of and within a theological horizon exceed religion as an individual, private commitment as well as socially perceived as a cultural foundation. Just as Benjamin insists in one of his notes that "*Nicht ist Moral: Gesinnung* [Morality is not: ethos],"[13] theology is not faith. Theological discourses elaborate both an implicitly binding sense of experience while at the same time containing within themselves a heterogeneity of critiques, disagreements, and reinterpretations. In his brief "Theological-Political Fragment" (1919) Benjamin interprets transience itself as messianic, insofar as transient existence can be a passing away in *Glück* (happiness, fortune). This interpretation of the messianic allows Benjamin both to affirm the experience of demise and to refuse uncritical affirmations of suffering as well as the postponement of redemption to afterlife.[14] Hence Benjamin's overlay of the concept of the messianic onto the experience of transience compels a critical scrutiny of the conditions under which worldly demise is experienced. On the one hand, this messianic temporality of demise provides an immanent but nevertheless theological critique of the sedimented frameworks of experience in history by making reference to the need for redemption and refusing to settle with the facticity and unilinearity of history. On the other hand, Benjamin's insistence on a messianic temporality of demise points toward the task of elaborating nonsubjective affective registers to transform those conceptual networks, the continuously emergent metaphysics that orient our experience.

Messianic Metaphysics of Transience

At different moments in his career, Benjamin stresses different aspects of the theological concepts that he invokes. Recourse to these concepts, however, is a constant feature of his work, and they provide critical resources for his approach to history and experience. In "On the Program of the Coming Philosophy," Benjamin sets up what is arguably his most programmatic philosophical argument for the conceptual relationship between philosophy and theology. In this essay, Benjamin positions theology as the metaphysics of experience. "Meta-physics," literally "what comes after physics (science)," has in a standard way been interpreted to mean the transcendence of experience. As opposed to this common meaning, Benjamin recuperates the term to describe instead a nonsubjective, nonindividual, but immanent reality of transient experience.

Metaphysics for Benjamin does not exist as a transcendent structure of reality beyond experience; rather, his metaphysics arises out of experience. The privileged discourse within which Benjamin sees metaphysics surviving in the modern world and being continuously elaborated is theology, especially in its pervasive contribution of concepts that structure our experience of history.

In particular, Benjamin criticizes the prevalent understanding in Weimar culture of history as progress as an experience in which the concept of salvation history that survives in secularized form.[15] The philosophical targets of his critique are the neo-Kantians and especially Kant himself. Benjamin criticizes both Kant's exclusion of theology from the epistemological grounding of experience and the theological underpinnings of Kant's treatment of history that exclude demise and dissolve suffering into the idea of progress.[16] Against the idealization of salutary progress, Benjamin introduces the messianic, understood as redemption in demise, as a critical framework through which to affirm the experience of transience without likewise affirming the historical conditions of this experience. Opposing Kant's and the neo-Kantians' ethical formalism, Benjamin's metaphysics of experience allows and compels a shift from ideas (and ideals) to material experience. His aim—to rid philosophy of Kantian subjectivity—seems to imply that there is no sustained philosophical ethics that he embraces, but his critique of the Kantian view of experience elaborates work on the conditions of life and experience as a theological as well as ethical critique of these conditions.

In this section, I argue that Benjamin's early critique of the Kantian formulation of experience offers us two useful ways to understand his critique of theological concepts. First, Benjamin's rejection and modification of Kantianism illuminates his invocation of theology as a metaphysics of experience. Second, the experience of transience becomes an occasion for critique to the extent that Benjamin interprets transience as redemptive, but only insofar as transience is understood as demise in happiness. I begin by exploring Benjamin's objections to the Kantian and neo-Kantian construal of objectively valid experience as systematic knowledge of nature. Against this view, Benjamin includes religion and history as systematic structures of experience that are irreducible to the experiences of empirical individuals. To clarify Benjamin's position on this issue, I turn to "On Perception" (1917) and "On the Program of the Coming Philosophy" and elaborate Benjamin's conceptualizing of a metaphysics of experience that can affirm "the dignity of transient experience" and what is at stake in understanding this approach as metaphysical.[17]

Benjamin refers to the neo-Kantians in general in "On the Program of the Coming Philosophy" and in its precursor essay, "On Perception." The summary reference understates the importance of Benjamin's engagement with Kantian philosophy. As early as 1913, Benjamin studied Hermann Cohen's work with Heinrich Rickert, the leading neo-Kantian of his day. Hence it is probable that both Cohen and Rickert are the foils for Benjamin's criticism of the neo-Kantian treatment of experience and theology found in these pieces, written only a few years later.[18] As Deuber-Mankowsky has demonstrated incisively, Benjamin's encounter with Cohen's philosophy runs deeper than a cursory reading and Benjamin's early work in particular should be read as a rigorous response and elaboration on the systematic challenges posed by Cohen's work. In the seminar with Rickert, Benjamin studied Cohen's *Kants Theorie der Erfahrung* (Kant's theory of experience; first published in 1871), which does not address religion nor does it work with theological concepts.[19]

By the time he writes *Ethik des reinen Willens* (1907), Cohen attributes a crucial role to messianism in order to frame the idea and ideal of a historical temporality within which human freedom and social justice can and must be accomplished. Finally, the posthumously published *Religion of Reason out of the Sources of Judaism* (1919) indicates that Cohen continuously called into question and rethought his own conceptual framework. Throughout his career and particularly in his late work, Cohen sought to demonstrate, on the one hand, how Judaism was not in contradiction with rational ethics and, on the other hand, how the rational ethical core of his neo-Kantian philosophy has always been aligned with and inspired by the scriptural and theological tradition. In his final work, Cohen stylistically takes a different approach from his previous work by reading biblical sources to elaborate systematically Judaism's rational, ethical core. But even though many readings that have split Cohen into the neo-Kantian philosopher of the *Logik der reinen Erkenntnis* (Logic of pure cognition, 1902), the *Ethik des reinen Willens* (Ethics of pure will, 1904), and *Ästhetik des reinen Gefühls* (Aesthetics of pure feeling, 1912) and the Jewish thinker of the *Religion of Reason out of the Sources of Judaism*, Cohen's *Religion of Reason* continues to elaborate his philosophical commitments and arguably takes the place of a fourth intended systematic work on philosophical psychology.[20] As it is, for Cohen, ethics out of religious sources is and has to be nonetheless rationally and philosophically justified; the religious tradition and its theoretical reflection is merely a site where the progress of reason both advances and still needs to be advanced. Despite the rationalist commitments, the material in *Religion of Reason* provides inroads for reformulating Cohen's concept of experience and his insistence on establishing a unity of ethics and religion within pure reason.

Cohen himself did not pursue these paths, which may have led to further revisions of his Kantianism. Instead, throughout his work, including *Religion of Reason*, Cohen remains committed to restricting his concept of experience to the Kantian view of experience as systematic knowledge of the world according to scientifically established laws of nature. In *Kants Theorie der Erfahrung*, Cohen embraces Kant's aim: "He [Kant] aimed especially at . . . constituting the unity of experience as the unity of the mathematical natural science, in order to obtain from it the norm for all other kinds of *wissenschaftlicher* (scientific, scholarly) certainty and for the distinguishing value of objective knowledge."[21]

Kant seeks, Cohen explains, to ensure the certainty of knowledge as experience by conceiving of experience as derived from the ordering of individual experiences according to the laws of nature, immutable laws that yield a systematic conceptual unity among these disparate individual experiences. Kant elaborates this understanding of experience in the *Critique of Pure Reason* and the *Prolegomena to Any Future Metaphysics* by way of explaining his transcendental method, which aims at grounding the possibility of objective knowledge through abstaining from making claims about the things in themselves and by locating the conditions of knowledge and experience in the subject of knowledge itself.[22] In the *Critique of Pure Reason*, Kant introduces the transcendental turn by explaining that while all *Erkenntnis* (knowledge, cognition) begins with experience, not all knowledge need derive from experience: "But although all our cognition commences with experience, yet it does not on that account all arise from experience."[23] While temporally no knowledge exists prior to experience, we can discern conditions that are logically prior to and independent of that experience that make this experience possible.[24] The transcendental turn aims to ensure the certainty of knowledge by discovering the a priori conditions of the possibility of experience and knowledge, rather than by making claims about the nature of experience and of the objects themselves.

Kant's intent to establish the certainty of theoretical knowledge without recourse to speculative metaphysics also led him to reformulate the philosophical concept of experience. In the opening of the A version of the introduction to the *Critique of Pure Reason*, Kant distinguishes between experience and the "raw material" of sense-perceptions. In contradistinction from sensory perception, experience is a reflective awareness of these sensations organized by our understanding (*Verstand*): "Experience is without doubt the first product that our understanding brings forth as it works on the raw material of sensible sensations."[25] The (for Kant) passive faculty of sensibility is affected by objects and provides intuitions (*Anschauungen*) as the mechanism by which the raw material of perception is to be cognized by understanding. Understanding determines these intuitions conceptually and so produces experience. Since Kant requires experience be dependent on sensibility, all experience for him must be spatiotemporal. In other words, for Kant both experience and theoretical knowledge are limited to the possibility of empirical consciousness.

In *Kants Theorie der Erfahrung*, Cohen presents Kant's circumscription of experience as an accomplishment for philosophy, because with this theory of experience Kant develops the fundamentals of natural scientific knowledge as the ideal for all philosophical knowledge. Cohen follows Kant in restricting the concept of experience to the perception and knowledge of nature in accordance with its laws; for Cohen this approach is critical because of the foundational role Cohen—to an even greater extent than Kant—attributes to the natural sciences and their theoretical grounding in natural laws. In *Ethik des reinen Willens*, Cohen identifies his aim as "*die Fixierung der Erfahrung in den Wissenschaften* [anchoring experience in the sciences]."[26] Already in *Logik der reinen Erkenntnis*, Cohen parts with Kant, however, by severing the concept of experience completely from that of empirical consciousness, which the Kantian account retains as cofoundational. Cohen does so in order to elaborate a purely functional account of the philosophical concept of experience that is thoroughly independent from the empirical perception of sense-data at the heart of Kant's argument. With the advance in the sciences, what we can know with the help of scientific instruments far exceeds the "raw material of sensible sensations." Instead, Cohen moves to a purely methodological epistemological account of philosophical experience within which to ground the certainty of objective and universal philosophical knowledge.

With this move, Cohen seeks to get rid of what he considered metaphysical residues in Kant's account, namely, the presupposition of the entity of a subject who receives sensory stimuli.

Cohen's main concern is that this presupposition of a subject introduces a speculative assumption and so becomes uncritical. Consequently, from *Logik der reinen Erkenntnis* on, Cohen eliminates the subjective dimension from the methodological grounding of knowledge. Instead, the subject becomes the issue of the fourth part of the system, philosophical psychology, which Cohen, however, never writes. Instead he writes the *Religion of Reason*, where he introduces the unique systematic contribution of religion as introducing attention to the individual, emotions, and the concrete consequences of actions. At the level of grounding philosophical knowledge, however, Cohen excises history and subjectivity. Benjamin, as I read him, actually agrees with the critique of anchoring experience and knowledge in subjectivity, transcendental or empirical, because it eviscerates the concept of the world. However, Benjamin sees Cohen's resolution of a purely epistemological, methodological account of experience and knowledge to exacerbate this latter problem of worldless experience, since Cohen's scientificity of philosophical knowledge is won at the expense of either ignoring or not taking seriously the singular, unrepeatable material transience (*Vergänglichkeit*) of experience as affecting philosophical knowledge.[27]

In Cohen, this exclusion of transience is the underlying philosophical commitment that compels him to elaborate ethics as a framework of ideas and concepts on which the possibility of rational agency and ethical progress can be grounded. For Cohen, ethics does not, need not, and cannot concern itself philosophically with empirical experience, because the validity of ethical ideas depends on their independence from empirical experience. In *Religion of Reason*, Cohen explains to this end that while ethics cannot and may not concern itself with consequences, it is therefore the task of religion to deal with consequences and experiences: "While according to ethics . . . [reason] is not responsible for anything that happens beyond its borders and basically, therefore, is also not interested in the outward success or failure of moral duty, here, too, religion objects to this indifference."[28] But these insights do not affect the ethical ideas in return, since those ideas have been and have to be grounded a priori. In the place of the elaboration of ethical ideas to orient actions, Benjamin examines experience and the ways in which our experience of transience is formed. In Benjamin, an ongoing theoretical critique of experience and the attempt to rework philosophical experience takes the place of philosophical ethics.[29]

In "On Perception" and "On the Program of the Coming Philosophy," Benjamin criticizes Kant and especially the neo-Kantians such as Cohen for narrowing the conceptual grounding of experience to the scientific—that is, mechanical and psychological—production and consequent representation of experiences. In his *Critique of the Power of Judgment*, Kant attempted to mitigate the rift between nature and freedom and between theoretical and practical knowledge through aesthetics and a theory of judgment.[30] However, the grounding of this mediation remains subjective, and the validity of transindividual experience is only hypothetical through reference to common sense, which Kant argues must be assumed as an a priori condition of possibility for subjective cognition to become objective knowledge. But aesthetic experience lacks a definite objective principle and hence Kant must deny its unconditioned necessity. His argument in Section 22 demonstrates the subjective limitation of experience that implies that aesthetic experience can never be objectively universal: "The common sense, of whose judgment I here offer my judgment of taste as an example and on account of which I ascribe *exemplary* validity to it, is a merely ideal norm."[31] The common sense to which aesthetic experience appeals neither arises out of shared experience nor bears on elaborating this framework of experience further. Common sense is solely an ideal norm that must be presupposed. Kant renders common sense epistemologically necessary through his analysis of the possibility and structure of judgments of taste, but in this turn also shows exemplarily how he epistemologizes metaphysics, dissolving the possibilities of experience into the conditions we are forced to assume so that experience is possible in the first place.

In "On Perception," Benjamin reminds us of the distinction between two different understandings of experience that Kant and especially Cohen tend to gloss over. First, there is experience in the sense of the individual empirical events we experience; Benjamin terms this kind of experience as "immediate and natural" experience. He distinguishes this first meaning of experience from the second meaning as in "*der Erfahrungsbegriff des Erkenntniszusammenhangs* [the concept of experience in the context of knowledge]."[32] This second meaning of experience is not different from the first in the sense that there is something new added, but the concept of experience in this second case denotes the transformation of experiences into a different form than that of discreet individual instances: "[E]xperience as the object of knowledge is the unified and continuous manifold of knowledge."[33] Experience does not lose its variegated character in the context of knowledge, but insofar as experience sediments into knowledge, the multiplicity of instances creates a unity and continuity, similar to that of a scaffolding, as Benjamin describes it later in *The*

Arcades Project.[34] Benjamin insists that all experiences—including those that are intangible, such as religion, magic, or hallucinations—need to be considered as possibly contributing equally to this scaffolding. While Kant and the neo-Kantians do not discard unity and continuity as crucial to the philosophical concept of experience, their idea of the unity of experience within the context of knowledge is an impoverished one, because they limit the concept of experience as epistemic context (*Erkenntniszusammenhang*) to the possibility of scientific experience that arises out of a priori concepts.[35] The problem is not simply that empirical experience is excluded from ever reaching the status of knowledge, but that empirical experience is not taken seriously as bearing on and reshaping the conditions of the possibility of knowledge themselves. For Kant, time and space are the transcendental forms of apperception and as transcendental they are unaffected by history. For Benjamin, as I argue, the forms of apperception are shaped and reshaped by experience, but they are not therefore arbitrary, subjective, or open to easy reworking at anyone's will.

According to Benjamin, Kant's critical limitation of experience breaks with the pre-critical philosophers' speculative interests to establish "the closest possible continuity and unity—that is, to create the closest possible connection between knowledge and experience through a speculative deduction of the world."[36] Benjamin's main critique is that Kant and the neo-Kantians sever experience from knowledge in the sense that no certainty of knowledge can ever be derived from experience. For Kant empirical experience remains an occasion for knowledge, but his concept of the certainty of knowledge refers only to the conditions of the possibility of experience and of the possible objects of experience, not to experience itself.

Moreover, Benjamin contends, Kant has no interest in the unity of all variations of experiences or in the world as a totality of experience, where the concept of the world stores up and gives rise to experiences of all sorts.[37] Kant limits the sense of the unity of experience that is philosophically relevant for the production of knowledge to the discovery of regularity in empirical chance occurrences (*Zufälligkeiten*), which can then be used to infer the structure of experience in the integration of the individual instances with each other through the laws of nature. For Kant, concepts like God, freedom, the soul, or the world as a whole have nothing to do with experience, because they involve the extension of concepts of the understanding beyond any possible spatiotemporal realization. Whatever does not have a corresponding intuition (*Anschauung*) in time and space cannot be an object of experience. From the perspective of knowledge, such over-extended concepts are "empty": "Without sensibility no object would be given to us, and without understanding none would be thought. Thoughts without content are empty, intuitions without concepts are blind. It is thus just as necessary to make the mind's concepts sensible (i.e., to add an object to them in intuition) as it is to make them understandable (i.e., to bring them under concepts)."[38] Hence concepts like God, freedom, the soul, or the world as a whole must be regarded as ideas of reason and can only have regulative use. For Benjamin, this Kantian formulation of experience and its adoption by his successors give experience an "erstaunlich geringes spezifisch metaphysisches Gewicht [astonishingly small specifically metaphysical weight]."[39] Specifically, after Kant, with the privileging of a scientific grounding, ethical, aesthetic, and religious experiences no longer have any weight philosophically and are relegated to solely private, individual, or group-specific claims to meaning. Ironically, Kant's so-called Copernican revolution grounds philosophical certainty and universality in transcendental subjectivity and the transcendental unity of apperception, but the consequent epistemological focus of philosophy renders this subject worldless to a degree unparalleled even by pre-Kantian speculative metaphysics.[40]

Despite his criticisms of the Kantian and neo-Kantian view of experience, Benjamin is not seeking to return to pre-critical metaphysics. In aspiring to "*die Umprägung der 'Erfahrung' zu 'Metaphysik'* [the re-embossing of 'experience' into 'metaphysics']" Benjamin is not proposing a restoration of the speculative deduction of the world from first principles nor the establishment of the concept of a transcendent totality such as spirit or substance as grounding all existence beyond history.[41] Instead, Benjamin insists on both the transience of experience and the experience of transience as crucial to recuperating metaphysics. Early in the "Program" essay, Benjamin explains that both Kantian and neo-Kantian philosophy neglect any philosophical treatment of transience. Understanding transience, he argues, is one of the two tasks for philosophical critique after Kant: "First of all, there was the question of the certainty of knowledge that is lasting, and, second, the question of the dignity of an experience that was *vergänglich* [transient, perishable]."[42] Kant addressed the first question, but neglected the second. Hence Benjamin's essay focuses on the unity of transient experience. Benjamin concludes his essay by stating that he has arrived at a new formulation of metaphysical knowledge that makes transient experience central qua its relation to *Dasein* (existence): "To say that knowledge is metaphysical means in the strict sense: it is related via the original concept [*Stammbegriff*] of knowledge to the concrete totality of experience—that is to *existence* [*Dasein*]."[43] The transient totality of experience is nothing other than existence (*Dasein*). This totality in turn cannot be observed or experienced from an external vantage point. As a totality of experience that is rendered concrete in existence, this totality is not the sum of individual increments of facts or events. The sense of *Dasein* implies a continuum that cannot be broken into particulars. The particulars and singularities do not bear on *Dasein* as independent and discrete quantities but as intensities. Philosophical knowledge is metaphysical and exceeds epistemology insofar as it is formed in relation to and also bears on an encompassing, underlying, and indivisible sense of our existence as material and transient, as perishable and perishing.

One difficulty of Benjamin's very condensed prose is that it is unclear whether *Dasein* as the concrete totality of experience is individual existence or collective existence or whether it implies both, but then the relation between the two aspects of existence would need to be clarified further. Another difficulty of Benjamin's interpretation of the experience of transience is that within this one concept both the transience of both history and existence converge. Benjamin seems to seek to bring both aspects of transience to bear on each other, but he is not very forthcoming in explaining this relation. It is relatively easy to grasp how a more general sense of history and historical experience bears on and inflects our experience of our own transience, yet Benjamin seems to be more interested in the second relation, namely in how our experience of our own transience infiltrates and bears on the general sense of transient history. Benjamin's approach to transient experience counters Kant's dissolving of historical events and experiences into the idea of progress, an aim that becomes most clear in Kant's "Idea for a Universal History from a Cosmopolitan Point of View."[44] In this short essay, Kant seeks to develop an "idea of how the course of the world would have to go if it were to conform to certain rational ends."[45] He admits that this idea sounds like fiction, but argues that the idea is necessary so that "there will be opened a consoling prospect into the future (which without a plan of nature one cannot hope for with any ground)."[46] For Kant this systematic framework for making sense of individual instances in history is not affected by history itself, since he derives the idea of progress in history out of a rational necessity. Moreover, in the conclusion of his argument, Kant suggests that the theological issue of affirming the creation as good rationally compels the "justification of providence" on which his argument relies. Although Benjamin opposes, as has been pointed out, the Kantian assumption of a progressive teleology in history, Benjamin does not oppose the Kantian reliance on theological concepts to develop a concept of history. In fact, Benjamin seems to agree that philosophy of history is theology; philosophy of history is metaphysical because it develops a unity of meaning, and philosophy of history is theological because it aims to redeem individual historical instances.

Theological Tradition as Historical Laboratory of Experience

In this section, I will read Benjamin as opposing the mostly disavowed theological dimension of Kant's concept of history in two ways. First, whereas Kant reduces the unity of history to an immutable idea of history necessitated by reason, Benjamin considers this unity as developed through and transmitted by traditions, whose affective and historical force cannot be simply opposed by the judgment of reason. Second, Kant excludes from his idea of history the material experience of history as not only time passing, but also as demise. Kant dissolves the demise of individuals into the idea of the overall progress of the species and justifies suffering as the ploy by which nature propels humanity to overcome its laziness and toward incremental perfection. Viewing history under the idea of progress subsumes all suffering in history into this account of progress, which, according to Kant, reveals suffering as the cunning providence of nature to coax humans into an effort to overcome adversity and thus make progress by inventing solutions. In the fourth proposition of his essay "Idea for a Universal History from a Cosmopolitan View," he writes: "The human being wills concord; but nature knows better what is good for his species: it wills discord. He wishes to live comfortably and contentedly; but nature wills that out of sloth and inactive contentment he should throw himself into labor and toils, so as, on the contrary, prudently to find out the means to pull himself again out of the latter."[47] While nature inflicting pain and discord may seem like the works of an "evil spirit," Kant argues that such an interpretation suffers from a limited point of view. Once we take on the point of view of the species and a view of history that extends beyond the lives of any individual, we come to understand that the individual and momentary conflicts and painful experiences are incentives and purposeful for the overall progress of the species "betray the ordering of a wise creator."[48] Against this Kantian idealist theodicy of history and the elision of the experience of transience, Benjamin introduces the messianic as redemption in worldly demise.

As discussed, Benjamin's appropriations of theological concepts need to be positioned within the context of his attempts to recuperate a postcritical metaphysics of experience. The central texts for this analysis are "On the Program of the Coming Philosophy" and its draft version, "On Perception."[49] Benjamin's turn to theological concepts has often been interpreted as motivated by his melancholic character or his despair in light of his historical circumstances.[50] While these motivations may play a part in animating Benjamin's indeed often obscure and quirky metaphysical and theological claims, to reduce them to his personal or historical circumstances limits these arguments also to precisely these circumstances and preempts taking them philosophically seriously. In the process of trying to unpack the philosophical impact, I have been arguing that theological concepts make their appearance in Benjamin's work precisely at those points where he insists on metaphysical claims, especially in reference to the transience of life and history.

In what follows, I examine the critical purchase of Benjamin's distinctive way of rendering theology metaphysical—an effort that to contemporary ears may sound outrageous and indeed it is this metaphysical aspect that is the very core of the problem with religion. Yet what seems productive to me about Benjamin's approach is not a matter of simply celebrating theology as metaphysics, but that it implies how in order to work critically on the effects of theological concepts, we need to first understand the affective force of theological concepts as exceeding personal or group-specific commitments. For Benjamin, as I read him, theological thinking becomes a matter of grasping our experience of transience in life and history in a nonindividual, nonpersonal, yet not in an ahistorical or transhistorical way.

The implications of insisting on the philosophical dignity of transience reach beyond a simple effort to include forms of experience other than the scientific by allowing additional objects of experience. Rather, Benjamin's critique reformulates the very philosophical grounding of experience and knowledge in the Kantian transcendental unity of apperception. Benjamin insists that a recuperation of post-critical metaphysics needs to work with a nonsubjective elaboration of a unity of experience in transience. This unity or concrete totality, as Benjamin calls it, is neither transcendent nor monolithic, but is instead fragmented and marked by decay. Benjamin moves beyond Kant as well as neo-Kantians such as Cohen by articulating the source of philosophical knowledge and experience as both historical and material in transience.[51]

Benjamin introduces *Lehre* (teaching, doctrine, and in a wider sense, tradition) as the medium for what he terms the "unity of experience" or "concrete totality of experience," an implicit integrating sense of our existence in history that is a socially pervasive sensibility. Earlier in the "Program" essay, Benjamin invokes the scientific sensibilities of the Enlightenment as example of how experience is a historically constituted "horizon" or *Weltanschauung*, which Kant could not acknowledge as "*singuläre zeitlich beschränkte* [singularly temporally limited]" experience.[52]

Benjamin suggests we must understand these "horizons" through tradition and *Lehre* in particular, because of the way in which traditions are both historical and nonrelative, and neither immutable nor easy to switch or transform. In reaction to his reading of Kant and the neo-Kantians as well as to his perception of Hegel, Benjamin does not formulate the unity of transient experience as an abstract absolute unity that is beyond critical engagement or as a preestablished reality or force, waiting only to manifest itself in this world. Rather, Benjamin conceives of this totality of existence as immanent—that is, existence refers to the experience of transience in the world.[53] He therefore grounds the unity of transient experience neither psychologically empirically nor epistemologically. Indeed, to be precise, transient experience cannot be grounded at all, but must be elaborated on historically. Nonetheless, this historical immanence is also precisely how for Benjamin metaphysical experience exceeds epistemology:

> However, the original and primal concept [*Stamm- und Urbegriff*] of knowledge does not reach a concrete totality of experience in this context [of an epistemological-critical inquiry], any more than it reaches a concept of existence [*Dasein*]. But there is a unity of experience that can by no means be understood as the sum of experiences, to which the concept of knowledge as teaching [*Lehre*] is *immediately* related in its continuous development.[54]

We can gather two insights from this passage. First, Benjamin indicates that the concrete totality of experience as transient existence can be experienced, but not philosophically grounded. Second, this ungroundedness is what allows Benjamin to consider this totality as both nonsubjectively and historically formed. Benjamin rejects the idea that either the concrete totality of experience or even the concept of existence could be derived by summing up empirical experiences and then finding their most basic commonality. While concrete, Benjamin's concept of totality does not denote a psychological process of integrating experiences made over time with all others. In fact, Benjamin suggests that the experience of our existence cannot be split into individual elements. At the same time, this experience is also more than pure facticity; as Benjamin argues, we encounter this unity of experience in its concrete elaborations as *Lehre*, as teachings, as doctrines, as traditions. Knowledge of this experience is historically passed on as *Lehre*—as traditions and our understanding of life and of the world that we derive from these traditions that orient our awareness of our existence in this world in a visceral, albeit implicit and prereflective sense.

Through the elaboration of the unity of experience into knowledge, this knowledge becomes *Lehre* (doctrine, teaching), a part of tradition. In the epistemological critical prologue of *The Origin of German Tragic Drama*, Benjamin explains that "Philosophical teaching [*Lehre*] rests on historical codification [*Philosophische Lehre beruht auf historischer Kodifikation*]."[55] Historical codification lends authority to the philosophical doctrine as it sediments into a presentation of truth. Benjamin argues that the mode of presentation in philosophy cannot be a methodological manual for how to attain knowledge. Philosophical presentation, Benjamin suggests, should follow a method of contemplation to produce experience. But the argumentative force of the text itself and of thinking cannot force the insights to turn into *Lehre*. *Lehre* cannot be scientifically proven (or falsified), but undergoes historical elaboration through passing into a collective, general imaginary and thus shapes the reality of experience.[56]

Experiences, insofar as they are integrated into the metaphysical, undergo what Benjamin describes as an *Umprägung* (reembossing, reminting), a material transformation into frameworks and traditions. The sense of experience is not anchored in subjective categories of cognition but in *Lehre*; history sediments into experiential truth without the mediation by subjectivity. Benjamin's consideration of the unity of experience nonsubjectively means that there is no interiority within which this unity is forged. Time, which in the Kantian transcendental aesthetic is the form of interior representations, in Benjamin becomes historical as external form. The implication for practical philosophy that we can mark at this point is that Benjamin's metaphysics of experience shifts the attention from a key concern with how we *think* about the world and how we *ought to think* about it to one in which we consider how the world makes itself *felt* and how our *affective orientation* and our sense of life and history are shaped and can be reshaped by our experiences.

In the "Program" essay, Benjamin follows up this interpretation of metaphysics as immanent and historical in *Lehre*, in tradition, by suggesting that religion, as tradition, is more than simply one kind of possible experience under this new conception of experience. For Benjamin, religion is the privileged site where philosophy encounters the metaphysics of experience: "The object and the content of this *Lehre* (teaching), this concrete totality of experience, is religion, which, however, is presented to philosophy in the first instance only as *Lehre* (teaching)."[57] Metaphysics and religion here seem to merge in the terminology of *Lehre*, especially as Benjamin suggests that the "object and content" of the concrete totality of experience is religion. Later in the essay he corrects himself, suggesting that theology may be more what he means than religion. We might reformulate Benjamin here to consider religion as a concretion of this unity of experience in history and theology as that which more specifically emerges from the commentary on this unity of experience.[58]

Benjamin puts forth this idea of a commentary on reality as inherently theological later in *The Arcades Project*, in "Convolute N: On the Theory of Knowledge, Theory of Progress" where Benjamin advises emphatically: "Bear in mind that commentary on a reality (for it is a question here of commentary, interpretation in detail) calls for a method completely different from that required by commentary on a text. In the one case, the scientific mainstay [*Grundwissenschaft*] is theology; in the other case, philology."[59] In this note, Benjamin casts reality as a legible surface to be interpreted, but he carefully distinguishes what he calls the legibility of reality from the legibility of texts.[60] Whereas the meaning of texts can be established through philological insight, which elaborates on the world internal to the text and stays within the text, reality produces a theological reading that reaches beyond the world of the text, its accounts, and its characters.

Benjamin ends the "Program" essay without further clarifying why or how the metaphysical reformulation of experience is either religious or theological. In the argument that follows, I will turn to Benjamin's interpretation of the transience of existence as messianic to elaborate on his theological critique of the conditions of experience. At this point, however, I would like highlight that by considering theology as a metaphysics of experience, as Benjamin seems to do, he offers a different approach to theology and religion than one that would take religion or theology as primarily connected to individual commitments and acts of faith. Theological and religious experience as *Lehre*, as a metaphysical framework, is precisely neither limited to nor grounded in private beliefs and practices.

Benjamin's critique of Kant demonstrates that the Kantian restriction of objective experience to scientific experience undergirds later approaches that understand religion as primarily a private, individual matter that might or might not be supported in the public sphere. Because of the commitment to transcendental subjectivity as grounding the account of experience and as necessitating the split between understanding (*Verstand*) and reason, (*Vernunft*) the Kantian approach produces a restricted perspective on religion as individual faith, universalizable only as ethics, and as a political matter only with regard to the institutional location of theology in the university and the church in the state. Against Kant, Benjamin's approach foregrounds religion as historically transmitted and theological concepts as furnishing our very sense of life, history, and the world. Rather than centering on private faith or on theological normative stipulations for individual actions, Benjamin brings into focus the idea that theological concepts attain their binding, nonrelative character out of history itself through shaping the experience of transient existence and a related outlook on life and the world.

Taking this experiential metaphysical dimension of religion and theology seriously implies that any critique of religion and theology becomes a question of how to affect the metaphysical force of these traditions. The Kantian resources for such a critique are in the end rather anemic because of Kant's and the neo-Kantians' focus on an epistemological account and on the concordance of religious practice and theological accounts with the demands of reason. Benjamin's own approach in the "Program" essay, unlike in his later works, still seems rather similar to a Kantian response, insofar as Benjamin simply insists on a confrontation of the religious *Lehre* with philosophy and philosophical critique. He writes, "The philosophical concept of existence must answer to the religious concept of teachings [*religiösen Lehrbegriff*], but the latter must answer to the epistemological original concept [*Stammbegriff*]."[61] Admitting that "all of this is only a sketchy indication," Benjamin does not explain the force of this *must*, which seems more an ideal of what ought to happen than a description of a critical confrontation that is bound to happen.

As I mentioned previously, the "Program" essay ends without Benjamin's resolving how or why we are to understand the experience of existence in its transience, not only in metaphysical terms but also more specifically in theological terms. To clarify this theological dimension in Benjamin and suggest that theology itself carries an ethical-critical potential, it is helpful to examine Benjamin's "Theological-Political Fragment," written at the same time as "On the Program of the Coming Philosophy." In the profane world—the world that is *pro fano*, "out in front of the temple"—according to Benjamin's interpretation in this fragment, we encounter the messianic only in the form of natural transience. In this assertion, he departs from traditional eschatological expectations of a linear progression toward the final goal of eternal salvation that results in the end of history, expectations that live on in Kant's eschatology of progress. Considering transience as messianic enables a critique of the historical conditions of the experience of transience and thus counters Kant's move—which Cohen repeats in a slight alteration—to abstracting from those historical conditions to find in them evidence for an idealized hope for progress.[62] Benjamin's insistence on transience as a messianic mode, far from exuberantly extolling a heroic embrace of death, provides a critical perspective on history and on the future because it raises the question of the conditions of this natural demise and the livability of demise within these events. In the following, I will argue that this conceiving of transience in happiness as messianic introduces an ethical qualification into Benjamin's metaphysics of experience, because the completion or totality of this undoing and passing away that is the messianic cannot be taken for granted, nor can it be accomplished by being indifferent about or even desiring one's own death. Rather, passing away in happiness is a matter of the conditions and circumstances under which life in this world is allowed, rather than forced, to perish.

The theological-political argument in the fragment centers on Benjamin's rejection of theocracy through his insistence on a messianic framing of history. Denouncing any attempt at ordering the profane world in accordance with divine principles, Benjamin argues for a stringent discontinuity between messianism and the profane world in which we live and act.[63] For Benjamin, politics and history are in the first place profane and are in need of redemption. While insisting on the discontinuity that exists between the profane and the messianic, Benjamin also recovers an intimate, yet indirect relationship between the two:

> For in *Glück* (happiness) all that is earthly seeks its *Untergang* (downfall), and only in happiness is it destined to find its downfall. Whereas admittedly the immediate messianic intensity of the heart, of the inner man in isolation, passes through *Unglück* (unhappiness), as suffering. The spiritual *restitutio in integrum*, which introduces into immortality, corresponds to a worldly restitution that leads to an eternity of *Untergang*, and the rhythm of this eternally transient worldly existence, transient in its totality, in its spatial but also in its temporal totality, the rhythm of messianic nature, is *Glück*. For nature is messianic by reason of its eternal and total *Vergängnis* (transience, passing away).[64]

Benjamin frames transience as messianic insofar as transience is both the rhythm of nature and the path to a worldly restitution. Unlike in a salvation paradigm, which presents as its goal an incorruptible body and eternal life, for Benjamin worldly, material restitution and integrity can be found precisely in the natural rhythm of perishing, not in the overcoming of this perishing. Benjamin seems to distinguish this worldly restitution from a spiritual one that leads to immortality, but after this single mention, spiritual immortality immediately drops out of his argument, never to return. While Benjamin does not explain himself further, this distinction between spiritual and worldly restitution does not seem to indicate that Benjamin is some sort of modern-day Gnostic looking to overcome the imperfect or sinful bodily, earthly world through its destruction, aspiring thereby to find a purer form of the life of the soul beyond the body. Instead, Benjamin emphasizes both body and soul as inseparable in the individual bodily experience that is at the same time the experience of the "inner heart." It is this worldly existence in its finitude that Benjamin understands as messianic. However, Benjamin likewise does not cast this finitude as a final limitation toward which existence tends, but rather as an inner-worldly rhythm and experience of aging and, in Benjamin's terms, decaying.[65] The decline and transience that we humans—but not only or even especially we humans—undergo with all nature is not opposed to redemption but is part of it.[66] The time of redemption, for Benjamin, is a rhythm of completion found in undoing, rather than either in a mythic penance for one's imperfect existence or in a salutary new beginning in which this life and this world are exchanged for eternal perfection.

Bringing the messianic to bear on the profane allows Benjamin to introduce a critical perspective on the conditions of life in the profane world by insisting on the redemption of life as transient without declaring the demise of life as directly redemptive. This perspective is critical, because, as Benjamin insists, "*only* in happiness is its downfall [*Untergang*] destined to find it [the worldly]."[67] Benjamin sets up happiness as the exclusive condition for and sole medium by which this *Untergang*—the going under and passing away of the worldly—becomes possible. So demise as such is not necessarily redemptive, but becomes so in those moments when demise and happiness coincide.

The fragment is brief and extremely condensed. Benjamin's concept of *Glück* in this context does not receive extensive commentary. Given the slow and often painful experience of bodily and mental decay and given Benjamin's rejection of the glorification of suffering, the coincidence with happiness seems to mark out an impossible or at least subjectively uninhabitable and uncontrollable temporality. Benjamin's *Glück* seems not to be a state of mind, but rather to be akin to a state of life, perhaps closer to when *Glück* is used in translating the Aristotelian *eudaimonia* in German, which, however, is not at all meant to suggest an equivocation between the Benjaminian and Aristotelian notions of happiness.[68] Unlike in Aristotle, where happiness is a matter of an equilibrium, in Benjamin, happiness connotes completion. The convergence of demise and happiness means that this happiness is not the fulfillment of a promise to be found on the other side of this life's demise; it is part of life in this world. Benjamin thus renders redemption thoroughly immanent and profane; life in this world is redeemed as it passes away fully and totally into happiness in this world. In contradistinction from the Christian *visio beatifica* that renders happiness salutary as eternal and transcendent, for Benjamin happiness itself becomes redemptive only insofar as it is transient and immanent. Even so, Benjamin insists that the individual does not directly experience what he calls the rhythm of demise as happiness. Benjamin here seems to distinguish the messianic rhythm of demise from a romanticized version of redemptive suffering and with this argument denies anyone their aspirations to actively seek happiness and reconciliation in death. The individual suffers the demise untransfigured as decline, even if it may be a passing away in happiness. Or in the words of the oft-cited last line of Benjamin's Goethe essay, "There is hope only for the hopeless."[69]

For Benjamin transience is neither a failure nor deficiency of life in this world whose overcoming theology can and must promise. At the same time, Benjamin's twin concepts of transience and redemption do not justify the suffering and pains of demise, neither as penance that will lead to perfection and reconciliation nor as an inevitable condition that must be affirmed and embraced as such. Rather, Benjamin figures demise as redemptive only when passing away becomes fully and totally possible, when individuals, nature, and history can all pass away without continuing to haunt the present as the unredeemed past. The experience of transience is neither redemptive per se nor perceived as such by the individual. Instead, the nonsubjective focus of Benjamin's account of transience reorients our perspective from our own individual experiences to that of seeking to alter the conditions of life itself such that they can enable this full passing away in happiness.

To reformulate the reading this essay has advanced, we might understand Benjamin's attempt to articulate the philosophical dignity of transience in a material metaphysics of experience along the lines of Theodor Adorno's suggestion that "*die Metaphysik geschlüpft ist in das materielle Dasein* [metaphysics has slipped into material existence]."[70] As Adorno argues, we become especially attentive to this material life of metaphysics insofar as we refrain from seeking an epistemological-critical grounding for insights in order to guarantee their philosophical certainty and instead acknowledge their experiential foundation. Adorno made this remark in his 1965 lecture course on metaphysics to explain that the material reality of suffering inflicted on and intensified by human action delivers a new categorical imperative, namely, that this suffering ought not to be.[71] However, this imperative carries within it a metaphysical moment, a metaphysical experience, if we but acknowledge the material, historical, and experiential source of this imperative. This imperative, according to Adorno, cannot and should not be deduced from nor grounded in logical principles, even though it can and must be subjected to critical reflection. The demonstration of the certainty, validity, and necessity of this principle can be attained only at the price of neglecting the material origins of this imperative and the contingency of this experience. Similarly, Benjamin's positioning of theology as the metaphysics of experience moves theology from an absolute, eternal, and unchanging transcendence into transient existence. His interpretation of transient existence through the rhythm of demise as what he describes as messianic introduces a critical perspective on the conditions of the experience of demise, insofar as this passing away is only complete and redemptive in happiness. Understanding theological concepts as precipitating a metaphysics of experience does not insulate them against critique, but rather directs the task of theological critique to attending to and attempting to reshape the infrastructures of our collective affects.

Notes

1. Jürgen Habermas asserts Benjamin's importance for critical theory and distinguishes Benjamin's understanding of critique from the type of criticism that seeks to raise awareness about injustices in his essay "Consciousness-Raising or Redemptive Criticism: The Contemporaneity of Walter Benjamin," *New German Critique*, no. 17 (Spring 1979): 30–59. As Habermas explains, Benjamin's understanding of critique works through its unique conception of history, which is characterized by an "impulse to rescue and redeem" (38). Habermas suggests that in retrieving Benjamin's understanding of critique in the contemporary debates on critical theory, the "mystical causality" (38) that Benjamin attributes to the critique of history would need to be reconsidered, since religion (in Habermas's estimation) has retreated into private belief. Habermas's assessment in this essay has been taken up by his successor at the Institut für Sozialforschung, Axel Honneth in "A Communicative Disclosure of the Past," in *The Actuality of Walter Benjamin*, ed. Laura Marcus and Lynda Nead (London: Lawrence and Wishart, 1998), 118–134.

Hamacher offers a thorough reading of Benjamin's understanding of *Jetztzeit* (now-time) and of the concept of historical time in Benjamin in " 'Now': Walter Benjamin on Historical Time," in *Walter Benjamin and History*, ed. Andrew Benjamin (London: Continuum, 2005), 38–68. However, without further commentary, messianism in Hamacher's argument eventually only figures as a trope of the constitutive possibility and impossibility of history's redeemability. In my estimation, the problem with many readings of Benjamin's messianism is not simply that eventually it is no longer clear what is theological about this argument. As I argue in my book project on Walter Benjamin and Hermann Cohen, Benjamin's understanding of the messianic implies the continuous undoing of the theological—distinctively transcendent and religious—dimension of the messianic itself. In my interpretation, however, I part from interpretations such as Hamacher's. I find it important to mark precisely the *Stillstellung* (arrest) and undoing of theology and oppose the quasi-transcendentalism of deconstruction through Benjamin's recuperation of metaphysics. For another example of a reading that renders the messianic into a quasi-transcendental framework of history, see Dimitris Vardoulakis, "The Subject of History: The Temporality of Parataxis in Benjamin's Historiography," in *Walter Benjamin and History*, ed. Andrew Benjamin (London: Continuum, 2005), 118–136.

A great number of interpretations take up the theological specificity in Benjamin's work in various ways; see especially Eric Jacobson, *Metaphysics of the Profane: The Political Theology of Walter Benjamin and Gershom Scholem* (New York: Columbia University Press, 2003), and Astrid Deuber-Mankowsky, *Der frühe Walter Benjamin und Hermann Cohen: Jüdische Werte, kritische Philosophie, vergängliche Erfahrung* (Berlin: Vorwerk 8, 2000). Howard Caygill argues that paying attention to theology is an appropriate theoretical move, because theology has never disappeared and continues to undergird purportedly secular conceptions of history and time; see Caygill, "Non-Messianic Political Theology in Benjamin's 'On the Concept of History,'" in *Walter Benjamin and History*, ed. Andrew Benjamin (London: Continuum, 2005), 215–226. Gillian Rose makes a similar case and substantiates the interpretation of Benjamin's own vocabulary by contextualizing it with reference to Jewish religious sources in her essay "Walter Benjamin: Out of the Sources of Modern Judaism," in *Judaism and Modernity: Philosophical Essays* (Oxford: Blackwell, 1993), 175–210. Susan Handelman, *Fragments of Redemption: Jewish Thought and Literary Theory in Benjamin, Scholem, and Levinas* (Bloomington: Indiana University Press, 1991) and Susan Buck-Morss, *The Dialectics of Seeing: Walter Benjamin and the Arcades Project* (Cambridge, MA: MIT Press, 1989) both anchor the discussion of Benjamin's theology in readings of Scholem's studies on Kabbalah. Robert Gibbs draws on Rosenzweig's work to offer a theological discussion of Benjamin's reference to a liturgical temporality in "On the Concept of History"; see Gibbs, "Messianic Epistemology: Thesis XV," in *Walter Benjamin and History*, ed. Andrew Benjamin (London: Continuum, 2005), 197–214, In his *The Messianic Reduction: Walter Benjamin and the Shape of Time* (Stanford, CA: Stanford University Press, 2011), Peter Fenves examines Benjamin's early work in relation to phenomenology and argues that the messianic introduces a plasticity into history that upends its unilinearity. For a comprehensive survey of philosophical themes in Benjamin, see also Eli Friedlander's reading of Benjamin against Kant's metaphysics of experience in *Walter Benjamin: A Philosophical Portrait* (Cambridge, MA: Harvard University Press, 2012). Friedlander follows my *Fate, Guilt, and Messianic Interruptions: Ethics of Theological Critique in Hermann Cohen and Walter Benjamin* (2009), published as open access document at http://gradworks.umi.com/34/11/ 3411051.html. Friedlander, however, does not engage with Cohen and neo-Kantianism, which in my opinion Deuber-Mankowsky, Pierfrancesco Fiorato, and Tamara Tagliacozzo convincingly show as crucial to Benjamin's philosophical formation. See Fiorato, "Die Erfahrung, das Unbedingte und die

Religion: Walter Benjamin als Leser von *Kants Theorie der Erfahrung*," in *Hermann Cohen's Philosophy of Religion: International Conference in Jerusalem, 1996*, ed. Stéphane Mosès and Hartwig Wiedebach (Hildesheim: Georg Olms, 1997), 71–84, and Tagliacozzo, *Esperienza e Compito Infinito Nella Filosofia Del Primo Benjamin* (Macerata: Quodlibet, 2003).

2. Walter Benjamin, "Über den Begriff der Geschichte," in *Gesammelte Schriften*, vol. 1.2, ed. Rolf Tiedemann and Hermann Schweppenhäuser (Frankfurt am Main: Suhrkamp, 1974), 691–704; "On the Concept of History," in *Selected Writings*, 4:389–400.

3. Jacobson, *Metaphysics of the Profane*, 5.

4. See in particular Benjamin's conclusion to his essay "Critique of Violence," in *Selected Writings*, 1:236–252. On profanation and the undoing of theology itself as part of Benjamin's understanding of theology, see Werner Hamacher's commentary on "Das Theologisch-politische Fragment," in *Benjamin-Handbuch: Leben—Werk—Wirkung*, ed. Burkhardt Lindner (Stuttgart: J. B. Metzler, 2006), 175–192. Theologically inventive transpositions of Benjamin's theological concepts into Christian theology include, among others, Johannes Baptist Metz, *Memoria Passionis: Ein provozierendes Gedächtnis in pluraler Gesellschaft* (Freiburg im Breisgau: Herder, 2006); Helmut Thielen, *Eingedenken und Erlösung: Walter Benjamin* (Würzburg: Königshausen und Neumann, 2005); and Benjamin Taubald, *Anamnetische Vernunft: Untersuchungen zu einem Begriff der neuen Politischen Theologie* (Münster: LIT Verlag, 2001). These readings appropriate Benjamin to offer critical reformulations of Christian theology, but they also tend to bypass Benjamin's attempt at undoing theology.

5. On the discussion of the theological versus the materialist tendencies in Benjamin's thinking and Brecht's, Scholem's, and Adorno's influences, see Rolf Tiedemann, *Dialektik im Stillstand: Versuche zum Spätwerk Walter Benjamins* (Frankfurt am Main: Suhrkamp, 1983) and *Mystik und Aufklärung: Studien zur Philosophie Walter Benjamins, mit einer Vorrede von Theodor W. Adorno und sechs Corollarien* (Munich: Edition Text & Kritik, 2002); Richard Wolin, *Walter Benjamin: An Aesthetic of Redemption* (New York: Columbia University Press, 1982); Richard Lane, *Reading Walter Benjamin: Writing through the Catastrophe* (Manchester: Manchester University Press, 2005); Terry Eagleton, *Walter Benjamin: Or Towards a Revolutionary Criticism* (London: Verso, 1981); and Buck-Morss, *Dialectics of Seeing*.

6. Walter Benjamin, "An Werner Kraft, 25.5.1935," in *Gesammelte Briefe*, vol. 5, *1935–1937*, ed. Christoph Gödde and Henri Lonitz (Frankfurt am Main: Suhrkamp, 1995), 115. Walter Benjamin, *Das Passagen-Werk*, in *Gesammelte Schriften*, vol. 5, ed. Rolf Tiedemann (Frankfurt am Main: Suhrkamp, 1982), translated by Howard Eiland and Kevin McLaughlin as *The Arcades Project*, ed. Rolf Tiedemann (Cambridge, MA: Harvard University Press , 2002).

7. Buck-Morss, "Is This Philosophy?," in *Dialectics of Seeing*, 217–252. Specifically Buck-Morss argues that "for Benjamin, theology functions as an

axis of philosophical experience, and . . . this differs from the function of 'religion' as part of the ideological superstructure" (248–249), and consequently theology has a critical function for Marxism, just as the Marxist materialism has a critical function for theology: "Without theology (the axis of transcendence) Marxism falls into positivism; without Marxism (the axis of empirical history) theology falls into magic" (249). While I agree with the interpretation that theology in Benjamin carries a critical force, I hope the following examination of what I call Benjamin's "metaphysics of transience" will make clear how I see a different theological materialism at play especially in the early Benjamin.

8. Jacobson, *Metaphysics of the Profane*, 5.

9. In "Walter Benjamin: Out of the Sources of Modern Judaism," Rose suggests that "Strictly speaking, there is no Judaic theology—no *logos* of God . . . Talmud Torah means the teaching of the teaching, or the commentary on the law" (182). In response to this claim that there is no Jewish theology, David Kaufmann argues that while there is no systematic elaboration of a Jewish creed—no dogmatics—if one looks to the Middle Ages, there is a tradition of Jewish theological texts concerned with speculations on creation, revelation, and redemption. Theology, in other words, need not only be restricted to the dogmatics of faith, but can be extended to speculative commentary; in Benjamin and Adorno, their sense of theology revolves around the concept of redemption in particular. See David Kaufmann, "Beyond Use, within Reason: Adorno, Benjamin and the Question of Theology," *New German Critique*, no. 83 (Spring–Summer 2001): 151–173.

10. Jacobson's interpretation of the theological character of Benjamin's metaphysics in *Metaphysics of the Profane* works out the crucial links among language, justice, and politics in Benjamin's work. Here I am concerned more with the issue of experience. On theological critique and its bearing on experience and affect, see also Idit Dobbs-Weinstein, "The Power of Prejudice and the Force of Law: Spinoza's Critique of Religion and Its Heirs," *Epoché* 7, no. 1 (2002): 51–70.

11. Walter Benjamin, "Über das Programm der kommenden Philosophie," in *Gesammelte Schriften*, vol. 2.1, ed. Rolf Tiedemann and Hermann Schweppenhäuser (Frankfurt am Main: Suhrkamp, 1977), 157–171, translated by Mark Ritter as "On the Program of the Coming Philosophy," in *Selected Writings*, 1:100–110. For an examination of this text as a critique of Cohen in particular, see Deuber-Mankowsky, *Der frühe Walter Benjamin und Hermann Cohen*, 80–89. In her argument Deuber-Mankowsky does not consider Benjamin's claim that we encounter metaphysics especially by way of theology, which is the claim that I want to turn to in order to suggest that Benjamin offers theology as a theory of nonsubjective experience, which is to be cast as a metaphysics of transient experience.

12. In the background of my approach to this interpretation of metaphysics in Benjamin is Adorno's 1965 lecture course on metaphysics, published as *Metaphysik: Begriff und Probleme*, ed. Rolf Tiedemann (Frankfurt am Main:

Suhrkamp, 1998). On Benjamin's attempt to think experience beyond interiority and subjectivity, see also Martin Jay, "Walter Benjamin, Remembrance, and the First World War," *Benjamin Studien/Studies* 1, no. 1 (2002): 185–208, and "Lamenting the Crisis of Experience: Benjamin and Adorno," in *Songs of Experience: Modern American and European Variations on a Universal Theme* (Berkeley: University of California Press, 2005), 312–360.

13. Walter Benjamin, "Zum Problem der Physiognomik und Vorhersagung," in *Gesammelte Schriften*, vol. 6, ed. Rolf Tiedemann and Hermann Schweppenhäuser (Frankfurt am Main: Suhrkamp, 1985), 93.

14. On *Glück* (happiness, fortune), demise, and the messianic in Benjamin, see also Deuber-Mankowsky, "Walter Benjamin's *Theological-Political Fragment* as a Response to Ernst Bloch's *Spirit of Utopia*," in *Leo Baeck Institute Yearbook* 47 (2002), 3–19; and "The Image of Happiness We Harbor: The Messianic Power of Weakness in Cohen, Benjamin, and Paul," *New German Critique* 35, no. 3 (Fall 2008): 57–69; Elissa Marder, "Walter Benjamin's Dream of 'Happiness,'" in *Walter Benjamin and* The Arcades Project, ed. Beatrice Hanssen (London: Continuum, 2006), 184–200; and Hamacher, "Das Theologisch-politische Fragment."

15. On Benjamin's own understanding of secularization, see Walter Benjamin, *Ursprung des deutschen Trauerspiels*, in *Gesammelte Schriften*, 1.1:203–430, translated by John Osborne as *The Origin of German Tragic Drama* (London: Verso, 1998); and "Kapitalismus als Religion," in *Gesammelte Schriften*, 6:100–103, translated by Rodney Livingstone as "Capitalism and Religion," in *Selected Writings*, 1:288–291. In "Capitalism as Religion," Benjamin comments critically on Max Weber's understanding of secularization in *Die protestantische Ethik und der "Geist" des Kapitalismus*, ed. Dirk Kaesler (Weinheim: Beltz Athenäum, 1993). See also Hamacher, "Guilt History: Benjamin's Sketch 'Capitalism as Religion,'" *Diacritics* 32, no. 3–4 (2002): 81–106. For rethinking theology and secularization beyond the dichotomy of reason versus religion, see Hans Blumenberg, *Legitimität der Neuzeit* (Frankfurt am Main: Suhrkamp, 1966); Jacob Taubes, *Vom Kult zur Kultur: Bausteine zu eine Kritik der historischen Vernunft*, ed. Aleida Assmann, Jan Assmann, Wolf-Daniel Hartwich, and Winfried Menninghaus (Munich: Wilhelm Fink, 1996); Anthony J. Cascardi, "Secularization and Modernization," in *The Subject of Modernity* (Cambridge: Cambridge University Press, 1992), 125–178; Talal Asad, *Formations of the Secular: Christianity, Islam, Modernity* (Stanford, CA: Stanford University Press, 2003); Charles Taylor, *A Secular Age* (Cambridge, MA: Harvard University Press , 2007), and my "Theological-Political Ruins: Walter Benjamin, Sovereignty, and the Politics of Skeletal Eschatology," *Law and Critique* 24, no. 3 (2013): 295–315.

16. Hermann Cohen parts with Kant since he rejects Kant's natural teleology, but Cohen retains the Kantian idealization of progress. For an account of the differences and connections between Kant and Cohen in their philosophy of history, see William Kluback, "Hermann Cohen and Kant: A

Philosophy of History from Jewish Sources," *Idealistic Studies* 17 (1987): 161–176. On the issue of theodicy and the justification of suffering in Cohen in the name of progress, see Christoph Schulte, "Theodizee bei Kant und Cohen," in *Hermann Cohen's Philosophy of Religion: International Conference in Jerusalem, 1996*, ed. Stéphane Mosès and Hartwig Wiedebach (Hildesheim: Georg Olms, 1997), 205–230, and Andrea Poma, "Suffering and Non-Eschatological Messianism in Hermann Cohen," in *Hermann Cohen's Critical Idealism*, ed. Reinier Munk (Dordrecht, NL: Springer, 2005), 413–428.

17. Walter Benjamin, "Über die Wahrnehmung," in *Gesammelte Schriften*, 6:33–38; translated by Rodney Livingstone as "On Perception," in *Selected Writings*, 1:93–96.

18. On experience in neo-Kantianism more generally, see Alan W. Richardson, "Conceiving, Experiencing, and Conceiving Experiencing: Neo-Kantianism and the History of the Concept of Experience," *Topoi* 22, no. 1 (2003): 55–67.

19. Hermann Cohen, *Kants Theorie der Erfahrung* (Hildesheim: Georg Olms, 1987). On Benjamin's studying Kant and Cohen's *Kants Theorie der Erfahrung*, see Deuber-Mankowsky, *Der frühe Walter Benjamin und Hermann Cohen*, 29–80, and Fiorato, "Die Erfahrung, das Unbedingte und die Religion."

20. Hermann Cohen, *Ästhetik des reinen Gefühls* (Hildesheim: Georg Olms, 2005); *Ethik des reinen Willens* (Hildesheim: Georg Olms, 1981); *Logik der reinen Erkenntnis* (Hildesheim: Georg Olms, 1977); and *Die Religion der Vernunft aus den Quellen des Judentums* (Leipzig: G. Fock, 1919), translated by Simon Kaplan as *Religion of Reason out of the Sources of Judaism* (Atlanta, GA: American Academy of Religion, 1995).

21. "Vor allem galt und galt es ihm [Kant] [*sic*], die Einheit der Erfahrung als die Einheit der mathematischen Naturwissenschaft zu konstituieren, um an ihr die Norm zu gewinnen für alle anderen Arten wissenschaftlicher Gewissheit, und für den auszeichnenden Wert objektiver Erkenntnis" (Cohen, *Kants Theorie der Erfahrung*, 753). All translations of excerpts from Cohen's works with the exception of passages from *Religion of Reason* are my own.

22. Immanuel Kant, *Prolegomena zu einer jeden künftigen Metaphysik, die als Wissenschaft wird auftreten können*, ed. Konstantin Pollok (Hamburg: Felix Meiner, 2001). Immanuel Kant, *Kritik der reinen Vernunft*, ed. Wilhelm Weischedel (Frankfurt am Main: Suhrkamp, 1956), translated and edited by Paul Guyer and Allen W. Wood as *Critique of Pure Reason* (Cambridge: Cambridge University Press, 1998).

23. Kant, *Pure Reason*, 136. Paul Guyer and Allen W. Wood in their translation of Kant's *Critique of Pure Reason* render *Erkenntnis* as "cognition." However, it seems to me that *Erkenntnis*—in particular for Benjamin—denotes more than solely the action of cognizing. *Erkenntnis* also implies knowledge in the sense of insight.

24. See, for instance, the B introduction of the *Critique of Pure Reason*: "Wenn aber gleich alle unsere Erkenntnis mit der Erfahrung anhebt, so

entspringt sie darum doch noch nicht eben alle aus der Erfahrung" (Kant, *Kritik der reinen Vernunft*, B1, 45).

25. Kant, *Pure Reason*, 127. "Erfahrung ist ohne Zweifel das erste Produkt, welches unser Verstand hervorbringt, indem er den rohen Stoff sinnlicher Empfindungen bearbeitet" (Kant, *Kritik der reinen Vernunft*, A2, 48).

26. Cohen, *Ethik des reinen Willens*, 85.

27. In his countering the Kantian and neo-Kantian focus on a natural-scientific ideal of knowledge, questions of philosophy of language are also at issue for Benjamin. Benjamin's own early work on philosophy of language needs to be read in this context of a reformulation of the Kantian epistemological critique. An examination of Benjamin's philosophy of language is beyond the scope of this project, which foregrounds his philosophy of history and the ethical implications arising from the theological concept of the messianic in Benjamin's work. On redemption and Benjamin's philosophy of language, see Handelman, *Fragments of Redemption*. On language and epistemological critique in Benjamin, see Howard Caygill, "Language and the Infinities," in *Walter Benjamin: Colour of Experience* (London: Routledge, 1998), 13–22; Rodolphe Gasché, "Saturnine Vision and the Question of Difference: Reflections on Walter Benjamin's Theory of Language," in *Benjamin's Ground: New Readings of Walter Benjamin*, ed. Rainer Nägele (Detroit, MI: Wayne State University Press, 1988), 83–104; Peter Fenves, "The Paradisial *Epoche*: On Benjamin's First Philosophy," in *Arresting Language: From Leibniz to Benjamin* (Stanford, CA: Stanford University Press, 2001), 174–226; and Eli Friedlander, *Walter Benjamin: A Philosophical Portrait*, chap. 1, 9–36.

28. Cohen, *Religion of Reason*, 20; translation modified. The original German reads: "Und während nach der Ethik . . . [die Vernunft] unverantworlich ist für alles, was außerhalb ihrer Grenzen geschieht, . . . und daher auch eigentlich gar nicht interessiert ist für den Erfolg, den die Pflicht nach außen erlangt oder nicht erlangt—so erhebt auch hier die Religion Einspruch gegen diese Indifferenz" (Cohen, *Religion der Vernunft*, 23–24).

29. See also Deuber-Mankowsky, *Der frühe Walter Benjamin und Hermann Cohen* on critique as an ethical commitment and her foregrounding the role of transience as key to Benjamin's critique. In the sections that confront Benjamin and Cohen on the philosophical role of transience, Deuber-Mankowsky emphasizes the importance of transience as Benjamin's way of inscribing contingency against Cohen for whom contingency threatens *wissenschaftliche Erkenntnis* (scientific knowledge), as Deuber-Mankowsky demonstrates. My focus here lies more on the claim to a specifically metaphysical dimension that Benjamin elaborates through the emphasis on transience and what the conjunction of theology and transience mean for recuperating a material metaphysics.

30. Immanuel Kant, *Kritik der Urteilskraft*, ed. Wilhelm Weischedel (Frankfurt am Main: Suhrkamp, 1957), translated by Paul Guyer as *Critique of the Power of Judgment*, ed. Eric Matthews (Cambridge: Cambridge University Press, 2000).

31. Kant, *Critique of the Power of Judgment*, 123.

32. Benjamin, "Wahrnehmung," 6:36.

33. Benjamin, "On Perception," in *Selected Writings*, 1:95. "Erfahrung als Gegenstand der Erkenntnis ist die Einheitliche [*sic*] und Kontinuierliche [*sic*] Mannichfaltigkeit [*sic*] der Erkenntnis" (Benjamin, "Wahrnehmung," in *Gesammelte Schriften*, 6:36).

34. "So hat auch der Historiker heute nur ein schmales, aber tragfähiges Gerüst—ein philosophisches zu errichten, um die aktuellsten Aspekte der Vergangenheit in sein Netz zu ziehen" (Benjamin, *Passagen-Werk*, in *Gesammelte Schriften*, 5:572). "The historian today has only to erect a slender but sturdy scaffolding—a philosophic structure—in order to draw the most vital aspects of the past into his net" (Benjamin, *Arcades Project*, 459, N1a,1).

35. In the *Critique of Pure Reason*, the first sense of experience would be the "raw material" of sense-perceptions, which understanding determines conceptually and so produces experience. However, Kant makes no clear distinction between the two senses when he states: "But although all our cognition commences with experience, yet it does not on that account arise from experience" (Kant, *Critique of Pure Reason*, B1, 136). Experience here seems to include and also denote experience in the sense of sensations and impressions. "Wenn aber gleich alle unsere Erkenntnis mit der Erfahrung anhebt, so entspringt sie darum doch noch nicht eben alle aus der Erfahrung" (Kant, *Kritik der reinen Vernunft*, B1, 45).

36. Benjamin, "On Perception," in *Selected Writings*, 1:94. The full passage here reads in German: "Es ist überaus merkwürdig, daß Kant im Interesse der Apriorität und Logizität da eine scharfe Diskontinuität u[nd] Trennung macht wo aus dem gleichen Interesse die vorkantischen Philosophen die innigste Kontinuität und Einheit zu schaffen suchten, nämlich durch spekulative Deduktion der Welt die innigste Verbindung zwischen Erkenntnis und Erfahrung zu schaffen" ("Wahrnehmung," in *Gesammelte Schriften*, 6:35).

37. Totality in Benjamin needs to be understood through his use of the monad, which creates a multiplicity of totalities that are in themselves fragmented. On the monad as a critical category in Benjamin, see Rainer Nägele, "Das Beben des Barock in der Moderne: Walter Benjamins Monadologie," *MLN* 106, no. 3 (1991): 501–527.

38. Kant, *Pure Reason*, 193–194. "Ohne Sinnlichkeit würde uns kein Gegenstand gegeben, und ohne Verstand keiner gedacht werden. Gedanken ohne Inhalt sind leer, Anschauungen ohne Begriffe sind blind. Daher ist es ebenso notwendig, seine Begriffe sinnlich (d.i. ihnen den Gegenstand in der Anschauung beizufügen), als, seine Anschauungen sich verständlich zu machen (d.i. die unter Begriffe zu bringen)" (Kant, *Kritik der reinen Vernunft*, A51/B75).

39. Benjamin, "Programm," in *Gesammelte Schriften*, 2.1:159; translation mine. The English translation by Mark Ritter in *Selected Writings* mistakes the relationship between the adverbs and adjectives here. This issue of the metaphysical weight of experience is at the heart of Benjamin's essay

"Erfahrung und Armut," in *Gesammelte Schriften*, 2.1:213–219, translated by Rodney Livingstone as "Experience and Poverty," in *Selected Writings*, 2.2:731–736. In his later work, Benjamin continues to examine the decay of experience as in "Über einige Motive bei Baudelaire," in *Gesammelte Schriften*, 1.2:605–653, translated by Harry Zohn as "On Some Motifs in Baudelaire," in *Selected Writings*, 4:313–355; and "Der Erzähler: Betrachtungen zum Werk Nikolai Lesskows," in *Gesammelte Schriften*, 2.2:438–465, translated by Harry Zohn as "The Storyteller: Observations on the Works of Nikolai Leskov," in *Selected Writings*, 3:143–166.

40. In general, Benjamin seems to agree with some of Hegel's critique of Kant, but rejects Hegel's solutions, in particular Hegelian teleology and mediation (see Caygill, *Colour of Experience*, 2). In a letter to Scholem from January 31, 1918, Benjamin expresses his being repelled by Hegel's work and calls him an "intellektueller Gewaltmensch [intellectual thug, person of intellectual violence]": "Von Hegel dagegen hat mich das was ich bisher las durchaus abgestoßen. Ich glaube wir würden wenn wir uns einige Sachen auf kurze Zeit vornehmen würden bald auf die geistige Physiognomie kommen die daraus blickt die eines intellektuellen Gewaltmenschen, eines Mystikers der Gewalt, die schlechteste Sorte, die es gibt: aber auch Mystiker" (*Gesammelte Briefe*, vol. 1, *1910–1918*, ed. Christoph Gödde and Henri Lonitz [Frankfurt am Main: Suhrkamp, 1995], 422–423). It is not clear what Hegel Benjamin read or how extensive his Hegel studies might have been. In his *Mystik und Aufklärung*, Tiedemann suggests that there are strong affinities between Benjamin and Schelling in Benjamin's rejection on conceptual knowledge of the absolute (19–44).

41. Benjamin, "Programm," in *Gesammelte Schriften*, 2.1:169.

42. Benjamin, "Program," in *Selected Writings*, 1:100. In German, this passage reads: "Es war erstens die Frage nach der Gewißheit der Erkenntnis die bleibend ist; und es war zweitens die Frage nach der Dignität der Erfahrung die vergänglich war" ("Programm," in *Gesammelte Schriften*, 2.1:158). The English translation is problematic, since it renders *Dignität* into "integrity" and *vergänglich* into "ephemeral" without any commentary to explain these choices. Moreover, the translation elides that the German uses the past tense to describe this transience of experience, in contrast to asserting the lasting certainty in the present tense.

43. Benjamin, "Program," in *Selected Writings*, 1:110. "Eine Erkenntnis ist metaphysisch heißt im strengen Sinne: sie bezieht sich, durch den Stammbegriff der Erkenntnis auf die konkrete Totalität der Erfahrung, d.h. aber auf *Dasein*" ("Programm," in *Gesammelte Schriften*, 2.1:170–171).

44. Immanuel Kant, "Idee zu einer allgemeinen Geschichte in weltbürgerlicher Absicht," *Schriften zur Anthropologie, Geschichtsphilosophie, Politik und Pädagogik*, ed. Wilhelm Weischedel (Frankfurt am Main: Surhkamp, 1964), 31–50, translated by Allen Wood as "Idea for a Universal History with a Cosmopolitan Aim," in *Essays on Kant's "Idea for a Universal*

History with a Cosmopolitan Aim," ed. Amélie Rorty and James Schmidt (Cambridge: Cambridge University Press, 2009), 9–23.

45. Kant, "Idea," 21.

46. Ibid., 22. The full passage reads in German: "[S]o wird sich, wie ich glaube, ein Leitfaden entdecken, der nicht bloß zur Erklärung des verworrenen Spiels menschlicher Dinge . . . dienen kann . . . ; sondern es wird (was man, ohne einen Naturplan vorauszusetzen, nicht mit Grunde hoffen kann) eine tröstende Aussicht in die Zukunft eröffnet werden, in welcher die Menschengattung in weiter Ferne vorgestellt wird, wie sie sich endlich doch zu dem Zustande empor arbeitet, in welchem alle Keime, die die Natur in sie legte völlig können entwickelt und ihre Bestimmung hier auf Erden kann erfüllt werden" ("Idee," 49).

47. Kant, "Idea," 14. "Der Mensch will Eintracht; aber die Natur weiß besser, was für seine Gattung gut ist: sie will Zwietracht. Er will gemächlich und vergnügt leben; die Natur will aber, er soll aus der Lässigkeit und untätigen Genügsamkeit hinaus, sich in Arbeit und Mühseligkeiten stürzen, um dagegen auch Mittel auszufinden, sich klüglich wiederum aus den letzteren heraus zu ziehen" ("Idee," 38–39).

48. Kant, "Idea," 14.

49. For a summary explication of the main arguments of "On the Program of the Coming Philosophy," see Peter Fenves, "'Über das Programm der kommenden Philosophie,'" in *Benjamin-Handbuch*, 134–150. For an incisive disarticulation of Benjamin's reading of four different understandings of metaphysics in "On Perception," see also Deuber-Mankowsky, *Der frühe Walter Benjamin und Hermann Cohen*, 80–85. For a careful philosophical analysis of "On the Program of the Coming Philosophy," see Caygill, "The Programme of the Coming Philosophy," 1–32, in Caygill, *Colour of Experience*.

50. In *Walter Benjamin: An Aesthetic of Redemption*, Wolin tends to mitigate the systematic, philosophical challenge of Benjamin's theological claims either by considering religion a "regulative idea" (36) or by personalizing Benjamin's turn to theology as a leap of faith compelled at first by his melancholic psychic disposition and later by his despair in the face of fascism (see especially 203–207). As Caygill indicates at the end of his reading of the "Program" essay, Benjamin's concern with experience is mostly considered in the context of his critique of modernity and is presented as an issue with the disintegration of experience (see Caygill, *Colour of Experience*, 29–31). In *Songs of Experience*, Martin Jay points out that the theological grounds of Benjamin's arguments remain un- or under-examined in most arguments that appropriate Benjamin's critiques in the context of cultural theory. Jay concludes that Benjamin's theoretical framework and his efforts to offer an alternative understanding of experience are in the last instance "frankly dogmatic and based on a doctrinal belief in the Absolute, which could somehow manifest itself in mundane experience" (341). It is hard to tell whether Benjamin indeed held such a belief, since his letters paint a complex picture of Benjamin's avowed beliefs and

commitments, which also vary significantly depending on the addressee of the letter. Taking up Jay's concern that the theological aspect in Benjamin requires attention, but differing with it insofar as I do not consider the question as one of "frankly dogmatic" assertions, I read Benjamin's metaphysical elaborations as a diagnostic of how to frame the affective force of theological concepts in their bearing on experience.

51. On Benjamin's unique materialism, see Caygill, *Colour of Experience* and Buck-Morss, *Dialectics of Seeing*. With attention to Benjamin's understanding of materialism especially in his book on German tragic dramas, see Pensky, *Melancholy Dialectics*. On Benjamin's examination of surrealism to find a different account of materialism, one against nineteenth-century mechanical materialism, see Margaret Cohen, *Profane Illumination: Walter Benjamin and the Paris of Surrealist Revolution* (Berkeley: University of California Press, 1993). On Benjamin's appropriation of historical materialism, see Christoph Hering, *Die Rekonstruktion der Revolution: Walter Benjamins messianischer Materialismus in den Thesen "Über den Begriff der Geschichte"* (Frankfurt am Main: Peter Lang, 1983) and Roland Beiner, "Walter Benjamin's Philosophy of History," *Political Theory* 12, no. 3 (1984): 423–434.

52. Benjamin, "Programm," in *Gesammelte Schriften*, 2.1:158.

53. Benjamin's use of "totality" as a nonindividual, nonsystematic, fragmented totality constantly in demise is complicated and would demand further examination, for instance especially through the *"Erkenntniskritische Vorrede* (Epistemo-Critical Prologue)" of *The Origin of German Tragic Drama*. The concept of the totality of experience contains the kernel of a critical potential that Benjamin's later work brings to full fruition as an interruptive contraction of the continuum of time into a single moment. In Thesis XVII of "On the Concept of History," Benjamin explains his methodology of historical materialist historiography as the production of monads to contract history into just such a totality, where an image contains the entire history of an era (and presumably its metaphysics as well). These monads can then enter into constellations with each other, so that history no longer appears as a continuous development and progress, but reveals occasions for critique and action. It seems to me that the early work elucidates the philosophical underpinnings of these later invocations of monadic totalities in relation to Benjamin's theory of experience.

54. Benjamin, "Program," in *Selected Writings*, 1:109. In German this passage reads: "Jedoch kommt der Stamm- und Urbegriff der Erkenntnis in diesem Zusammenhang nicht zu einer konkreten Totalität der Erfahrung, ebensowenig zu einem Begriff von Dasein. Es gibt aber eine Einheit der Erfahrung die keineswegs als Summe von Erfahrungen verstanden werden kann, auf die sich der Erkenntnisbegriff als Lehre in seiner kontinuierlichen Entfaltung *unmittelbar* bezieht" ("Programm," in *Gesammelte Schriften*, 2.1:170).

55. Benjamin, *Origin*, 27; Benjamin, *Trauerspiel*, in *Gesammelte Schriften*, 1.1:207.

56. In connection with Benjamin's recuperation of tradition as a critical category, not as content, but as process, see also Adorno's last lecture of his metaphysics course (Adorno, *Metaphysik*, 214–226). Adorno cautions against an uncritical rejection of traditional knowledge, because such a rejection tends to forego the possibility of reckoning with the force of traditions and hypostasizes rational autonomy without reflecting on how the sense of the incontrovertible truth of reason as more compelling than other humbug is part of a tradition itself and derives its persuasiveness out of this tradition of rational scientificity (see Adorno, *Metaphysik*, 216)

57. Benjamin, "Program," in *Selected Writings*, 1:109; translation modified. In German this passage reads: "Der Gegenstand und Inhalt dieser Lehre, diese konkrete Totalität der Erfahrung ist Religion, die aber der Philosophie zunächst nur als Lehre gegeben ist. Die Quelle des Daseins liegt nun aber in der Totalität der Erfahrung und erst in der Lehre stößt die Philosophie auf ein Absolutes, als Dasein, und damit auf jene Kontinuität im Wesen der Erfahrung in deren Vernachlässigung der Mangel des Neukantianismus zu vermuten ist" ("Programm," in *Gesammelte Schriften*, 2.1:170).

58. This focus on experience does not mean that Benjamin embraces life-philosophy. To the contrary, he is vehemently critical of life philosophy's organicist accounts of life. On Benjamin's anti–life-philosophy, see Jay, "Lamenting the Crisis of Experience." On Benjamin's criticism of Stefan George and the proximity of the *Georgekreis* to life-philosophy, see Deuber-Mankowsky, *Der frühe Walter Benjamin und Hermann Cohen*, 164–203, and Lane, "Goethe and the *Georgekreis*," 75–100, in *Reading Walter Benjamin*.

59. Benjamin, *Arcades*, 460, N2,1. In German this passage reads: "Sich immer wieder klarmachen, wie der Kommentar zu einer Wirklichkeit (denn hier handelt es sich um den Kommentar, Ausdeutung in den Einzelheiten) einer ganz anderen Methode verlangt als der zu einem text. Im einen Fall ist Theologie, im anderen Fall Philologie die Grundwissenschaft" (*Passagen-Werk*, in *Gesammelte Schriften*, 5:574).

60. The question of metaphysics, totality, and reality as a surface with a linguistic structure would require further elaboration in relation to Benjamin's theory of allegory in *The Origin of German Tragic Drama*.

61. Benjamin, "Program," in *Selected Writings*, 1:110. In German this passage reads: "Der philosophische Daseinsbegriff muß sich dem religiösen Lehrbegriff, dieser aber dem erkenntnistheoretischen Stammbegriff ausweisen" ("Programm," in *Gesammelte Schriften*, 2.1:171).

62. My argument here is indebted to the critical force Deuber-Mankowsky attributes to Benjamin's recuperation of transience and demise against Cohen's focus on futurity and progress. See Deuber-Mankowsky, *Der frühe Walter Benjamin und Hermann Cohen*, 80–90, 112–120 as well as Deuber-Mankowsky, "The Ties between Walter Benjamin and Hermann Cohen: A Generally Neglected Chapter in the History of the Impact of Cohen's Philosophy," in *Hermann Cohen's Ethics*, ed. Robert Gibbs (Leiden, NL: Brill,

2006), 127–146, and "Walter Benjamin's *Theological-Political Fragment* as a Response to Ernst Bloch's *Spirit of Utopia*." For a different approach to the critical force of happiness in Benjamin through its relation to Cohen's account of human weakness, see Deuber-Mankowsky, "The Image of Happiness We Harbor."

63. On the distinction between profane and messianic as crucial to the argument in the "Theological-Political Fragment," see also Hamacher, "'Das Theologisch-politische Fragment,'" 175–192, in *Benjamin-Handbuch*.

64. Benjamin, "Theological-Political Fragment," in *Selected Writings*, 3:305–306; translation modified. In German this passage reads: "Im Glück erstrebt alles Irdische seinen Untergang, nur im Glück aber ist ihm der Untergang zu finden bestimmt. Während freilich die unmittelbare messianische Intensität des Herzens, des inneren Menschen durch Unglück, im Sinne des Leidens hindurchgeht. Der geistlichen restitutio in integrum, welche in die Unsterblichkeit einführt, entspricht eine weltliche, die in die Ewigkeit eines Untergangs führt und der Rhythmus dieses ewig vergehenden, in seiner Totalität vergehenden, in seiner räumlichen, aber auch zeitlichen Totalität vergehenden Weltlichen, der Rhythmus der messianischen Natur, ist Glück. Denn messianisch ist die Natur aus ihrer ewigen und totalen Vergängnis" ("Theologisch-politisches Fragment," 204).

65. This aspect of decay would require further elaboration through Benjamin's interpretation of natural history in *The Origin of German Tragic Drama*, where he suggests that nature and history converge in transience, because nature is historical in its transience, which is the way in which time leaves its mark on objects. On this interpretation of natural history, see also Theodor Adorno, "Die Idee der Naturgeschichte," in *Philosophische Frühschriften* (Darmstadt: Wissenschaftliche Buchgesellschaft, 1998), 345–365, and Bainard Cowan, "Walter Benjamin's Theory of Allegory," *New German Critique*, no. 22 (Winter 1981): 109–122.

66. Even though this understanding of demise as totally encompassing the world in its entirety bears similarities to the sensibilities that Benjamin uncovers in the Baroque quasi-eschatology, this messianic demise is different insofar as Benjamin neither hastens nor anticipates a final catastrophe and spectacular destruction. Benjamin's messianic rhythm of nature is not the path to a final catastrophe in which the entire world will end to exist, but rather for him the worldly passes away *eternally*. I argue against subsuming Benjamin under an apocalyptic heading, as Mark Lilla does in *The Stillborn God: Religion, Politics, and the Modern West* (New York: Knopf, 2007).

67. Benjamin, "Theological-Political Fragment," 305 (emphasis added).

68. Benjamin makes no allusion to Aristotle in this context or in any of the other brief notes on politics and *Glück*. It is not clear how much Aristotle beyond the *Poetics* he might have read and engaged with.

69. "Nur um der Hoffnungslosen willen ist uns die Hoffnung gegeben" (Benjamin, "Goethes Wahlverwandschaften," in *Gesammelte Schriften*, 1.1:201). For a discussion of Benjamin's argument against glorifying suffering and death

in his work on Goethe, and how this argument is pitched against the cultic heroism of the George Circle in particular, see Deuber-Mankowsky, *Der frühe Walter Benjamin und Hermann Cohen*, 234–281; Lane, "Goethe and the *Georgekreis*," 75–100, in *Reading Walter Benjamin*; and Stanley Corngold, "Genuine Obscurity Shadows the Semblance Whose Obliteration Promises Redemption: Reflections on Benjamin's 'Goethe's *Elective Affinities*,'" in *Benjamin's Ghosts: Interventions in Contemporary Literary and Cultural Theory*, ed. Gerhard Richter (Stanford, CA: Stanford University Press, 2002), 154–168.

70. Adorno, *Metaphysik*, 183.

71. The passage—a single sentence—on this point in Adorno's lecture reads in full: "Wenn ich Ihnen sage, dass eigentlich der Grund der Moral heute in, ich möchte fast sagen: in dem Körpergefühl, in der Identifikation mit dem unerträglichen Schmerz beruht, so zeige ich damit etwas von einer anderen Seite her an, was ich Ihnen vorhin in einer viel abstrakteren Form anzudeuten versucht habe,—nämlich daß die Moral, das was man moralisch nennen kann, also die Forderung nach dem richtigen Leben, fortlebt in ungeschminkt materialistischen Motiven; daß also gerade das metaphysische Prinzip eines solchen 'Du sollst'—und dies 'Du sollst' ist ja ein metaphysisches, ein über die bloße Faktizität hinausweisendes Prinzip—, daß das selber seine Rechtfertigung eigentlich finden kann nur noch in dem Rekurs auf die materielle Wirklichkeit, auf die leibhafte, physische Realität und nicht an seinem Gegenpol, als reiner Gedanke; daß also, sage ich, die Metaphysik geschlüpft ist in das materielle Dasein" (Adorno, *Metaphysik*, 182–183).

Completion Instead of Revelation
Toward the "Theological-Political Fragment"

PETER FENVES

This essay is concerned with the act of the Messiah. According to a brief sketch that Walter Benjamin read to Theodor and Gretel Adorno in the winter of 1937–1938 and that has since acquired the title of "Theological-Political Fragment," there is a single messianic act, the description of which requires three separate terms. Two of these terms can be easily translated into English, for they belong to a long tradition of theological speculation that encompasses a broad group of languages, including German and English. But the word through which Benjamin identifies *the* act of the messiah—namely, *vollenden*—cannot be easily translated, for it does not belong to a similarly long-standing theological lexicon. In the following translation of the opening of the "Fragment," this word is left in its original form: "Only the Messiah himself *vollendet* all historical occurrence, and indeed in the sense that he first redeems, *vollendet*, creates the relation of historical occurrence to the messianic itself."[1] Not only does *vollenden* designate the act of the Messiah; it also describes one of the attributes of this act—as though this word, akin to Spinoza's *deus sive natura*, must be conceived only in and through itself. And even if the sense of the word can also be conceived through other terms, the centrality of its position between *redeems* (*erlöst*) and *creates* (*schafft*) provides an indication of what it means by way of negation. The term that would be expected to stand between *creation* and *redemption* is *revelation*. Whatever else *vollenden* may mean in the context of the fragment, it also says "no revelation"—or, in other words, "no apocalypse," now or ever.

The first two sections of this discussion reconstruct the tradition in which *Vollendung* functions as a cardinal concept of religion; the final section briefly examines the "Theological-Political Fragment" in light of this short-lived and now forgotten tradition.

A Lecture Course in the Summer of 1913

In the summer semester of 1913 Heinrich Rickert, holding the chair of modern philosophy at the University of Freiburg, offered a series of lectures in which he laid out, for the first time, his own philosophical system. The official title of the lecture course was Logic (Foundations of Theoretical Philosophy).[2] But far from being an introduction to the premises of theoretical philosophy, much less a review of the principles of logic, the lecture course was an opportunity for Rickert to publicize a philosophical program that would replace *Lebensphilosophie* ("philosophy of life" or "vitalism"), which he associates not only with the thought of Nietzsche and Bergson but also with the work of Kierkegaard and William James.[3] The defining characteristic of *Lebensphilosophie*, for Rickert, is that it concerns itself only with "bare life" (*bloßes Leben*) and cannot therefore pose the philosophical question of how life gains value and thus acquires meaning and direction. In order to dissuade the educated strata of German youth from accepting *Lebensphilosophie* as a valid alternative to academic studies, Rickert proposes what he calls—using a phrase that I will initially leave untranslated—"die Philosophie des vollendeten Lebens." What distinguishes *Lebensphilosophie* from its replacement is that the former is concerned with "bare life," while the latter aims for its *Voll-endung*. Separated into its components parts in accordance with Rickert's own practice of hyphenation, the central term of the new philosophical system is easily captured in English as "full-ending." The word as a whole, however, is less amenable to translation. "Perfection" is one possibility, especially since Rickert sometimes uses *Vollkommenheit* in conjunction with *Vollendung*. A story Robert Musil published in 1911, "Vollendung der Liebe," generally appears in English under the title "Perfection of a Love." And translations of Benjamin's "Political Theological-Fragment" often use "consummate" in its opening sentence. For the purposes of this paper, however, *Vollendung* will be translated by "completion," which at least has the advantage of suggesting the idea of fullness via its Latin root. As for the advantage of the "philosophy of completed life" over the "philosophy of bare life," the following remark is what Rickert told his students in one of the early sessions of the lecture course he gave in the summer semester of 1913: "The active life does not simply consist in ethical willing but also in the realization of entirely different goods. For this reason, the determination of the ethical as autonomy is not the violation of life [*Vergewaltigung des Lebens*] but, rather, the one-sided moralism of *Lebensphilosophie*, and for this reason, too, the other part of the system is needed, beyond ethics, in the philosophy of an active, social-personal life."[4]

This passage comes from the typescript Rickert himself prepared for his lectures, which is preserved in the library archive of the University of Heidelberg.[5] The typescript is incomplete, missing the first few lectures; but the first page of the extent document briefly describes in the form of a question the aforementioned "other part" of the emerging system: "Can we find completion only in the highest level of monistic contemplation? Is there not a realm of completed life that is not found in the asocial, contemplative, nonpersonal sphere and, instead, raises itself into the social, active, personal sphere, even beyond the social-ethical? A completion of 'fullness' [*Eine Vollendung der 'Fülle'*], a truly pluralistic 'completion' of richness?" Rickert answers his own question in the affirmative by making it into a systemic imperative: a "full," "pluralistic," and therefore "rich" *Vollendung* "must emerge as a demand of the system, since the aim toward which it strives cannot simply lie in scientific, artistic, social-ethical, or transcendent-religious life."[6] Thus, in brief, Rickert outlines the ultimate goal of his as yet unwritten system: it seeks to find the region of "completed life" that lies beyond science, art, ethics, and any religion that defines itself in terms of a lone believer directed toward a transcendent God. As a form of value philosophy, the system is not concerned with the status of the subject or the nature of the object but, rather, with the articulation of the neutral sphere of "validation" (*Gelten*) in which "meaning" (*Sinn*), beyond being, can be found. In order to delineate the particular regions of this sphere, Rickert distinguishes social values from asocial ones and identifies three interrelated modes of completion: "infinite totality," "completed particularity," and "completed totality." Multiplying two by three, Rickert arrives at six different regions of values, each of which is governed not so much by laws or principles as by its own "completion-tendency" (*Vollendungstendenz*). As he argues in "On the System of Values" (1913), every philosophical system is only a completed particularity, but all of them nevertheless strive to be completed totalities. This means that philosophical inquiry can be both fully systematic and "open" at the same time. The "peculiar situation" that philosophers must confront when they wish to construct a system is that they can do so only by arresting the "current of cultural development"—an act of resistance to the continuous flow of cultural history that can be justified only under the condition that the proponent of the system be convinced that it is "more comprehensive and more unified than its predecessors."[7] That the "philosophy of completed life" stands opposed to *Lebensphilosophie* is not, therefore, an accident of recent cultural history but is, rather, a sign of its systematic intention: every system has a more or less evident counter-cultural purpose.

Only at the end of the lecture series does Rickert make good on his promise to present the part of the system that transcends science, art, ethics, and religion, understood as a relation to a single, transcendent being. And it is here that Rickert outlines the features of a "religion of fullness" (*Religion der Fülle*), which not only completes the "philosophy of completed life" but also completes "completed life" for this reason. By discovering the region where "completed life" can be found, the system comes to a provisional perfection—"provisional" only because the flow of cultural history continues anew. If the wider aim of the lecture course Rickert offered under the rubric of Logic lies in the demonstration that the "philosophy of value of completed life" is superior to *Lebensphilosophie*, its specific purpose lies in introducing a new "pluralistic" concept of religion. As long as religion tends toward asocial, impersonal, and passive contemplation of the deity, it devalues "the earth" and thus forecloses any access to the value region of "completed life." In this context, "bare life" becomes the only viable value, that is, a value in the absence of values, which antiphilosophy in the form of *Lebensphilosophie* exploits in the form of its "one-sided moralism." Despite the fact that the word *religion* must retain a consistent meaning in order for it to enter into the lexicon of systematic philosophy, the difference between the "religion of poverty," which knows only a single, transcendent God, and the "religion of fullness," in which each individual has his or her own God, tends to tear the word apart:

> The pluralistic religion of fullness just as decisively affirms the world and earthly life as mysticism denies such life. The religion of fullness does indeed have a meaning: to liberate our earthly, temporal existence [*Dasein*] in its lively, personal activity and individuality from its imperfections [*Unvollkommenheiten*]. . . . It must be a religion that brings the eternal into the temporal and the divine into the human, the absolute into the relative, the completed into the endless and the finite, totality into particularity itself.[8]   *Romanticism*

Two Students

It has been reported that all of "literary Freiburg" attended the lectures in which Rickert inaugurated his system of value philosophy.[9] Among the auditors was Martin Heidegger, who, shortly after the lecture course was completed, wrote a letter to Rickert in which he expressed his "heartfelt thanks for the strong philosophical incitement and instruction that I was able to acquire from your lectures."[10] Heidegger was not simply ingratiating himself with a professor who would soon oversee his habilitation; much of the work he undertook in this period was stamped by the concept of *Vollendung* that Rickert introduced in the summer of 1913. Thus, at the beginning of the inaugural address Heidegger delivered in 1915 upon receiving the *venia legendi* (authorization to teach), he defines the concept of science—but not that of philosophy—in terms of completion. None of the sciences can be completed, according to Heidegger, for the task of inquiry remains infinite; but there can be no science in the strict sense without the concept of its completion, which defines the tendency of the relevant research.[11] And with regard to the idea of "completed life," Heidegger repeats the step of Rickert by replacing the laxness of *Lebensphilosophie* with the rigors of philosophical inquiry, which not only constructs its own concepts but also deconstructs—the term *Destruktion* enters Heidegger's lexicon in precisely this context—the notions of life that occlude the phenomenon itself. In the lecture course Heidegger gave in Freiburg in the summer semester of 1920, he thus revises his teacher's own revision of *Lebensphilosophie*. Instead of outlining the totality of value regions in terms of their characteristic completion-tendencies, he constructs the concept of *Vollzug* ("carrying out" or "accomplishment"; literally "full-draft") in order to give an indication how life is actually lived. In any genuine *Vollzug*, "self-worldly *Dasein*" carries itself out in the absence of an end or purpose that would be external to the movement of the *Vollzug* itself.[12] This means that a genuine *Vollzug* takes the form of *renewal*, where the end is always already achieved. Thus, despite the difference between *Voll-endung* and *Voll-zug*, the concept Heidegger constructs in his 1920 lecture course does not so much criticize as retrieve the line of argument Rickert pursued some seven years earlier. And even as Heidegger abandons Rickert's lexicon in the lecture hall, he retains it for his private correspondence. Fully Germanizing the term *Vollendungstendenz* by replacing *-tendenz* with "auf dem Wege," Heidegger in 1918 provides Elisabeth Blochmann with an abbreviated version of the "philosophy of completed life":

> Because spirit as life is alone real, living being-for-another can work wonders. But it places the greatest demand on the existence of the ownmost personality and its value completion [*Wertvollendung*]. . . . And where a life of personality with inner truthfulness is on the *way* to completion [*auf dem* Wege *der Vollendung*]—and we are nevertheless *essentially underway*—there necessarily belongs to this life the

acerbity of being split apart, the relapses and new attempts, the unbearable suffering from whatever is problematic and questionable: these are essential parts; they belong to the ethos of truly scientific und spiritual human beings.[13]

It is no accident that the addressee of Heidegger's exposition of "value completion" is a woman who was just beginning her academic studies, for this is very much in line with its original intention. Rickert carefully constructed his "philosophy of completed life" so that it would be as appealing to his female students as to their male counterparts. Far from being a mere biological datum, valueless in itself, the sexualization of the human species is an irreducible dimension of "completed life." The "completion tendency" characteristic of sexuality is called eros. In accordance with the basic structure of value philosophy, which does not seek to describe empirical reality but, rather, constructs certain timeless types, Rickert conceives of masculinity under the value-philosophical category of infinite totality and femininity under that of completed particularity. In terms of the value-character of temporal modes, the future is assigned to infinite totality, in which goods always remain unfinished, whereas the present is the home of completed particularity. The latter category is particularly important for the system, because it governs the construction of the concept of philosophy and the concept of femininity. Rickert thus demonstrates that woman as type is incapable of engaging in the highest scientific and ethical projects but is nevertheless—or indeed for this very reason—representative of systematic philosophy. Another student who attended the lecture course in the summer of 1913, Walter Benjamin, describes its overall intention to a friend of his, Carla Seligson: "[Rickert] reads a sketch of his system as an introduction to his logic, a system that grounds a completely new philosophical discipline: the philosophy of perfect life [*vollkommenes Lebens*]. (Woman as its representative.) As interesting as it is problematic."[14] Benjamin expresses a similar ambivalence about the appeal of the lecture course in a letter to his former teacher, Gustav Wyneken, where he also describes how the women in attendance responded to Rickert's ex cathedra pronouncements about the representational relation between femininity and philosophy:

[The lecture course] is value philosophy. [Rickert] grounds an entirely new discipline, "value region of completed life [*Wertgebiet des vollendeten Lebens*]" (alongside logic, aesthetics, ethics, the philosophy of religion). Only in connection to "completed life" does the principle of femininity retain its meaning. Here is a German professor, holding a chair in philosophy, who has now spoken upwards of five hours about women and the relation between the sexes. Do not presume that the term "completed life" makes the whole thing into a matter of sterile aestheticism! This, it certainly is not—but what it is, that's also not clear. For me, what he says is unacceptable, for he declares that women are in principle incapable of the highest ethical accomplishment—they receive their asylum in "completed life." The women students are beside (!) themselves with joy.[15]

Unlike Heidegger, who remained in Freiburg except for a brief sojourn in Marburg, Benjamin left the university immediately after the end of the summer semester in 1913. Nevertheless, like his fellow student, with whom he shared at least three courses, all taught by Rickert, he retained the terminology he encountered in Logic (Foundations of Theoretical Philosophy). Just as Heidegger writes a letter to a young woman in which he describes the path of "value completion" as always already completed, so Benjamin adopts Rickert's terminology in his letter to Seligson: "in every human being who is ever born and ever becomes young, there lies— not 'improvement' but, rather, completion [*Vollendung*]: the goal that [Viktor] Hueber feels so messianically, how close it is to us. Today I feel the enormous truth of Christ's words: See the Kingdom of God is not here and not there but in us."[16] And just as Rickert's terminology informs the methodological preamble of his first major philosophical essay, so it guides the opening paragraph of Benjamin's first major publication, "The Life of Students" (1915). As with Heidegger's "Concept of Time in Historical Science," Benjamin's essay arose out of an inaugural lecture. Whereas Heidegger delivered his lecture before a group of professors in conjunction with his acceptance into the German academic establishment, Benjamin spoke to a group of students upon assuming the presidency of the Berlin free student movement. The two inaugural lectures, as represented in the two published essays, are nevertheless concerned with the very same problem: how can a concept of historical time be constructed? And despite the use of contrasting terms—*Vollendung* in Heidegger's essay, *Vollkommenheit* in Benjamin's—they are both rooted in the terminological tradition Rickert inaugurated when he sought to replace *Lebensphilosophie* by a philosophy of either completed or perfected life. And just as Heidegger begins his essay on the concept of time in historical scholarship with an exposition of the sciences in terms of their completion, so Benjamin begins his essay with reference to a "state of perfection":

There is a conception of history that, confident in the infinitude of time, distinguishes only the tempo . . . with which human beings and epochs advance along the path of progress. This accords with the incoherence, lack of precision, and laxity of demand such a conception imposes on the present. The following meditation, by contrast, concerns a particular state [*Zustand*] in which history rests concentrated as a focal-combustive point [*Brennpunkt*], which it is what it has been in the images of thinkers from time immemorial. The elements of the final state do not appear as formless progressive tendencies but are deeply embedded into every present moment as the most endangered, scandalous, and ridiculed creations and thoughts. The historical task consists in purely forming this immanent state of perfection, making it visible and dominant in the present.[17]

The "state of perfection" under discussion in "The Life of Students" lies in those "creations and thoughts" that escape the ends and purposes that are ascribed to life for the tautological purpose of making life purposive. And if one were to ask who assigns purposes to life for this purpose, the answer, for Benjamin, would obviously be: teachers, from whom students must break in order to live their individual-collective life. In the section of *Being and Time* concerned with the structure of "being-at-the-end," Heidegger makes an acerbic comment about the cardinal concept of Rickert's philosophical system: "With its ripeness the fruit *completes* itself [*vollendet sich*]. . . . 'Incomplete' *Dasein* also ends. Then again, it is so little necessary that *Dasein* come to fruition with its death that it can have already overstepped fruition before its end. For the most part, it ends in incompleteness [*Unvollendung*], broken down and exhausted."[18] "The Life of Students" is guided by a similar insight that is derived from a complementary eschatology. Instead of reflecting on the condition in which *Dasein* by and large ends—"broken down and exhausted"—Benjamin locates where the "final state" currently lies: "in the most endangered, scandalous, and ridiculed creations and thoughts." Far from being the function of supposedly free agents, who make their lives meaningful by positing ends for themselves, the "final state" is always already achieved. It can be characterized as both "perfect" and "immanent" for this reason. And the discovery of where the "final state" lies "embedded" in the present defines the "historical task" in both senses of the term: the task of accounting for historical occurrences and the corresponding task of making an occurrence historical.

In contrast to adult life, which acquires meaning by positing certain norms of conduct, the life of students is directed toward only a single place, which Benjamin identifies in the passage above as a *Brennpunkt*. This term can be translated in two ways: in spatial terms as "focal point" and in the temporal terms as "point of combustion." The complete spatio-temporal point of orientation guides both Benjamin's brief theory of history and his more expansive exposition of student life. Whenever students are indeed students, they are as concentrated and combustive as the "focal-combustive point in which history rests concentrated." The more intensely they engage in their studies, the more they live the singular life of students, the less thoroughly they are dominated by the various models that can be drawn from their teachers, and the more revolutionary combustive they become. This counter-norm of student life holds in the life of eros as well: the higher the degree of focus, the more explosive. In a number of contemporaneous writings Benjamin develops a concept of eros that elaborates on the brief comments he made in response to Rickert's lectures: "The philosophy of perfect life. (Woman as its representative.) As interesting as it is problematic." Instead of following the model of the elderly philosophy professor, who presents eros solely in terms of heterosexual norms, Benjamin distinguishes among various level of completion and identifies the highest with love between women. Thus, he includes the following remark in his Nietzsche-inspired polemic against Socrates: "among all the levels of [desiring] love . . . the most glorious and in both erotic and mystical terms the most complete, indeed the almost radiant (if it were not entirely nocturnal) level is woman-woman love."[19] For Rickert, the feminine type is characterized by the category of completed particularity, which he likewise locates in the temporal mode of the present, where the "present goods" (*Gegenwartsgüter*) of domesticity are also to be found. For Benjamin, by contrast, the highest level of completion lies in woman-woman eros, which is indeed so perfect that it can appear in finite language only in the form of the past perfect, where all action has always already been accomplished. According to the "Metaphysics of Youth," which Benjamin probably wrote soon after his departure from Freiburg, the perfection of such love makes it impossible for "Sappho and her friends" to say anything that has not already been said. And for the very same reason—because they say nothing new—the lovers can see something, namely where the completion of their love has taken shape: "How did Sappho speak to her friends? Language is veiled like the past, future-directed like silence. . . . Silent women are the speakers of what had been spoken. They escape from the circle; they alone see the completion of its roundness."[20]

Toward a "Religion of Fullness"

While appropriating Rickert's concept of *Vollendung* in his 1915 inaugural lecture, Heidegger makes no mention of the problem in which his lectures in the summer semester of 1913 culminated, namely the problem of deciding whether systematic philosophy could construct a "religion of fullness" that would transcend and encompass the value regions of art, science, ethics, and monistic religion. Nevertheless, there is reason to suppose that Heidegger's interest in Rickert's lectures and seminars derived in no small measure from the fact that a professor of *modern* philosophy was demonstrating how the construction of philosophical concepts ultimately leads to religion—and indeed a "full" religion that, valuing works as much as faith, can be described as "catholic" in a limited sense. For a student like Heidegger who had been trained in a starkly antimodern form of Catholicism, this probably came as a welcome surprise. Those Catholic authorities who sought to present all of modern philosophy as so many stages of God-denial were clearly wrong. In his initial letter to Rickert, Heidegger says as much. While emphasizing that his philosophical "orientation" remains Catholic-Aristotelian, he commends Rickert's courses in 1913 for demonstrating the error of those who see modern philosophy as the spawn of "'godlessness' and the like."[21] And from a diametrically opposed direction, something similar happens with Benjamin. As he enigmatically tells Carla Seligson, he was prompted to study in faraway Freiburg because of Kierkegaard,[22] and although he wrote no ingratiating letters to Rickert, soon after he arrived in the provincial city he did publish an essay, "The Religious Attitude of New Youth," in which his Kierkegaardian orientation converges with Rickert's new system.

At the beginning of "The Religious Attitude of New Youth" Benjamin appeals to *Either/Or* as the point of departure for the ensuing discussion: "The educational path of the young generation is meaningless without [religion]. It remains empty and agonizing without the place at which it bifurcates into a decisive either-or."[23] Just as in the second part of *Either/ Or* Judge Vilhelm urges a young aesthete to make the ethical decision, so Benjamin asks of new youth that it recognize its religious "attitude" or "position" (*Stellung*). And just as the ethical decision, according to Judge Vilhelm, does not consist in the choice of marriage over nonmarriage—as though they were equivalent forms of life—but, rather, in the absolute choice to choose the act of choosing over an irresolute and thus "aesthetic" absence of choice, so, for Benjamin, the "decisive either/or" of youth does not consist in a decision among future professions but in the absolute decision to decide in favor of a life of decision over a life defined and determined by models of progression. The future is not therefore wiped away by this decision to decide; rather, it is disconnected from prevailing norms and becomes the very "religion" that youth—as both word and life—means: "youth that avows itself to itself *means* a religion that is not yet [*Die Jugend, die sich zu sich selbst bekennt, bedeutet Religion, die noch nicht ist*]."[24] This, in short, is the religious "attitude" or "position" of youth: in vowing to be itself, youth rejuvenates itself and thus becomes the signifier of something called "religion," which has yet to emerge. The current emptiness of this signifier is the promise of its fulfillment.

The religion of rejuvenating youth thus resonates with the "religion of fullness." And even if Rickert would classify Kierkegaard among the proponents of *Lebensphilosophie*, he draws on two characteristically Kierkegaardian terms—*paradox* and *decision*—in the concluding lectures of his course. The paradox of the new religion lies in its pluralistic character: there is only one God, to be sure; but each and every individual has his or her own God, so that the affirmation of God does not require a corresponding self-negation. Only in this way can the value-region of religion transcend the world-annihilating tendency of monistic religiosity, which sees in God the source of all goodness and can find nothing other than evil in the world. The "religion of fullness," by contrast, affirms the partial goodness of the world, and each individual is called upon to make the world completely good. Explicitly posing the question whether the task of world-improvement can be accomplished under the premise that God alone remains absolutely good, Rickert provides a response that Benjamin, for one, would have recognized as Kierkegaardian: whereas Kant famously claims at the beginning of the *Foundations of the Metaphysics of Morals* that the good will alone is altogether good, Rickert concludes the lecture course Logic (Foundations of Theoretical Philosophy) with the claim that the goodness of the world can be found in each individual's decision to decide—an absolute decision that is not necessarily *for* goodness over evil but is the foundation of any goodness that can be predicated of the world. If, moreover, the world-annihilating tendency of the "religion of poverty" is based on the claim that the self must be denied because its evilness is irreconcilable with divine goodness, the discovery of worldly goodness in the act of decision generates the conditions under which monistic religion can turn into a pluralistic one: God can become my God *and* yours. It is of no concern from the perspective of value-philosophy whether or not anything resembling such a religion has ever arisen in history. Just as, according to Benjamin, "youth . . . means a religion that is not yet," so, for Rickert, the value-philosophical system intends a religion that may never correspond with an empirically recognizable form of religious belief or ritual practice.

In the final lectures of his course in 1913, Rickert launches an indirect attack on Kierkegaard that accords with Kierkegaard's own critique of systematic philosophy: "Of course, the mystic can always flee into the *credo quia ad absurdum*," Rickert tells his students, using a recent phrase made famous by translations of Kierkegaard's works, and immediately adds: "He can 'believe.' But he cannot bring about a philosophy of this belief, for a philosophy can never be absurd."[25] Drawing on this unstable distinction between paradox and absurdity, Rickert arrives at the culmination of his course. Allusions to Kierkegaard's *Concluding Unscientific Postscript* are replaced by paraphrases of the concluding pages of Nietzsche's *Toward the Genealogy of Morality*: "In short," Rickert tells the assembled students, "not to recognize the good in the world and not therefore to recognize the evil in the world as that which is there to be overcome means: wanting nothingness, which means: wanting nothing: not being. It is absolute nihilism: death."[26] At this point the ultimate rationale for replacing *Lebensphilosophie* with a philosophy of complete life emerges: only the latter can forestall the "European nihilism" of which Nietzsche writes. In Rickert's words, "we must therefore learn to think otherwise, if we want to philosophize in general. We take it as a point of departure that we are and that we want to be. Furthermore, we want freely to complete ourselves, and we want to understand how completion is possible."[27] But as Rickert immediately adds, wanting to understand is not the same as understanding; on the contrary, understanding the possibility of completion is predicated on a constitutive want of understanding. Far from retreating from the circularity of the resulting argument, according to which the understanding of completion is possible only on the basis of complete non-understanding, Rickert makes the circle into the figure in which his lecture course concludes:

> We have reached the final limit of understanding that is possible for us as finite, individual, and at the same time free beings. To want the world to be different always means: to want that we not be what we now facticly are [*nun einmal faktisch sind*], finite beings that not only can complete ourselves but that necessarily perish [*zu Grunde gehen*]; it is to want that we, therefore, in general not be. If it appears as though a circle lies in this thought, it is precisely a circle from which one can never escape and that one must therefore, speaking with Lotze, perpetuate purely as a circle.[28]

It is only a short step from this passage from Rickert's lecture to the beginning of *Being and Time* where Heidegger, too, insists on the necessity of entering into the circle rather than seeking a way out.[29] And it is an even shorter step from the conclusion of Logic (Foundations of Theoretical Philosophy) to the end of "The Religious Attitude of New Youth," where Benjamin adopts the term *imperfection* as a designation of the current situation of youth. The essay is ostensibly a contribution to the discussion among members of the youth movement concerning the proper mode of responding to the renewed hostility emanating from various academic, journalistic, and political institutions. For Benjamin, the struggles of the movement against its enemies should not be allowed to determine its attitude or position. And youth can remain untouched by polemics only if its struggles are redefined, so that they do not presuppose either enmity or resistance but are, instead, the very places in which the "decisive either/or" occurs. Benjamin represents the difficulty of finding terms for the redefined struggle by presenting the conclusion of his argument in a series of broken-up sentences:

> To struggle [Kämpfen] does not mean condemning the enemy. Rather, the struggles of youth are its divine judgments. Struggles in which this youth is prepared to gain victory or be defeated. Because it is only important that the holy reveal itself in its shape and form out of these struggles [aus diesen Kämpfen das Heilige in seiner Gestalt sich offenbare]. This struggling is far removed from the mysticism that only pretends to offer salvation to the individual as long as there is as yet no religious community. Youth knows that struggling does not mean hating; it knows that if it still finds resistances—if everything is not yet permeated by youth—it is only because of its own imperfection [Unvollkommenheit].[30]

With this formulation—youth is "imperfect" as long as it does not permeate and interpenetrate "everything"—Benjamin adopts and transforms the very last lecture he heard in Freiburg, where Rickert, discussing the "riddle of the world," establishes the limit of value-philosophical system-construction. In the final hour of the lecture course, the professor explains the ultimate paradox of his system, which lies in the impossibility of its construction:

> We can, of course, form the concept of an absolutely perfect world in which there is no dualism [between the temporal and the finite, on the one hand, and the eternal and the infinite, on the other]; but we cannot wish that our world be absolutely perfect in a monistic sense, for at that very moment it would cease to be our world. . . . In other words, we cannot want to be absolute, complete, and eternal without wanting not to be. And if we are not, we cannot be absolutely completed.[31]

Something along these lines is, for Benjamin, the religious attitude of new youth: it wants nothing other than its own perfection, which is to say, it wants to be itself, without an opponent or antagonist that would determine its position or attitude. As Rickert sees it—but he is without doubt blinded by the obfuscating norms of bourgeois adulthood—perfection would preclude all forms of struggle. For the professor, the absence of struggle would be the end of willing, and in the absence of willing, there can be no decision, and in the absence of decision, no individual; finally, in the absence of the finite-temporal individuality, there can be only the monistic God. For the student, however, the state of youthful perfection is not the end of the struggle but, rather, its transformation into something that adults, with their struggles against the enemies that define their lives, could never recognize. Instead of the struggle taking the form of resistance to hostile forces, it becomes the medium in which "the holy reveals itself in its proper shape and form." If an image of such a struggle is difficult to form, it is only because it would have to be one of the "utopian images of thinkers," which, as he writes at the opening of "The Life of Students," breaks with any conception of history that represent historical occurrences in terms of "formless progressive tendencies."[32] At this point, combustive as well as concentrative, the imperfection of new youth becomes a paradoxical dimension of its perfection, for only in this triple resistance to childhood, to the old (conception of) youth, and to adulthood can new youth define its attitude.

The Act of the Messiah

Benjamin's "Theological-Political Fragment" was written long after the publication of his "Religions Attitude of New Youth." Precisely how long— fewer than ten or more than twenty-five—may never be known; but at least this much is clear: the opening sentence of the fragment draws on the terminology that Rickert introduced into systematic philosophy for the purpose of constructing a "religion of fullness" in the summer semester of 1913.[33] To say that "the Messiah himself alone completes all historical occurrence" means that every supposed occurrence in the absence of the Messiah remains incomplete, including the occurrence of life. It follows that there can be no such thing as "completed life." Instead of contradicting the lecture course, the opening sentence of the "Theological-Political Fragment" can be seen as its corroboration, for, even if "completed life" remains impossible, the very occurrences of life can still be defined in terms of their "completion tendencies." The second part of the first sentence, however, immediately reveals the erroneous character of this inference: "and indeed in the sense that he first redeems, completes, creates the relation of historical occurrence to the messianic itself." Not only is "historical occurrence" incomplete in the absence of the messianic, but so, too, is the relation to any state of completion. This means, above all, that the concept of completion-tendency is no longer applicable to historical occurrence, since, in the absence of a relation to completion, no degrees of incompletion can be determined. The governing directionality of the value-philosophical system from lower to higher degrees of completion is therefore lost, and with the loss of this concept-constructive directionality, the nihilism that Rickert sought to overcome returns in full: action is pointless not only in the sense that there is nothing to be gained by initiating an action but also, and more importantly, in the sense that no action—other than the act of the messiah—can secure a relation to its own completion.

As soon as the concept of completion-tendency is rendered invalid—and this is what happens in the second part of the first sentence of the "Theological-Political Fragment"—the imperfection Benjamin attributes to "new youth" at the end of his essay on its "religious attitude" can be seen as a perfection in its own right, and this, in turn, can become the paradoxical aim of any action other than the messianic one: to strive toward a state of perfected imperfection, which can only be done when striving is no longer conceived in terms of struggling, and struggles are no longer seen as the medium in which the holy reveals itself. The radicality of the fragment in contrast to the essay expresses itself, above all, in the fact that the former makes no reference to revelation—and effectively hides the absence of revelation by replacing *revelation* with *completion*. Insofar the holy is the name of the medium in which a Holy One reveals itself, the absence of any revelation, whether as act or occurrence, means that the order under consideration in the fragment is not simply "profane" but a redoubled "profane order of the profane."[34] And this order can be constructed only on the basis of the idea of "happiness" (*Glück*) insofar as the occurrence of happiness is a matter of luck or happenstance, not the achievement of a goal or the activation of a tendency. While the messianic act alone consists in completion, all other acts become transient venues for happiness. The paradoxical preservation of this transience, which requires the complete removal of completion-tendencies, thus becomes the task of "world politics."[35]

Just as Benjamin transforms the transcendental reduction to a point where it would be unrecognizable to Husserl, so does he radicalizes the system-constructive concept proposed by the prior occupant of the chair of modern philosophy at the University of Freiburg.[36] "Completed life" is not the telos of the philosophical system but is, rather, the messianic act: the completion of the historical occurrence that is life. For this reason, there can be only "bare life" in the absence of the messianic act. Only one thing can be accomplished under this stringent condition: the incompleteness of every historical occurrence can itself be made complete by declining to assign a goal or direction to any particular occurrence, much less to history as a whole. There thus arises the perfected state of "teleology without final purpose."[37] At the end of the "Theological-Political Fragment" Benjamin uses the term "nihilism" to characterize the procedure through which completion-tendencies are methodically removed;[38] but this nihilism has nothing to do with the denial of the world and the annihilation of the self. The lectures Rickert delivered in the summer of 1913 sought to demonstrate how a "religion of fullness" can both transcend the inherent nihilism of monistic religion and overcome the implicit nihilism of contemporary *Lebensphilosophie*. As a belated response to these lectures and in preparation for a further inquiry into "European nihilism," Heidegger, yet again a professor in Freiburg, having been demoted from rector, tells a roomful of students at the beginning of the summer semester of 1939 that Nietzsche is "the thinker of the completion of metaphysics,"[39] By contrast, a short time earlier, Benjamin, living in exile, reads a fragment to a couple of older students, Theodor and Gretel Adorno, which begins with an affirmation that "the Messiah alone completes historical occurrence" and concludes with a highly abbreviated program for a pluralistic nihilism of fullness.

Notes

1. Walter Benjamin, "Theologisch-Politisches Fragment," in *Gesammelte Schriften*, vol. 2.1, ed. Rolf Tiedemann and Hermann Schweppenhäuser (Frankfurt am Main: Suhrkamp, 1972), 203. All translations here as elsewhere are my own. For a discussion of the dating of the text along with an extensive commentary, see Werner Hamacher, "Das Theologisch-Politische Fragment," in *Benjamin-Handbuch*, ed. Burkhardt Lindner (Metzler: 2006), 175–192.

2. A list of the classes Rickert taught in Freiburg can be found as an appendix to Martin Heidegger and Heinrich Rickert, *Briefe 1912 bis 1933 und andere Dokumente*, ed. Alfred Denker (Frankfurt am Main: Vittorio Klostermann, 2002), 152.

3. Several years later Rickert presented his critique of *Lebensphilosophie* in book form; see *Philosophie des Lebens: Darstellung und Kritik der philosophischen Modeströmungen unserer Zeit* (Tübingen: Mohr, 1920). It should be noted that the term *Vollendung* is also important for Hegel, especially in the conclusion to the *Phenomenology of Spirit*. A major aim of Rickert's work in this period is to demonstrate that, contra Hegel, a system can preserve its "openness" to future developments without compromising its systematicity. It should also be noted that, despite certain Christian connotations of the term, recognizable through the Greek word *pleroma* or *fullness*, Luther rarely used *Vollendung* or its cognates in his translation of the Bible. Thus, for instance, when Jesus, according to the Gospel of John (19:30), says that "it is finished," the word is *vollbracht*, not *vollendet*.

4. Quote from the typescript stored in the University Library Archive at Heidelberg University under the title "Heid. Hs. 2740." The quoted passage appears on the first page of the typescript and then, after the ellipses, on the seventh and eighth. I thank the library and Clemens Rohfleisch in particular for giving me access to this typescript. The typescript was worked over several times in Rickert's hand, and it probably served as the preliminary draft of the only volume of philosophical system that he managed to publish. In the preface to the volume Rickert indicates that the original version of the system was delivered as a series of lectures in the summer of 1913; see Rickert, *System der Philosophie: Erster Teil, Allgemeine Grundlegung der Philosophie* (Tübingen: Mohr, 1921), vii.

5. In 1915, Rickert accepted an offer from the University of Heidelberg to replace his recently deceased mentor Windelband, ceding to Edmund Husserl the chair in modern philosophy at Freiburg.

6. Heid. Hs. 2740, 1.

7. Heinrich Rickert, "Von System der Werte," *Logos* 4 (1913): 325.

8. Heid. Hs. 2740, 225.

9. See Benjamin's letter to Carla Seligson from June 1913, reprinted in Walter Benjamin, *Gesammelte Briefe*, vol. 1, *1910–1918*, ed. Christoph Gödde and Henri Lonitz (Frankfurt am Main: Suhrkamp, 1995), 112.

10. Heidegger and Rickert, *Briefe*, 11.

11. Martin Heidegger, "Der Zeitbegriff in der Geschichtswissenschaft," first published in *Zeitschrift für Philosophie und philosophische Kritik* 161 (1916); repr. in *Frühe Schriften*, ed. Friedrich-Wilhelm von Hermann (Frankfurt am Main: Klostermann, 1978), 416.

12. Martin Heidegger, *Phänomenologie der Anschauung und des Ausdrucks*, ed. Claudius Strube (Frankfurt am Main: Klostermann, 1993), 75.

13. Martin Heidegger and Elisabeth Blochmann, *Briefwechsel, 1918–1969*, ed. Joachim Storck (Marbach: Deutsche Schillergesellschaft, 1989), 7.

14. Benjamin, *Gesammelte Briefe*, 1:112. Benjamin may have misremembered the content of Rickert's early lectures, substituting *Vollkommenheit* for *Vollendung*; it is also possible that he correctly recorded the opening lectures (the typescript for which has been lost), where Rickert may have defined the goal of the lecture course in terms of "perfect life" (rather than "completed life"). Occasionally, especially in the final pages, he uses "vollkommen" in conjunction with "vollendet." In any case, as Giorgio Agamben has aptly noted, only two of the philosophy professors with whom Benjamin studied can be seen to exercise any influence over his line of thought: Rickert at the University of Freiburg and Moritz Geiger at the University of Munich; see Agamben, "Cronologia della opera di Walter Benjamin," in Walter Benjamin, *Metafisica della gioventù: Scritti 1910–1918* (Torino: Einaudi, 1997), xix. See also the detailed reconstruction of Benjamin's first philosophical itinerary in Tamara Tagliacozzo, *Esperienza e compito infinito nella filosofia del primo Benjamin* (Marcerata: Quodlibet, 2003), esp. 19–52.

15. Benjamin, *Gesammelte Briefe*, 1:117.

16. Ibid., 1:175.

17. Benjamin, "Das Leben der Studenten," in *Gesammelte Schriften*, 2.1:75.

18. Martin Heidegger, *Sein und Zeit*, ed. Friedrich Wilhelm von Hermann (Frankfurt am Main: Klostermann, 1977), 244. In one of the last letters in the Heidegger-Rickert correspondence, Heidegger responds to an angry Rickert, who had read a report about the Davos-disputation, where Heidegger apparently cast aspersions on the entire neo-Kantian movement, including Rickert along with Hermann Cohen and others. Heidegger assures Rickert that he does not simply lump him among the neo-Kantian, for he (Rickert), according to his former students, was also concerned, above all, with "finitude [*Endlichkeit*]" (*Gesammelte Briefe*, 1:63). This may have been largely a ruse on Heidegger's part; but it is also possible to see that the *-endung* character of *Voll-endung* can be interpreted altogether on the side of *Endlichkeit*, that is, as its fulfillment.

19. Benjamin, "Sokrates," in *Gesammelte Schriften*, 2.1:130.

20. Benjamin, "Das Tagebuch," in *Gesammelte Schriften*, 2.1:96.

21. Heidegger and Rickert, *Briefe*, 12.

22. Benjamin, *Gesammelte Briefe*, 1:92.

23. Benjamin, "Die religiöse Stellung der neuen Jugend," in *Gesammelte Schriften*, 2.1:73.

24. Ibid., 2:73.

25. Heid. Hs. 2740, 218.

26. Heid. Hs. 2740, 219.

27. Heid. Hs. 2740, 219.

28. Heid. Hs. 2740, 219–220. Rickert refers to Hermann Lotze, *System der Philosophie* (Leipzig: Hirzel, 1874), 471.

29. See Heidegger, *Sein und Zeit*, 7–8.

30. Benjamin, "Die religiöse Stellung der neuen Jugend," in *Gesammelte Schriften*, 2.1:74.

31. Heid. Hs. 2740, 223. Rickert added "timeless" to the list of adjectives (absolute, complete, eternal) in the typescript.

32. Benjamin, "Das Leben der Studenten," in *Gesammelte Schriften*, 2.1:75.

33. Benjamin does not, of course, refer to Rickert; but a trace of his work is lodged in Benjamin's fragment, for the reflections that issue into the only text to which it refers, *Geist der Utopia*, emerge out of Bloch's doctoral dissertation, *Kritische Erörterungen über Rickert und das Problem der modernen Erkenntnistheorie* (Ludwigshafen: Baur, 1909). Benjamin returned to Rickert twice, so to speak: first, when encountering him again in Heidelberg in 1921, described him as "grey and angry" (*Gesammelte Briefe*, 2:173), and then again in 1940, when he learned that Adorno, for whatever reason (perhaps because Benjamin suggested it), wrote a review of a posthumous collection of Rickert's writings. Benjamin asks for a copy of Adorno's review and adds: "I am indeed a student of Rickert (just as you are of Cornelius [who rejected Adorno's first *Habilitationsschrift*]" (*Gesammelte Briefe*, 6:455). It is therefore not surprising

that Rickert's two-volume *Grenzen der naturwissenschaftlichen Begriffsbildung* can be found on a list of works Benjamin prepared for his reflections on the concept of history; see Walter Benjamin, *Über den Begriff der Geschichte*, ed. Gérard Raulet (Frankfurt am Main: Suhrkamp, 2010), 154.

34. Benjamin, "Theologisch-Politisches Fragment," in *Gesammelte Schriften*, 2.1:204.

35. Ibid.

36. For a discussion of Benjamin's transformation of the Husserlian idea of reduction, see Peter Fenves, *The Messianic Reduction: Walter Benjamin and the Shape of Time* (Stanford, CA: Stanford University Press, 2011). What Benjamin does with Rickert's system is thus similar to what he does to Husserl's method: hyperbolize its imperative, so that it becomes consonant with its radicality.

37. Benjamin, "Zwei Gedichte von Friedrich Hölderlin," in *Gesammelte Schriften*, 2.1:109.

38. Benjamin, "Theologisch-Politisches Fragment," in *Gesammelte Schriften*, 2.1:204.

39. Martin Heidegger, *Nietzsches Lehre vom Willen zur Macht als Erkenntnis* (= *Gesamtausgabe*, vol. 47), ed. Eberhard Hanser (Frankfurt am Main: Klostermann, 1989), 1. At the end of the lecture course Heidegger presents the value-philosophy of Windelband and Rickert as derivative response to Nietzsche's thought that only confirms his status as the "completer" of metaphysics, which completes itself in "European nihilism" and forms the subject matter of his subsequent lecture course.

Fidelity, Love, Eros
Benjamin's Bireferential Concept of Life as Developed in "Goethe's Elective Affinities"

SIGRID WEIGEL

Fidelity certainly does not rank among the central themes of Walter Benjamin's work.[1] Likewise, it has garnered little attention in critical reception of his work so far—one will mostly look in vain for the term in the indexes of scholarly works on Benjamin.[2] The word nevertheless occupies a crucial position in Benjamin's conception of life. It appears to have played an indispensable role in the elaboration of a fundamental facet of Benjamin's thought: the double determination of human life as both creaturely (or natural) and supernatural, and thus of a concept of life derived from its relationship to these "two spheres."[3] The marginal attention that the concept of fidelity in Benjamin's writings has found so far is particularly eye-catching in regard to his essay, "Goethe's *Elective Affinities*," a text in which fidelity arises as "logos of [marriage's] divine component."[4]

On the Blind Spot of "Fidelity"—Habitual Evasion in the Reception of Benjamin

The reflections on fidelity and marriage in Benjamin's essay are among those passages in his writings that prove particularly difficult, if not wearisome, in discussion with students. This is not only because of the essay's immense density, which makes it difficult to grasp its arguments, but due even more to the mystification or complete chagrin that is regularly aroused in students by claims that appear anachronistic to them at the beginning of the twenty-first century and furthermore hardly fit the image of Benjamin that has been otherwise conveyed to them: that of an idiosyncratic thinker with connections to the avant-garde and sympathies for the radical currents of his time. Statements such as those from "Goethe's *Elective Affinities*" that claim the morality of marriage "could only prove as fidelity" are considered to belong to a bourgeois morality that can hardly be harmonized with Benjamin's usual thought and lifestyle (347). In academic discussions on Benjamin, there seems to be a tacit and habitual (or rather, unconscious) resistance to this topic. Although uses of the concept in the figurative sense are among the most frequently cited formulations of Benjamin's—for instance, in the passage on "fidelity to things"—the reflections on fidelity in "Goethe's *Elective Affinities*" rank among the most evaded passages in Benjamin's writings. Irritation, resistance, and willful ignorance are frequent reactions to passages such as the commentary on Mozart's *The Magic Flute* in this essay:

> For to the extent that this is possible in opera, *The Magic Flute* takes precisely conjugal love as its theme. . . . The subject of the opera is not so much the desires of the lovers as the steadfastness of husband and wife. They must go through fire and water not only to win each other but to remain united forever. Here, however much the spirit of freemasonry had to dissolve all material bonds, the intuition into the content has found its purest expression in the feeling of fidelity. (300)

Ought Walter Benjamin, a thinker who has become known as a radical intellectual, turn out to be the voice of a bourgeois morality of marriage? Such an initial suspicion can be quickly disposed of, since immediately following his comments on *The Magic Flute*, Benjamin returns to Goethe's novel and submits the Mittler's sermon, in which marriage is described as the base and pinnacle of culture, to a biting criticism. He describes the sermon as being "the words of a grim blusterer" (300), judges these words to be a disgusting mishmash, and in the process cites idioms from the section on the "Transition from Popular Moral Philosophy to Metaphysics of Morals" in Kant's *Groundwork of the Metaphysics of Morals*. It is thus already clear that the meaning Benjamin ascribes to fidelity in the context of love and marriage is to be found beyond any moral discourse and moral-philosophical determinations. However, the tension inherent in the concept of fidelity—whether conceived as Logos or as morality—can only be illuminated by a more detailed reading of Benjamin's essay on Goethe.

At first glance, the limited attention paid to the role of marriage and fidelity in this text may appear to be justified by the fact that in the section, "Marriage in *Elective Affinities*," Benjamin himself expressly declares: "The subject of *Elective Affinities* is not marriage" (302). Yet when he continues, "Nowhere in this work are its ethical powers to be found," things certainly become more complicated, for with these statements it becomes clear that even though Benjamin's foremost concern may not be marriage, its moral powers most certainly are. And fidelity is indeed brought into connection with the moral dimension of marriage several times in this text. Following the just-cited clarification of the subject of *Elective Affinities* and his own text, Benjamin continues: "From the outset, they are [the moral powers] in the process of disappearing, like the beach under water at floodtide. Marriage here is not an ethical problem, yet neither is it a social problem. It is not a form of bourgeois conduct. In its dissolution, everything human turns into appearance, and the mythic alone remains as essence" (302). Thus in Benjamin's condensed interpretation of Goethe's novel, the mythical character of human relations becomes visible when they lose their human face through the dissolution of marriage. These thoughts are affirmed seven pages later in light of the equally apodictic conclusion that the mythic is the material content [*Sachgehalt*] of the book (309).

Even though marriage may not be the subject of the novel, Benjamin does not lose sight of it in his reading. For him, marriage presents itself as that scene in which the mythic searches for a passage through which it can reveal itself. In order to clarify Goethe's divergence from his literary figures in this case, Benjamin points out that the poet did not, unlike Mittler, aim at establishing marriage, but rather "to show the forces that arise from its decay. Yet these are surely the mythic powers of the law and in them marriage is only the execution of a decline that it does not decree." And a bit later: "With this, however, Goethe in fact touched on the material content of marriage" (301). Up to this point it can be summarized that marriage, according to Benjamin, is indeed not the subject of *Elective Affinities*. The morality of marriage is, however, the subject of Benjamin's essay, "Goethe's *Elective Affinities*," where he relates it to the mythic, which is the actual subject of Goethe's novel.

As is well known, Benjamin's text begins with the distinction between commentary and critique: commentary is that which is dedicated to the material content [*Sachgehalt*] of a work, whereas critique relates to its truth content [*Wahrheitsgehalt*]. Therefore, we must take note of formulations such as those in the passage on *The Magic Flute* that state that the "intuition into the content" would be given expression in a "feeling of fidelity," because as Benjamin initially described, the interpretation of the material content is a "prerequisite" for critique (297). That is to say, the path of critique, which seeks the truth content of a work (and this is the actual concern of his analysis of Goethe's novel and its reception) proceeds through the interpretation of its material content. It can thus be assumed that Benjamin's observations regarding marriage and fidelity, as well as the mythic and the moral, are prerequisites leading to something else beyond these elements: to something that does not disclose itself at first glance.

Benjamin's Critique of Kant's Definition of Marriage as between Nature and Law

In order to understand the meaning of "the moral" for Benjamin, his critique of and differentiation from Kant's *Metaphysics of Morals* must first be discussed. From the subheadings of an outline for "Goethe's *Elective Affinities*" which was not included in the published version, it is evident that this critique and differentiation takes place in a passage titled: "Marriage as Mythic Legal Order."[5] Benjamin had insisted that the subheadings be deleted for its 1924–1925 publication in the *Neue Deutsche Blätter*, edited by Hugo von Hofmannsthal. However, he added them again to his personal copy that was to have served as preparation for its publication in book form. As with his other writings, these subheadings reveal the system of his argumentation as well as the dialectic composition of the whole text. Thus we can derive, just from the disposition of his work on *Elective Affinities*, the role that the topic of marriage has in forming the structure of Benjamin's argumentation. It is the only theme that emerges several times in the outline. In the first part of the main heading—II A: "Marriage as Mythical Legal Order"—it appears in the first, "Marriage in the Enlightenment," and the second, "Marriage in *Elective Affinities*." In section C: "Marriage in the Novel," it appears in the third part, "Passion and Affect."

Benjamin develops his concept of marriage as a mythical legal order out of Kant's definition of marriage. In this context, he describes it as "[the philosopher's] gravest mistake" that Kant "supposed that from his definition of the *nature* of marriage, he could deduce its *moral* possibility, indeed its moral necessity and in this way confirm its *juridical* reality" (299; emphasis added). He therefore criticizes that Kant establishes the relation between nature, morality, and law qua deduction; more specifically: his deduction of morality and law from what is commonly referred to as "nature." For this reason, we should look more closely at the deduction in question. In paragraphs 24 to 27 of the section on civil law, Kant identifies marriage as *natural sexual union according to the law*. This definition implies a number of provisions that are partly moral and partly systematic in nature. The term *natural* here stands in opposition to *unnatural* (which Kant equates with homosexuality or sodomy), from which—reinforced through a distance from concepts of morality that changed over time—the normative or judgmental connotation of such a concept of "natural" becomes recognizable: It does not define something given by nature but rather conditions that are regarded as natural and therefore as to be normal. For Kant, opposition to what operates "according to the law" constitutes on the contrary a behavior "in accordance with mere animal nature." He thereby introduces a systematic differential criterion by which human behavior sets itself apart from animal behavior qua law. If for Kant sexual union defines itself in the reciprocal use "one human being makes of the sexual organs and capacities of another,"[6] then this definition is due to an ultimate purpose [*Zweck*]. The relation between nature and law is already problematic enough in this complex definition of marriage because it represents a juridical sanction of relationships assumed to be natural, yet the subject becomes more complicated still when Kant relates it to the aim [*Zweck*] of bearing children. This becomes clear by virtue of the fact that he immediately needs to establish limits to its importance. He determines that although it is the aim of nature to bear children, this alone cannot found the legality of marriage, "otherwise marriage would be dissolved when procreation ceases." He continues: "Even under the condition of desire for using each other's sexual attributes, the marriage contract is not a contract whichever but rather one that is necessary by the law of humankind."[7]

When Kant deduces the necessity of the marriage contract from the "law of humankind," it indicates that he conceives of this law as a natural law of man. Although such a natural law of man is not fully identical with the aim of nature to bear children, it is nevertheless indirectly explained by it since he states that it is for the goal of childbearing that nature "implanted the inclinations of the sexes for each other." Therefore, Kant's deduction of marriage as a legal relationship does not follow directly from nature, but rather indirectly through the inclination or pleasure that nature would have implanted in humans for its own purpose. Kant's deduction, rejected by Benjamin, thus leads from the aim of nature, through the inclination of the sexes (which presents itself as a law of humankind), to the necessity of marriage as a legal form for the exercise [*Ausübung*] of this inclination, which in turn is defined as sexual union according to the law. Presented as a kind of closed circle in which the law created ("implanted") by nature is transmuted into the law as a legal relationship, this deduction represents nothing less than the classic case of a modern myth:[8] it retransforms historical processes into seemingly natural conditions by grounding a certain cultural-specific idea of sexuality and marriage in nature. In this way positive law gets deduced from natural law.

Benjamin responds to the ambiguity that attaches to the concept of law in this deduction through entirely different semantics, in which he replaces the ambiguous term *law* (as legal and natural law) with the words *law* and *love*. Benjamin writes: "Yet in truth, marriage is never justified in law (that is, as an institution) but is justified solely as an expression of continuance in love," and further, that love "by nature seeks this expression sooner in death than in life" (301). For Benjamin, marriage is therefore the expression of the continuance of love and as such not derived from nature but is rather a different expression of it. It is a sort of counterpart to the very expression with which love "by nature" seeks permanence—that is to say, rather in death than life. Thus marriage is virtually introduced as the antipodal expression of the nature of love. Proceeding from the inconstancy of love (that functions here as an unnamed assumption), Benjamin identifies two opposed expressions of the desire to overcome impermanence: death and marriage. While death, as an expression of the desire for eternal love, is assigned to the "nature" of love, marriage (which obviously doesn't come by nature) represents a different answer to the phenomenon of inconstancy. Marriage therefore appears as an unnatural expression of the wish for permanence, or, in other words, as a non-natural form for the survival of love.

Correspondence of Benjamin's Critique to Freud's Dialectic of the Death Drive and Eros

These thoughts on the nature of love (or more precisely, to that which love seeks by nature) obviously refer to Sigmund Freud's theory of life and death drives that he developed in *Beyond the Pleasure Principle.*[9] On the one hand, Freud describes the death drive as the tendency of an organism to approximate [*angleichen*] the inorganic and inanimate that was there prior to the organic and living; on the other hand, he presents the life drive or sexual drive as a countermotion, understood as a "circuitous path to death" or described as "a movement with a vacillating rhythm" and named after the mythical god Eros.[10] Freud based his rewriting of the Eros-Thanatos motif on his theory of drives, which he developed in association with contemporary theories of mortality and reproduction in the biological sciences, in particular in reference to August Weismann's theories on life spans and the death of organisms.[11] Freud's essay appeared in 1920, which is exactly the time Benjamin was working on his text on *Elective Affinities*.

Although Freud is never explicitly named in his text,[12] Benjamin does not, as is widely held, first cite *Beyond the Pleasure Principle* in his work on Baudelaire with the famous sentence: "Consciousness emerges at the place of the memory trace."[13] He had cited it already in "Goethe's *Elective Affinities*." The reference to the Freudian term *death drive* in particular can be seen as evidence that he read *Beyond the Pleasure Principle*. Thus Benjamin alludes to Freud's remarks on the "inertia inherent in organic life,"[14] when he writes of Ottilie that "In her death drive, there speaks a longing for rest" (336). The way Benjamin describes the fading of Ottilie as "mournful end" may well be read as a case study of the process Freud regarded as an approximation of the organic to the inorganic. For Ottilie this process was initiated in the very moment when Eros vanished, that is, when her life drive gave up countering her death drive or the ongoing mortality of organic life. There are also traces of Freud recognizable in Benjamin's remarks on Eros—significant differences aside. This becomes clear in the relation between perfection and Eros. In *Beyond the Pleasure Principle* Freud dismisses the belief in an inherent drive in human beings toward perfection "which has brought them to their present high level of intellectual achievement and ethical sublimation and which may be expected to watch over their development into supermen."[15] He rather interprets that "[which] appears in a minority of human individuals as an untiring impulsion towards further perfection" as "a result of repression of drives" and as a product of a persistent tension which develops from the fact that the repressed drive never ceases "to strive for complete satisfaction."[16] Finally, he asserts the probability "that the efforts of Eros to combine organic substances into ever larger unities probably provide a substitute for this 'drive towards perfection' whose existence we cannot admit."[17] Freud thereby characterizes Eros as the driving power of "dynamic conditions" of the living.[18] From a theoretical point of view, Eros takes the place of a metaphysical idea of humankind or an evolutionary explanation of perfectibility.[19]

Excursus on the Correspondence of Messianism to Psychoanalysis

Benjamin took up Freud's thoughts on the theory of drives directly and reformulated them within the context of his messianic understanding of history in what is known as "Theological-Political Fragment." Here, he defines the dynamis of the profane as the striving of everything mundane toward happiness, which is only to be found in decay [*Untergang*]. In the fragment—which Benjamin himself called a "teaching of the philosophy of history"[20]—messianic intensity and the dynamis of the profane are conceived of as analogous to the Freudian opposition of the death drive to Eros; as forces which, although they follow along two paths leading in opposite directions, nonetheless support and advance each other. In this context Benjamin links Freud's constellation of the organic with the messianic topos of the "end of history," which is at the same time both consummation and endpoint, and brings both together in a concept of "messianic nature." As he writes: "For nature is messianic by reason of its eternal and total passing away."[21]

Sigmund Freud's thoughts on Eros—which is at the same time the product of an instinctual drive and its repression, and which strives for consummation and thereby edges its way toward death—must have seemed familiar to Benjamin, trained as he was to perceive messianic structures. The process Freud describes is indeed structurally similar to the notion of a process that strives toward a vanishing point that appears as end, salvation, and completion. *Life* takes a position in Freud's conception of drives analogous to that of *history* in messianism—the end of life in Freud and the consummation [*Vollendung*] of history in Benjamin. Neither concept is temporal, but rather qualitatively determined by an absolute end, which signifies both its completion and simultaneous transition into another status. Thus Benjamin's text can be read as an attempt, stimulated by Freud's writings, to introduce nature into a messianic theory of history. For this attempt, he chose the mode of analogy: "To the spiritual *restitutio in integrum*, which introduces into immortality, corresponds a worldly restitution that leads to the eternity of downfall, and the rhythm of this eternally transient worldly existence, transient in its totality, in its spatial but also in its temporal totality, the rhythm of messianic nature, is happiness."[22] In Benjamin's scheme, happiness therefore occupies that place that in Freud is taken by Eros: "For in happiness all that is earthly seeks its downfall, and only in happiness it is destined to find downfall."[23]

Benjamin doesn't develop this attempt to bring together the philosophies of history and nature any further. He will, however, take up the motif of happiness in another context and work further on the correspondences between Psychoanalysis and messianism. In his essay "Franz Kafka: On the Tenth Anniversary of his Death," for instance, he establishes a connection between the concepts of 'disfiguration' [*Entstellung*] and 'redemption' [*Erlösung*].[24] Therefore his unfinished text, posthumously entitled as "Theological-Political Fragment," should perhaps better have been ti-tled the "Fragment on Messianic Nature."

To return to the *Elective Affinities* essay: It is about love rather than happiness and therefore also about Eros. Benjamin sees the "presentiment of the life of bliss" as the origin of love and not the will to happiness that he here connects instead to the *vita contemplativa*: "It is not from the will to happiness—which only fleetingly lingers unbroken in the rarest acts of contemplation, in the 'halcyon' stillness of the soul—that love has arisen. Its origin is the presentiment of the life of bliss" (352). It need not be pointed out that origin [*Ursprung*] is not meant as beginning [*Anfang*] or descent [*Herkunft*]. It is rather to be read in the sense of that from which something arises [*entspringt*]. One finds these reflections in the third part of the essay (in the section on "Loving Couples"), where the motif of Eros-Thanatos emerges precisely at the point Benjamin speaks of love. It is concerned with the impossibility of the perfection of love that is due to the deepest imperfection of human nature. The latter is, as Benjamin for-mulates, fully *realized* [*eingelöst*] in Eros—he refers to "the dark conclu-sion of love, whose daemon is Eros" (345; emphasis added). With this description of Eros as daemon, Benjamin leads it back again to its origin [*Herkunft*] in the classical mythology while at the same time (exactly like Freud) putting it in relation to an idea of perfection. However, while Freud views perfection in relation to culture, Benjamin relates it to love: "the true ransoming of the deepest imperfection which belongs to the nature of man himself. For it is this imperfection which denies to him the fulfill-ment of love" (345). With this relation, however, a completely different concept of love as thought within the limits of a theory of drives comes into play, by which Benjamin's concept of love distances itself from Freud's Eros: "Therefore, into all loving that human nature alone determines, af-fection [*Neigung*] enters as the real work of *Eros thanatos*—the admission that man cannot love" (345). Benjamin thus defines love as an idea that overcomes human nature and its imperfection. In this context, he attri-butes to Eros the role of translating passion into affection, and that way again plays into the hands of Freud's proposition that the genesis of cul-ture comes with sublimation. In Benjamin, Eros thus occupies the central position in a dialectic conception: love as the idea of perfection arises from the realization of the imperfection of human nature in Eros. Impor-tant for our context (the meaning of fidelity) is that through this imper-fection Benjamin's conception of perfect love is not only referred to an extra-natural realm, but more so to the sphere of godly dominion: "Love becomes perfect only where, elevated above its nature, it is saved through God's intervention" (345).

Fidelity as Logos of the Supernatural Duration of Love

Subsequent to these reflections, Benjamin again takes up his thoughts on death and marriage as two contrasting forms of expression for a lasting love, this time in the context of the breaking of love in Goethe's novel. According to Benjamin, this break reveals that "every love grown within itself must become master of this world" (345). Regarding the possibilities Benjamin mentions for a literal, earthly dominion of love, he again proposes two opposing avenues: a "natural exitus" in shared death, and love "in its supernatural duration, marriage" (345). Thus a supernatural component comes to marriage through the fact that it has to secure the existence of love against its own nature. This exact element cannot be derived either from a natural law (or aim of nature) or be founded as law. Marriage rather aims at establishing a seemingly natural relation through *decision*; this is evident in the fact that marriage constitutes kinship. On these grounds, Benjamin installs marriage beyond the sphere of choice and nature: "In any case when relation [*Verwandtschaft*] becomes the object of a resolution; it strides over the stage of choice to decision. This annihilates choice in order to establish fidelity: only the decision, not the choice, is inscribed in the book of life. For choice is natural and can even belong to the elements; *decision is transcendent*" (346; emphasis added). With this he pinpoints the central transgression of the novel's characters: the confusion of the regularities of human conduct with the natural laws of the elements, which the chemical metaphor calls "elective affinity" [in German *Wahlverwandtschaft*, literally: chosen kinship].

Noteworthy in the cited passage is the formulation "book of life," which refers to the biblical notion of a register of names that includes all righteous men, men whose conduct pleases God. Whereas the *sefer chajim*, the biblical book of life, is mostly connected to the idea of a divine bookkeeping—because entry into this book depends on a righteous conduct of life—Benjamin's term refers above all to those aspects through which this book differs from the laws of nature: "Only the decision, not the choice, is inscribed in the book of life." Goethe's simile of the chemical elective affinities is thus indirectly assigned to the book of nature, respectively into natural history, whereas the concept of life originates only by separating from it: through the notion of humans who act and make decisions. The relationship between the two books is just as dialectically conceived as that between Eros, love, and marriage, since choice is annihilated by decision in order to establish marriage. And the decision for the constancy of love in marriage bears the name of fidelity. Thus for Benjamin, human culture does not originate in nature, whether such a deduction is thought of as natural philosophy or as evolutionary theory. Rather, through *deciding* another dimension comes into play that conveys a meaning to the couple's relation that goes beyond any physical or social ties. Benjamin calls this dimension supernatural [*übernatürlich*] in the sense of more than natural, and sees in it a moment of transcendence in which the idea of the "book of life" actively resonates. This reading is quite similar to Hannah Arendt's conception of the *Vita Activa*, for which *promise* and *contract* play a crucial role in order to establish a specifically human culture of acting. There she also refers to a religious prehistory when discussing the sacred inviolability of agreements and treaties (*heilige Unverletzbarkeit von Verträgen und Abkommen*) and traces it back to both Abraham and the biblical Covenant.[25]

In this passage of Benjamin's text it becomes clear once more how little the concept of *decision* in Benjamin's thought has in common with that of Carl Schmitt's theology of sovereignty. If Benjamin judges the decision to be transcendent, then love gains a meaning through the decision to marry that is more than and different from the nature of love. Benjamin calls this meaning supernatural. It turns marriage into a paradigmatic setting for his concept of life, which is grounded in a double reference to the natural and the supernatural. In Benjamin's concept of marriage this is represented through Eros and fidelity, respectively: Eros as the redeeming manifestation of human imperfection, fidelity as the decision for supernatural constancy. The latter is a moral act by virtue of which people seek to transcend both nature's and their own inclination. It is not until then that something worthy of the name *human nature* comes into existence.

The opposition of *choice* and *decision*—and their correlation to the opposition of nature and transcendence—belongs to an entire register of conceptual distinctions on which Benjamin is working in the *Elective Affinities* essay. As a kind of structural leitmotif he contrasts words from a profane register—that is, from a human or worldly order—with meanings that are associated with a divine order: for instance, *Gebilde* versus *Geschöpf* (product of culture versus creature), *Aussöhnung* versus *Versöhnung* (reconciliation among humans versus divine atonement), or *Aufgabe* versus *Forderung* (worldly task versus divine requirement).[26] In this sense, Benjamin marks fidelity as Logos of a divine momentum of marriage (326). It is important to consider that fidelity is not conceived as *the* divine momentum in marriage, but rather as its Logos. This is to be understood literally, because fidelity in the religio-historical perspective in fact goes back to a term that stands for a superhuman capacity to which only God is entitled. We encounter the idea of divine fidelity repeatedly in Paul's letters, often in a homonymic idiom, "God is faithful."[27] Fidelity represents that word or principle in whose name the unnatural duration of love is transferred into a supernatural form, marriage, and is thereby transcendent. In other words, fidelity *signifies* the supernatural momentum of love. From the perspective of the history of the human species, the idea of fidelity is thus a central category for anthropological distinction—that is to say for concepts to organize mutual behavior of humans and to develop a kind of life distinct to that of other living creatures.

In the popular phrase *sexual fidelity*, however, the origin of the concept as well as its transcendental element are altogether misrecognized, because fidelity is recommitted to that sphere that Benjamin understands as the "natural component of marriage—sexuality" (326). Furthermore, sexual behavior is turned into an indicator: when sexuality becomes evidence for that aspect of love that points precisely beyond sexuality. A still greater confusion of concepts materializes in the passage on sexual infidelity, a phrase that—with reference to human as well as animal behavior—has garnered pertinence in contemporary ethology and is the subject of a wide range of empirical research. This use of the term is a symptom of the mingling of moral concepts (such as fidelity or loyalty) and those of behavioral biology (such as polygamy and monogamy) in the field of evolutionary theory, in which sexuality is defined as the mere goal of the production of species or types. However, the semantics of fidelity *cannot* be derived from natural laws, instead it is based in a decision to overcome them in shaping human culture.

It should have become clear by now that Benjamin's concept of ethicality cannot be situated within the framework provided by the theorems of moral philosophy. Nor is it a theological concept. The theological and biblical register represents rather that field of meaning in which the desire for transcendence has traditionally found expression. In this sense, the history of religion conveys an archive to us of those concepts that articulate the human desire to transcend mere, naked life (that is to say, to leave behind our "creaturely" existence). Yet, at the same time Benjamin always insists that nothing worldly or human equates exactly to theological concepts (and/or those concepts that originate in the idea of a divine order). Mundane institutions' claim on these concepts will always involve an inherent difference or gap between the divine and human existence. This is not only explicit in his critique of and dissociation to Gundolf, whose characterization of marriage (as simultaneously a mystery, sacrament or enchantment and animal act) Benjamin describes as "bloodthirsty mysticism" (326); it is also apparent in those passages that thematize the older Goethe's affiliation with religion and distinguish it as nonreligious: "Access to religion by any kind of conversion" was not permitted to him; to the contrary, he abhorred precisely this tendency in the romantics. "But," continues Benjamin, "the laws that those vainly sought to satisfy by converting, and thus in the moment of extinguishing their lives, kindled in Goethe—who also had to submit to these laws—the highest flame of his life" (329).

With the opposition of denomination to law, Benjamin's concept of law—one standing beyond the Kantian ambiguity of natural law and rights—refers to a sphere preceding positive law, that is to say to a sphere of rite or religion understood as cult. The fact that he does not approach "access to Religion" in terms of denomination but rather in terms of ritual, taking cult to be the foundation of culture, sheds light on the development of his thinking through Jewish tradition—indeed even where he is concerned with problems of Christian secularization. "Nothing but strict attachment to ritual . . . can promise these human beings a stay against the nature in which they live" (303), writes Benjamin in the first part of his essay, in which he comments on the famous graveyard scene in Goethe's novel. The scene depicts Charlotte's violation of burial rites: She removes gravestones from their proper place, classifying them by age and arranging them according to an aesthetic rule. It also relates Eduard's habit of always making his way *around* the cemetery. Taking advantage of the ambiguity of the word *ground*, Benjamin describes Eduard's habit as avoidance [*Scheu*] of the grounds of the graveyard: "One cannot imagine a more conclusive liberation from tradition than that liberation from the graves of the ancestors, which, in the sense not only of myth but of religion, provide a foundation for the ground under the feet of the living" (302). Thus, when Benjamin talks of religion or ethicality this means first of all his talking of ritual—the ritual as the human species' footing against both the nature in which we live and the nature of our life; or, in other words, the footing of natural life in the supernatural.

Benjamin's Concept of Life

Analogous to Benjamin's statement that the subject of Goethe's novel is not marriage, but myth, one may now conclude that the subject of Benjamin's essay "Goethe's *Elective Affinities*" is not marriage—or love, Eros, myth, and so on—but rather a *concept of life* that Benjamin arrives at after debating all these terms and topics. Human life is, on the one hand, defined in relation to an extra-human [*außermenschlich*] nature that Benjamin calls superhuman [*übermenschlich*] and which he discusses above all in the passages on the telluric and water. On the other hand, human life is defined in reference to a supernatural sphere whose conceptions are traditionally determined by religious notions. In Benjamin's science, the concept of life always gains its determination from this double reference, which also puts "Goethe's *Elective Affinities*" in accordance with the "Critique of Violence," on which he worked around the same time. The most direct connection to this text, right up to literal correspondences, appears in the section on "Guilty Life," in the chapter on "Fate." There, Benjamin not only concisely discusses the concept of life; he also develops a specific concept of guilt [*Schuld*].

His succinct definition reads: "With the disappearance of supernatural life in man, his natural life turns into guilt, even without him committing an act contrary to ethics" (308). He is therefore concerned with a concept of guilt that precedes each individual, concrete, or specific transgression. By this is meant neither juridical nor moral guilt, but rather a disregard of that which constitutes "the human" and consists of the connection of a natural to a higher life, exceeding bare life. In remarkable contrast to the widespread notion of original innocence, Benjamin instead assumes that when the human being remains bound to the "league of mere life," life "manifests itself as guilt" (308). Importantly however, it is not the idea of "original guilt" that is the ground for his concept of life here, because any concept of "mankind" as marked by mere nature—be it innocence or guilt—is simply unthinkable for Benjamin. "Man cannot, at any price, be said to coincide with the mere life in him,"[28] he argues in "Critique of Violence."

Consequently, the disregard of those moments in which the concept of the human points beyond the natural, mere, or bare life (and in this way creates the human being) leads into the "nexus of guilt [*Schuldzusammenhang*] among the living," which is often regarded as fate and thereby misunderstood (307). Precisely this, however, is the case with the characters in Goethe's novel, who interpret life as destiny in misrecognition of their self-produced mythical context. They have set in motion their own analogy to the elements of nature, through which the chemical equivalence of "elective affinities" is transferred to self-experimentation on one's own life. Aligned with natural laws in such a manner, life changes back into mere nature. "In this circle, the powers that emerge from the disintegration of the marriage must necessarily win out" (308).

In his commentary on Goethe's novel, the disintegration of marriage is for Benjamin obviously a subject that provides him an opportunity to develop something that exceeds it, namely a concept of life energized by the double reference to both natural and supernatural life. His engagement with Freud will have played no small part in this development, because through it he could find the analogy of humans to the elements (acted out in Goethe's novel) reflected within the horizon of the assimilation of the organic to the inorganic that Sigmund Freud thematizes in his theory of drives. Through a critical discussion of Kant's deduction of law from nature, in reference to the assimilation of Goethe's protagonists to the elements of nature, and by way of the dialectic of Freud's drive theory, Benjamin was able to lend more exact contours to his thoughts on law in the ritual sense. It is also from this perspective of law that he later develops his reservations about Ludwig Klages, discussing the latter's philosophy of life [*Lebensphilosophie*] after the publication of Klages's book *Kosmogonischer Eros* (1922). In 1926 he writes to Gershom Scholem: "A confrontation with Bachofen and Klages is unavoidable; of course there is much that says that this can be strictly conducted only from the perspective of Jewish theology. This, of course, is where these important scholars scent the archenemy and not without cause."[29] To reiterate, Benjamin's reading of Klages—and through him of Bachofen—took place during a period in which his own concept of life had already gained its clear contours ("Critique of Violence," "Goethe's *Elective Affinities*"). Thus he was not so much interested in Klages's concept of life but was rather fascinated, on the one hand, by his discussion of the image—especially by the distinction of image from the (Platonic) idea: the image "which appeals to the soul, and which, when the soul in pure passivity admits it, imbues it with symbolic content."[30] On the other hand, he was drawn to the cosmic context in which Klages discusses mankind's struggle with nature, especially through the development of technology. This is obvious in the thought image of the "Planetarium" in *One-Way Street* (1928), where Benjamin interprets technology as a new, unprecedented possibility for the "wooing of the cosmic . . . on a planetary scale—that is, in the spirit of technology."[31] The disregard of this planetary dimension through the use of technology as a means merely of mastering nature during war leads to the point where technology turns against humankind.

With his reflections on the concept of life, Benjamin occupies a third space, as it were—beyond the opposition in which *Lebensphilosophie* posits itself against scientific definitions of organisms or species and their evolution by taking either the biographical coherence of life, as in Dilthey, or the corporeal experience of perception and lived time, as with Bergson, or the unity of the body and soul, as in Klages, as the ground for its philosophical constructions. Contrary to the overestimation of creativity and a momentary experience [*Erlebnis*] in *Lebensphilosophie*, Benjamin has always emphasized that experience [*Erfahrung*] which is structured by tradition and heritage[32]—impregnated with culturally transmitted meaning, which turns the momentous experience [*Erlebnis*] into experience as such [*Erfahrung*]. In this context he and other authors of the cultural sciences

[*Kulturwissenschaft*][33] share the insight into the crucial role of the afterlife or survival [*Nachleben*] of mythic, cultic, and religious notions throughout the course of history. It is only from beyond the opposing concepts of human life as developed in sciences and humanities, from beyond the contrast of the laws of nature and metaphysical definitions of life that Benjamin can draw and develop his idea of human culture. Insofar as one can register, at present, a comprehensive reconceptualization of human behavior with parameters taken from nature—riding the waves of the recent research in the neuro- and biological sciences—Benjamin's work on the concept of life is perhaps indispensable as never before for a cultural historically informed life-science.

Translated by Chadwick Smith

Notes

1. [There is a wide range of options in the English lexicon for translating *Treue*, from which I have chosen *fidelity*. One could also render *Treue* as loyalty, fealty, constancy, or faithfulness, all of which are intimately related, like *Treue*, to both truth and allegiance. I have chosen *fidelity* because of its frequent use in the cited translations of these texts by Benjamin and because of its common use in connection both with marriage and other interpersonal relationships and adherence to a legal, ethical, or moral code—such as a *true friend*.]

2. Indeed, *fidelity* is missing from the index of Burkhardt Lindner, ed., *Benjamin-Handbuch: Leben—Werk—Wirkung* (Stuttgart: Metzler, 2006). There is also no contribution on fidelity in Michael Opitz and Erdmut Wizisla, eds., *Benjamins Begriffe* (Frankfurt am Main: Suhrkamp, 2000).

3. Walter Benjamin, "Critique of Violence," in *Selected Writings*, 4 vols., ed. Michael W. Jennings et al. (Cambridge, MA: Harvard University Press, 1996–2003), 4:251. This double determination of *life* in Benjamin's writings is a leitmotif in Sigrid Weigel, *Walter Benjamin: Images, the Creaturely, and the Holy* (Stanford, CA: Stanford University Press, 2012), esp. chaps. 1 and 3.

4. Walter Benjamin, "Goethe's *Elective Affinities*," in *Selected Writings*, 1:297–360, 326. Hereafter cited in text by page number in parentheses.

5. [All headings from Benjamin's outline are translations of the annotations in Walter Benjamin, *Gesammelte Schriften*, vol. 1.3 (Frankfurt am Main: Suhrkamp, 1974), 835–837.]

6. Immanuel Kant, *The Metaphysics of Morals* (Cambridge: Cambridge University Press, 1996), 61–62.

7. Ibid., 62.

8. Cf. Roland Barthes's work on this process in *Mythologies* (New York: Farrar, Straus and Giroux, 1972).

9. Sigmund Freud, *Beyond the Pleasure Principle* (New York: W. W. Norton, 1961).

10. Ibid., 46, 49.

11. Freud explicitly mentions three works by Weismann: *Über die Dauer des Lebens* (1882), *Über Tod und Leben* (1884), and *Das Keimplasma* (1892) [translated as: *The Germ-Plasm: A Theory of Heredity* (New York: Scribner's, 1893)]. Cf. Sigrid Weigel, "Jenseits des Todestriebs: Sigmund Freuds Lebenswissenschaft an der Schwelle von Natur- und Kulturwissenschaft," *Kultur Poetik: Journal for Cultural Poetics* 12, no. 1 (2012): 41–57.

12. In Benjamin's *Verzeichnis der gelesenen Schriften* [List of books read], Freud's *Beyond the Pleasure Principle* appears only as no. 1076, after another title published in 1928. Walter Benjamin, *Gesammelte Schriften*, vol. 7.1 (Frankfurt am Main: Suhrkamp, 1989), 437–519. According to this note, 1928 would be the earliest year for Benjamin's reading of this text. Conspicuously, however, and in complete contrast to the other titles in the listing, he names neither date nor place of publication here, indicating that Benjamin added the title from memory and therefore possessed Freud's text earlier than this. Particularly since the title appears a second time (no. 1680), and then with specific information: 3rd ed., Vienna, 1923. This entry indicates that he used this edition for the rereading of Freud's text which took place in the context of his work on Baudelaire. The acquisition of this edition indicates that in exile he no longer possessed the first. There is evidence for the fact that he knew *Beyond the Pleasure Principle* already in 1921 through a letter to the philosopher David Baumgardt (June 9, 1921) for whom Benjamin had purchased Freud's book (the price was 10,75 Mark). Walter Benjamin, *Gesammelte Briefe*, vol. 2, *1919–1924*, ed. Christoph Gödde and Henri Lonitz, (Frankfurt am Main: Suhrkamp 1996), 159. And in the period in question (1918 and after), Benjamin had noted already a number of other titles by Freud in the list, such as his book on jokes (no. 540), the work on the Schreber case, the text on narcissism (no. 549), and *Five Lectures on Psycho-Analysis* (no. 609), indicating a close reading of Freud during the years prior to the publication of *Beyond the Pleasure Principle*.

13. Benjamin, *Selected Writings*, 4:317. Whereas Benjamin inserts a *the*, in Freud's text it reads: "Consciousness arises instead of a memory-trace" (*Beyond the Pleasure Principle*, 28). For extensive treatment of this topic, see Sigrid Weigel, *Body- and Image-Space: Re-reading Walter Benjamin* (London: Routledge 1996), 109–127.

14. Freud, *Beyond the Pleasure Principle*, 43.

15. Ibid., 50.

16. Ibid.

17. Ibid., 51.

18. Ibid.

19. On Freud's place in the history of the concept of sublimation, see Eckart Goebel, *Jenseits des Unbehagens: "Sublimierung" von Goethe bis Lacan* (Bielefeld: Transcript, 2009).

20. Walter Benjamin, *Reflections: Essays, Aphorisms, Autobiographical Writings* (New York: Schocken, 1986), 312.

21. Ibid., 313.

22. Ibid.

23. Ibid., 312.

24. For more on these psychoanalytical reformulations of *Erlösung*, see also Weigel, *Body- and Image-Space*, 25–27, 142–145.

25. Hannah Arendt, *The Human Condition* (Chicago: Chicago University Press, 1958), 243–244, translated as *Vita Activa oder vom tätigen Leben* (München: Piper, 1981), 239.

26. Cf. Weigel, *Walter Benjamin*, chap. 4.

27. 1 Cor. 1:9, 10:13; 2 Cor. 1:18 (King James Version).

28. Benjamin, "Critique of Violence," in *Selected Writings*, 1:251.

29. Walter Benjamin, *The Correspondence of Walter Banjamin, 1910–1940* (Chicago: University of Chicago Press, 1994), 288.

30. Translator's note: My translation, from Walter Benjamin, "Johann Jakob Bachofen," in *Walter Benjamin. Text + Kritik*, no. 31–32 (1970): 36.

31. Walter Benjamin, "One-Way Street," in *Selected Writings*, 1:486.

32. Regarding the contrast between *Erlebnis* and *Erfahrung* in Benjamin's writing, see especially Walter Benjamin, *Charles Baudelaire: A Lyric Poet in the Era of High Capitalism* (London: New Left Books, 1973).

33. Different from cultural studies today, the term *Kulturwissenschaft* stands for a group of authors—including Freud, Warburg, Benjamin, Simmel, and Cassirer—who around 1900 developed readings of cultural history beyond a single discipline and beyond the two-culture distinction.

The Will to Apokatastasis
Media, Experience, and Eschatology in Walter Benjamin's Late Theological Politics

MICHAEL W. JENNINGS

> The end is always like the beginning.
>
> *—Origen of Alexandria*

To begin with the ending: Walter Benjamin's much discussed and little understood allegory of the Turkish puppet in his last known text, "On the Concept of History," raises one central question for the entirety of his work: exactly *how* might politics take theology into its service, and to what effect?[1] Throughout his career, Benjamin's use of theological concepts and motifs is invariably bound to the formulation of a politics; but how are we to trace the invisible strings that allow theology to ensure that historical materialism always wins? Benjamin's deployment of theological motifs and his political commitments are of course in and of themselves complex and often contradictory; and they are anything but stable across the full spectrum of his career as a writer. It is thus hardly surprising that simplifying myths have grown up around the signature "Walter Benjamin." Of these, those describing the purported forms of his religiosity have been among the most tenacious. I use the term *purported* because there is no evidence that Walter Benjamin held any religious beliefs whatsoever. Benjamin's upbringing in an assimilated German-Jewish family of the haute bourgeoisie provided him neither with practice in religious observance nor with even the barest trappings of religious ideas. Insofar as there *were* religious traditions in the Benjamin household, they were secularized Christian customs—the Christmas tree or the Easter egg hunt. This remainderlessly secularized man, the very quintessence of the displaced and alienated denizen of the modern urban jungle, thus never hinted at a belief structure to which he adhered.

This is not to say, of course, that theology did not play a leading role in his intellectual production. As Benjamin himself says, "My thought is related to theology as the blotter to ink. It is saturated with it. If it were just a matter of the blotter, however, then nothing that was written would remain."[2] Yet even as it tries to discern the ink on the blotter, much of the Benjamin scholarship has shown itself content to attribute broad and consistent theological positions to Benjamin: the rhetoric of the "messianic" Benjamin is only the most pervasive of these.[3] The theologeme "messianism" can thus serve as a brief case study of Benjamin's deployment of theological concepts. Messianic motifs indeed play an important role in Benjamin's work—but only at two widely separated points, the period 1919–1923 and the year 1940. The first period follows on the intensive discussions between Benjamin and Gershom Scholem during their years in Switzerland; the period 1919–1923 is also the period of Benjamin's extensive engagement with Ernst Bloch's *Spirit of Utopia* and Franz Rosenzweig's *Star of Redemption*, both of which deploy varying understandings of messianism.[4] This involvement surfaces in such Benjaminian texts from this period as the "Theological-Political Fragment" and "The Task of the Translator." In the years that followed, roughly 1924–1939, messianism plays virtually no role in Walter Benjamin's writings. The massive torso of *The Arcades Project*, which spans the years 1927–1939, provides us with a convenient test sample: the terms *Messiah* and *messianic* occur precisely seven times in Benjamin's text, and all but one of these are either quotations or paraphrases from nineteenth-century socialist and utopian theorists: Fourier, Marx, and Saint-Simon. The sole exception—the statement, "The authentic concept of universal history is a messianic concept"[5]—speaks less to messianism than to the impossibility of universal history. It is only in the winter of 1939–1940 that messianic motifs reenter Benjamin's writing; these are the months in Paris in which he read and discussed the manuscript of Scholem's *Major Trends in Jewish Mysticism* with Hannah Arendt and Heinrich Blücher. The effect was immediate: he began to interweave messianic motifs with the revolutionary historiography he had developed in convolute N of *The Arcades Project* (which develops its epistemology and historiography without recourse to messianism), and the result is the theses on the philosophy of history, "On the Concept of History" (1940). This example of the uses of messianism demonstrates two things. First, that Benjamin's use of theological material is always local: it is deployed within a specific *local* context in his work, often in support of a political position under development. The result is a "situational" theological politics oriented to the task at hand. And second, in constructing these local constellations, Benjamin draws freely on a number of traditions: Christian and Jewish theology, but also upon secularized theological thought such as German romanticism and French utopian socialism.

If Benjamin's theological rhetoric is local and specific, his articulation of his political commitments tends to be more consistent—and, for the period after 1924, somewhat better understood. We can discern two broad arcs in his politics. Up to 1924, Benjamin patiently constructed an idiosyncratic theological politics. Gershom Scholem long ago characterized Benjamin's position in this period as "theocratic anarchism"; more recently, Anson Rabinbach has called it "anarcho-messianism." The full publication of Benjamin's letters, together with new archival research, suggests that neither of these designations is fully satisfactory. In the years 1920 to 1925, Benjamin mapped out the complex political and theological terrain in which he moved, assembling a theological politics in these years that drew in equal measure on Judaic and Christian motifs and positions, and resulted in a politics that moved gradually from a rather straightforward anarchism toward a constructive and engaged theological politics situated to the left of center.[6] The story after 1924 is somewhat clearer: Benjamin's gradual movement leftward saw an equivocating and shifting identification with different strands of Marxist thought. First, he never moved completely away from his first Marxist inspiration, Georg Lukàcs, and the strongly philosophical engagement with historical materialism that shaped *History and Class Consciousness*; Lukàcs's ideas on reification and its effect on consciousness remained central at every moment after 1924. Second, Benjamin's understanding of an engaged, class-conscious leftism was kindled by his association with the Latvian theater director Asja Lacis; its strongest formulations, though, derive from his friendship with Bertolt Brecht. And finally, those more distanced and hesitant approaches to Marxism are consonant with the thinking of the circle around Theodor Adorno and Max Horkheimer.[7] In sum, over the course of Benjamin's life we find a rather consistent political arc punctuated by a shifting, situational deployment of theological motifs.

In order to demonstrate the resultant complexity, I will present a fuller case study: a view onto the eschatology that is implicit in Benjamin's late work. There is, of course, no explicit eschatology in the key texts here: neither the series of essays that grew out of his attempt to write a book on Baudelaire nor the *Arcades Project* nor any of the late writings on technological media speak plainly of the coming of the last days. Yet the attentive reader certainly feels the tug of the undercurrent of eschatological expectation in these texts. Benjamin's theory of modernity is not merely analytical: it subtends an understanding that the proper use of technologized media *accelerates* the erasure of the conditions that currently obtain. It is, in short, an apocalyptic eschatology.

"The Work of Art in the Age of Its Technological Reproducibility" examines the possibilities open to human experience under the conditions of modern capitalism.⁸ The essay proceeds from the conviction—best articulated in "Experience and Poverty"—that one of capitalist modernity's principle effects is the destruction of the conditions for an adequate human experience. Within this broad horizon, the artwork essay offers a complex and often seemingly contradictory understanding of technological media: for Benjamin, technology is at once a main cause of this destruction of experience and its potential solution. On the one hand, as Benjamin puts it in "Eduard Fuchs, Collector and Historian," human experience has been denatured by our own "bungled reception of technology."⁹ This bungled reception has ensured that modern technology has produced anesthesia—a deadening of the human sensory capacities—while at the same time aestheticizing and masking what are at their base brutal conditions of production and domination.¹⁰ Yet that very technology nonetheless has the potential not so much to *liberate* human experience from its bondage, not so much to effect the construction of a new, emancipated humanity, but rather the potential to *reveal* to human cognition the conditions that obtain, and thus to create conditions under which they might be erased.

If this central argument is not often recognized as central, that is because it is embedded in a deep doubleness at the heart of Benjamin's essay. Benjamin uses the term *apparatus* in two distinct ways without clearly differentiating them. The first meaning, which we might think of as the *lower-case* or *basic* apparatus, is the sum of the equipment necessary to produce and reproduce films; the second meaning, which we might think of as *upper-case* or *extended* apparatus, designates a conceptual and immaterial—yet absolutely objective—arrangement that serves to position the subject as a point of view. For Benjamin, this latter apparatus is nothing more and nothing less than the phantasmagoria that defines life under modern urban capitalism. Benjamin—as well as Adorno—of course derived this term itself from an eighteenth-century optical device, a kind of precinematic Plato's cave. At times, Benjamin understands phantasmagoria as an objective, although largely passive, condition of modern life: we live under phantasmagoria as under a second nature, in which everything is illusory, yet we take it to be real and inevitable—with distorting and denaturing consequences for the human subject. In the artwork essay, though, the term *apparatus*, while often coterminous with phantasmagoria, is more proactive. In fact, it is largely coextensive with what Foucault in the *History of Sexuality* would call the *dispositif*—an assemblage of heterogeneous mechanisms that "capture" and "transform" living beings into subjects in the process of which the "dimension of power" plays a crucial role.[11] This is clearly what Benjamin intends in a sentence such as this: "The function of film is to train human beings in the apperceptions and reactions needed to deal with a vast apparatus whose role in their lives is expanding almost daily."[12] The artwork essay is, then, a demonstration of how this apparatus might be refunctioned and appropriated for humane ends—or, as Benjamin puts it, for resistance to fascist aestheticization. Freedom from what Benjamin calls "enslavement to the apparatus" can come only when a reformed humanity can come to ✓ terms with the new productive forces present but unexploited in technology. Benjamin envisions such a process in one late sentence in the essay, a sentence in which the term *apparatus* moves from its extended meaning through its basic meaning and arrives, after a dialectical process, at a kind of sublated and potentiated form of the apparatus that can now be turned to human purposes: "For the majority of city dwellers, throughout the workday in offices and factories, have to relinquish their humanity in the face of an apparatus. In the evening these same masses fill the cinemas, to witness the film actor taking revenge on their behalf not only by asserting *his* humanity (or what appears to them as such) against the apparatus, but by placing that apparatus in the service of his triumph."[13] Much as Aristotle's spectator experiences catharsis through the fall of the hero on the stage, Benjamin's spectator experiences and participates in the actor's triumph against the lower-case apparatus on the screen as a figurative model for the spectator's resistance to the upper-case apparatus—a device for the reproduction of images of control—within which she lives. In Miriam Hansen's wonderful translation, Benjamin's utopian vision reconceives the apparatus within which we live as a "room for play," drawing on one of the most famous passages in the essay:

> The most important social function of film is to establish equilibrium between human beings and the apparatus. Film achieves this goal not only in terms of man's presentation of himself to the camera but also in terms of his representation of his environment by means of this apparatus. On the one hand, film furthers insight into the necessities governing our lives by its use of close-ups, by its accentuation of hidden details in familiar objects, and by its exploration of commonplace milieu through the ingenious guidance of the camera; on the other hand, it manages to assure us of a vast and unsuspected field of action/room for play [*Spielraum*].[14]

The artwork essay attributes to film, then, the capacity to effect profound changes in the very structure and capacities of the human sensorium. New apperceptions and reactions are necessary if humans are to confront—indeed even to recognize—the vast and inimical social apparatus currently in place. Yet—and we now reach a central divide in the understanding of Benjamin's late work—the power of that apparatus cannot be modified. Benjamin was no meliorist: he sought to think, write, and act "always radically, never with consequences." The apparatus cannot be changed, but only destroyed, annihilated with what he calls the "whetted ax of reason." The erasure intended here would, in Benjamin's historiography, bring us to the end of days. I have claimed earlier that his work includes no concept of religion. At this point, let me modify that claim: the late work is shot through with a sense that religious experience might be possible only *after* the end of days. This line in Benjamin's late thought is organized not by the concept of messianism, but by the theological concept of apokatastasis.

In his late work, Benjamin deploys the term *apokatastasis* in a variety of contexts, signaling a sense of its very broad applicability. Here, I am concerned with one instance that has largely escaped critical attention: In the first section of the convolute labeled "social movement" in *The Arcades Project*, Benjamin speaks of the "will to apokatastasis" as the resolve to gather again, in revolutionary action and in revolutionary thinking, precisely the elements of the "too early" and the "too late" of "the first beginning and the final decay."[15] I will turn later to a fuller reading of the term itself, but for now let me assert proleptically that the will to apokatastasis is in this sense *the* political will, the will to bring an end to what is in the hope that, in a cosmological turn, something better might succeed it.

What I have suggested so far is that, in Benjamin's late work, three things flow together in an explosive way: the theory of modern media; an advanced understanding of the effect of these media on the human sensorium; and the relationship of these two elements to Benjamin's late theological politics, here considered under the eschatological rubric "apokatastasis." In what follows, I will reconstruct the discursive field from which this set of keywords—eschatology, experience, and media—originally arose. And, in a manner utterly typical of Walter Benjamin's patterns of thought, that field was constructed many years before these terms bubbled to the surface of his writing in the late 1930s. In fact, he constructed this field in the early 1920s. And the names that correspond to those keywords are Adolf von Harnack, Laszlo Moholy-Nagy, and Erich Unger. Let me turn to Unger first.

Erich Unger is hardly a household name, even among Benjamin scholars. He was a disciple of the Jewish mystagogue Oskar Goldberg. By the end of World War I, Goldberg had begun to propagate an esoteric doctrine of Judaism that held that the Jews' special relationship to God was founded on a set of ritual practices in "prehistoric" Judaism, on a Judaism that has left traces in the Pentateuch.[16] At the heart of the mythic, prerational age that Goldberg purports to have uncovered was the practice of magic. An investment in magic guaranteed, then, not just the proper relation to the divine, but especially a fundamental existential unity that alone could serve as the basis of an integrated, holistic human being and, in turn, of a proper Jewish people. For Goldberg, historical Judaism is nothing more than a falling away from this ancient, unified, magical Hebraism. Contemporary religion, mysticism, philosophy, and indeed every cultural practice are for Goldberg nothing more than disunified, disjunctive approximations of the original magic unity. Scholem famously characterized Goldberg's doctrines as a "biological Kabbalah."[17] In the hands of Goldberg's principle disciple Unger, however, these unambiguously religious ideas were given the *appearance* of a secularized philosophical form. In Unger's *Politik und Metaphysik* (1921), the word *religion* appears not a single time; and the terms *myth* and *magic*, which are the central concepts of Goldberg's project, appear only in a derogatory sense. This *apparent* secularization was, however, self-consciously constructed as the necessary philosophical pendant to Goldberg's project; Unger's theories function as the *propaedeutic* to the possibility of what he took to be genuine religious experience.

The transmission and apparent secularization of Goldberg's ideas through Unger would have remained a deeply buried footnote in the history of Jewish esoteric thought if Walter Benjamin had not encountered Erich Unger in the early 1920s. In those years, Benjamin's enthusiasm for Unger and his work knew no bounds; he characterized *Politik und Metaphysik* as the "most significant piece of writing on politics in our time."[18] Significant shared assumptions laid the ground for Benjamin's positive reception of Unger. Each man was persuaded that philosophical thought must move beyond a Kantian model that for them was based upon an inadequate understanding of human experience and knowledge.[19] Each was deeply invested in a polemic against the rationalistic activism of Kurt Hiller.[20] Each man's politics was informed by a deep-seated distrust of democracy and its attendant procedures such as compromise and negotiation. And each of them saw in the mind/body problem a determinative analogy for any understanding of politics.[21]

Erich Unger's *Politik und Metaphysik* is nothing less than the attempt to reconceive experience under the conditions of modernity such that a return to myth might be possible.[22] As such, the book formulates a metaphysics through which apperception of what Unger calls an "ideal condition" might be possible. Thus his *credo ex negativo* on page one: "Every establishment and every survival of uncatastrophic human orders—every uncatastrophic politics—is unmetaphysically not possible."[23] Unger's idealist politics aims to restore to humanity a direct, unified relation to the categories of "life, vitality, and death," categories attainable only through their organization under the category *Geist*. The question raises itself, then, as to just what a thinker of the stature of Walter Benjamin might have seen in Unger's untidy mixture of vitalism, Hegelianism, and mystagogy.

At the core of Unger's book lies a radical theory of the reformation of the human sensorium, a proposal that sets it apart from other positions within the German conservative revolution and brings it into dialogue with a range of thought across the political spectrum. Unger begins by asserting that *Geist* can intervene in the world—in what he calls "corporeal, economic existence"—without falling prey to its "dislocations and ailments" because this intervention occurs as a form of what he calls *Fernwirkung* or "distant effectivity" (*PM*, 18). The sole evident paradigm for the kind of remote control he has in mind, and thus for the possibility of spiritual intervention in the catastrophic contemporary world, is the remote control evident in "the physiological mastering of the body through spiritual factors." Unger begins to stake out new ground when he asserts that the spaced or distant intervention of *Geist* in the corporeal world "according to the manner of the body" is conceivable only if nature— what he calls the "naturally given elements of the psychophysiological phenomenon"—is itself "modifiable" (19). And this modifiability itself can only, in turn, be based on a reformation of the concept of *Anschauung*— of an intuition based on observation of the phenomenal world. Unger thus calls for the creation of what he calls a *reine Sinnlichkeit* (pure sensuousness) that is the dialectical product of the modifiability of the sensorium and the modifiability of nature (20).

The reconstruction and reformation of the human sensorium is, in *Politik und Metaphysik*, thus the key to a reconsideration of the very concept of experience and, more importantly, an expansion of the field constituted by the possible objects of experience. "More and different material circumstances must be brought within the field of vision of politics in order that the physical world might be governed. Any political undertaking fails not because of the extensiveness but because of the restriction of its scope" (*PM*, 21). On this basis, Unger claims that the modifiability of the consciousness of empirical individuals can achieve a "potentiation" that might produce an "extension of the borders of accessibility into heretofore closed regions" (26). The reformation of the sensorium envisioned here allows, in other words, for the "intuition" of a radically broadened range of phenomena—and such a reformation remains the *precondition* of religious experience. It is important to underline that, for Unger, these objects of experience are not in themselves religious.

Walter Benjamin certainly encountered a thoroughgoing argument for the reformation of the sensorium for the first time in Unger's book. Soon after his reading of Unger, though, Benjamin's circle of friends and intellectual partners began to intermingle with a very different group of Berlin intellectuals, a group now referred to as the "G-Group."[24] In late 1922 and early 1923 a new avant-garde had begun to form in Berlin. The group met in the ateliers of a number of artists and architects, among them Laszlo Moholy-Nagy, Mies van der Rohe, El Lissitsky, and Hans Richter. A small inner circle soon formed, a circle intent on propagating a new direction for European culture. At the edges of the group, a few Berlin intellectuals soon found their way into the intensive discussions. This was a group of friends centered around Walter Benjamin. It included his wife, Dora, and his close friend Ernst Schoen, a musician and music theorist who would go on to become the cultural director of one of the national radio stations.

Especially as a result of his conversations with Moholy, Benjamin had by 1923 begun to rethink the implications of his reading of Unger, and Unger's call for the reformation of the sensorium as the precondition for religious experience. Under Moholy's influence, Benjamin begins to reformulate this transformation as the result of material, and especially of visual processes that are shaped by the human encounter with modern media. By 1923 he had read Moholy's essay "Production/Reproduction," in which Moholy discriminates two forms of art: art that merely *reproduces* the phenomenal world characteristic of capitalist modernity, and thus substantiates and perpetuates that world, and art that *produces* new relationships among its elements.[25] And Moholy claims that this art, productive art, is itself the catalyst for major changes in the human sensorium, changes that might potentially allow for a revision and new understanding of our world. The reformation of the sensorium through the encounter with art becomes for Moholy the precondition not for religious revival, but for social change. Walter Benjamin, however, clearly envisioned a reformation of the sensorium that drew on both Unger and Moholy: in his refunctioning of their ideas in the theory of modern technological media that he formulated in the course of the 1930s, the reformed sensorium

alone can raise the actual conditions that obtain to the level of consciousness. Once these conditions are disclosed, he felt that violent social change—
revolt—was inevitable. This account begs the question, of course, as to how
religious experience might be enabled by this process.

Benjamin's reading habits at this time provide a third, still wider horizon that suggests an answer to this question. While still in Switzerland
and writing his dissertation in 1918–1919, he had read the prominent liberal theologian Adolf von Harnack's three-volume *History of Dogma*.[26] It
is certainly significant that Benjamin turned to Harnack while in self-
imposed exile during World War I. Harnack was not merely the leading
liberal theologian in the German-speaking world; he was also something
like the state theologian of the German empire. It had been Harnack who
had written the speech delivered by the Kaiser in 1914 announcing the
beginning of the war. Now, in 1923, as Benjamin undertook the broad
preparatory work for his second dissertation on the German Baroque
Trauerspiel, he *re-read* all three weighty volumes. Although we could trace
a remarkable number of impulses that go out from Benjamin's reading of
Harnack, one is of particular importance for us here: Benjamin encountered there for the first time the theology of Origen of Alexandria
(185–254 A.D.), one of the earliest church fathers. And a central postulate
of Origen's theology is the idea of apokatastasis.

The simple version of this term sees it as the belief in universal salvation: no soul is ever lost to redemption. The term occurs in only one biblical passage, in Acts 3:21, a discussion of the end times. Apokatastasis
there points to the possible *restitutio in integrum*, the restoration of all
things *after* the end times.[27] This temporal element is deeply inscribed not
only in the biblical passage, but in Origen as well. In Origen, though, the
temporal aspect is the residue of a persistent *cosmological* dimension of the
term. A cosmological understanding of apokatastasis is typical of Platonism,
Stoicism, and Gnosticism; all these share a belief in the rigorous *alterna-
tion* of ages of cosmic culmination and cosmic restitution. In Stoicism,
the term *apokatastasis* refers to the idea that, in an all-encompassing con-
flagration, the cosmos is reduced to its primal element—fire. Only then
can the rebirth of all existing things come about. How, though, do residues of these ideas inform Origen, and thus the beginnings of a Christian
orthodoxy?[28]

Origen was a process theologian: he believed that our capacity to understand the divine concepts was a dynamic process, a process that led to a
gradual transformation not just of our knowledge, but of our very being.
A central stage of this education was in fact the fire of punishment, which
is not an instrument of eternal torment, but of divine instruction and

purgation—both of which are necessary preconditions for any apokata-static restitution. Just as there are many stages of our education, many different stages of the soul, there are many ages through which humans rise, fall, or come to an end. In his major work *De Principiis*, Origen offers an explanation of the term *apokatastasis* that, in its emphasis on the cyclical nature of salvation history, reveals its cosmological dimension:

> The end is always like the beginning: and, therefore, as there is one end to all things, so ought we to understand that there was one beginning; and as there is one end to many things, so there spring from one beginning many differences and varieties, which again, through the goodness of God, and by subjection to Christ, and through the unity of the Holy Spirit, are recalled to one end, which is like unto the beginning.[29]

The beginning is thus like unto the end that necessarily precedes it: the cosmological and cyclical dimensions of Origen's project, first discovered in the early 1920s, bubbled to the surface of Benjamin's writing in the late 1930s. And his ever-present nihilism—like D. H. Lawrence, he liked to think of the world going "pop"—ensured that the element of confla-gration was retained and indeed deployed in a manner utterly foreign to Origen.

Taking into account these varying strands, Benjamin's evocation of the "will to apokatastasis" after 1935 clearly intends a complex action. Through the proper reception and deployment of modern media, this will might effect a broad historical change in the structure and capacities of human sense perception; such a reformed perceptive capacity might, on the basis of a newly enabled "now of recognizability" lead to a revolt against the conditions that obtained in the world, conditions that had previously been veiled;[30] and the envisioned erasure of current conditions might pro-vide a new "body space" within which religious experience is possible.[31] This is, admittedly, a preliminary and rather abstract formulation of the "will to apokatastasis" and its effects.

Benjamin's most important work of the late 1930s, however, the great, unfinished book on Charles Baudelaire, provides a very concrete example of how Benjamin envisioned the cosmological speculation embedded within the term *apokatastasis* as it might be realized under conditions of modernity. It does so by reading Baudelaire himself precisely as an incar-nation of the will to apokatastasis. The Baudelaire book, which had the working title *Charles Baudelaire: A Lyric Poet in the Era of High Capital-ism*, had a complex genesis. It grew, beginning in 1937, out of the massive studies undertaken after 1927 for Benjamin's projected book on the origins of urban commodity capitalism in the Paris of the nineteenth century that are now published as *The Arcades Project*. Convinced by his supporters at the Institute for Social Research in New York to commence work on a project that might yield near-term results, Benjamin turned his focus to the great French poet, whom he had increasingly come to see as one of the organizing figures of the larger study of the arcades.[32] The basis for the Baudelaire book was thus a systematic revision and reordering of the arcades materials. Benjamin arrived at a tripartite schema, a book comprised of major sections called "Baudelaire as Allegorist," "The Paris of the Second Empire in Baudelaire," and "The Commodity as Poetic Object." It is this last section that is of particular interest to us here. Its chapters are titled "The Commodity," "Nouveauté," "Eternal Return," "Spleen," "Loss of the Aura," "Jugendstil," and "Tradition." The book would have ended thus:

> The ideologies of the rulers are by their nature more changeable than the ideas of the oppressed. For not only must they, like the ideas of the latter, adapt each time to the situation of social conflict, but they must glorify that situation as fundamentally harmonious. To undertake to salvage the great figures of the bourgeoisie means not least: to conceive them in this most unstable dimension of their operation, and precisely from out of that to extract, to cite what has remained inconspicuously buried beneath—being, as it was, of so little help to the powerful.[33]

The key phrase here is "the most unstable dimension of their operation." Benjamin locates this dimension in the construction of cosmological allegories by three "great figures of the bourgeoisie": Baudelaire himself, Friedrich Nietzsche, and August Blanqui. He sees in the very audacity of these constructions the potential to reveal the fissures and incoherencies in the harmonious façade bodied forth by the capitalist metropolis.[34]

The final pages of the Baudelaire book thus stage a reconstruction of these three allegories. For Benjamin, the allegories of stellar constellations as networks of commodities that recur in *Les Fleurs du mal* make of Baudelaire's poetry a conjuration of the temporal phantasmagoria of modernity—with its main feature, the appearance of newness—from the misery of the Second Empire. Far from serving as rational analyses of the state of life under capitalism, these cosmological conjurations condense and exacerbate central, if hidden features of time as sameness and repetition. Similarly, Nietzsche's idea of the eternal return reveals the constitutive emotional fantasies of capitalist life as the ineradicable "phantasmagoria of happiness of the *Gründerjahre*." These phantasmagorias are, much like the modern media analyzed in "The Work of Art in the Age of Its Technological Reproducibility," the product of crisis. Yet, also like these media when properly deployed, they have the unusual ability to indicate and intensify that crisis itself.

> The idea of eternal recurrence transforms the historical event itself into a mass-produced article. But this conception also displays in another respect—on its reverse side, one could say—a trace of the economic circumstances to which it owes its sudden actuality. This was manifest at the moment when the security of conditions of life was considerably diminished through an accelerated succession of crises. The idea of eternal recurrence derived its luster from the fact that it was no longer possible, in all circumstances, to expect a recurrence of conditions across any interval of time shorter than that provided by eternity. The quotidian constellations quite gradually began to be less quotidian. Quite gradually their recurrence became a little less frequent, and there could arise in consequence the obscure presentiment that henceforth one must rest content with cosmic constellations.[35]

The evocation of this obscure presentiment—that the apparent regularity and predictability of life was a pernicious illusion—is the first chink in the otherwise harmonious temporal façade of capitalism. An epoch does not simply awaken from the bad dream of history: it must have its uneasy sleep punctuated by a nightmare vision of a cruelty to awaken the dead. It is in this sense that Benjamin can characterize the buried man as "the transcendental subject of history."[36]

The final hero in Benjamin's series is Auguste Blanqui, that professional insurrectionist who had the distinction of being incarcerated for each major upheaval of the French nineteenth century. In the 1939 exposé of *The Arcades Project*, Benjamin calls Blanqui's book "one last, cosmic phantasmagoria which implicitly comprehends the severest critique of all the others."[37] He ascribes to Blanqui's text "an extreme hallucinatory power." Blanqui's phantasmagoria shows a society, or so Benjamin hoped, about to be nudged by this horror out of its long, phantasmagoric sleep and to awaken not, like the allegorist of the *Trauerspiel* book, in the redeemed world, but in a world conscious of its own structures, mechanisms, and possibilities. Only then might revolution come, only then might all things be first erased and then restored, only then might religious experience become possible once again.

The apokatastatic dimension of the theological politics developed in the Baudelaire book might well have remained unnamed: like the ink in the metaphor with which we commenced, apokatastasis could have remained invisible. Yet he did name it. The cosmological speculation of the book's final chapters is saturated with Benjamin's very particular inflection of the patristic concept—an understanding shaped not just by his reading of Christian dogma, but by meditation on esoteric Judaism and the espousal of a utopian media theory. Apokatastasis emerges in *Charles Baudelaire: A Lyric Poet in the Era of High Capitalism* as nothing less than the invisible linkage suggested by Benjamin's last text, "On the Concept of History." The puppet that is historical materialism might well, using the dwarf that is theology, vanquish every opponent . . . if apokatastasis is present as the invisible string linking the two.

Notes

1. Walter Benjamin, "On the Concept of History" in *Selected Writings*, 4 vols., ed. Michael W. Jennings et al. (Cambridge, MA: Harvard University Press, 1996–2003), 4:389: "There was once, we know, an automaton constructed in such a way that it could respond to every move by a chess player with a counter move that would ensure the winning of the game. A puppet wearing Turkish attire and with a hookah in its mouth sat before the chessboard placed on a large table. A system of mirrors created the illusion that this table was transparent on all sides. Actually, a hunchbacked dwarf—a master at chess—sat inside and guided the puppet's hand by means of strings. One can imagine a philosophic counterpart to this apparatus. The puppet, called 'historical materialism,' is to win all the time. It can easily be a match for anyone if it enlists the services of theology, which today, as we know, is small and ugly and has to keep out of sight."

2. Walter Benjamin, *The Arcades Project* (Cambridge, MA: Harvard University Press, 1999), N7a,7, 41. Hereafter cited in the notes by convolute number.

3. To take only strong instances of this tendency, cf. Irving Wohlfarth, "Immer radikal, niemals consequent . . . Zur theologisch-politischen Standortsbestimmung Walter Benjamins," in *Antike und Moderne: Zu Walter Benjamins "Passagen,"* ed. Norbert Bolz and Richard Faber (Würzburg: Königshausen und Neumann, 1986), 116–137, and Giorgio Agamben, "Die Struktur der messianischen Zeit," in *Aisthesis. Zur Erfahrung von Zeit, Raum, Text und Kunst*, ed. Nikolaus Müller-Schöll and Saskia Reither (Schliengen: Verlag Schmitt-Langelot, 2005), 172–182.

4. Howard Eiland and Michael W. Jennings, *Walter Benjamin: A Critical Life* (Cambridge: Harvard University Press, 2014), 74–176.

5. Benjamin, *Arcades Project*, N18,3.

6. For a full account of Benjamin's politics in this period, see Michael W. Jennings, "Towards Eschatology: The Development of Benjamin's Theological Politics in the early 1920's," in *Walter Benjamins Anthropologisches Denken*, ed. Carolin Duttinger, Ben Morgan, and Anthony Phelan (Freiburg: Rombach

Verlag, 2012), 41–58. Also cf. Anson Rabinbach, *In the Shadow of Catastrophe: German Intellectuals Between Apocalypse and Enlightenment* (Berkeley, University of California Press, 1997), 59, and Uwe Steiner, "The True Politician: Walter Benjamin's Concept of the Political," *New German Critique*, no. 83 (Spring–Summer 2001): 72.

7. Benjamin's heterodox Marxism has, if anything, occasioned even more—and much fiercer—debate than has his theology. The debate began already in his lifetime, as Bertolt Brecht, Adorno, and Scholem all struggled to "correct" Benjamin's political line. Long after his death, the writer Helmut Heissenbüttel published an attack in 1967 in the prominent journal *Merkur* on Adorno's stewardship of Benjamin's legacy, making accusations that were echoed in other quarters. From very different political vantage points, both the West Berlin journal *Alternative* and Hannah Arendt amplified Heissenbüttel's charge that Adorno's editorial practices essentially continued the censorship of Benjamin's writing undertaken by the Institute of Social Research in New York in the late 1930s. What began as a debate about philology became a fierce war of words concerning the use and abuse of Marxist politics in the West. These debates, and the many that followed them, could be said to culminate in the title of T. J. Clark's article: "Should Benjamin Have Read Marx?" *boundary 2* 30, no. 1 (2003): 31–49.

8. The remarks that follow are deeply indebted to Miriam Bratu Hansen's lifelong engagement with the artwork essay and in particular to the chapters on Benjamin in her magisterial *Cinema and Experience: Siegfried Kracauer, Walter Benjamin, and Theodor W. Adorno* (Berkeley: University of California Press, 2011).

9. Benjamin, *Selected Writings*, 3:266.

10. Cf. esp. Susan Buck-Morss, "Aesthetics and Anaesthetics: Walter Benjamin's Artwork Essay Reconsidered," *October* 62 (Autumn 1992): 3–41.

11. Michel Foucault, *The History of Sexuality*, vol. 1 (New York: Random House, 2012), 8–10.

12. Benjamin, *Selected Writings*, 3:107–108. All quotations are from the second version of the essay that Miriam Hansen first dubbed the "Urtext."

13. Ibid., 3:111.

14. Ibid., 3:117.

15. "Since the Surrealists constantly confuse moral nonconformism with proletarian revolution, they attempt, instead of following the course of the modern world, to relocate themselves to a historical moment when this confusion was still possible, a moment anterior to the Congress of Tours, anterior even to the development of Marxism: the period of the 1820s, '30s and '40s." Emmanuel Berl, "Premier Pamphlet," *Europe*, no. 75 (March 15, 1929), 402. And that is certainly no accident. For, on the one hand, we have here elements—anthropological materialism, hostility toward progress—which are refractory to Marxism, while, on the other hand, the will to apokatastasis speaks here, the resolve to gather again, in revolutionary action and in revolutionary

thinking, precisely the elements of the "too early" and the "too late," of the first beginning and the final decay [a1,1].

16. Oskar Goldberg, *Die Wirklichkeit der Hebräer: Einleitung in das System des Pentateuch* (Berlin: David Verlag, 1925). For a thorough study of Goldberg and his circle see Manfred Voigts, *Oskar Goldberg: Der mythische Experimentalwissenschaftler. Ein verdrängtes Kapitel jüdischer Geschichte* (Berlin: Agora Verlag, 1992).

17. Gershom Scholem, *Walter Benjamin: The Story of a Friendship*, trans. Harry Zohn (New York: Schocken Books, 1982), 96–97.

18. Walter Benjamin, *The Correspondence of Walter Benjamin, 1910–1940*, trans. Manfred R. Jacobson and Evelyn M. Jacobson (Chicago: University of Chicago Press), 172.

19. Cf. Benjamin, "On the Program of the Coming Philosophy," in *Selected Writings*, 1:100–110.

20. On Hiller and his "revolutionary pacifism," see Brigitte Laube, *"Dennoch glaube ich an den messianischen Geist." Kurt Hiller (1885–1972): Aspekte einer deutsch-jüdischen Identität* (Essen: Klartext, 2011).

21. For Benjamin's ideas on the mind-body problem, see his (posthumously published) fragment "Outline of the Psychophysical Problem," in *Selected Writings*, 1:393–401.

22. For an important general reading of the intellectual relationship between Benjamin and Unger, see Margarete Kohlenbach, "Religion, Experience, Politics: On Erich Unger and Walter Benjamin," in *The Early Frankfurt School and Religion*, ed. Margarete Kohlenbach and Raymond Geuss (London: Palgrave, 2005), 64–84.

23. Unger, *Politik und Metaphysik*, ed. Manfred Voigts (Würzburg: Königshausen und Neumann, 1989), 3. All translations are my own. Hereafter cited in text as *PM*.

24. For an introduction to the group and its journal, *G: Materials for Elemental Form-Creation*, see Michael W. Jennings and Detlef Mertins, "Introduction: The G-Group and the European Avant-Garde," in *G: An Avant-Garde Journal of Art, Architecture, Design, and Film, 1923–1926*, ed. Michael W. Jennings and Detlef Mertins (Los Angeles: Getty Research Institute, 2010), 3–20. For a broader characterization of Benjamin's relations with the European avant-garde, see Michael W. Jennings, "Benjamin and the European Avant-Garde," in *The Cambridge Companion to Walter Benjamin*, ed. David Ferris (Cambridge: Cambridge University Press, 2004), 18–34.

25. Laszlo Moholy-Nagy, "Production/Reproduction," in *Photography in the Modern Era*, ed. Christopher Phillips (New York: Metropolitan Museum of Art, 1989), 79–82.

26. Adolf von Harnack, *Lehrbuch der Dogmengeschichte*, 3 vols. (Freiburg: J. C. B. Mohr, 1888–90).

27. It is this understanding of the term that informs Irving Wohlfarth, *"Et cetera? Der Historiker als Lumpensammler,"* in *Passagen. Walter Benjamins*

Urgeschichte des Neunzehnten Jahrhunderts, ed. Norbert Bolz and Bernd Witte (Munich: Wilhelm Fink, 1984), 70–95.

28. In this context, see esp. Rowan Williams, "Origen: Between Orthodoxy and Heresy," in *Origeniana Septima*, ed. W. A. Bienert and U. Kuhneweg (Leuven: Leuven University Press, 1999), 3–14.

29. Origen, *On First Principles*, trans. G. W. Butterworth (Gloucester, MA: Peter Smith, 1973), 58.

30. The "now of recognizability" is the key element in the epistemology Benjamin developed as the theoretical armature of the arcades project. See *Arcades*, N3,1. For an account of the role played in the late work by the theory of the dialectical image developed, see Jennings, *Dialectical Images: Walter Benjamin's Theory of Literary Criticism* (Ithaca, NY: Cornell University Press, 1987), 121–163.

31. "Body space" and "image space" are the highly suggestive, albeit insufficiently contoured keywords in Benjamin's essay "Surrealism: The Last Snapshot of the Intelligentsia," in *Selected Writings*, 2:207–221. On this twinned conceptual pair, see especially Sigrid Weigel, *Body- and Image-Space: Re-reading Walter Benjamin* (London: Routledge, 1996).

32. For an account of the gestation of the book, see Eiland and Jennings, *Walter Benjamin*, 576–646. A version of the full draft of the book has now been published in Italian: *Charles Baudelaire. Un poeta lirico nell'età del capitalismo avanzato*, ed. Giorgio Agamben, Barbara Chitussi, and Clemens-Carl Härle (Vicenza: Neri Pozza Editore, 2012). For a full philological account of the book, see Michel Despagne and Michael Werner, "Vom Passagen-Projekt zum Charles Baudelaire: Neue Handschriften zum Spätwerk Walter Benjamins," *Deutsche Vierteljahresschrift für Literaturwissenschaft und Geistesgeschichte* 58 (1984): 593–657. For a fuller account of the role of the stellar phantasmagorias in the Baudelaire book itself, see Jennings, "On the Banks of a New Lethe: Commodification and Experience in Walter Benjamin's Late Work," *boundary 2* 30, no. 4 (2003): 89–104.

33. Quotations from the draft of the Baudelaire book are cited according to their location in *The Arcades Project*; here, J77,1.

34. For a reading that emphasizes the role of these cosmological allegories in the Baudelaire book itself, see Jennings, "On the Banks of a New Lethe," 89–104.

35. Benjamin, *Arcades Project*, J62a,2.

36. Ibid., J67,5.

37. Benjamin, "Paris, Capital of the Nineteenth Century: Exposé <of 1939>," in *Arcades Project*, 25.

Historical, Religious, and Philosophical Influences

Walter Benjamin's Jewishness

HOWARD EILAND

Benjamin's Jewishness was at first no more than an exotic "aroma" in his life. He grew up in a thoroughly assimilated household of the liberal Jewish bourgeoisie in Berlin. His mother's side of the family felt some allegiance to the Jewish reform community in Berlin, while his father's side inclined to the orthodox rite, but all during Benjamin's protected childhood his family celebrated Christmas in high style and organized Easter egg hunts for the children—these occasions are commemorated in his *Berlin Childhood around 1900*—whereas the young Benjamin knew next to nothing about the Jewish holidays.[1] In the vignette "Sexual Awakening" (1932) in *Berlin Childhood*, he tells of a misadventure during the Jewish High Holy Days that prevented his attendance at services in the synagogue, a slip-up and deviation he traces in part to his own "suspicion of religious ceremonies, which promised only embarrassment." The boy's anxiety at having lost his bearings in an unfamiliar neighborhood where he was supposed to meet a relative quickly gives way, however, to indifference ("So be it—I don't care") and to "a dawning sensation of pleasure," wherein the profanation of the holy day is combined with the pandering of the street, "which here, for the first time, gave me an inkling of the services it was prepared to render to awakened instincts."[2] The profane services rendered on this holy day by "the street" are associated with an instinctive awakening of powers more intellectually and spiritually fruitful than organized religious services could ever be, catering as they do to what he would call, in his "Dialogue on the Religiosity of the Present" in 1912, "the useless energy of piety" (*EW*, 75).

It was Benjamin's experience with the antebellum German youth movement in his last years in high school and first years of university study, and especially with the contingent of students around the leading educational reformer Gustav Wyneken, many of whom were Jews, that first occasioned his reflection on his own Jewishness. In this regard, the four lengthy letters to a fellow student and poet, Ludwig Strauss, written by the twenty-year-old Benjamin between September 1912 and January 1913, provide insight into his thinking about the "Jewish problem" at this time. Indeed, these letters constitute the only extended direct reflection on his Jewishness that we have today from Benjamin.[3]

At the outset of the exchange with Strauss, he raises the vexed question of the German-Jewish relationship, and this question hangs over the entire exchange (prompted as it evidently was by a public debate on the subject in the pages of the Munich literary journal *Kunstwart*, a debate to which Strauss had recently contributed).[4] "Although in ourselves we have two sides, Jewish and German, up until now we have been wholly and quite willingly absorbed in the German. The Jewish was often, it would seem, only an exotic, southern (or worse: sentimental) aroma in our production and in our life" (*GB*, 1:61–62). He mentions his liberal upbringing to Strauss, as something that would be self-evident to him, and adverts to the two years (1905–1906) he spent at the country boarding school Haubinda, where he first studied under Wyneken, a popularizing Nietzschean who introduced him to philosophy in his class on German literature. "I had my decisive intellectual and spiritual experience before Judaism ever became important or problematic to me. What I knew about it was really just anti-Semitism and a vague piety. As religion it was remote from me, and as national feeling altogether unknown" (69–70). Now, however, that has changed, and he feels Judaism and the Jewish to be at his core ("als mein Kernhaftes"). The "decisive influence," in this development, was his encounter with the charismatic non-Jew Wyneken, who in 1906 cofounded the progressive coeducational Freie Schulgemeinde (Free School Community) in the Thuringian village of Wickersdorf in central Germany.[5] Among those active in the "enlightened reform work" growing out of the Wickersdorf pedagogic program, says Benjamin, it was for the most part Jews who were in the forefront. "This all has become clear to me in the past few months. On the basis of Wickersdorf—not by speculative means, and not simply by means of feeling either, but on the basis of outer and inner experience—I have found my Judaism. What to me was the highest in ideas and in people—I have recognized this as Jewish.[6] And to reduce all that I've discovered to a formula: I am a Jew, and if I live as a conscious man, I live as a conscious Jew" (71). The element of the "Jewish" pervades conscious being at the same time that it manifests what is highest. The Jewish is a principle of both universalism and exclusivism.

Strauss had evidently invited Benjamin to collaborate on a planned journal of Jewish affairs (*GB*, 1:76–77), and Benjamin expressed an interest in writing for the journal so long as this did not mean promoting Zionism, the problem of which he has given much thought to, he says, although he has not had time to look into the literature (62). He is careful to distinguish his newfound sense of Jewishness and "Jewish spirit" from "political Zionism" and "practical Zionism." He is interested in furthering a broad educational-cultural program, but "not as dogma!" (70). "Assuming one can know the Jewish spirit, can one then build on it more than a provisional realm—a cultural realm? More generally: what do those who are capable of judgment expect from the *artificial* instauration of a culture-state [*Kulturstaat*]?" (62). The problem with Zionism in its present manifestation is, on the one hand, the philistinism of its membership—"they make propaganda for Palestine and then get drunk like Germans" (72)—and, on the other hand, the fundamental nationalism of its mission (82). For culture is valid, first and last, as *human* culture, and, however localized its origins, its appeal should not in principle be restricted to any one *part* of humanity (77). In his letter of October 10 to Strauss, Benjamin sums up the issue as follows: "I see three kinds of Zionist Judaism: the Palestine Zionism (a necessity of nature), the German Zionism in its half-heartedness, and the cultural Zionism [*Kultur-Zionismus*] that sees Jewish values *everywhere* and works for them. I stand with the latter, and, as I think, you too must take your stand there" (72).[7] In his letter of January 7, however, there is a more unqualified repudiation of Zionism as a whole: "I cannot make Zionism my political element. (And for that reason I shall naturally have to combat it in radical politics.)" (82). He glances at the possibility of an emancipated "Zionism of the spirit [*Zionismus des Geistes*]," which would promote "a certain Jewish gesture" that he knows from Strauss and one or two others, but "such a Zionism remains an idea and is thoroughly esoteric" (82–83). Moreover, it is not only Zionist tenets, both practical and esoteric, from which he keeps his distance; a "rigorous engagement with the Jewish sphere is something denied me" (77).

Judaism, he argues, cannot become an end in itself but may serve as "a preeminent vehicle and representative of the spiritual [*des Geistigen*];" in fact, "Jews constitute an elite in the ranks of intellectuals [*der Geistigen*]" (*GB*, 1:75). It is *jüdischer Geist*—Jewish spirit and intellect—that he is concerned with, and in his first surviving letter to Strauss he suggests that the Jewish spirit shows itself in its nature more readily in the field of culture, of artistic endeavor, than in "Jewish religious life" (61).[8] In the whole *Komplex* of his convictions, he tells Strauss in January, the Jewish plays but a partial role (83). And he remains incapable of defining more closely what for him is at issue in the notion of a fruitful *Kulturjudentum*. What he has in mind here is "more an image than a line of thought": "It is the reverse of the Tower of Babel: the biblical peoples pile ashlar upon ashlar, and their spiritual desideratum [*das geistig Gewollte*]—the tower that reaches heaven—fails to materialize. / The Jews handle ideas like ashlars; the origin, the matter [*Materie*], is never attained. They build from above, without reaching the ground" (84).[9] That Benjamin himself does not exactly "build from above" is indicated by a statement made toward the beginning of the letter of January 7–9, where it is not any teleological deduction that is decisive for his thinking but recurrent and ever-changing sudden confrontation (which will become the principle of montage): "Once again it seems to me that I am now for the first time confronted with [*nun erst bei*] the ultimate and essential" (81). In the letter of September 11 to Strauss, he writes that "the best Jews today" are bound up with a valuable process of struggle and formation taking place in Western European society, and in this connection he paraphrases a rhetorical question of Heinrich Mann's: "What would spirit, art, and love mean for us without the Jews?" (64). This comes at the end of a brief excursus on "the literati" (compare his later reference to "today's intellectual literary Jew [*Literaten-Jude*]" [83]) and their role in the formation of a new social consciousness and new modes of living—the excursus being an amplification of his thesis that the Jewish spirit is most fully expressed in the cultural sphere.

Benjamin prescinds from the customary negative connotation of "literati" (as a species of café-dweller or bohemian), insisting on the cultural and indeed religious importance of this type for the present day. The literati, he says, draw the ultimate consequences from "our famous enlightenment and freedom from prejudice." It is not enough for them to be open-minded under cover of bourgeois security; they seek out new ways of living that are in accord with the spirit of today's artistic expression. "They have their most serious mission in this: out of art, which they themselves cannot make, to win spirit for the life of the times" (*GB*, 1:63). The idea of the literary man—or "the man of letters (as idea)"—is for Benjamin associated, paradoxically enough, with a "modern asceticism," which extends even to the café culture. The literati "take the present day as seriously as Tolstoy takes the culture of Christianity. . . . [They are] called upon to be, in the new social consciousness, that which 'the poor in spirit, the downtrodden [*Geknechteten*] and the humble' were for early Christianity.[10] One can only wonder whether this social consciousness will seek and find metaphysical formulas, whether it will become a general or broader class consciousness" (63–64).

Several themes of these letters are rehearsed in the posthumously published "Dialogue on the Religiosity of the Present," which Benjamin completed in October 1912, and which he mentions to Ludwig Strauss at this time. There he further elaborates the idea of "the literati," associating them with a Zarathustrian "mania for exposing and overleaping abysses" and with "the mighty will to see everything unmoored—that is, not so peacefully and self-evidently anchored in the 'I' as it customarily appears to be" (*EW*, 72). His speaker remarks that he both loves and fears "this cynicism." To Strauss Benjamin characterizes the literati as *zukunftsvoll*, full of the future, and in the dialogue on religiosity he writes that "religion . . . will once again emerge from what is enslaved and downtrodden [*vom Geknechteten*]. But the class that today endures this necessary historical enslavement is the class of literati. They want to be the honest ones, want to give shape to their artistic enthusiasm, . . . but society repudiates them; and they themselves, in pathological self-destructiveness, must root out in themselves everything 'all too human' needed by one who lives . . . . We will never spiritualize conventions if we don't seek to infuse these forms of social life with our own personal spirit. And to that end we are helped by the literati. . . . I look upon them as bearers of religious spirit in our times" (73–74).[11] There is no little irony in the ambivalence Benjamin's high-minded speaker feels toward a social stratum that prefigures the author's own "downtrodden" condition of exile after 1933.

The question of the metaphysical bearing of social consciousness is also elaborated in the 1912 dialogue on religiosity, which characteristically conjoins the religious question to the sociopolitical as well as the aesthetic. Religious feeling is said to be rooted in "the totality of the time," and so any authentic religious reform will naturally involve all areas of life. According to Benjamin—and this is just the baldest expression of something axiomatic in all his writings—our social activity has lost its metaphysical seriousness and become a matter merely of public order and personal respectability. The spiritualizing of convention—by which a new dignity might be imparted to daily life, along with a sense of "something eternal in our daily labors" (*EW*, 66)—this new religious grounding to communal life has as correlate "a new consciousness of personal immediacy," an appreciation of "the abundance and weightiness of individuality" (78), or of what he suggestively calls "the natural being of the personality" (71). This is where the literati (as exemplary idea) can contribute. For "the culture of expression is the highest" (75). But such dynamic individuality cannot develop in a vacuum; and Benjamin remains skeptical of both the individual and the social taken in themselves. A genuine community—which would necessarily be a community of individual consciences—presupposes the cultivation of solitude,[12] but meaningful solitude can flourish only within a fruitfully encompassing spiritual-intellectual atmosphere. The circle is inescapable, especially considering that "religion must be born from a deep and almost unknown need [Not]" (76).

The "Dialogue on the Religiosity of the Present" is concerned with the awakening and fostering of a new worldly religiosity, something neither mystical nor conventionally pious, neither pantheistic nor conventionally dualistic. To be sure, the principal speaker in the dialogue refers to "the honesty of dualism" (EW, 77)[13]—by which he means both the contemporaneous "dualism of social morality and personality" and the traditional duality of nearness and distance with regard to humanity's relation to divinity (71, 68). He also remarks on "the mortal sin of making the spirit natural, taking it as self-evident, as merely causal in its functioning" (77). But at the end of the dialogue he states that "in the last analysis a religion can never be simply dualism," and he speaks, in an emphatically Nietzschean manner, of the importance of discovering anew "the bodily sensation [Körpergefühl] of . . . personal spiritual being [geistigen Persönlichkeit]" (78–79). Elsewhere in the early writings (ca. 1915), he underlines "the properly spiritual essence of the senses" in their capacity for reception, even as he continues to assume that spirit is not something self-evident and not something reducible to cause and effect (218). Clearly, the concepts of spirit and nature here, with all their *moral* force, belong within the framework of neither idealism nor empiricism in a traditional sense; already at this early stage Benjamin has worked through this classical antinomy.

The same may be said for his attitude toward the distinction between Jewish and Christian; this, too, comes across predominantly in his early writings, which, despite the obvious differences in focus, subject matter, and voice, are in fundamental respects theoretically consistent with the better known later writings. In a letter of 1913, which tells of sometimes fleeing Kant for Kierkegaard, Benjamin mentions the latter's appeal to "Christian ethics (or Jewish ethics, if you will)."[14] And we've seen how he invokes the spirit of early Christianity—adducing in this connection the late writings of Tolstoy—as a precursor of the new socioreligious consciousness of the literati.[15] Likewise, in his culminating article on educational reform, "The Life of Students" (1914–1915), he laments the failure of "that Tolstoyan spirit," which he associates with "the most profound anarchists" and "Christian monastic orders," to take root in student life, and he refers to the idea of the *civitas dei* among early Christians as a model community in certain respects (*EW,* 201, 206). What Benjamin has in mind with the invocation of a primitive Christianity in the context of a modern religiosity becomes clearer in two other short texts from the period before World War I. In "The Religious Position of the New Youth," published in May 1914, he writes of the struggle of youth to awaken to its own "religious seriousness" and "religious objectivity." In the midst of "a scarcely comprehensible life," full of devotion and skepticism, this youth "may dismiss no object, no person, for in each (in the advertising kiosk and in the criminal) the symbol or the sacred can arise." Yet it cannot entirely entrust itself to any one thing or person either, for the relation to "the ultimate and essential—to the sacred—is dark and uncertain. As uncertain as our own I." It is this attentiveness to the finitude and contingency of any sacred or symbolic advent—here is plausibly the kernel of his later interest in the "detritus of history"—it is this youthful readiness for the eternal in the transient that furnishes the link with the figure of the early Christian: "It would seem that this youth shares many traits with the first Christians, to whom the world likewise appeared to be so utterly overflowing with the sacred—which could arise in each and all [*in jedem*]—that it deprived them of the power to speak and act." The movement of awakening youth is for Benjamin a collective sign indicating "the direction of that infinitely distant point at which we know religion." Youth "*signifies* religion, which does not yet exist." This intensive betokening of what is other and not yet, involving as it does a strange interweave of nearness and distance, he understands as *waiting*, something which again unsettles the customary distinction of active and passive. Youth makes ready, in the present "chaos" of its existence, for a moment of decision, one in which it will choose between the sacred and the unconsecrated, and in the process find itself. But "meanwhile" the soul of youth must struggle, Hamlet-like, for "it will not be able to choose with utmost seriousness until by some grace the holy and unholy have been newly created [*bis die Gnade das Heilige und Unheilige neu geschaffen hat*]." The religious position of the new youth is thus no *position*, for in its constitutive openness it is "removed from all religions and all ideological alliances" (168–170).

Benjamin had written Ludwig Strauss concerning the desire of the literati to see everything "unmoored." Such a dangerous and salutary assault on bourgeois complacency would mean dissolution of what Henri Bergson names "the logic of solids," the logic informing our customary atomistic way of looking at things.[16] Back of this radical liquidation maneuver lies the Nietzschean critique of classical metaphysical substance and causality in favor of a thoroughgoing "oceanic" conception operating beyond the traditional opposition of static and dynamic. In the transformation of metaphysical or "ontotheological" categories that comes in the wake of the Nietzschean eventism, the idea of waiting is divested of all object-oriented certainty. Benjamin's usage intimates the modern crisis of identity concealed beneath bourgeois security and the instrumentalizing of education. Implicit in the waiting that is not impatient fixture on a determinate goal but concentrated attention on its own dark horizon is the possibility of education as actualization. At an infinite distance from the incipient goal (namely, true religion), one may nevertheless heed its transformative imperative and gain a sort of direction, a seminal impetus and calling. Which brings us to the second short text I mentioned in connection with Benjamin's early theoretical appropriation of what he conceives to be ur-Christian teaching.

Writing on September 15, 1913, to his comrade-in-arms Carla Seligson—who had asked, "How is it possible?"—Benjamin characterizes the phenomenon of waiting (later explored in its more profane aspects in *The Arcades Project*) as a kind of gravitating of attention toward some ungraspable source of attraction, some presence eventuating—insofar as we are sufficiently resolved and dissolved to receive it, to actualize it—in our very midst:

> Today I felt the awesome truth of Christ's words: Behold, the kingdom of God is neither here nor there, but within us. I would like to read with you Plato's dialogue on love, where this is said more beautifully and thought more deeply than probably anywhere else.
>
> This morning I gave this some more thought: to be young means not so much serving the spirit as *awaiting* it. . . . This is the most important thing: we must not fasten on any particular idea, [not even] the idea of youth culture. . . . For then (if we do not turn ourselves into mere workers in a movement), if we keep our gaze free to see the spirit wherever it may be, we will be the ones to actualize it. Almost everybody forgets that *they themselves* are the place where spirit actualizes itself. But because they have made themselves inflexible, turned themselves into pillars of a building instead of vessels or bowls that can receive and shelter an ever purer content, they despair of the actualization we feel within ourselves. This soul is something *eternally actualizing* [*ist das* Ewig-Verwirklichende]. Every person, every soul that is born, can bring to life the new reality. We feel it in ourselves and we also want to establish it from out of ourselves.[17]

"Actualization" here and elsewhere in Benjamin bespeaks a temporality of intermittences, of disjunction and renewal—continuous discontinuity—something casually signaled in the comment to Ludwig Strauss quoted above: "once again . . . for the first time." At issue in such interruption and punctuation of chronology is what Benjamin by 1916 had begun to call messianic time. (In the letter to Carla Seligson just cited, at a point right before the invocation of Luke 17:21, he refers to the "messianic" feelings among the Wynekenians.) Already in the Bergson-influenced "Metaphysics of Youth" of 1913–1914, Benjamin distinguishes "immortal time" (also called "youthful time" and "pure time") from "calendar time, clock time, and stock-exchange time," and he speaks of the "resurrections of the self" taking place at intervals in the recurrent radiation and gravitation of the spatiotemporal medium we embody (*EW*, 150–152). Everything that happens, Benjamin declares in this essay, surrounds us as landscape, and "we, the time of things" therefore befall ourselves; in ourselves we transcend ourselves, constituting the possibility and task of self-transcendence. Time sends us forth, flooding back toward us. Forth from "the womb of time . . . the self radiates outward. And fate is: this countermovement of things in the time of the self." The self is an intrinsic reflection in the mirror-play of time, a variable focus of temporal energies and a fateful midpoint; the self awaits itself—"await[s] the new radiance"—in consciousness of death ("the great interval") and in face of "the unnameable despair that flows in every soul." It is the nearness of death, made vivid through the distantiation of the reflective interval, that "for a single moment gives us immortality" (156). This is not an escape from time so much as a reorientation to the concrete and dynamic multidimensionality of time. "Past things become futural . . . [sending] forth the time of the self anew." As a consequence of this temporal bearing and plasticity, this elemental tiding of time, "what we do and think is filled with the being of our fathers and ancestors" (144).[18] The past is a virtual reservoir of unplumbed dream-energies, which we tap at moments of waking and presence to ourselves, and to which we are prey at other moments. But latent every moment is something eternal: "In that self to which events occur and which encounters human beings . . . in that self courses immortal time" (151). At stake in the realization of such precipitous temporality is what he calls here redemption. That this always involves the experience of failure and despair is indicated by another statement made in a letter from this period: "the redemption of the unredeemable . . . is the universal meaning we proclaim."[19] Which of course is not just a philosophical and theological (or perhaps atheological) but also a political proclamation; the metaphysics of youth is an indirect politics.

The Nietzschean-Bergsonian eventism given expression in Benjamin's posthumously published "Metaphysics of Youth" thus conditions his adoption of the concept of actualization, and indeed his whole religious outlook. The letter of September 15, 1913, to Carla Seligson employs this concept to characterize youth's singular collective task of self-deliverance to the world of awakening spirit. The prospect of a momentary gestation of immortal time, as unfolded in the central section of "Metaphysics of Youth," shows that the concept has been incorporated into the theory of historical remembrance. For in the moment's summons is actualized the self-renewing intelligibility of the past; the "dead field" of a dream-past occasions new growth in recollection and conversation. This idea of critical-creative renewal reappears in the concept of "afterlife"—a profane, historical afterlife—in Benjamin's 1919 dissertation, *The Concept of Criticism in German Romanticism*.[20] At that point in his career the theological as such begins to mask itself and go underground, having become "small and ugly" in modern times, as we read in Benjamin's last known work.[21] But the messianic and specifically ur-Christian doctrine of readiness for sudden grace, adduced as hermeneutic-ethical model in the youth theory, retains its relevance in the metropolitan world of flâneur, collector, and gambler. It may be said, moreover, that the emphasis, early and late, on a redemption of the everyday effectively differentiates the Benjaminian religiosity from the Nietzschean, though Nietzsche's deconstruction of the principle of identity likewise retains its importance.

The suggestion that Benjamin's thinking displays a certain proximity to "early Christian" modes of thought—a suggestion emanating from the young Benjamin himself—runs counter to the blanket assertion of his close friend and later editor, Gershom Scholem: "Christian ideas never held any attraction for him."[22] Recent opinion on this question of an idiosyncratic "Christian" dimension to Benjamin's thinking tends to assume a less absolute division between Jewish and Christian scriptural traditions. I will mention two prominent examples, the first from a man who once spoke of his own "uneasy Ahasueric lifestyle at the borderline between Jewish and Christian," where things "get so hot" one is inevitably burned.[23] In a short course of lectures on Paul's Letter to the Romans given in Heidelberg in 1987, a few weeks before his death, the Jewish philosopher of religion Jacob Taubes traces an oblique line of influence from Paul through Nietzsche to Benjamin, proposing that Paul's quasi-antinomian theology in Romans, above all in the "great jubilation" of Romans 8, the passage on creation's unceasing collective "groaning" and the fruits thereof, has its closest parallel in Benjamin's "Theological-Political Fragment," though a distance of nearly nineteen hundred years separates the two writings.[24] He argues that Paul and Benjamin write from "out of the same experience." Benjamin is said to have a Pauline notion of creation, that is, creation without visible hope. The penultimate sentence of the "Theological-Political Fragment" is cited: "For nature is messianic by reason of its eternal and total passing away [Vergängnis]"). Such a catastrophic notion in both cases leads to a highly paradoxical formulation of messianism, though Taubes also stresses the difference between Benjamin and Paul, insofar as the former posits an autonomy of the profane, the historical dynamic in itself having no messianic telos that would ground a political theocracy (and there is of course a richly detailed, if infernal, world of things [Dingwelt] elsewhere in Benjamin). Taubes suggests that it is "quite possible" to understand Benjamin's text from the perspective of Karl Barth's epoch-making commentary on Romans (a work Benjamin himself claims never to have read[25]), and his own approach, for all its sober humanism, betrays something of Barth's "hardness," his gnostic insistence on the unknowability of God, the inner abyss of grace, the possibility of deliverance only as coming "from the other side."[26]

For Taubes, as for a line of radical interpreters preceding him, the historical development of the Christian community from a provincial adventist sect, working in principle against the flourishing cult of the emperor, to an institutionalized universal church tends to conceal the all-important element of protest in Christian scripture: "Christian literature is a literature of protest. . . . All the Christian concepts I know are highly political and explosive, or become so at a certain moment."[27] The proviso to this observation, which concerns the triggering of the latent subversive charge of the New Testament at certain *moments* in history, recalls Benjamin's theory of the dialectical image, according to which an historical object, an image of the past, becomes legible and intelligible not at any given moment (as historicism assumes) but only in "the now of recognizability," in a present day capable of recognizing it, which is to say, realizing its potential. Only as relevant to the construction of historical "now-time"—source of what Taubes, in a seminar on Benjamin, designates *geballte Geschichte* (encapsulated history)—does the past first come to itself and yield up its meaning.[28] Nietzsche's critique of nineteenth-century linear historicism clearly resounds through this latter-day enunciation of the Now, and Taubes explicitly acknowledges Nietzsche as his best guide to thinking about Paul. In his Heidelberg lectures on Romans, Taubes echoes the Nietzschean dictum that the last Christian died on the cross: "Christianity is no longer Christian, but is a kind of mishmash in modernity";[29] a veil of amnesia overspreads church history, for as soon as the early church erects a textual canon against perceived heresies, he argues, it no longer comprehends the texts it has canonized. At the same time, Taubes underscores the Jewish character of what was originally Christian. Paul's diasporic Jewishness is manifest not only in the wealth of his visible and invisible citation of the Hebrew Bible but also in his critical spiritual zeal, which has a political significance in the context of Jewish-Hellenistic mission-theology. Taubes even suggests a connection with the Jewish Zealots whose revolt would precipitate the destruction of the Second Temple. This Paul, whose radically conflicted Jewishness has been essentially blotted out by the church, and for whom the word *Christian* does not exist, "is a fanatic!"

> Paul is a zealot, a Jewish zealot, and for him this step is a tremendous one. The spiritual costs that he must bear he doesn't take upon himself for the sake of some blather in the spirit of this great nomos liberalism. . . . This is someone who answers . . . with a protest, with a transvaluation of values. It isn't *nomos* but rather the one who was nailed to the cross by *nomos* who is the imperator! This is incredible, and compared to this all the little revolutionaries are *nothing*. This transvaluation turns Jewish-Roman-Hellenistic upper-class theology on its head. . . . This is nothing like nomos as *summum bonum*.[30]

In its overcoming ("dying to") both natural law and state law, both Greek rationalism and Jewish legalism,[31] in its decisive setting-apart of truth from all possession (of knowledge, of property), Paul's strategic and explosive political theology can become—despite what has appeared to many as its ultimate *apology* for state authority—the prototype of Benjamin's nihilist messianism, his salvaging of eternity in universal downfall.[32]

For insight into the "messianic logic" of Paul's "excited texts," Taubes recommends chapter 8 of Scholem's *Major Trends in Jewish Mysticism* (1941)—the chapter concerned with the religious anarchism and "mystical nihilism" of the Sabbatian movement in the seventeenth and eighteenth centuries—which he considers more instructive than "the entire exegetical literature."[33] Another recent commentator on Romans, the Italian philosopher and Benjamin editor Giorgio Agamben, in *The Time That Remains* (2000), quotes a 1965 publication of Scholem's in which Paul is characterized as "the most outstanding example known to us of a revolutionary Jewish mystic."[34] Agamben goes on to note Scholem's ambivalence toward the apostle Paul and to suggest that Scholem himself may have recognized the "closeness between Benjamin's thought and Paul's" and, if so, must have been bothered by it. Agamben mentions Taubes as the only scholar to have discerned the "possible influence" of Paul's letters on Benjamin (*TR*, 140)—something for which there is no direct evidence, although we know that Benjamin read pretty widely in Christian theology—and he backs up Taubes's observations with further philosophical exposition, making it plausible that Benjamin as a thinker has "positioned himself at the singular intersection of Christianity and Judaism."[35]

Agamben argues in particular for the "secret presence of the Pauline text" in Benjamin's last known writing, the famous theses "On the Concept of History," whose entire vocabulary appears to him to be "stamped Pauline." His analysis focuses on the problem of presence and the present moment, and specifically on the correspondence between Benjamin's concept of *Jetztzeit*, actuality as now-time,[36] and Paul's concept of *kairos*, the critical moment of messianic time, a term used afterward with various acceptations and emphases in the gospels (for example, Luke 12:56: "Why do you not know how to interpret the present time [*ton kairon*]?" and 19:44: "you did not recognize the moment [*kairon*] of your visitation"—to which one may compare Isa. 43:19). In this perspective, the evangel is an announcement not of some far-distant future but of a present eventuality—present, if nonobjective and inconspicuous. *Chronos*, conceived in terms of quantifiable motion or sequence, is classically distinguished from the motionless quality of eternity, but Agamben's interpretation subverts ontological dualism as much as linear eschatology. In fact, he pointedly differentiates messianic time, the only real time for Paul, from eschatological time and the apocalyptic *eschaton* (*TR*, 62). As he sees it, the kairological—*kairos* means also "due measure"—is really a *transformation* of the chronological, or of the relation between them, just as, for Benjamin, immortal time is potential within the flow and eddy of developmental time (as opposed to being its ultimate goal).

In an effort to clarify the metaphysical structure at issue here, Agamben introduces the category of uni-duality. The messianic eventuality is that through which "being is beside itself in the present" (*TR*, 70). The term *parousia* in Paul does not in essence refer to a second coming of Jesus, understood as the culmination of a temporal sequence, but means presence as a being-beside (*par-ousia*).[37]

> [The] Pauline decomposition of presence . . . [brings out] the innermost uni-dual structure of the messianic event, inasmuch as it is composed of two heterogeneous times, one *kairos* and the other *chronos*, . . . which are coextensive but cannot be added together. Messianic presence lies beside itself, since, without ever coinciding

with a chronological instant, and without ever adding itself onto it, it takes hold of this instant and brings it forth to fulfillment. (70–71)

Agamben cites an ancient Hippocratic text in which *chronos* and *kairos* are conceived as being within each other, and he comments: "what we take hold of when we seize *kairos* is not another time but a contracted and abridged *chronos*," the latter comprising "something like a time within time . . . which only measures my disconnection with regard to it" (*TR*, 69, 67). To seize upon *kairos* is to seize hold of nothing substantial but only my own being seized, or being called, which is to say, my saving disjointedness with respect to chronological time—"saving" because the bitter estrangement occasioned by "messianic vocation" is necessary for any resurrection (69, 78, citing Phil. 3:12). The "messianic tension" does not tend elsewhere but works from within, contracting the extension and taking the measure of human perduration, as an "implosion" into eternity (63). In this untoward decomposition-and-fulfillment, where we are decidedly and productively beside ourselves, and where, as Benjamin likes to say, truth *strikes* us, the distinction between promise and realization is all but abrogated. What is called the kingdom of God is at once present and absent, already and not yet here. The meaning of its coming exceeds the logic of noncontradiction.

Likewise exceeded is the framework of chronicle and chronology. The messianic experience of time discloses a plastic transparency across which expectation and remembrance play into and off one another (much as in the temporality of a poem or of a melody). This experience of time is determinative for biblical narrative, in its many-layered redaction and dense motivic unity, and for the traditions arising out of it. Through an "economy of salvation," events are there concentrated, crystallized, *allegorized*— are set resonating, backward and forward, in anticipatory-retrospective figuration and "vertiginous abbreviation" (*TR*, 77). In the intertwined temporality of the biblical universe, everything is inherently quotable, is potentially a parable for teaching; a single passage in the narrative may adumbrate the entire historical trajectory of the people, just as a particular object, in the eyes of Benjamin's allegorizing "collector," encapsulates as remnant the whole history of its production and subsequent acquisition. (In the theses on history, which explicitly propound a monadological conception of the historical object, Benjamin states that now-time, "as a model of messianic time, comprises the entire history of humankind in a tremendous abbreviation [*ungeheueren Abbreviatur*].")

At stake in this interpenetrating textuality and expansive contraction of history is not just prefiguration (Agamben refers to Erich Auerbach's theory of mimesis and figural understanding) but constellation of temporal dimensions. Thus, in discussing Paul's creative recapitulation of the past—"these things happened unto [the Israelites] by way of figure [*typikōs*], and they were written for us, for our admonition, upon whom the ends of the ages are come to face each other" (1 Cor. 10:11)—Agamben points to "the typological relation established by messianic *kairos* between present and past. The fact that we are dealing not only with a prefiguration but with a constellation and quasi unity between the two times, is implicit in the idea that the entire past is summarily contained, so to speak, in this present" (*TR*, 73, 76–77). In such "summary recapitulation" of historical happening, whereby the present is defined in terms of an "exigency of fulfillment," a certain past acquires its "true meaning" (as awakened to the historian's present) and hence is "saved." Reborn in the guise of today's concerns, the past becomes "my past," and "what once happened to the Jews is *recognized* as a *figure and reality* for the messianic community" (77; emphasis added). The past becomes "possible" again—of possible use—in its newly emergent legibility for the Now of historical remembrance.[38]

Agamben indirectly elaborates Taubes's point about the autonomy of the profane in Benjamin as something at variance with the Pauline world view: "While, for Paul, creation is unwillingly subjected to caducity and destruction and for this reason groans and suffers while awaiting redemption, for Benjamin, who reverses this in an ingenious way, nature is messianic precisely because of its eternal and complete caducity, and the rhythm of this messianic caducity is happiness itself" (*TR*, 141). We may be reminded here of what the young Benjamin calls the redemption of the unredeemable. It is precisely in the fallenness and eternal groundlessness of worldly existence, in the rhythm (Benjamin's term) of transience, that the messianic potential resides. Which is no doubt to cast a revolutionary light on the old complacent *felix culpa* doctrine. The messianic world, in Agamben's presentation, signifies a kind of threshold—a subtle but decisive displacement of the everyday chronological world, the world of logic and law, closure and possession. The messianic instance is not the abolition but the "deactivation" of law, that which paradoxically fulfills the spirit of the law. Agamben refers to Paul's "aporetic" treatment of the problem of law.[39] In his invocation of the faith of Abraham, Paul reaches back, with a certain hermeneutic violence, to a time before the institution of the Mosaic statutes and ordinances, for the codifications bring in their wake an atrophy of the law, wherein the originary nearness to the word is increasingly eclipsed by dogmatic confession. The figure of Abraham here stands for a sphere of "prelaw" that is at once juridico-political and religious, an archaic realm of "magic indifference" between promise and *nomos*

(119).[40] The prioritizing of the "promise" made to Abraham over the "law" given to Moses has in view the possibility of "justice without law" (Rom. 3:21), a condition realizable through an anomic "space of grace" knowing trial and ordeal, a struggle within the law itself. More precisely, the revocation or suspension of the "law of works" entails "the indiscernability of an outside and inside of the law" (*TR*, 106–107). It is not a matter of simply obeying the law or following established procedure, nor of simply going one's own way, but rather of opening oneself, as vessel, to the tidal being of what is encountered: "the world of faith . . . [is] not a world of substance and qualities, not a world in which the grass is green, the sun is warm, and the snow is white . . . but a world of indivisible events, in which . . . I am transported and displaced in the snow's-being-white and in the sun's-being-warm" (129).[41] As Paul puts it in his singular idiom, "through the law I died to law . . . : it is no longer I who live but the Messiah who lives in me" (Gal. 2:19–20), a passage cited by Agamben in this context.

In a messianic perspective, there are degrees of living and dying in any life; one may live a "death," and one may "die" daily so as in some sense to live more justly. If one dies to law *through* the law, this is first of all because one willy-nilly inhabits the law and traverses it; the law, as seen so clearly in Kafka, has no outside. Nevertheless one may come to live at a distance from the law, being—as a "stranger"—effectively "set apart" from the world and from oneself. One may be divided from the law *through* the law because law itself, *nomos*, is the principle of division and apportionment (*TR*, 47). To die to the law in thought and action would be, then, to decompose its dogma, its externality, by internalizing its spirit. These interarticulations of the functions of living and dying are not mere figures of speech but operations of a dialectical comportment in a field of tension beyond the dogmas of substance and identity. And that means beyond the concept of law as obligation, as command and prohibition. For law is essentially not punitive but educative. The mortification and dissolution of substance is the birth of eternal transience—threshold to witnessing the world-play from the perspective of the dead.[42] In messianic time the saved world coincides with the irretrievably lost (42). What redeems the unredeemable would accordingly be the recognition of its parable-character, its possible teaching and summary judgment.[43] Thus Paul comes to regard the law as no longer a prescriptive norm but only the knowledge of guilt, just as he comes to regard himself no longer under the regal name of "Saul" but only as *paulus*, "little," as one allied to what the world accounts weakness. In allegorical perception, especially as this is theorized in Benjamin's later studies of Baudelaire, the empirical world is transformed from within, and reality in all its immediacy and contingency becomes script, "book of life," spatiotemporal palimpsest. The variable interplay of modernity and antiquity in historical afterlife is the structural principle of such perception. Presupposing as it does the groundless ground of language in all things, the Judeo-Christian turn to allegory—as a mode of experience—conditions virtually all the perceived parallels between Paul and Benjamin, both of whom, Agamben emphasizes, were writing in the midst of crisis.[44]

Benjamin would have early on been made aware of the Jewish side to these ur-Christian ideas through his relationship with Scholem. When they met in the summer of 1915 in Berlin, Gershom Scholem, five-and-a-half years Benjamin's junior, was in his first semester at the university, studying mathematics and philosophy. Already at this period the dedicated young Zionist and socialist was a student of ancient and medieval Hebrew texts, while his thinking was inspired as much by Kierkegaard as by Hermann Cohen. In his often intensive and wide-ranging conversations with Benjamin during the war years, he stimulated, as is well known, his friend's investigations into the nature of language, which Benjamin conceived, in his great fragmentary essay of 1916 on the subject, in terms drawn directly from the opening chapters of Genesis ("creative word," "naming word," "judging word"). Scholem, in turn, was shaken to the core by his friendship with Walter Benjamin, which he quickly recognized as the most decisive in his life. His diaries from these years bear witness to the influence not only of Benjamin's personal being—which the younger man compares somewhat breathlessly to that of the Old Testament prophets and Lao Tzu—but also of his messianic nihilism. He writes on November 3, 1917: "Walter once said that the messianic realm is always present [*immer da*], which is an insight of *stupendous* importance—though on a plane which I think no one since the prophets has achieved. Revelation and the messianic realm are the foundation of the Jewish conception of history."[45] Several months later, in an entry of June 17, 1918, he writes down some "Remarks on Time in Judaism," in which Benjamin's "stupendous" idea is buttressed by Cohen's and his own approach to the problem of messianic time, especially as this problem is focused in the eschatological refrain of the prophets (one thinks, above all, of Second Isaiah) concerning the coming "day" of deliverance. He quotes Cohen's late work, *The Concept of Religion in the System of Philosophy*, on the intertwining of present and future tenses in God's definition of his own being in Exod. 3:14: "When the meaning of the present tense is shared by the future tense, then the difference between present and future is thereby diminished also. Being is not fixed in the present but hovers above it. Present and future are bound together in this being of God [*Sein Gottes*]."[46] Here is a further index to the linguisticality of messianic thinking, and perhaps also to the rootedness of the kairological paradox, of what is at once present and on the way, in the originary play of Yahweh's self-attesting discourse on Mount Horeb. Scholem goes on, in the diary entry of June 17, to construe the meaning of God's "I am/will be" as "the I of time":

> The foundation and, at the same time, expansion of all empirical time is divine time, which is eternal presence [*ewige Gegenwart*], for what God will be is what he *was* through all generations. . . . The messianic realm is the presence of history, history in the present [*die Gegenwart der Geschichte*]. The prophets could speak about this idea only hypothetically by using the image of the future. What does "in those days" mean? If you think it through, you see that "those days"—are *these* days. The kingdom of God is the *present* [ist Gegenwart], for it is origin and end. . . . Time in religion [*die religiöse Zeit*] is always decision, which is to say, the present. . . . The future is a *command*, . . . the command to spread holiness into the present moment [*das reine Antlitz, die Gegenwart dieser Heiligkeit zu entfalten*— literally, "to disclose the pure countenance, the presence, of this holiness"][47]

In other words, the present—and here Scholem appropriates Cohen's terms *Ursprung* and *Nichts*—has its true being as origin: out of its deep and fecund "nothingness" springs eternal time.[48] The task is to wake to this burden of nothingness in the medium of every moment, for the messianic day—whose sign is the festival (*das Fest*) and, in particular, the Day of Atonement—lies enfolded within the everyday as its animating and annihilating principle. Hence the prophetic admonition (as construed by the young Scholem) to learn to read the "face" of the present moment, as it were the presence of the present, which is ordinarily too near to be apperceived. The schema of the dialectical image as "focal point" of history,[49] as messianic convergence of times, the whole theory of the monadological character of truth, is adumbrated in what Scholem, following hints in Cohen, understands to be "the Jewish conception of history," the conception of history's veiled and condensed operativity in the present.

Benjamin and Scholem devoted part of the summer of 1918, during their shared "exile" in the Swiss village of Muri, to daily reading and discussion of Cohen's influential early work, *Kant's Theory of Experience*, as a follow-up to Benjamin's recent "On the Program of the Coming Philosophy," in which he sought to overcome precisely that theory of experience. Both men expressed serious misgivings about Cohen's "transcendental method," his effort to deduce the a priori continuity of experience, that is, continuity as a law of thought—an effort perfectly in line with what Benjamin had represented to Ludwig Strauss as the Jewish penchant for building from the top down. Benjamin even referred to the great man's "transcendental confusion" and termed this Kant book "a philosophical vespiary."[50] In the long run, however, Cohen's antipsychologist and problem-historical orientation spoke to them both, as did his magisterial philosophic interpretation of biblical messianism. Scholem, for his part, felt a strong identification with this foremost Jewish philosopher of the day, despite the insistent rationalism, rigid dualism, and Victorian optimism of his system. In a diary entry written the day after Cohen's death on April 4, 1918, he remarks that the Jewish people (!) have lost "something very great" with his passing, and adds: "I wish for myself nothing else than a life like his."[51] A week later: "Cohen's existence is Torah: it will be passed on. It is worthy of being passed on, worthy of tradition. I am his disciple [Schüler]. This I shall be."[52] On July 24 and 25, amid mounting dissatisfaction with the Kant book, Scholem makes some surprising and revealing notations, having become aware of what he takes to be a concealed and "most dangerous mysticism" in Cohen's argumentation, an "unimaginable demonic of absolute ambiguity":

> This is the ontology of the devil. The reality of what cannot become object [des Gegenstandslosen] is proven by the demand for methodical unity. . . . Criticism is mysticism—that is the fundamental principle of Cohen's unscrupulousness. To these enlightened generations one can present the truth, which is precisely mysticism, only in enlightened garb; I speak that way myself for this reason. But then he would have to confess himself a mystic, for only then is the principle legitimate and profound. This criticism is a mystification, not mysticism.[53]

The last sentence of the entry for July 24 reads: "Cohen celebrates brutality as transcendental messiah"—likely alluding to Cohen's vigorous public defense of Germany's role in the war, a position seemingly at odds with his professed socialism and ideal of world peace. Elsewhere Scholem faults Cohen for his "self-deception" regarding German-Jewish relations, his faith in Jewish assimilation to a society that never welcomed the Jews.[54] And in his *Major Trends in Jewish Mysticism*, he sets up a contrast between Cohen's relegation of evil to the world of myth and the feeling of the

Kabbalists (as "true seal-bearers of the world of myth") for the reality of evil and "the dark horror that is about everything living." It is experience of the abyss that first brings to light "the symbolic nature of all that exists." The challenge for theology, Scholem says here, is to attain an understanding of "myth" that does not lead away from monotheism—that is, the monotheism evolving from myth.[55]

Benjamin's approach to the problem of myth, with which he was occupied throughout his career, from the essay on Hölderlin up through the late stages of the arcades project, is likewise more dialectical than Cohen's,[56] and this points to an acknowledged basic tendency of his thought: the overcoming and transformation—not abandonment—of classical antitheses. Truth and myth are in a relation of mutual exclusion, according to Benjamin's essay on Goethe's *Elective Affinities*, and yet for him, as for Scholem, the possibility of truth's presence is conditioned on the recognition of myth—myth understood as a primordial realm of indifference between truth and error or truth and mere semblance.[57] Predicated at every moment on the undifferentiated and metamorphic, the antithesis remains vital to the correlation. Indeed, Benjamin's Jewishness may be said to emerge especially clearly here, with this momentous 1924–1925 publication, in his strictures against Friedrich Gundolf's brute "conflation of truth and myth." On the other hand, the nonobjectifiable process of truth is not the expression of any classic "ascent" from bodily darkness and dissolution (the motif of ascent is central to Cohen's writings on religion); what matters is the refraction of the radiant in the nocturnal.[58] Truth and myth coexist ambiguously within a field of tension in things. The mythic can be seen to inform, more or less surreptitiously, practically every level of discourse, from the etymological on up. It is with myth and fable as it is with dream in Benjamin's texts (or as it is with metaphor in his words): this manifold "undergrowth" of our historical being and language is collectively at issue in the "dialectics of awakening." Awakening is dialectical because it must recollect and undergo what was dreamed, down to its deepest recesses, if it is in some measure to emerge from (gain distance on) the dream world. This is the strategy of Benjamin's primal history of the nineteenth century in *The Arcades Project*, with its materialist allegoresis: to set thinking in motion, as intimately and widely as possible, in broaching a recent epoch of "that dream we name the past," to cite and thereby summon the "lived life" of that epoch in tracing its characteristic milieux and detailing its forgotten thing-worlds, and to articulate the submerged sociomythological ramification of that once familiar life into the present. In this kerygmatic reading of the past as precursor, thinking is repeatedly exposed to what is obscure and inexplicable in the historical object, while at each address of the object, occasioning at once reception and conception, the (self-)interpreting present is absorbed and "distilled" as inmost essence, as particular fulfillment, of what has been.[59] The coming-to-presence of truth is just this singular, historically and mythically laden "now of recognizability."[60]

For Benjamin, awakening from and to the immanent being of myth is the ongoing task of art and philosophy. It is a task of recurrent excavation—the mining, namely, of "latent 'mythology'"[61]—and it calls into play a critical mimesis of the myth such that its eternal return in phenomena and in our ways of conceiving phenomena is both realized and broken through.[62] Although mythology may be considered "the dark shadow that language casts upon thought,"[63] it might also be said that the mythic word steps outside itself in the language of reflection, making possible a higher concreteness. This nearness distilled from distance is a resultant of close study and historical consciousness; Benjamin actually refers in *The Arcades Project* to the technique of nearness (*Technik der Nähe*), which he pits against the leveling intellectual "'empathy' [of Rankean historicism] that makes everything abstract."[64] And just as nearness in distance defines the ethos of (philosophical) community, so study and studious play—what the young Benjamin invokes as cultural education—can be understood to form the gateway to justice. In the long history of the Jewish people, devotion to study (to "the teachings") was certainly crucial to individual and collective spiritual renewal, and for this reason study could become "the foundation of the Jewish religion."[65] It is a peculiarly dislocated and provisional foundation, to be sure, the site of constantly renewed wrestling with the angel.[66] We've seen that Benjamin consciously assumes a precarious position simultaneously outside and within the traditional parameters of this religion, considered as a body of teachings, and that his worldly messianism in its way harks back to Paul's threshold theology as much as to the fierce adventism of the prophets. We might speak of a Jewish pietism in this regard, although it is clear that Benjamin himself was neither a pious Jew nor a secular Jew; what we can call his religiosity was virtually indistinguishable from his nihilism. This is demonstrated in the attempt to think the rhythm of redemption in that of transience. Precisely here the modern collides full-tilt with antiquity. The result is allegory, the antidote to myth.[67] Exile and remembrance—wilderness and witness: these guiding threads of the biblical salvation history are intricately interwoven in the very texture and tragic consistency of Benjamin's existence.

Notes

An early version of this essay was presented in the Graduate Speaker Series of the Department of German at Northwestern University in January 2012, in an event organized by Professors Peter Fenves and Samuel Weber. My thanks to the participants for their valuable comments.

1. Benjamin's ignorance of the Passover Seder ritual is depicted in Walter Benjamin, "Diary, Pentecost 1911," in *Early Writings 1910–1917*, trans. Howard Eiland et al. (Cambridge, MA: Harvard University Press, 2011), 34–35; hereafter cited in text as *EW*. His close friend Gershom Scholem mentions that "the problem of religious ritual . . . did not interest Benjamin" (*From Berlin to Jerusalem: Memories of My Youth*, trans. Harry Zohn [New York: Schocken, 1980], 82).

2. Benjamin, "Sexual Awakening," in *Berlin Childhood around 1900*, trans. Howard Eiland (Cambridge, MA: Harvard University Press, 2006), 124.

3. The letters to Ludwig Strauss, dated September 11, October 10, and November 21, 1912, and January 7–9, 1913, are in Benjamin, *Gesammelte Briefe*, 6 vols., ed. Christoph Gödde and Henri Lonitz (Frankfurt: Suhrkamp, 1995–2000), 1:61–88. Hereafter cited in text as *GB*. A fifth letter to Strauss, written in February 1913, is not substantive. There were exchanges in the fall of 1912 on the question of Judaism and Zionism between Benjamin and a high school senior, Kurt Tuchler, who helped found the Zionist youth group "Blue-White"; these letters were lost during the Nazi period. See Walter Benjamin, *The Correspondence of Walter Benjamin 1910–1940*, ed. Gershom Scholem and Theodor W. Adorno, trans. Manfred R. Jacobson and Evelyn M. Jacobson (Chicago: University of Chicago Press, 1994), 17–18n2. Ludwig Strauss (1892–1953) later became Martin Buber's son-in-law and a literary historian at Hebrew University in Jerusalem. His letters to Benjamin are not preserved. The letters to Strauss are excerpted and placed in an illuminating cultural-historical context, made up of selections from Strauss, Tuchler, Buber, Scholem, Gustav Wyneken, Moritz Goldstein, Ahad Ha'am, Erich Gutkind, and Oskar Goldberg, in Hans Puttnies and Gary Smith, *Benjaminiana* (Giessen: Anabas, 1991), 38–91.

4. In the March 1912 number of *Kunstwart*, Moritz Goldstein (1880–1977) published an article, "Deutsch-jüdischer Parnaß [German-Jewish Parnassus]," in which he called on Jews to give up their leading role in many areas of German culture and to develop an independent cultural and spiritual life based on Jewish traditions. His article provoked a number of responses, both Zionist and anti-Semitic, which were published in subsequent issues of the journal (*Gesammelte Briefe*, 1:66n). See Irving Wohlfarth, " 'Männer aus der Fremde:' Walter Benjamin and the 'German-Jewish Parnassus,' " *New German Critique*, no. 70 (Winter 1997): 3–85. An account of Strauss's pseudonymous contribution to the *Kunstwart* debate (it appeared, without a title, in August 1912 and is excerpted in Puttnies and Smith, *Benjaminiana*, 45), can be found in Paul Mendes-Flohr, *German Jews: A Dual Identity* (New Haven, CT: Yale

University Press, 1999), 46–52. The attribution of a "Zionism of the spirit" to Benjamin himself remains questionable; I discuss the relevant passage (from the letter of January 7) later in this essay.

5. Benjamin describes Wyneken's educational program in his essay, "The Free School Community" (1911), published under the pseudonym "Ardor" in the youth journal *Der Anfang*. See Benjamin, *Early Writings*, 39–45.

6. Strauss's contention that it is precisely through study of Goethe that one comes upon "the Jewish way [*die jüdische Art*]" is cited approvingly by Benjamin (*Gesammelte Briefe*, 1:84).

7. The concept of "cultural Zionism" derives from the Russian-born Hebrew essayist Ahad Ha'am (Asher Ginsberg; 1856–1927), a liberal leader and internal critic of the Zionist movement who called for a revival of Hebrew and Jewish culture as prelude to an envisioned "national awakening." See the excerpts in Puttnies and Smith, *Benjaminiana*, 60–61, and "The Spiritual Revival," in *Selected Essays by Ahad Ha'am*, trans. Leon Simon (Philadelphia: Jewish Publication Society of America, 1912), 253–305. In a diary entry of August 23, 1916, Scholem notes a conversation with Benjamin on Ahad Ha'am, remarking (despite his friend's explicit critique of nationalism) "how near Benjamin stands to Ahad Ha'am," by which he refers in particular to a shared appreciation of "the role of 'justice' in Judaism" (Scholem, *Tagebücher 1913–1917* [Frankfurt: Jüdischer Verlag, 1995], 386). See also *Selected Essays by Ahad Ha'am*, 133–135, 312–316. Ha'am, who lived in Tel Aviv during his last years, defended the rights of native Palestinians.

8. His argument at this point recalls Martin Buber's invocation of a deep-seated "Jewish religiosity," a consciousness irreducible to the dogmas and norms of institutional Judaism, in his *Drei Reden über das Judentum* (Three Addresses on Judaism, 1911), a text cited also by Ludwig Strauss in his *Kunstwart* contribution. In the letter of October 10, 1912, to Strauss, Benjamin refers to Buber's concept of "the essence of the Jewish [*das Wesen des Jüdischen*]" (*Gesammelte Briefe*, 1:71), as expounded in the second and third of these highly influential addresses (the first address, delivered in Prague in 1909, grounds the Jewish essence in "blood"). The three addresses are translated by Eva Jospe in Buber, *On Judaism*, ed. Nahum N. Glatzer (New York: Schocken, 1967), 11–55. In a letter to Buber written ca. November 1915, Benjamin maintains that "the problem of the Jewish spirit is one of the most important and persistent objects of my thinking" (*Gesammelte Briefe*, 1:283). Concerning Benjamin's reservations about Buber, who—after Benjamin had refused his offer of wartime collaboration in 1916 (Benjamin, *Correspondence*, 79–81)—would later help finance Benjamin's two-month visit to Moscow in 1926–1927 and publish his essay "Moscow" in a literary journal he coedited, see Scholem, *Walter Benjamin: The Story of a Friendship*, trans. Harry Zohn (New York: Schocken, 1981), 7, 25, 27–29.

9. Compare Søren Kierkegaard: "[religion] deduces its origins from above" ("Two Notes Concerning My Work as an Author," 1848), as cited in Jacob

Taubes, *Occidental Eschatology*, trans. David Ratmoko (Stanford, CA: Stanford University Press, 2009), 173.

10. Benjamin's quotation seems to conflate phrases from Matt. 5:3 ("the poor in spirit"), Isa. 66:2 ("The man I look to is a man downtrodden and distressed"), and Isa. 57:15 ("I dwell in a high and holy place with him who is broken and humble in spirit").

11. In the third of his *Three Addresses on Judaism*, Buber writes similarly that "the great ambivalence, the boundless despair, the infinite longing and pathetic inner chaos of many of today's Jews provide more propitious ground for the radical shake-up that must precede . . . a total renewal than does the normal and confident existence of a settler in his own land" (*On Judaism*, 39). He goes on to stipulate, as Benjamin will do, that such spiritual renewal must "penetrate the day's reality" (54).

12. In an essay of 1913, "Moral Education," published in a journal edited by his mentor Wyneken, Benjamin suggests "that all morality and religiosity originates in solitude with God" (*Early Writings*, 110). See also Benjamin, *Correspondence*, 50–52 (letter of August 4, 1913, to Carla Seligson).

13. Benjamin's letter of October 10 to Ludwig Strauss likewise adverts to "a rigorously dualistic conception of life. . . . Buber, too, speaks of this dualism" (*Gesammelte Briefe*, 1:71). In the second of his *Three Addresses on Judaism*, Buber emphasizes the contradictoriness of the Jewish character, abject and exalted, as reflected in the biblical narratives. A yea and a nay coexist within the Jew, and such "creative contradiction," as well as the redemption from all dualism, the "striving for unity," is determinative for Judaism—"The creative Jews are the conquerors of duality" (*On Judaism*, 23–29).

14. Benjamin, *Correspondence*, 20.

15. Buber's *Three Addresses on Judaism* contains numerous comments on "early Christianity" as a distinctive epoch of authentic Jewish religiosity. From the third address: "[What is,] erroneously and misleadingly, . . . called early, original Christianity . . . could with greater justification be called original Judaism . . . for it is much more closely related to Judaism than to what is today called Christianity. . . . Whatever was creative in the beginnings of Christianity was nothing but Judaism." He calls on Jews to overcome their "superstitious horror of the Nazarene movement" and to place it "where it belongs: in the spiritual history of Judaism" (*On Judaism*, 45–47). Buber later sought to qualify this interpretation of early Christianity. Concerning Benjamin's interest in German interfaith movements in the years following World War I, see Howard Eiland and Michael W. Jennings, *Walter Benjamin: A Critical Life* (Cambridge, MA: Harvard University Press, 2014), 184.

16. Henri Bergson, *Creative Evolution*, trans. Arthur Mitchell (1911; repr. New York: Dover, 1998), ix. With little outward enthusiasm, Benjamin attended Heinrich Rickert's seminar on Bergson's metaphysics at Freiburg University in the summer of 1913, the period at which he probably began his "Metaphysics of Youth." That essay testifies to his thoroughgoing and highly

original appropriation of Bergson's ontological theory of memory. (Also enrolled in Rickert's seminar on Bergson in 1913 was the twenty-three-year-old Martin Heidegger.)

17. Benjamin, *Correspondence*, 54–55; translation modified.

18. On "temporal plasticity and spatial happening [*zeitliche Plastik und räumliches Geschehen*]," see "Two Poems by Friedrich Hölderlin" (1914–1915), in Benjamin, *Early Writings*, 186–192.

19. Benjamin, *Correspondence*, 34 (letter of June 23, 1913, to Herbert Blumenthal). The formula "Erlösung des Unerlösbaren" may derive from Blumenthal (later known as Herbert Belmore).

20. Benjamin, *Selected Writings*, 4 vols., ed. Michael W. Jennings et al. (Cambridge, MA: Harvard University Press, 1996–2003), 1:164. Concerning the historical afterlife of works, see also *Selected Writings*, 1:254 ("The Task of the Translator," 1921), and *The Arcades Project* (1927–1940), trans. Howard Eiland and Kevin McLaughlin (Cambridge, MA: Harvard University Press, 1999), 460 (N2,3). There are three German terms at issue here: *Überleben* (1919), *Fortleben* (1921), and *Nachleben* (1927). The concept of *Nachgeschichte* (after-history) is developed in convolute N of *The Arcades Project*.

21. Walter Benjamin, "On the Concept of History," in *Selected Writings*, 4:389. This text of 1940 instances a dramatic resurfacing of the theological concern that had generally ceased to be explicit after Benjamin's second dissertation, *Origin of the German Tragic Drama*, composed 1923–1925. At every stage of his career, however, Benjamin's thinking is "saturated" by theology, as affirmed in a well-known passage in *The Arcades Project* (N7a,7).

22. Gershom Scholem, "Walter Benjamin," trans. Lux Furtmüller, *Leo Baeck Institute Yearbook* 10, no. 1 (1965): 133 (lecture at the Leo Baeck Institute in New York). Cf. Wohlfarth's identification of "the 'Christian' moment within Benjamin's Jewish Messianism—the element which helps save it from being reducible to 'only awaiting' the Messiah" ("Männer aus der Fremde," 41–42). See also Samuel Weber, *Benjamin's -abilities* (Cambridge, MA: Harvard University Press, 2008), 214–218, on Scholem's "exclusionary" perspective.

23. Jacob Taubes, *The Political Theology of Paul*, trans. Dana Hollander (Stanford, CA: Stanford University Press, 2004), 143.

24. Ibid., 70. Benjamin's "Theological-Political Fragment," dating probably from 1920–1921, is translated by Edmund Jephcott in *Selected Writings*, 3:305–306.

25. Benjamin, *Correspondence*, 606 (letter of June 8, 1939, to Karl Thieme).

26. Taubes, *Political Theology*, 75–76. See also Taubes's essay, "Theodicy and Theology: A Philosophical Analysis of Karl Barth's Dialectical Theology" (1954), in *From Cult to Culture* (Stanford, CA: Stanford University Press, 2010), 177–194. Taubes highlights concerns in Barth's work, especially in the second edition of his commentary on Paul's Letter to the Romans (1921), that have close parallels in Benjamin's work: the concern with a dynamic, anti-Aristotelian "logic of events," with a "dialectic of antithetical terms," and

atological actualism (*Aktualismus*). In his view, Barth opens up the
f a religious language in an age characterized by the eclipse of the

es, *Political Theology*, 16, 71.
es, "Walter Benjamin: Geschichtsphilosophische Thesen," in *Der*
sianismus, ed. Elettra Stimilli (Würzburg: Königshausen und
!006), 87 (notes of a participant in a seminar given by Taubes at the
Freie Universität in Berlin during the winter semester 1984–1985). On
Benjamin's "messianic actualism" and the "condensation of history," see 75–76.

29. Taubes, *Political Theology*, 81.

30. Ibid., 24.

31. Writing in 1953 for the American magazine *Commentary*, Taubes
distinguishes the ancient Jewish concept of law, *halacha*, the "way" of justice as
articulated in daily life and its detail, from a subsequent "dead legalism." It is
only when halacha is reduced to a bundle of folkways, and the practice of
justice to a juridical device, that the "arbitrariness of love" can be exalted above
the "yoke of the law." See "The Issue between Judaism and Christianity: Facing
Up to the Unresolvable Difference," in Taubes, *From Cult to Culture*, 45–58.

32. In an article attacking Scholem's distinction between Judaism and
Christianity in terms of historical/public versus ahistorical/inward, Taubes
delineates a revolutionary Marcionite-Gnostic patrimony (stretching from Paul
through Marcion and Joachim of Fiore to Karl Marx) for Benjamin's
theological-political discourse: "Walter Benjamin—ein moderner Marcionit?,"
in *Antike und Moderne. Zu Walter Benjamins "Passagen*," ed. Norbert W. Bolz
and Richard Faber (Würzburg: Königshausen and Neumann, 1986), 138–147
(repr. in *Der Preis des Messianismus*, 53–65). As Taubes sees it, the "protest" of
Gnosticism originates in confrontation with the problem of the origin of evil in
the world, a problem left unresolved in the monotheistic doctrine of God's
creation and omnipotence. See Taubes, "The Dogmatic Myth of Gnosticism"
(1971) and "The Iron Cage and the Exodus from It, or the Dispute over
Marcion, Then and Now" (1984), in *From Cult to Culture*, 61–75, 137–146;
in his *Occidental Eschatology* of 1947, he argues that "Apocalypticism and
Gnos[ticism] inaugurate a new form of thinking which, though submerged by
Aristotelian and Scholastic logic, has been preserved into the present and was
taken up and further developed by Hegel and Marx" (35). The second-century
Christian heretic Marcion considered himself a disciple of Paul; he elevated the
unknown alien God of love, to whom Jesus witnessed, above the jealous
demiurgic Creator-God of the "Old Testament," driving apart creation and
redemption. The thin thread linking gospel to law, such as still obtains in Paul,
effectively snaps in Marcion (Taubes, *Political Theology*, 56–61). To this
full-fledged antinomianism may be compared Benjamin's concept, in his 1921
"Critique of Violence," of a suspension of law (*Entsetzung des Rechts*) and his
concept of an expiatory "educative power . . . outside the law," an immediate
and unbloody "divine violence" that "calls a halt to" the "mythic violence" at

the basis of all legal order; for there is "something rotten in the law," and both lawmaking and law-preserving forms of violence are in this perspective "pernicious" (*Selected Writings*, 1:242–252). It must be added, however, that insofar as "Marcionism" denotes an attitude of world-denial, it runs counter to the Benjaminian gnosis. See Giorgio Agamben, *The Open: Man and Animal*, trans. Kevin Attell (Stanford, CA: Stanford University Press, 2004), 81–82, for a distinction, contra Taubes, between Marcion's "undervaluation" of nature and Benjamin's "transvaluation."

33. Taubes, *Political Theology*, 50.

34. Agamben, *The Time That Remains: A Commentary on the Letter to the Romans*, trans. Patricia Dailey (Stanford, CA: Stanford University Press, 2005), 144 (citing Scholem, *On the Kabbalah and Its Symbolism*). Hereafter cited in text as *TR*.

35. Agamben, *The Kingdom and the Glory*, trans. Lorenzo Chiesa, with Matteo Mandarini (Stanford, CA: Stanford University Press, 2011), 8.

36. Benjamin, *Selected Writings*, 4:395–397 ("On the Concept of History"). Benjamin's concept of *Jetztzeit* in this text should be compared to his concept of *Jetztsein* (now-being) and of the *Jetzt der Erkennbarkeit* (now of recognizability) in *The Arcades Project*, convolutes K2,3 and N3,1, respectively. See also *Selected Writings*, 1:276–277 (1920–1921).

37. Agamben at this point echoes Heidegger's wide-ranging analysis of the history of the concept of presence. Earlier in the text he refers to the second part of Heidegger's 1920–1921 lecture course on the "Phenomenology of Religion," with its explication of Paul's idea of *parousia* and of an ur-Christian "life experience" (neither Jewish nor Greek) in which one's life "remains unchanged but is radically changed nevertheless" (cited in *Time That Remains*, 33–34; see also Heidegger, *Gesamtausgabe*, vol. 60 [Frankfurt: Klostermann, 1995], 67–156, esp. 117–119, 149–150). Cf. Agamben's comments on paragraph 9 of Heidegger's *Being and Time* (1927), in particular the problem of the "apophantic 'as,'" in *The Coming Community*, trans. Michael Hardt (Minneapolis: University of Minnesota Press, 1993), 98–100. On the kairological, see also Agamben, *Infancy and History: The Destruction of Experience*, trans. Liz Heron (London: Verso, 2007), 105, 111–115, 165; and *The Signature of All Things: On Method*, trans. Luca D'Isanto with Kevin Attell (New York: Zone, 2009), 72–74.

38. Benjamin's theory of "now-time," like Karl Barth's concept of the Now of historical "communing" in his commentary on Romans 4:23–25, has its immediate provenance in the philosophy of Friedrich Nietzsche, specifically in the principle that the past can be understood only from out of the highest energy of the present (*höchsten Kraft der Gegenwart*), for "the past always speaks as an oracle." Nietzsche, *On the Advantage and Disadvantage of History for Life* (1874), trans. Peter Preuss (Indianapolis, IN: Hackett, 1980), 37–38 (section 6). This treatise, forming part 2 of Nietzsche's *Untimely Meditations*, is a sustained attack on nineteenth-century Rankean historicism, with its idea of attaining the past "as it really was;" it is cited by Benjamin as early as 1913 (*Early Writings*, 96). Also crucial for Benjamin's concept of intertwined time (*verschränkte Zeit*)

is the work of Marcel Proust; see the 1929 essay "On the Image of Proust" (*Selected Writings*, 2:244).

39. Cf. Benjamin's view, in "Critique of Violence," on the "ultimate undecidability of all legal problems" (*Selected Writings*, 1:247; trans. modified). On the deactivation of law, compare his 1934 essay "Franz Kafka": "The law that is studied but no longer practiced [*praktiziert*] is the gateway to justice" (*Selected Writings*, 2:815). These two passages are cited in Agamben's *State of Exception*, trans. Kevin Attell (Chicago: University of Chicago Press, 2005), 53–54, 63–64. See also the discussion of Sabbath inoperativity in Agamben, *Nudities*, trans. David Kishik and Stefan Pedatella (Stanford, CA: Stanford University Press, 2011), 104–112.

40. The concept of prelaw (*pré-droit*), stemming from Louis Gernet, is discussed further in Agamben, *The Sacrament of Language: An Archaeology of the Oath*, trans. Adam Kotsko (Stanford, CA: Stanford University Press, 2011), 16–17, 27, where it is stipulated that prelaw "cannot be merely a more 'archaic' law," just as what stands before religion, as we know it historically, is not simply "a more primitive religion."

41. Compare Alain Badiou, *Saint Paul: The Foundation of Universalism* (1997), trans. Ray Brassier (Stanford, CA: Stanford University Press, 2003), 14–15: "Since [for Paul] truth is evental, or of the order of what occurs, it is singular. It is neither structural, nor axiomatic, nor legal. No available generality can account for it, nor structure the subject who claims to follow in its wake. Consequently, there cannot be a law of truth . . . Truth . . . neither claims authority from nor (this is obviously the most delicate point) constitutes any identity . . . for truth is a process."

42. See Theodor W. Adorno, "Zu Benjamins Gedächtnis" (1940), in *Über Walter Benjamin* (Frankfurt: Suhrkamp, 1990), 72: "Gone . . . is the gaze that saw the world from the perspective of the dead."

43. Among the paralipomena to Benjamin's theses "On the Concept of History" is a reference to a note of Franz Kafka's from ca. 1917–1918: "It is only our concept of time that makes us call the Last Judgment by this name. Actually it is a kind of summary justice [*ein Standrecht*]." Benjamin compares this to a saying from the New Testament Apocrypha, which he interprets to mean that "the Day of Judgment . . . would not be distinguishable from other days" (*Selected Writings*, 4:407).

44. On the ontological priority of language, see Benjamin, *Early Writings*, 251–252 (1916); on perception as reading, see *Selected Writings*, 1:92–96 (1917); and on allegorical perception and allegorical experience, see *The Arcades Project*, convolute J53a,1 and J67,2–J68,2, especially J67,4: "The experience of allegory, which holds fast to ruins, is properly the experience of eternal transience [*ewigen Vergängnis*]."

45. Scholem, *Lamentations of Youth: The Diaries of Gershom Scholem 1913–1919*, trans. Anthony David Skinner (Cambridge, MA: Harvard University Press, 2007), 192.

46. Scholem, *Lamentations of Youth*, 245 (trans. modified). Original text in Hermann Cohen, *Der Begriff der Religion im System der Philosophie* (Giessen: Alfred Töpelmann, 1915), 22. Cohen argues that the function of the future tense here is to further "the abstraction, the withdrawal" from the "sensuous present" and hence to augment the conception of "God as being" (20).

47. Scholem, *Lamentations of Youth*, 245–246 (trans. modified).

48. In his *Logik der reinen Erkenntnis*, 2nd ed. (1914; repr. Hildesheim: Georg Olms. 2005), 84–85, Cohen writes: "The origin of something [*der Ursprung des Etwas*] is not to be found in that thing itself. Therefore judgment cannot avoid taking a venturesome byway [*Umweg*] if it wishes to search out something in its origin. This adventure in thinking [*Abenteuer des Denkens*] makes the *nothing* manifest [*stellt das* Nichts *dar*]. *By the roundabout way of the nothing, judgment makes manifest the origin of something.* . . . The nothing is not the erecting of a non-thing that would stand opposed to a something; rather, it is a monstrous deliverance [*eine Ausgeburt*] of deepest logical perplexity, which however does not allow of despair in the effort to comprehend being." Cohen refers in this context to the *Kreuzweg des Nichts* (Golgotha-Way of nothingness) as a station in the path of questioning. Cohen's student and critic Franz Rosenzweig comments on these passages and on Cohen's novel "*Ursprungs-Logik*," as it was called, his doctrine of particular origin and particular nothingness, in *Star of Redemption* (1921), trans. William W. Hallo (Notre Dame, IN: University of Notre Dame, 1985), 21 (introduction to part 1).

49. The idea of the historical focal point (*Brennpunkt*), a striking anticipation of the concept of dialectical image, is introduced at the beginning of Benjamin's essay of 1914–1915, "The Life of Students" (*Early Writings*, 197–198).

50. Scholem, *Walter Benjamin: The Story of a Friendship*, 59–60. Scholem writes: "We each at different times had attended courses or individual lectures given by Cohen in Berlin during his advanced years, and we were full of respect and indeed reverence for this figure; thus we approached our reading with great expectations. . . . But Cohen's deductions and interpretations seemed highly questionable to us; we dissected them with great severity." In *From Berlin to Jerusalem*, Scholem mentions that he heard talks by Cohen in Berlin (ca. 1915–1916) on themes from his work-in-progress, *Religion of Reason out of the Sources of Judaism* (68). See also Benjamin, *Gesammelte Briefe*, 2:107 (letter of December 1, 1920, to Scholem), documenting Benjamin's brief but favorable first impression of the recently published text of *Religion of Reason*.

51. Scholem, *Tagebücher 1917–1923* (Frankfurt: Jüdischer Verlag, 2000), 167.

52. Ibid., 175.

53. Ibid., 276.

54. Scholem, *From Berlin to Jerusalem*, 26–27. Cohen's essay of 1915, "Deutschtum und Judentum," expresses a faith in the triumph of German arms and the concomitant full integration of Germanness and Jewishness in German society and the German university.

55. Scholem, *Major Trends in Jewish Mysticism*, trans. George Lichtheim (New York: Schocken, 1961), 36, 38. Scholem distinguishes symbol from allegory, associating the former with the mystical, the latter with the philosophical tradition within Judaism.

56. See Winfried Menninghaus, "Walter Benjamin's Theory of Myth," trans. Gary Smith, in *On Walter Benjamin: Critical Essays and Recollections*, ed. Gary Smith (Cambridge, MA: MIT, 1988), 300: "Cohen's notion [of myth] . . . emphasizes exclusively the negative. Benjamin's 'dialectic' of blasting apart *and* redeeming is radically unfamiliar to Cohen's as well as to the Enlightenment notion." In a letter of December 22, 1924, Benjamin writes Scholem of their ongoing "critique of Cohen's system" (*Gesammelte Briefe*, 2:512). At this same period, in the foreword to his book on the seventeenth-century German *Trauerspiel*—published in English as *The Origin of German Tragic Drama*, trans. John Osborne (London: Verso, 1977)—Benjamin criticizes the origin-logic developed in Cohen's *Logic of Pure Knowledge* (see note 48) as insufficiently historical (46); this is a defect he will remedy in his own conception of particular origin within "the Jewish contexts of history" (*Arcades Project*, N2a,4). There are related criticisms of Cohen in *Selected Writings*, 4:140 (1939) and *Gesammelte Briefe*, 2:215n. Cohen's ideas on ethics and aesthetics are taken up by Benjamin in such works as "Fate and Character" (1919), "Critique of Violence" (1921), "Goethe's *Elective Affinities*" (1921–1922), "Franz Kafka" (1934), and in letters before 1922.

57. In Stanley Corngold's translation: "And where the presence of truth [*Gegenwart der Wahrheit*] should be possible, it can be possible solely under the condition of the recognition of myth [*Erkenntnis des Mythos*]—that is, the recognition of its crushing indifference [*vernichtenden Indifferenz*] to truth" (*Selected Writings*, 1:326). In "Benjamin's *Einbahnstrasse*" (1955)—included in Theodor W. Adorno, *Notes to Literature*, vol. 2, trans. Shierry Weber Nicholsen (New York: Columbia University Press, 1992)—Adorno speaks similarly of "the myth that thought must approximate in order to gain control of itself and thereby break the spell of myth" (325). Cf. the formulation by Ernst Bloch, in his 1968 study of "an underground Bible," *Atheism in Christianity*, trans. J. T. Swann (London: Verso, 2009), 27: "destroying and saving the myth in a single dialectical process, by shedding light upon it."

58. Benjamin writes in his short essay "Socrates" (1916): "The radiant is true only where it is refracted [*wo es sich bricht*] in the nocturnal" (*Early Writings*, 234; cf. Benjamin, *Correspondence*, 224, on art's redemption of "night"). Socrates is "the figure in whom Plato annihilated the old myth and received it;" he represents a logical bulwark against the myth while being himself a kind of "satyr" (*Symposium*, 215–216), or, rather, a "terrible mixture of castrato and faun" (*Early Writings*, 233, 235).

59. Reference is to *The Arcades Project*, N1,4 ("undergrowth of delusion and myth"); "Materials for the Exposé of 1935," no. 8 ("dialectics of awakening");

convolute K1,3 ("that dream we name the past"); and "First Sketches," D°,6 ("distilling the present as inmost essence of what has been").

60. Benjamin, *Selected Writings*, 1:276.

61. Benjamin, *Arcades Project*, D°,7 ("First Sketches"). Despite the analogies here to the Freudian paradigm of the unconscious, Benjamin's method of "dream interpretation" is to be understood as historical or psycho-historical rather than narrowly psychological. Closer to Benjamin's conception of latent myth is Nietzsche's: "For it is the fate of every myth to creep by degrees into the narrow limits of some alleged historical reality and to be treated by some later generation as a unique fact with historical claims" (*The Birth of Tragedy*, trans. Walter Kaufmann [New York: Vintage, 1967], 75).

62. Benjamin, *Arcades Project*, D10,3: "'Eternal return' is the *fundamental* form of the *urgeschichtlichen*, mythic consciousness. (Mythic because it does not reflect.)" See also J22, 5: "abyss of myth . . . at every step."

63. This formulation by the nineteenth-century popularizing philologist Max Müller is cited in Agamben, *Sacrament of Language*, 15.

64. Benjamin, *Arcades Project*, S1a,3.

65. Cohen, *Religion of Reason out of the Sources of Judaism*, trans. Simon Kaplan (Atlanta, GA: Scholars Press, 1995), 349, 444, 450. The theme of study is sounded, in connection with the critique of myth, at the conclusion of Benjamin's 1934 essay on Kafka, where it is said, apropos a quotation from Plutarch on the two primal forces (one leading out and the other driving back), that "reversal [*Umkehr*] is the direction of study which transforms existence into script [*Schrift*]" and, further, that "the gate to justice is study" (*Selected Writings*, 2:815). The association of study with (Jewish) humor in the Kafka essay recalls Cohen's argument (459).

66. "One definition of Judaism which is not that bad," notes Agamben, "is that of an implacable reflection on the paradoxical situation arising from the desire to establish juridical relations with God" (*Time That Remains*, 117).

67. Benjamin, *Selected Writings*, 4:179 ("Central Park," section 28).

Benjamin's Natural Theology

HOWARD CAYGILL

> I am standing on the threshold about to enter a room. It is a complicated business. In the first place I must shove against an atmosphere pressing with a force of fourteen pounds on every square inch of my body. I must make sure of landing on a plank travelling at twenty miles a second around the sun—a fraction of a second too early or too late, the plank would be miles away. I must do this while hanging from a round planet head outward into space, and with a wind of aether blowing at no one knows how many miles per second through every interstice of my body. The plank has no solidity of substance. To step on it is like stepping on a swarm of flies.
>
> —A. S. Eddington, *The Nature of the Physical World*

One of Benjamin's more unexpected citations can be found in his letter to his friend Gershom Scholem, dated Paris June 12, 1938. As far as I am aware it is the only time that he cites at length from a Gifford Lecture, the distinguished series founded in 1888 and intended "to promote and diffuse the study of natural philosophy in the widest sense of the term—in other words, the knowledge of God." I am referring to the citation from Arthur Stanley Eddington's influential presentation of the revolutionary advances in early twentieth century cosmology (the theory of relativity and subatomic physics) in the Gifford Lectures of 1927 published in 1928 as *The Nature of the Physical World*. Benjamin's extended citation is taken from the 1931 German translation *Das Weltbild der Physik und ein Versuch seiner philosophischen Deutung* and any surprise at his interest in such a text testifies to the widespread critical underestimation of his fascination with contemporary science, especially cosmology, and his sustained efforts to develop a modern natural theology.[1] The significance of Benjamin's interest in cosmology has been obscured by the critical focus on his messianic theology, whose orientation toward the historical world seems at first glance to be wholly incompatible with the cosmological concerns of a natural theology. Yet it can be shown not only that Benjamin possessed and pursued an intense interest in cosmology and natural theology, but also that it served as an indispensable complement to his understanding of the significance of the messianic.

This said, Benjamin's understanding of cosmology and of its role in natural theology might not have been immediately recognizable to Adam Lord Gifford, nor to many of those who lectured on natural philosophy under his auspices. Yet it was not as distant from their concerns as it may initially seem. Benjamin worked with two understandings of the range and character of cosmology: one was largely religious and indebted to Gnostic precedents that were antagonistic toward the created cosmos and its creator God or demiurge, the other emerged from the tradition of natural philosophy that developed into the modern scientific cosmology revolutionized in the early twentieth century by Einstein and Bohr. The two approaches to cosmology enjoyed a perplexing proximity, with the Gifford Lectures founded on an anti-Gnostic position with respect to the relationship between God and his creation and the knowledge of both through natural philosophy. For Gifford, natural philosophy was knowledge of the beneficent creation of the single and benevolent God, not knowledge of the fallen created cosmos and its evil creator. Yet the Gnostic and the scientific understandings of the cosmos were never entirely separate and William Blake was not alone in regarding the Newtonian laws of Urizen as those imposed on a fallen creation by a mad and evil demiurge.

Benjamin's interest in Gnostic religious cosmology was part of a broader, contemporary interest in Gnostic cosmology prompted by Adolf von Harnack's pioneering study of the first century heresiarch Marcion, *Marcion: Das Evangelium vom Fremden Gott* (1920), that left unmistakable traces in the work of his radical contemporaries Gershom Scholem, Ernst Bloch, Georg Lukacs, Hans Jonas, and later Jacob Taubes.[2] The Gnostic doctrine shadowing the major monotheisms proposed the existence of two divinities—the evil creator God and the good God beyond creation—and insisted on the unredeemably fallen character of the created world and its laws. It emphasized the rule of the demonic archons over the souls separated from the good but weak God and imprisoned in material creation; in some variants Gnosticism encouraged antinomian behavior as a form of resistance to the laws of the evil creation, but all Gnostics advocated knowledge or *gnosis* of the God beyond creation. This approach to the cosmos in terms of an ancient religious heresy seems worlds away from the advances in physics and astronomy that allowed the twentieth century to be described as the "cosmological century" and to which Eddington made distinguished contributions as a researcher and public teacher.[3] Benjamin is perhaps unique in bringing together the two understandings of the cosmos—there is nothing resembling his approach among his contemporaries, with the exception of Eddington himself and perhaps Kafka in whose work he found a similar proximity between Gnosticism and modern cosmology. For Benjamin, the two understandings of cosmology represented negative and affirmative relations to the created cosmos and he understood them as complementary aspects of a broader historical character of the relationship between humanity, the divine, and the cosmos.[4]

The Gnostic vision according to which the cosmos stands in a hostile relationship to humanity as the creation of a malevolent divinity is prominent in Benjamin's early writings and receives its most developed expression in *The Origin of German Tragic Drama* (1928) that explicitly discusses the historical character of the "binding together" of the "material and the demonic" characteristic of Gnosticism. In one of his many allusions in this book to the historical character of this relationship Benjamin points to the contribution of the Gnostic demonization of nature to the emergence of natural science: "not only did the middle ages come thus to impose strict limits on the scientific study of nature; even mathematicians were rendered suspect by this devilish essence of matter."[5] This reflection on the limits to science posed by the threat of the Gnostic demonization of matter formed part of the larger project pursued in *The Origin of German Tragic Drama*, one of whose objectives was to show how the complex equation of the human, the cosmos, and the divine undergoes and has undergone complex and sometimes unexpected historical transformations. Fundamental to the history of this equation is the violent transition from paganism to Christianity described by Benjamin in terms of the conflict between the guilt-laden physis of Christianity and the *natura deorum* of the pagan pantheon, a conflict provisionally resolved by the demonization of matter. The ancient Gods were regarded as demonized natural forces with the effect of conceding to Gnosticism a view of the created cosmos as essentially evil. Yet Benjamin wanted to show this resolution was itself historically contingent and unstable, with the Renaissance, Reformation and Counter-Reformation cited as moments of rupture in the Christian relation to the cosmos as modulations in the sense of guilt experienced before nature. The place and character of the cosmos in the history of perdition and salvation provides Benjamin with a methodological key for understanding broader shifts in the relations between humanity, the cosmos, and divinity.

The attention to the historical character of the link between humanity, divinity, and a fallen cosmos informing *The Origin of German Tragic Drama* is explicitly announced in one of Benjamin's earlier fragments,

"Capitalism as Religion" (1921). While often and not incorrectly understood as an early statement of Benjamin's critique of capitalism, the fragment also provides an important statement of his view of Gnostic cosmology. Its guiding proposition that "the Christianity of the Reformation period did not favour the growth of capitalism; instead it transformed itself into capitalism" announces not only an original critique of the Weber thesis concerning the religious origins of capitalism but also a more general historical investigation of a radical change in the relations between humanity, cosmos, and divinity.[6] The transformation of the Christian guilt-laden physis into a cosmos hostile to both humanity *and* God is understood in "Capitalism as Religion" in terms of the "universalization" of guilt up to the point "where God, too, finally takes on the entire burden of guilt" which is to say the "expansion of despair, until despair becomes a religious state of the world in the hope that this will lead to salvation."[7] Although departing from Gnostic premises of a guilty God occupying a hostile cosmos Benjamin does not adopt the bleak conclusions of its soteriology. For him salvation does not come from a God located beyond the cosmos— outside the guilt-laden physis of creation—nor from a messianic figure that enters cosmic history from without as an emissary of the removed divinity, but from within the fallen cosmos itself. Benjamin elaborates his soteriology, his view of the salvation of humanity and the fallen creation, by means of an ambivalent confrontation with Nietzsche's thesis concerning the death of God. While conceding that Nietzsche's thesis implies that "God's transcendence is at an end," Benjamin is careful to note: "But he is not dead; he has been incorporated into human fate [*Menschenschicksal*]."[8] The death or rather metamorphosis of the transcendent creator, here the evil God of Gnosticism into human fate—the divinization of historical law—is emphasized in Benjamin's description of the *Übermensch* as the "passage of the planet Human through the house of despair,"[9] where the human incorporates the evil God and becomes an *archon* or ruling planet moving through a fallen cosmos.[10] This election of evil, however, is quickly revealed as being the same gesture as the hope for salvation through the universalization of despair anticipated earlier in the fragment.

Benjamin reads Nietzsche's *Übermensch* in terms of the Gnostic distinction between *psyche* and *pneuma*, between the cosmic and the acosmic bodies of Gnostic soteriology. The first is the body enveloped by corrupt matter undergoing the "many deaths" assumed by the soul during its descent through the planetary cosmos, while the second is what Hans Jonas described as the "acosmic principle" or the soul that remains alien to and alienated from the created cosmos.[11] For Benjamin, Nietzsche's *Übermensch* emerging after the death or transformation of the evil creator God risks becoming a planet or archon, a shape of the evil creator God who finds himself estranged in a state of "absolute loneliness" in the alien cosmos of his own creation. It is at the extreme point of this estrangement that Benjamin locates salvation, a place that is at once continuous with and beyond the alien cosmos. Salvation emerges from the *intensification* of the loneliness of the archon "planet human" or *Übermensch*, through the invention of religious techniques that bring the level of estrangement to the point of explosion: "The idea of the superman transposes the apocalyptic 'leap' not into conversion, atonement, purification and penance, but into an apparently steady, though in the final analysis explosive and discontinuous intensification."[12] The passing of the creator God renders obsolete the techniques of propitiation and atonement suited to a fallen creature's relationship to its creator and the evil cosmos it is forced to inhabit. As the human approaches the condition of *Übermensch* through an intensification of its solitude in the cosmos and its decision to take responsibility for creation, it breaks with the sense of being a creature inhabiting a created cosmos. In a striking image for this transition Benjamin describes the *Übermensch* as the "historical man who has grown up right through the sky" and, following this image of continuous intensification describes this growth as eventually exploding in the "breaking open of the heavens by an intensified humanity."[13] In place of the descent of the soul through the levels of the created cosmos until it is incarnated in a human body, Benjamin proposes an ascent of the human, and through it the eventual destruction of the fallen cosmos and its evil creator God by the "intensified humanity" of the *Übermensch*.

With this view of the intensification of humanity and the explosive destruction of the alien cosmos through the breaking open of the heavens, Benjamin parts company not only with Nietzsche but also with Gnostic cosmology. For the intensification of humanity in the *Übermensch* and its estrangement from the created cosmos does not lead to an acosmic contemplation and gnosis of the God beyond creation "giving it in the beholding of the divine light an acosmic content of its own" but to a historical task.[14] Benjamin describes capitalism's unprecedented historical mission as "not the reform of being but its complete destruction" here understood as the rending of the sky of the created cosmos and overcoming its evil creator.[15] Benjamin's fragment moves to an incomplete conclusion by recognizing a connection between Gnosis or to use Benjamin's terms the "redemptive and murderous nature of knowledge [*Wissens*] and capitalism."[16] Both free the human creature from creation and its creator, but leave them having to find their own salvation. The murderers of God, according to Nietzsche's classic formulation in the *Gay Science*, murdered the evil creator God, but do not yet know or appreciate the import of their deed, nor the more than human responsibility for creation to which it has condemned them. The evil God of creation is dead and the good God beyond creation if not dead is by definition beyond life and death and hence even more remote than ever.

The Origin of German Tragic Drama culminates in a performance of the breakdown of this moment of gnosis, framed in terms of the guilt-laden physis of nature announced in "Capitalism as Religion," but it does so in a way that points toward an alternative, scientific natural theology to the Gnostic demonization of matter. The view of matter absorbing the demonic explored in "Capitalism as Religion" is now understood in terms of the elimination of the evil of creation and the possible purification of the world: "According to Gnostic-Manichean doctrine, matter was created to bring about the 'de-Tartarisation' of the world, and was destined to absorb everything devilish, so that with its elimination the world might display itself in its purity."[17] Both the tearing down of the sky by an intensified humanity described in "Capitalism as Religion" and the elimination of the demonic aspects of creation allow the cosmos to present itself in its purity. Yet both "Capitalism as Religion" and to a lesser extent *The Origin of German Tragic Drama* remain transfixed at this apocalyptic moment of the tearing open of the sky, pointing but not moving beyond it to a description of the cosmos revealed after the death of the creator God. *The Origin of German Tragic Drama* ends with a suspended apocalypse, at the point where allegory reveals itself to be but an allegory of the "arbitrary rule in the realm of dead objects, the supposed infinity of a world without hope."[18] This moment of revelation then abolishes itself in the intensified apocalyptic moment of unveiling or the tearing away of the sky and the discovery of a new heaven and a new earth: "All this vanishes with this *one* about-turn, in which the immersion of allegory has to clear away the final phantasmagoria of the objective and, left entirely to its own devices, re-discovers itself, not playfully in the earthly world of things, but seriously under the eyes of heaven."[19] The liberation of matter from guilt and from its demonization by the evil creator is certainly a form of gnosis, but one that proceeds under the eyes of a godless heaven in which there no longer dwells even the remote God beyond being of the Gnostics.

The theme of liberation from the gaze of God or the gods would later be central to the thesis of the politicization of art proposed in "The Work of Art in the Age of Its Mechanical Reproducibility." There the "aestheticisation of politics" is understood in terms of the gaze of the gods upon the spectacle of human history, following the itinerary of the angel of history from above. The extent of the potential perversity of the divine gaze—that version of the equation of humanity, cosmos, and divinity in which the divine spectates and the human is the spectacle—is affirmed in a short and little appreciated text almost contemporary with the *Trauerspiel* book. In his article "Books by the Mentally Ill," Benjamin begins by describing the problems of classifying the "motley collection" that is his "little library of pathology." He finds the family resemblance between his books to consist in the elaboration of a theological cosmology, which encompasses an enormous range of perverse and imaginative permutations of the relations between the human, the cosmos, and the divine. His collection includes Judge Schreber's celebrated *Denkwürdigkeiten eines Nervenkranken*, C. F. Schmidt's *Leben und Wissenschaft in ihren Elementen und Gesetzen*, a nameless Slavic author, and Carl Gehrman, *Körper, Gehirn, Seele Gott*. All offer elaborate temperamentally Gnostic cosmologies—reconstructions of the cosmos after the experience of the end of the world characteristic of extreme psychosis. In addition to Schreber's well-known sexualization of the relationship between God and humanity in his person, Benjamin finds in C. F. Schmidt a "construction of the universe" in the self-image of a God whose "life-giving gaze" informs the material and intelligible world. These and the cosmopolitical theology of *Der Ganz-Erden Universal Staat* and Gehrmann's "theological medical science" share a concern with the relationship between the human body, God, and the cosmos; each responds to the given historical character of this equation with the invention of deranged variants that Benjamin hints are not so different from the variant that historically we have been called to occupy.

At the same time as writing the historical reflections on the transformations of the relation to the cosmos in *The Origin of German Tragic Drama* and reflecting on the pathological variants proposed by the psychotic theorists of "Books by the Mentally Ill," Benjamin also completed the remarkable final reflection of *One-Way Street*, "To the Planetarium." Here too Benjamin begins with a distinction between the "teachings of antiquity" and the theology of the now waning Christian epoch. Benjamin encapsulates the former in the formula, "They alone shall possess the earth who live from the powers of the cosmos"; and he adds: "Nothing distinguishes the ancient from the modern man so much as the former's absorption in a cosmic experience scarcely known to later periods. Its waning is marked by the flowering of astronomy at the beginning of the modern age."[20] The final reflection of *One-Way Street* resumes the stalled history of science begun in *The Origin of German Tragic Drama* and maintains that modern astronomy first becomes possible with the liberation from Gnosticism or, in Benjamin's terms, by taking distance from the forces of the created cosmos. Benjamin indeed continues by citing some of the revolutionary figures who like the *Übermensch* literally tore down the sky, observing that their motivation was not simply cognitive: "Kepler, Copernicus, and Tycho Brahe were certainly not driven by scientific impulses alone" (*SW*, 1:486).

Benjamin understood modern astronomy in terms of the emergence of an exclusively optical relation to the cosmos, which differed widely from the *Rausch* or ecstatic trance that characterized the ancient "absorption in cosmic experience" (*SW*, 1:486). The optical connection with the cosmos succeeded the haptic communion with it that was corporeal and ecstatic.[21] *Rausch*, however, is a form of ecstatic gnosis arising from the tension between distance and nearness that would later characterize the phenomenon of aura: it "gives certain *knowledge* of what is nearest to us and what is most remote from us, and never one without the other' (486; emphasis added). Such experience, Benjamin underlines, is a "communal experience" and one whose power should not be underestimated or consigned to "individual poetic rapture of starry nights" (486). Benjamin obliquely cites the experience evoked by Kant at the end of the *Critique of Practical Reason*, where the visual spectacle of the cosmos provokes the intensifying *Rausch* of the "ever increasing awe" Kant evokes at the end of the *Critique of Practical Reason*—a union of optical perception and physical affect that Benjamin believes points to a closer, corporeal relation between humanity and the cosmos.

For Benjamin, however, the predominance of the optical relation to the cosmos as the object of modern science underestimates the continuing power of the haptic communion with its forces, noting with an enigmatic reference to Nietzsche's eternal return: "its hour strikes again and again, and then neither nations nor generations can escape it" (*SW*, 1:486). The most recent rendezvous was World War I, which for Benjamin was no less than "an attempt at new and unprecedented commingling with the cosmic powers" (486). By "commingling with cosmic powers" he seems to be referring to the outcome of the electromagnetic scientific and technical revolution inaugurated by James Clark Maxwell that became the acme of twentieth-century modernity.[22] Benjamin described the outcome of this revolution in terms of the difficult birth of a new relation to the cosmos characterized not only by the Gnostic intensification of alienation from the cosmos but also by the hope for a new covenant between God, creation, and humanity made possible by technology: "Human multitudes, gases, electrical forces were hurled into the open country, high frequency currents coursed through the landscape, new constellations rose in the sky, aerial space and ocean depths thundered with propellers, and everywhere sacrificial shafts were dug into mother earth" (486). Benjamin here describes once again the passage of the "planet Human" through the cosmos but facilitated this time by technology, a passage that he sexualizes as "an immense wooing of the cosmos enacted for the first time on a planetary scale" in the "spirit of technology" (487). The alienated optical relation to the cosmos bears with the hope of a creative union or *Rausch* whose haptic absorption in its object is figured sexually in metaphors of intercourse, orgasm, and birth.

The change in the relation to the cosmos effected by modern technology brought with it radical consequences for human nature: "Men as a species completed their development thousands of years ago; but mankind as a species is just beginning his. In technology a physis is being organised through which mankind's contact with the cosmos takes on a new and different form from that which it had in nations and families" (*SW*, 1:487). Just as Christianity created the guilt-ridden physis and its correlate cosmos of demonic matter, so now technology is preparing a new physis in the technologized body and an appropriate cosmic correlate. The perceptual equivalent of the new physis is the expanded sensorium described in "The Work of Art in the Age of Its Technological Reproducibility" essay. But just as the powers released by the latter were able to assume a destructive character in aestheticized politics, so too the absorption of Gnostic demiurge or creator God into the technological relation to the cosmos can become murderous. Technology emerges as the mediating term in the equation humanity, cosmos, and divinity, substituting for the creator God as the point of negotiation between humanity and the cosmos: "technology is the mastery not of nature but of the relation between nature and man" (487). Benjamin imagines technology making possible a vast expansion of human experience aimed at nothing less than the abolition of time, and with it the resentment (in Nietzsche's view) of the present with respect to the past and with that to a transcendent punitive divinity. However, his characterization of the new human physis as one transformed by "the experience of velocities by virtue of which mankind in now preparing to embark on incalculable journeys into the interior of time" should be understood not just as a fantasy of time travel but also in terms of the new cosmology released by the establishment of the constancy of the speed of light (487). The "ever-increasing awe" at the "starry heavens above" evoked by Kant as a spatial spectacle has now become a journey into the "interior of time" or the remote past of the cosmos that takes place with every glance at the heavens. The tearing open of the sky has revealed a cosmos of far greater power and scale than previously imagined by natural theologians and one for which the Gnostic opposition between the God of creation and the God beyond creation is no longer appropriate. ⌉

Benjamin thus returns to the ecstasy or *Rausch* that the ancients experienced in their contact with the cosmos. With the new *physis* the powerful affect provoked by the contact of humanity, cosmos, and divinity is understood literally as an unassimilable experience figured by Benjamin in terms of the neural intensifications of epileptic seizure or orgasm. Making a definitive break with the limitation of the cosmos to Latin nature, Benjamin insists on the paroxistic character of our relation to it, substituting paroxism or *Rausch* for gnosis: "The paroxism of genuine cosmic experience is not tied to that tiny fragment of nature that we are accustomed to call 'Nature'" (*SW*, 1:487). The cosmos makes a demand of us that we are scarcely capable of experiencing let alone knowing, one that shakes the very physis of the human. The convulsion or seizure occasioned by the technological expansion of the human physis—the explosive transition to the *Übermensch*—was for Benjamin experienced pathologically in warfare: "In the nights of annihilation of the last war, the frame of mankind was shaken by a feeling that resembled the bliss of the epileptic" (487). The latter experience is known medically as the aura of a seizure, the sense of wind moving up the body reported by victims of epilepsy or the "sacred disease." The sense of a growing estrangement or distance from self and world that is the prodroma of an epileptic seizure is an apt description of the state of unreality that made possible the destruction released by technology in World War I. Benjamin continues the parallel by describing the revolutions that followed the war as attempts to recover from the paroxysm provoked by technological experience or to "bring the new body under its control" even describing the "power of the proletariat" as the "measure of its convalescence" (487). Yet beyond this attempt to discipline the destructive energies is the thought of a creative paroxysm with which "To the Planetarium" and thus *One-Way Street* concludes: "Living substance conquers the frenzy of destruction only in the frenzy of procreation" (487). The erotic *Rausch* of creation is Benjamin's understanding of the explosive transition to the *Übermensch*, a transition that can be understood gnostically as the absorption of previously estranged cosmic and divine energies in an act of gnosis, but also in terms of the "breaking open of the heavens" that has freed space and time for modern cosmology.

The fragment "Capitalism as Religion" of 1921 and the diptych *Origin of German Tragic Drama* and *One-Way Street* of 1928 situate Benjamin's cosmology within a Gnostic and largely Nietzschean framework. Yet they also announce a growing fascination with the emergence of modern science and in particular the astronomical and the electro-magnetic revolutions which together gave birth not only to technological modernity but also to modern cosmology.[23] In this light it should perhaps not be too surprising to find Benjamin using a long citation of Eddington's technical scientific cosmology in his discussion of Kafka. Benjamin recognized not only the theological significance of the scientific and technological relation to the cosmos but also the redemptive significance of the "paroxysm of genuine cosmic experience" that reverberated in contemporary cosmology. It is a redemption that Benjamin understood in terms of natural rather than messianic theology, that is to say, precisely the conjuncture of contemporary cosmology and mystic theology that he found in Kafka but also in Eddington.

Before looking more closely at why Benjamin thought Eddington's cosmology could help in understanding Kafka, it is necessary to frame a little more explicitly the circumstances of Eddington's entry into his thought. In particular it is crucial to understand how Eddington's cosmology and its affirmative relation to the cosmos—its affirmative natural theology in short—enabled Benjamin to leave the nineteenth-century climate of Nietzsche's thought and to overcome the assumptions of Gnostic cosmology. It might be asked why Benjamin should have been drawn to Eddington's thought in the first place. The explanation is probably independent of Eddington's scientific work and is perhaps related to his political renown (or notoriety) as a pacifist (he came from a Quaker family and was a conscientious objector during World War I). Eddington's political activity may have brought him and his work to Benjamin's attention as a close follower of pacifist theory and practice. But once he encountered Eddington's *The Nature of the Physical World* he would have been intrigued by its foregrounding of the themes of the void and of the double world as well as by Eddington's claim at the outset of the Gifford Lectures that modern cosmology was initiated by Einstein's theory of relativity and Rutherford's atomic hypothesis. Yet, there were also a number of stylistic and metaphorical aspects to Eddington's text that would have specifically fascinated Benjamin and provoked the emergence of the unexpected constellation of his work with that of Kafka.

By way of illustration, consider a fragment from 1938—the same year as Benjamin's citation from Eddington in his letter to Scholem—on "Blanqui." In it Benjamin describes Blanqui's political cosmology *L'Eternité par les astres* as a critique of the nineteenth century "conceived on a cosmic plane" but also as a Gnostic political cosmology that regards the created universe as hell: "The conception of the universe that Blanqui develops in this book, taking his basic premises from the mechanistic natural sciences, proves to be a vision of hell." [24] Essential to this vision is the "eternal return" that Benjamin contrasts with the version informing Nietzsche's *Also Sprach Zarathustra*. He offers a long and for him "depressing" excerpt in which Blanqui suggests that a finite number of elements in infinite space will result in the eternal return of the same. This very moment and point in time has already been and will repeat itself infinitely in the future: "The universe repeats itself endlessly, marking time on the spot."[25] Blanqui illustrates this by reference to his immediate predicament: "What I am writing at this moment in a cell in the Fort du Taureau I have written and will write throughout eternity—at a table, with a pen, in circumstances absolutely identical to the present ones." This is followed by a series of claims linking the temporal eternal return with the phenomenon of spatial doubling: "we have innumerable doubles in time and space . . . these doubles have flesh and blood, trousers and overcoats, crinolines and chignons."[26] Benjamin's attention would have been struck by the curious doubling of Blanqui and Eddington (both of whom he compliments with a lengthy citation) for like Blanqui Eddington's cosmological meditation departs from the table on which he writes, in effect doubling Blanqui's obsession with doubling, but from the other side of the cosmological revolution of the early twentieth century. Eddington's understanding of space, matter, and the void makes his cosmic plane very different to Blanqui's and far removed from what Benjamin described as the "mechanistic natural sciences" of the nineteenth century that had been superseded by the electromagnetic and cosmological revolutions of the twentieth century.

Eddington, in characteristically genial vein, begins like Blanqui by evoking predicament of a man seated at his desk (also important for Kafka), but the differences between their cosmologies become quickly evident. After the electromagnetic and thermodynamic revolutions of the late nineteenth and early twentieth century, Eddington's table looks very different from Blanqui's solid nineteenth-century desk: "I have settled down to the task of writing these lectures and have drawn up my chair to two tables! Yes; there are duplicates of every object about me—two tables, two chairs, two pens."[27] But this is not the same double table that for Blanqui initiates the infernal sequences of the eternal return and repeated spatial doubling. Of Eddington's two tables, only one is inherited from the nineteenth century: "One of them has been familiar to me from earliest years. It is a commonplace object of that environment I call the world. How shall I describe it? It has extension; it is comparatively permanent; it is coloured; it is above all *substantial*" (*NPW*, xi). This same table however, also doubles as another, twentieth-century or scientific table: "My scientific table is mostly emptiness"—but unlike Blanqui's eternal spaces this emptiness is not the theatre for a repetition of finite combinations of elements, but something much more random and precarious for "parely scattered in that emptiness are numerous electric charges rushing about with great speed" (xi). This table is not made up of substance like Blanqui's, but is a dynamic equilibrium of forces, one such that when I lay the paper on it the little electrical "particles with their headlong speed keep on hitting the underside, so that the paper is maintained in shuttlecock fashion at a nearly steady level" (xii). The paper on which he writes is not "supported because there is substance below it" but rather is "poised as if on a swarm of flies and sustained in shuttlecock fashion by a series of tiny blows by the swarm underneath" (xiii). Eddington explains that the first table inhabits the world of human consciousness and habit while the other is the "object" of a knowing that is not "contaminated by conceptions borrowed from the other world." In departing from the world of consciousness we seem to enter a world of shadows, with Eddington warning us, "In the world of physics we catch a shadowgraph performance of the drama of familiar life" (xiv). But Eddington also imagines a world in the process of emerging from the shadows, a cosmos free of human consciousness, one that is "far removed from human preconception." Its indifference to what and how we think challenges our limits and forces us to change our relationship toward it. In place of understanding the world in terms of substance, Eddington proposes that we think of it as the refracted light of the rainbow: "The sparsely spread nuclei of electric force become a tangible solid; their restless agitation becomes the warmth of summer; the octave of ethereal vibrations becomes a gorgeous rainbow" (xv). The emergence of a new cosmos is announced by the rainbow, a phenomenon that for Eddington—as for Benjamin in his 1916 dialogue on the rainbow—announced the promise of a new covenant between humanity, god, and nature, even if this new cosmos, for Eddington if not for Benjamin, still contains suffering and evil. Nevertheless, for him as for Benjamin, humanity itself is transformed by its encounter with this new cosmos, which no longer respects the limits of human perception, habit or desire.

Eddington closes his introduction to the lectures by emphasizing that his view of the physical world is different "from that prevailing at the end of the last century" which as Benjamin noted underlay Blanqui and Nietzsche's views of the eternal return. Such a change in the understanding of the cosmos will bring with it a change in the relation between "human nature" and the cosmos. Eddington identifies the inauguration of the new cosmos in the "fundamental changes in our ideas of space and time" introduced by Einstein and Minkowski between 1905 and 1908 and more controversially in Rutherford's introduction of "the greatest change in our idea of matter since the time of Democritus" (*NPW*, 1). It is the latter revolution (paralleled with the Bolshevik Revolution) which Eddington considers most devastating: "the most arresting change is not the rearrangement of space and time by Einstein but the dissolution of all that we regard as most solid into tiny specks floating in the void" (1). This is apocalyptic, a revelation, or an unveiling of secrets, for "the *revelation* by modern physics of the void within the atom is more disturbing than the revelation by astronomy of interstellar space" (1; emphasis added). By way of illustration, Eddington sketched one of his more disquieting images of physical reduction: "If we eliminated all the unfilled space in a man's body and collected his protons and electrons in just one mass, the man would be reduced to a speck just visible with a magnifying glass" (1–2). If asked what is man or what is the creation, Eddington would answer—a void. But this is not the void of Blanqui, not just the theatre of the eternal return of finite combinations in an immense space: Eddington indeed explicitly criticized theories of eternal return at the end of chapter 4 of *The Nature of the Physical World* from the standpoint of entropy and the second law of thermodynamics.

Eddington's belief that the new cosmology would liberate humanity from its provincial assumptions, humbling and at the same time elevating it, is broadly sympathetic with Benjamin's views regarding the historical character of relations with the cosmos proposed at the end of *One-Way Street*. The new cosmology can potentially liberate us from the phantasms of the fallen cosmos—interestingly proposing a new form of gnosis, but one in which the created universe far exceeds current human consciousness and demands a change in or rather beyond its parochial limits. After ten chapters on the theory of relativity, thermodynamics, and particle physics, Eddington arrives at a new alignment between mysticism and modern cosmology, offering a defense of mysticism—as of 1927, he said, it was possible for a scientist to be religious. The traditional scission between an Aristotelian natural theology and a Platonic, Augustinian mysticism no longer holds with respect to the contemporary, atomic and relativistic concept of nature. Both mystical religion and twentieth century science point to aspects of reality that exceed the substantialist prejudices of traditional natural theology and everyday experience.

Benjamin adapts Eddington's argument for a complementarity between mysticism and cosmology to his description of Kafka's work, precisely pointing to his critique of substance. Benjamin begins his letter to Scholem dated Paris, June 12, 1938, with some critical comments on Brod's biography concluded by "some of [his] own reflections on Kafka at the end" which he explains subsequently are "more or less independent of [his] earlier reflections." It is in this context that he cites Eddington, adapting

Kafka's views on the complementarity of mysticism and contemporary cosmology. Benjamin introduces his new reflections on Kafka by describing his work as an ellipse, decisively and deliberately breaking with the figure of the circle and the circular orbits of ancient cosmology and alluding to Kepler's discovery of elliptical orbits: "Kafka's work is an ellipse whose widely spaced focal points are defined, on the one hand, by mystical experience (which is, above all, the experience of tradition) and, on the other hand, by the experience of the modern city dweller." Benjamin quickly specifies that the latter experience can mean different things. On the one hand, the "modern city dweller" is "the citizen of the modern state, confronted by an unfathomable bureaucratic apparatus whose operations are controlled by agencies obscure even to the executive bodies themselves, not to mention the people affected by them." This is the spectral realm of the police analyzed earlier in the "Critique of Violence" but this does not exhaust the concept of the modern human. Benjamin insists that "by 'modern city dweller' [he] also mean the contemporary of modern physicists." And it is at this point that Benjamin observes, before proceeding to his citation, "When you read the following passage from Eddington's *Nature of the Physical World*, it's almost as if you're listening to Kafka."[28] The tension between reading and listening, and the mistaken listening on which the impact of the citation depends—*reading* Eddington is like *listening* to Kafka—will be picked up subsequently with respect to tradition and the problem of listening. Here it is enough to note that Benjamin is citing the written text of an oral lecture and suggesting that it could be mistaken for Kafka, himself an avid public and semipublic reader of his own and other's work. The predicament is also important for Benjamin, since it points to the problem of the threshold and what it is to pass a threshold.

The passage cited by Benjamin arrives in the fifteenth and final lecture on "Science and Mysticism" and is indeed the culminating flourish of the entire series of Gifford lectures.[29] It is the culmination of Eddington's spirited review of recent cosmological work—from Einstein and Bohr to Schrödinger—that opened with "The Downfall of Classical Physics" and moved through accounts of relativity, time, thermodynamics, and entropy, gravitation, and quantum theory. It is in the final chapter that Eddington returns to the theme of the Gifford lectures with a reflection on the implications of the new cosmology for the understanding of divinity. The result is very far from traditional natural theology—Eddington does not believe for a moment that contemporary cosmology can make any contributions to arguments concerning the existence of God let alone divine power, goodness, and justice. But he does seem to believe that it underlies the importance of faith in the scientific and nonscientific outlooks and implicitly calls for a reconsideration of the relation between science and religion. The entire lecture series is dedicated to undoing the view that the world is made up of solid substances behaving in a law-like manner according to causality; for Eddington the world is more properly understood as a void occupied by a vast population of elementary particles whose behavior is a matter of statistical probability rather than causality.

On some occasions Eddington is not very far removed from a crypto-Gnostic or a Manichean understanding of the cosmos. At one point he describes, not without irony, the force of gravity as the work of a demon. Referring to the celebrated Newtonian falling apple, Eddington humorously observes that the deviation (or clinamen) of the apple from uniform motion has to be explained in terms of demonic agency: "This new phenomenon has to be accounted for by an unimaginable agency or demon called *gravitation* which persuades the apples to deviate from their proper uniform motion" (*NPW*, 138). He immediately clarifies that for him the demonic effect is epistemic, an effect of the limits of our perception: "the demon is simply the complication which arises when we try to fit a curved world in a flat frame" (138). But when we enter the quantum realm the epistemic demon seems even more uncanny, since for Eddington quantum events cannot be described in the substantialist and correlative spatial terms with which we experience the world.[30] In discussing the electron Eddington observes: "The tossing up of the electron is a conventional way of depicting a particular change of state of the atom which cannot really be associated with movements in space as macroscopically conceived. *Something unknown is doing we don't know what*—that is what our theory amounts to" (291). Confronted with this, Eddington draws two implications from contemporary cosmology for natural theology, the gist of which is his Gifford lectures. The first is to abandon concepts such as substance and reality and to experience divinity beyond reality and existence, the second is that there is no scientific answer to the Gnostic question of whether creation is divine or diabolic.

Eddington presents the first implication earlier in his lectures by referring to the Quaker idiom of the Inner Light—God is not known but can be experienced through the Inner Light that draws us toward divinity. According to this view, science and mysticism share the pursuit of the Inner Light and its de-substantialization of the world. In one of the many confessional passages of the lectures, Eddington mused:

> We all know that there are regions of the human spirit untrammelled by the world of physics. In the mystic sense of the creation around

us, in the expression of art, in a yearning towards God, the soul grows upwards and finds the fulfilment of something implanted in its nature. The sanction for this development is within us, a striving born with our consciousness or an Inner Light proceeding from a greater power than ours . . . Whether in the intellectual pursuits of science or in the mystical pursuits of the spirit, the light beckons ahead and the purpose surging in our nature responds. Can we not leave it at that? Is it really necessary to drag in the comfortable word "reality" to be administered like a pat on the back. (*NPW*, 327–28)

In this sense, the pursuit of the Inner Light through science or mystical experience is a form of proof of divinity, since the Inner Light proceeds from a "greater power than ours." But as it remains unknown even unknowable, there can be no certainty that its pursuit by way of nature is not as diabolic as it is divine, for "Science cannot tell us whether the world spirit is good or evil, and its halting arguments for the existence of a God might equally well be turned into an argument for the existence of a Devil" (*NPW*, 238). What science shows us according to Eddington is that we do not live in a world of reliably behaving law-abiding substances but are part of a vast population of atoms and their particles whose behaviors are at best probabilistic outcomes. This, the world of the modern physicist, is also for Benjamin the world of the modern citizen and the world of Kafka's writing.

After citing the passage Benjamin makes two arguments for the proximity of Kafka's writing with Eddington. The first argues to the unique proximity of Eddington and Kafka, with Benjamin confessing that "I know no passage in literature which displays the characteristic Kafka *gestus* to the same degree."[31] Benjamin aligns Eddington with Kafka's *gestus* not only in respect to his precarious universe without substance but also in terms of its distance from gnosis: for both Eddington and Kafka to cross a threshold it is better not to know what is involved, better not to know about the subatomic particles or the demonic archons that guard the subsequent gates to the law. Apart from the reference to the *gestus*, Benjamin also argues that Kafka's prose sentences could be juxtaposed with Eddington's physical descriptions of the aporia of the prevalence of accident over substance. Indeed, Benjamin believed that Kafka's most incomprehensible sentences are at home in Eddington. But beyond this complementarity between Kafka and Eddington's cosmology of the accidental universe—which is one focus of the ellipse that is the orbital path of Kafka's writing—is the enormous tension with the other focus, that of mystical experience. The centrifugal and centripetal forces that propel the "planet Kafka" through the houses of modern cosmo-political and mystical experience are complementary, but also maddening: the modern comes to Kafka through the mystical. But for this to be possible the mystical experience must have suffered a catastrophe—devastating occurrences that threw it off its proper orbit and brought it into an elliptical formation with modern experience, which has also suffered its own catastrophe not only in the formation of the modern state but also of the modern cosmos which is no longer the creation of a creator God.

Benjamin argues that the shock of modern reality—"theoretically in modern physics and in practice in military technology"[32]—is unassimilable by an individual, hence Kafka's recourse to the mystical tradition as a means to shape the experience. His writing is understood as the complement of modern experience, which in its nihilistic variant is the reality of extermination, or the movement beyond the paired good and evil Gods of Gnosticism to a complete indifference to creation. His surrender of the "consistency of truth" while maintaining fidelity to "transmissibility" drove him in Benjamin's reading to a fascination with the "products of its decomposition," namely the "rumour of true things" or the "whispered newspaper of the disreputable and obsolete."[33] Yet the relationship between the human, the cosmos, and the divine that survives in rumor and undergoes the strange variants of folly remain stalled at the same impasse of the end of the *The Origin of German Tragic Drama*. The double negation of the allegory of allegory is now seen in Kafka's hope that hope be infinite but not for us. Benjamin takes pains to insist to Scholem that Kafka is the figure of a failure, the chronicler of a fallen world, which even its evil creator God has abandoned.

The devastation of a creation without creator can be experienced as horror and exterminatory, as the ruined gate through which a messiah might pass, or it might be a theater of transformation. Eddington's cosmos that for Benjamin stands for the vacated cosmos of modern science cannot offer any reassurance concerning the existence of divinity, but it can challenge its human occupants to change their habits of occupying it. The vision of a transformation of nature and the human envisaged in *One-Way Street* is consistent with Benjamin's anti-Gnostic natural theology in which the cosmos is bereft of a creator, but also of evil. But it is also consistent with war and the view of the cosmos as an anticreation or theatre of extermination. The negative natural theology of an uncreated cosmos that Benjamin deduced from the collapse of Gnostic cosmology and that he found confirmed in Eddington's vision of modern scientific cosmology can either unleash the forces of extermination or point to new vistas for the relationship between cosmos, human and the divine.

Notes

1. Translated by Marie Freifrau Rausch von Traubenberg und Hermann Diesselhost for the natural science publisher Vieweg Verlag, Braunschweig.

2. Hans Jonas, *The Gnostic Religion*, 2nd rev. ed. (Boston, MA: Beacon Press, 1963), and Jacob Taubes, *From Cult to Culture: Fragments Toward a Critique of Historical Reason*, ed. Chalotte Elisheva Fonrobert and Amir Engel (Stanford, CA: Stanford University Press, 2010).

3. *The Cosmic Century* (Cambridge: Cambridge University Press, 2013). For Eddington's contribution, see John North, *The Measure of the Universe: A History of Modern Cosmology* (New York: Dover Publications, 1965) and *Astronomy and Cosmology* (London: Fontana Books, 1994).

4. For an analysis of this equation in terms of the new law following the rainbow—an explicit use of the metaphor of the rainbow as a symbol for a new covenant between God, the cosmos, and humanity following the flood, see my "Non-Messianic Political Theology in Benjamin's 'On the Concept of History,' " in *Walter Benjamin and History*, ed. Andrew Benjamin (London: Continuum Books, 2005), 215–226.

5. Walter Benjamin, *The Origin of German Tragic Drama*, trans. John Osborne (London: New Left Books, 1977), 227.

6. Benjamin, "Capitalism as Religion," *Selected Writings*, 4 vols., ed. Michael W. Jennings et al. (Cambridge, MA: Harvard University Press, 1996–2003), 1:290.

7. Ibid., 1:289.

8. Ibid.

9. Ibid.

10. For an analytical description of the planetary doctrine of the Gnostics see Jonas, *Gnostic Religion*, 156–158.

11. Ibid., 158.

12. Benjamin, "Capitalism as Religion," in *Selected Writings*, 1:289.

13. Ibid.

14. Jonas, *Gnostic Religion*, 158.

15. Benjamin, "Capitalism as Religion," in *Selected Writings*, 1:289.

16. Ibid., 1:290.

17. Benjamin, *Origin of German Tragic Drama*, 227.

18. Ibid., 232.

19. Ibid.

20. Benjamin, *One-Way Street*, in *Selected Writings*, 1:486. Hereafter cited in text as *SW*.

21. This is the first appearance of the distinction between the optic and the haptic axiomatic for the argument in the "The Work of Art in the Age of Its Technological Reproducibility," a direct continuation of the themes in "To the Planetarium."

22. This recognition also informs Aby Warburg's so-called snake ritual lecture at Kreuzlingen, which shows many similarities with Benjamin's views of cosmology and antiquity.

23. This is Alexander Koyre's description of the achievement of Copernicus and his contemporaries.

24. Benjamin, "Blanqui," in *Selected Writings*, 4:93.

25. Blanqui quoted by Benjamin in ibid., 94.

26. Ibid.

27. Arthur Stanley Eddington, *The Nature of the Physical World* (Cambridge: Cambridge University Press, 1928), x. Hereafter cited in text as *NPW*.

28. All excerpts in this paragraph are from Benjamin, "Letter to Gershom Scholem," in *Selected Writings*, 3:325. All excerpts in this paragraph are from page 325.

29. Eddington, *Nature of the Physical World*, 242.

30. To give just one example of Eddington's sustained critique of substance, one whose affinities with Bergson and Whitehead he explicitly noted: "So strongly has substance held the place of leading actor on the stage of experience that in common usage concrete and real are almost synonymous. Ask any man who is not a philosopher or a mystic to name something typically real; he is almost sure to choose a concrete thing" (274).

31. Benjamin, "Letter to Gershom Scholem," in *Selected Writings*, 3:325.

32. Ibid., 326.

33. Ibid.

Walter Benjamin—A Modern Marcionite?
Scholem's Benjamin Interpretation Reexamined

JACOB TAUBES

"The Devil is in the details." This *aperçu* of Aby Warburg applies not only to philology and history, but to philosophical and theological reflection as well. Gershom Scholem, a highly speculative mind, invoked Aby Warburg's words when he made his bold, imposing descent into the deep strata of Jewish history of religion, where he brought dark, dialectically fascinating, albeit profoundly demonic, forms of the Jewish spirit to light. A student once proposed that Scholem's "historical-rational" apparatus could be the bridge over which searching secular students could enter onto the path to the "nonrational" content of Jewish mysticism and its demonic consequences in the satyr play of messianism of the seventeenth century: Sabbatai Zevi and Jakob Frank. Scholem's answer has a magnificent air of scholarly asceticism: No, he countered: *not* rational, *only* historical. As if historical scholarship today stood in a universal civil war behind the front lines of the rational and irrational!

The subliminal, but bitterly waged culture war in the state of Israel represented an emergency for the spiritual and political potential of the Jewish religion, but even there Scholem saw himself as beyond the fronts of sacred and profane. This is because he believed in God. However, Jewish religious law—as it is ultimately codified in the *Schulchan Aruch* of Joseph Karo—did not declare itself as binding, and thus is reckoned as neither secular nor religious. In which God did Scholem believe? The Devil believes in God as well! Surely in the God of Israel, who, as scripture and tradition attest (the crisis of tradition aside) has called and sanctified us through his commands to become a holy people. But then, theocracy is at least virtually in sight.

It is easy for a mystical Marxist like Ernst Bloch to deny the political sense of theocracy with the utmost intensity and to insist only on a religious sense. Bloch floated untethered between the fronts—initially as an orthodox Marxist in the East, then, when the Berlin Wall went up, as a heretical Marxist in the West—as an atheist. His atheism is assuredly of a dialectical kind. "Only an atheist can be a good Christian, only a Christian can be a good atheist"[1]—this highly mystical proposition becomes false the moment that theologians of the Church, be they Catholic or Protestant, hold fast to it as a point of discussion with Bloch. It is understandable that Christian theologians cannot forgo the conversation, because at least *one* intellectual takes seriously their theology (which, according to Benjamin, "today is admittedly small and unsightly and in any case should not be seen"[2]), so seriously, that he mystically sublates it. However, the fact that theologians believe they have discovered in it a chance for an endless conversation, which they would not break off for any price, is another matter. Regardless of where one stands with regard to atheism in Christianity, Bloch would scarcely have been able to find this atheism in Judaism as well, even with all of the fine interpretive arts of which he was capable. If Bloch already turns the theocratic tendency inward in *The Spirit of Utopia*,[3] then he can take this path inward because he has detached himself from the classical Judaic tradition. Unlike Scholem, the conscious Jew who believed in God, the atheist Bloch did not live in the state of Israel. It is there that theocracy receives a deadly serious, concrete-historical sense that only illusionists could allow themselves to gloss over.

Bloch understands his work as a "witness to revolutionary gnosis"—in the spirit of the original heretic Marcion, the highly significant interpreter of the apostle Paul. His *Gospel of the Alien God* overturned the established table of values in such a revolutionary way that all church-going Christians, be they Catholic or Protestant, crossed themselves before Marcion's doctrine—if they were aware of him. Marcion is the classical case where anti-Semitism reaches a metaphysical status and religious depth. Against the terrible Moloch-god of the Old Testament, Marcion places the "good," "new" (for the first time in antiquity, the word *new* has a positive ring), and "alien" (to the world and its elements) God. Marcion proclaimed his new gospel as the "anti-thesis" (this is the title of his merely fragmentarily transmitted work), in which he tried to furnish the Christian of the second century with a Scripture that is purified of everything that reeked of the demiurgical Moloch-god of the Old Testament and its political promises. It was a starkly reduced and redacted version of the

Gospel according to Luke and extremely condensed letters of Paul. This Scripture was regarded as the canon in Marcionite Christian congregations, as Holy Scripture, which finally liberated them from the Jewish book of the Old Testament. As with the god, so with his people: The Jews insist on a political theocracy with an earthly goal as the end of historical development, which is left behind them as prehistory in order to enter finally into a historical realm of freedom. By contrast, Marcion's Christians regard themselves as foreigners on this Earth, as the congregation of a foreign god, who has nothing to do with this world as it is. Not only is this miserable world to be escaped, but the principle of this world is to be combated so that the spell of the Demiurge, who continually reproduces this miserable world, is broken. As the principle of this miserable world, the demiurgical, righteous (and also terrible) God of the Old Testament, which Marcion took so seriously, discloses himself.

Because Bloch sees the spirit of Marcion as operative throughout the history of heresy up to Karl Marx, he accepts the metaphysical anti-Semitism to which this opposition lends itself as part of the bargain. However, that theocracy would have no "political" but "only a religious sense" is the consequence of Bloch's revolutionary gnosis in the spirit of Marcion and Joachim of Fiore (who combines a severe *adversus Judaeos* alongside and *with* his three-stage doctrine).[4] Their earthly execution is found in Marx in the essay "Zur Judenfrage,"[5] where he places observant Jews and secular Jews under one "principle." It is not an occasional writing, not a lapse, but rather in line with Marcion and Joachim, systematically and consistently directed toward the secular world. (It is therefore an anti-Semitic socioeconomic text of the highest order and not a "slapdash job," as Scholem, who otherwise had sense and dialectical intuition even for the status of the opposite position, occasionally dismisses the work.[6]) "Thus we do not say with Bauer to the Jews: You cannot be politically emancipated without being radically emancipated from Judaism. Rather, we say to them: since you can be politically emancipated without completely and incontrovertibly renouncing Judaism, *political emancipation* itself is not *human emancipation*."[7]

We do not know whether Benjamin saw so clearly these relations between the idea of theocracy in a "merely religious sense" in the case of Bloch and his pedigree from Marcion, through Joachim of Fiore, and up to Marx. His review of *The Spirit of Utopia* is most likely irretrievably lost.[8] It is presumably Benjamin's view. It therefore seems to me to be too bold of Scholem when he wants to borrow just this purely spiritual form of theocracy (which Benjamin adopts from Bloch, or which connects him with Bloch's deeper intentions—that "essential lesson of the philosophy of history" that necessitates Benjamin's "mystical conception of history") as a piece of Jewish theology.[9] This lesson is, if anything, the harshly anti-Jewish—Christian, in Scholem's sense, in truth, however, Marcionite-Joachimite—part of Bloch's and Benjamin's theology. This causes Bloch early on, and later Benjamin, to end up—by means of arduous twists and turns—with a messianic Marxism. For Scholem, who was a historian, it was not necessary to book everything creative on the secret account Judaism, as established Jewish apologetics and theological and political Philo-Semitism did—as if such accounting would not revert into its exact opposite without any pressure. In Marx's case, Scholem is correct to the extent that he does not accede to the legend of prophetic Judaism in Marx as the secret source of the Marxist vision. In Bloch's case, he sees where his roots must be sought as well. One must accept what is surely more difficult: to see even Benjamin as ultimately in the second theoretical camp of the modern Marcionites. There can be no greater misunderstanding than to interpret Benjamin's early, highly significant, but difficult "Theological-Political Fragment" as seamlessly Jewish. Indeed, Benjamin divides the order of the profane from the order of the messianic in a way that runs contrary to the Jewish understanding of the messianic idea as promulgated by Scholem.

For Scholem insists upon nothing more vehemently than a demarcation between a Jewish and Christian understanding of the messianic idea. Jewish salvation is always a public (and therefore, I would argue, an earthly, and therefore political) event "on the stage of history and in the medium of the community."[10] Christian salvation is in the "spiritual [*geistlichen*]" (and why not intellectual [*geistigen*]?) realm,[11] invisible, an event in the soul of the individual, a conversion that corresponds to nothing external in the mundane world, "wondrous certainty of pure interiority," as Scholem half-seriously, half-ironically cites a professor of theology who has completely vanished from public consciousness as an authority.[12]

I want to leave undecided whether the bourgeois and late-bourgeois variants of Schleiermacher's "province of the soul," which operated in the nineteenth century and up to World War I as a "wondrous certainty of pure interiority," represent the relevant version of a Christian understanding of salvation. Only today, when we live with amnesia regarding the genuinely volatile and precarious configurations of the history of the Church and its self-conception for almost two thousand years—separated from any complex and assuredly ambiguous experiences of a Holy Roman Empire, separated from the idea of a *sacrum imperium*—can Scholem impress as a historical authority when he declares that Christian theology has been oriented from time immemorial toward that spiritual, inwardly directed sense of salvation, which has nothing to do with worldly realization.

I do not want to belabor Church history in order to demonstrate the one-sidedness of Scholem's argumentation. But an appeal to "Swabian Pietism" from Bengel up to the elder Blumhardt does not get stuck in the ghetto of Church history, but rather depicts the *prehistory* of that unique spiritual configuration of Germany: Hegel, Hölderlin, and Schelling. Scholem acts as if he had heard nothing of the younger Blumhardt, who led the quietist congregation of Pietism into an acute messianism (just at the time of the Hassidic movement in Judaism which, as Scholem himself brilliantly demonstrated, was *comparable* with Pietism). That "wondrous certainty of pure interiority" of Christian bourgeois belief surely goes brilliantly together with the general bourgeois interiority, which allows for Christian theology and ceremony as weekly gentle persuasion [*Seelenmassage*]. But why should those Swiss religious socialists, who tumultuously crowded into the medium of history, be forgotten and thereby be spiritually liquidated?

Is it really as Scholem declares (apodictically, as a historian) in his fundamental analysis "Toward an Understanding of the Messianic Idea," that it is "the particular position of Judaism" in the history of religion to have nothing, absolutely nothing at all of an "as it were chemically pure interiority"?[13] I ask, because in his magnificent essay Scholem himself presents evidence and indicates dialectical reversals that would entail a degree of interiorization of "his" Sabbatarians (who one might almost want to say admiringly and at the same time skeptically were discovered by him), who simply eliminated the points of orientation of inside and outside in distinction to the characteristics of the messianic idea specifically advertised as Jewish. Or, in order to say it more clearly: the point of the distinction between Jewish and Christian in the understanding of the messianic idea that Scholem makes is ironically denied in the development of the analysis, and the Eranos Circle, to which the analysis was initially offered, knew as much at the end of it as they did at the beginning. Or does Scholem have reasons—other than historical considerations, which he merely pretends to advocate—that force him to demarcate between Jewishness, which he identifies with exteriority, and Christianness, which he identifies with interiority ("swindle of interiority," a polemic theological proposition of Scholem that has become famous)?

If there is a point to that highly significant "theological-political fragment," then it is precisely the *contrast* of the direction of the "dynamic of the profane" and the "direction of messianic intensity," which as "immediate messianic intensity of the heart, of the inner individual human being, passes through unhappiness in the sense of suffering."[14] And then the Christian, even ultimately Marcionite sense of these sentences is almost palpable, even without Scholem's strict equation, where Jewish equals outer and Christian equals inner. The main sentence of this fragment states: "the spiritual *restitutio in integrum*, which ushers in immortality, corresponds to a worldly one, which leads to an eternal downfall."[15] From this passage Benjamin concludes: "to aspire" for transience, "even for those ranks of human beings that are nature, is the task of global politics [!], whose method must be called nihilism [!]."[16] However, anyone who claims that this is a piece of Jewish theology must introduce evidence that nihilistic global politics is a possible attitude of rabbinic or apocalyptic doctrine. Neither Scholem's authority as a historian (and in the guise of a historian as secret theologian) of the history of Jewish religion, nor his authority as a friend of Benjamin gives him any kind of privileged knowledge that would remain closed to others in principle. Scholem would be the first to sign on to this maxim. This authority is due more to a cult of personality than to Scholem himself. It was propagated in Germany (and not only here) with the researcher and scholar of Kabala for completely transparent reasons: a Jewish representative was needed and sought who could represent *the one* Judaism for the public after the death of Buber. This role adhered to Scholem, who studied the irrational and profound sides of Judaism historically. However, the aim of his work was precisely to repudiate this idea of *the* Judaism by developing its history. This view rubbed off on him after many years of friendship with Benjamin, even though it should not be forgotten that Scholem only met his friend in person two more times after 1923. Since 1923, Benjamin has taken several paths with often serpentine curves which he never revealed in his letters to Scholem.

The aura of Scholem's authority obstructed the intelligentsia's path—both on the left and the right—to a historical understanding of the *unity* of the Benjaminian program from the early "Theological-Political Fragment" up to the final, almost testamentary "Theses on the Philosophy of History." Scholem's thesis on Benjamin indeed presupposes the break, the detour, the sidetrack through Benjamin's illusory Marxist phase. Illusory in the most serious sense of the reproach in that Benjamin lulled himself into illusions concerning his own position.[17] The beginning and end of Benjamin's work is summarized as theses in brazen theological-political propositions. The question is only which kind of theology and which kind of politics?

Scholem's own assertiveness depends upon the concrete situation of a religious struggle in the state of Israel—a struggle for the self-conception of the state (which is subdued and deferred only through the external enemy, but which in truth is smoldering anyway). Scholem's utopian, albeit restorative, withdrawal to Zion (for which he existentially avows, as they say, even in speeches and presentations on his great annual travels in exile) cannot involve itself in such mystical explications of theocracy as Bloch and Benjamin do with various accents, but nevertheless unified in tenor.

For Scholem's Zion is no spiritual fool's paradise, no mere rational homestead, but rather the place of an experiment in historical responsibility. There are orthodox Jews in the state of Israel and in the United States who deny the sacral title "Israel" to this secular state, as to any earthly state at all before the arrival of the Messiah, and even in daily social dealings, even if they must do business with the authorities, they deny the sacral title of Israel to this state.

However, Scholem, who was familiar with everything the least historical, understood precisely his own withdrawal and the Jewish withdrawal to Zion to the state of Israel in general solely as "plotted by history."[18] He denounced all mysterious metahistory (i.e., salvation history) that clambered up clumsily into world history or that was welded onto it as Christian illusion and aberration. He did this even when it, in Scholem's opinion, turned up in the doubtlessly Christian-tinged phrases of ideologues of the modern Jewish orthodoxy. Thus he will naturally be unable to content himself, in a Jewish sense, with the completely apolitical implications of theocracy. For in the case of theocracy, there is always a political overtone heard along with the word *Jewish*. However, the term itself was coined by Josephus,[19] the ancient Jewish historian, in order to characterize the political constitution, the real constitution, of the first and second Jewish polities. In particular, Scholem will not be able to renounce the political tone in the term *theocracy* since Zionist ideology proclaims, more uninhibitedly since Auschwitz than ever before, the state of Israel as *atchalta di geula*, as "the beginning of salvation," accompanied by "overtones of messianism."[20] Even theocracy as a merely ideal perspective in a secular state today has implications that burst the talk of the liberal secular state of Israel—as if the separation of church and state originated from our tradition! Whoever claims this obscures the fact that the separation of church and state—over which the Jews of the United States, who are the financiers of the state of Israel, keep a jealous watch—was achieved in difficult inner struggles of the Calvinistic United States.

There were times when Scholem was still aware that "religious overtones of messianism," when taken more seriously, would be a phrase that could only compromise catastrophically the idea of Zionism for a Zionist, profane-historical perspective. Thus at one time, in 1929, he insisted with an iron consistency that was uniquely his own: the utopian withdrawal to

Zion would be "plotted by history" and would have nothing to do with messianic overtones. But what does "plotted by history" mean? In the end, should a secular state spring up in the Middle East, "a people like other peoples"? Or does "plotted by history" *also* mean plotted by one's own tradition, which, however broken it becomes when it forces itself into the medium of politics, virtually evokes a theocratic state, like the specter of Calvinist Geneva, the England of Cromwell and Micon, or Puritan New England with its strict Sabbath laws?

I have not invented the comparison between the theocracy of the Calvinistic Puritans and the theocracy of the Pharisees, who mold the tradition of classical Judaism to this day. It forms the axis around which the official Jewish scholarly analysis of the Pharisees turns, which Louis Finkelstein, the chancellor of the Jewish Theological Seminary in New York—one of the most important contemporary rabbinical institutions—put forward unchanged in three editions. Thus why should one "be ashamed" of the comparison with Calvinist Puritans when considering the case of the state of Israel?

If both rabbinical and New Testament historical scholarship are not to prostitute themselves to men of any fashion, then we must retain the comparison between Pharisees and Puritans, even if it does not sound so fashionable and honorable any more. The theocracy of the Pharisees not only has just a purely religious sense but is also mundanely meant as concretely political.

The *only ones* who did not come to some kind of arrangement with the Roman authorities, who did not want to realize the theocratic vision of the Pharisees *à la lettre*, and who risked the struggle to the end for this are the Zealots. They are denigrated by the "assimilated" Josephus,[21] who tries to sell the Jewish groups to the Romans as "philosophical schools" in his writings, as if the Romans would have to wage war against philosophical schools; they are also denigrated by the Pharisees, who portray a part of the Zealots as *sicarii*, as "assassins." So it stands to reason that one can learn about them only with difficulty. A few words of Jesus are all that can tell us something about the Zealots that validly sketches their aims and intentions. It is seldom noticed that Paul himself proudly calls himself a Zealot. The Pharisees, and doubtlessly their rabbinic line of succession, distance themselves from him, a distance that to this day determines both the theological and the profane-historical historiography of the Jews. This is so *even though* Paul, according to his own understanding, characterized himself, even *after* Damascus, only as a Pharisee, but *never* as a Christian (contrary to how some interpret his difficult identity crisis after Damascus and his tense relationship with the Jewish authorities in Jerusalem and the

Diaspora). It has not yet been noticed that Paul claims the title "Zealot" for himself in all seriousness, although admittedly in a dialectical packaging of the title. Paul is a Zealot, who includes in the covenant the pharisaic balance since Ezra, which inwardly makes possible and guarantees the Gentiles, the goy, as constitutive guarantors of the fulfillment of the law, be it in the private life of the individual or in the life of the people of Israel—in that he, as he says, supersedes the law backward in recourse to the covenants of Abraham and Sinai, and theoretically establishes a platform for a mission to convert the Gentiles. This intention appears to be fundamental in Paul's perspective; the rest has been commentary and scholarly dispute for generations.

What is put forward from the Jewish side in order to keep Paul out of the dialectic of a Jewish messianism—and thus not to pay the price that is involved in the premises of Jewish messianism—is not convincing. When Martin Buber focuses on the difference between the Hebrew *emuna* (trust) and the (in the case of Paul, self-articulating) Greek *pistis* (belief in) in the *Two Types of Faith*,[22] he overlooks that Paul's *pistis* is not a Greek concept, but is rather a messianic category, structurally built exactly like the messianic *emuna* of the Sabbatarians of the seventeenth century portrayed by Scholem.

Hans Joachim Schoeps investigates Paul's theology in light of Jewish history of religion and puts forward several things that *could* make possible a "repatriation of the heretics" in Jewish history of religion.[23] He sees the border as lying in the difference between the sacrifice of Isaac—where, according to Schoeps, the Jewish tradition places the entire emphasis on the character of temptation of the sacrifice of Isaac, with which only the obedience of faith is tested—and the doctrine of the sacrificial death of the divine son developed by Paul. The sacrificial victim himself, however—as distinguished from Paul's sacrifice theology, according to which God did not spare his own son and in the sacrifice of the son of God develops the bloody mystery—Schoeps explains, would not come into serious consideration for Jews: "The factical reality of the human sacrifice is for the Jewish tradition the most unthinkable and chilling thing there is."[24] Just as every apodictic declaration about what is possible or impossible in a Jewish sense becomes false, precisely this declaration of Schoeps is discounted by the material that he eruditely develops (and by much of what is expressed in the liturgy of the Jews beyond the horizon of Schoeps), but does not understand. The contrary is true. For the early Tannaitic tradition, Isaac is an *ola teminah*, a perfect sacrifice (i.e., he was offered up as a sacrifice, which Schoeps does not realize). According to another tradition, Isaac gave a quarter measure of blood on the altar, which means that he died, which Schoeps of course does not realize either. And since one passage reads "in all future generations, the ashes of Isaac are visible on the mountain of the Lord and ready for atonement" (Gen. 22:14), Isaac's ashes are naturally not, as Schoeps claims, those of the substitute ram, but rather what the text says if one reads it without apologetic glasses: the ashes of the sacrificed Isaac himself. It is not my intention in this context to wage a philological feud with Schoeps, whose body of work on Paul represents one of the few that is to be taken seriously, but rather only momentarily to illuminate how prejudiced dogmatic judgments can cripple even a respectable scholar, who is at least willing to pursue Paul's repatriation of the heretics within the dialectic of Jewish messianism.

It is not easy to break prejudices that prevail throughout two millennia and that have reinforced themselves through a violent history. Nevertheless, this break must be ventured in order to give room to a perspective in which the configuration of Paul as a spiritual Zealot can be debated. For in a world-historical perspective, he has been more than justified, I believe, in a claim to this title. For whereas the political Zealots in their resistance against Rome take upon themselves the military risk of a *universal* messianic war,[25] Paul continues the Zealotic total resistance against Rome, admittedly by means other than those of the national Zealots, that is, with spiritual means, through which he eventually forces Rome to its knees. The Zealots, who tragically perish in their desperate resistance against Rome in the retreat to the fortress Masada, were historically legitimized and avenged beforehand by Paul. The relation between the radically theocratic politics of the Zealots and Paul's theocratic vision, which appears to have a merely religious sense (but which even politically remains not without consequences), is yet another dark chapter of Jewish and Christian history of religion.

After World War II, when Buber sought after years of great affliction to reduce the sum total of events to a common denominator, he recalled the student of Paul, Marcion, and Harnack's monograph on the Gnostics:[26] "At the same time that Hadrian crushed Bar Kokhba's revolt, made Jerusalem into a Roman colony, and constructed a temple to Jupiter on the place of the Second Temple, Marcion came from Asia Minor to Rome and brought his own gospel as a spiritual contribution to the destruction of Israel."[27] In the case of Marcion, the redeemed soul stands on the one side, and the existing society stands on the other, and there is no thought of the improvement of the latter.

The Church did not follow Marcion. It knew that if creation and salvation were "torn apart, then it would be deprived of the foundation of its influence on the order of this world."[28] At this point Buber brings in Harnack's work on Marcion. Harnack, who was by no means an anti-Semite, but much rather a representative of a broad liberalism, held that preserving the Old Testament as a canonical document in the nineteenth century would be the "consequence of a religious and ecclesiastical paralysis."[29] Buber comments: "Harnack died in 1930; three years later, his thought, the thought of Marcion, was converted into action, not by means of the spirit, but by means of violence and terror . . . Marcion's gift to Hadrian was passed down to other hands."[30]

The complex of problems of gnosis and politics could not be stated more emphatically. In Buber's case, it occurs within the perspective of a concrete messianism, in which Bloch's *The Spirit of Utopia* stands as well. Thus a comparison of Bloch's and Buber's pro and contra Marcion could be instructive. Bloch has addressed the problem of Gnostic anti-Semitism as well; he coined the apt term "metaphysical anti-Semitism," but he interprets Marcion and conveys the legacy of this epoch completely differently than Buber. Yet *The Spirit of Utopia* says about Marcion:

> Precisely by conceiving of God as history, Marcion, a great man, places this contrast, this antithesis between the Demiurge and the hitherto unknown highest divinity, revealed through Christ,— places this apparently metaphysical anti-Semitism of the messianic spirituality closer than the entire subsequent, Old Testament– petrifying, economy of salvation, which weakened the succession of revelations to merely pedagogical measures and so kept the genuine theogonic process away from Heaven itself.[31]

The events of the Hitler years have done nothing to change this. Even *The Principle of Hope* (1959) eulogizes Marcion, "who felt himself as the consummator of the antithetical Paul,"[32] as teacher of the new God, the absolutely alien, "from whom there never came any tidings to humanity until Christ." "By admittedly breaking the bridge to the Old Testament, Marcion himself stands on this bridge." "In other words, Marcion comes not only from Paul, he comes just as well from Moses, the true or alien God dawns in the God of Exodus, between Egypt and Canaan."

In the case of Bloch, it becomes clear that "both utopia and messianism stand in opposition" to the doctrine of the Creation.[33] Even in his late work *The Spirit of Utopia* (1968), Bloch still recalls Marcion's doctrine as a "bold offence," which provided the key term of the antithesis: antilaw, antijustice, anti–world-creator and world-governor. Nevertheless, Marcion's antithetical key term has "certainly nothing" to do "with any worldly tension, even enmity toward the Jew (Marcion honored the Jew Paul as his master),"[34] as Bloch remarked in passing, as if he responded to Buber's great speech (from 1952).

In the wake of Bloch (and Benjamin), we should attempt to finally reclaim the tradition of the Zealots, Paul, Bar Kokhba, and Marcion from conformism and to present this configuration, which is freighted with chances for a new perspective on the past *and* the future—beyond all "official" and therefore boring and futile conversations between Judaism and Christianity with which the "official" representatives pass their time and cheat both Jews and Christians out of a real chance for the unity of their history. Who could dispute that such a bold leap into the past is not without risk?[35]

The first attempt of such a leap into the past will assuredly be ridiculed by the academic oligarchy and be trampled with footnotes. But a new generation, which is adept at critically scrutinizing footnotes, will not be impressed by the judgment of the academic oligarchy and will find ways to articulate the past historically, not only in the established form of the question, "how was it, actually?," but rather, as Benjamin says, to seize a memory as it flashes through one's mind in a moment of peril.[36]

In sum, the fronts—Judaism and Christianity, political and apolitical messianism—are faltering. Reflections of higher complexity, as Benjamin's theological-political theses present them, cannot be settled unambiguously. There are Marcionite vectors that determine the force field contrary to the Jewish ones. However overwrought it would be to portray Walter Benjamin as a modern Marcionite, it would be equally obfuscatory to read that "task of world politics, the method of which must be called nihilism," without a Marcionite thorn in one's side. None other than Scholem has instructed us that everything is possible in a Jewish sense in periods of plasticity. The decades after World War I were such a period of plasticity. Possibilities flashed up in them, which were later no longer visible: Leftists from the Right, rightists from the Left, Jewish Gnostics and Marcionites. I do not want to commandeer Benjamin for one orientation, but rather to indicate that he (with Bloch)—as a mystical Marxist—bears traits of which one hardly would have dreamt in cases such as Marxism and Jewish messianism.

Translated by Ryan H. Wines

Notes

This essay was originally published as *Walter Benjamin—ein moderner Marcionit? Scholems Benjamin-Interpretation religionsgeschichtlich überprüft*, in *Antike und Moderne. Zu Walter Benjamins "Passage,"* ed. Norbert Bolz and Richard Faber (Würzburg: Königshausen und Neumann, 1986), 138–147.

1. Cf. Ernst Bloch, *Atheismus im Christentum: Zur Religion des Exodus und des Reichs* (Frankfurt am Main: Suhrkamp, 1968), 15. *Atheism in Christianity: The Religion of the Exodus and the Kingdom* (New York: Herder and Herder, 1972).

2. Cf. Walter Benjamin, "Über den Begriff der Geschichte," in *Gesammelte Schriften*, vol. 1.2 (Frankfurt am Main: Suhrkamp, 1974), 693. "On the Concept of History," in *Selected Writings*, vol. 4, *1938–1940*, ed. Howard Eiland and Michael W. Jennings (Cambridge, MA: Harvard University Press, 2006).

3. Ernst Bloch, *Geist der Utopie* (München-Leipzig: Duncker und Humblot, 1918; repr: Frankfurt am Main: Suhrkamp, 1975). *The Spirit of Utopia* (Stanford, CA: Stanford University Press, 2000).

4. Cf. Walter Benjamin, "Theologisch-politisches Fragment," in *Gesammelte Schriften*, vol. 2.1 (Frankfurt am Main: Suhrkamp, 1977), 203. "Theological-Political Fragment," in *Selected Writings*, vol. 3, *1935–1938*, ed. Howard Eiland and Michael W. Jennings (Cambridge, MA: Harvard University Press, 2006), 305–306.

5. Marx-Engels, *Studienausgabe*, vol. 1 (Frankfurt am Main: Fischer Taschenbuch, 1966), 31–60. "On the Jewish Question," in *Karl Marx: Selected Writings*, 2nd ed., ed. David McLellan (Oxford: Oxford University Press, 2000), 46–63.

6. Cf. Gershom Scholem, *Walter Benjamin. Geschichte einer Freundschaft* (Frankfurt am Main: Suhrkamp, 1975), 276–278. *Walter Benjamin: The Story of a Friendship* (Philadelphia: Jewish Publication Society of America, 1981).

7. Marx-Engels, *Studienausgabe*, 1:45.

8. Cf. Walter Benjamin, *Gesammelte Briefe*, vol. 1, ed. Gershom Scholem and Theodor W. Adorno (Frankfurt am Main: Suhrkamp, 1978), 362. *The Correspondence of Walter Benjamin, 1910–1940* (Chicago: Chicago University Press, 1996).

9. Cf. Gershom Scholem, "Walter Benjamin" in *Walter Benjamin und sein Engel: Vierzehn Aufsätze und kleine Beiträge* (Frankfurt am Main: Suhrkamp, 1983), 28–34, and "Walter Benjamin und sein Engel," in ibid., 63–68.

10. Gershom Scholem, "Zum Verständnis der messianischen Idee im Judentum," in *Judaica* (Frankfurt am Main: Suhrkamp, 1963), 7. "Toward and Understanding of the Messianic Idea in Judaism," in *The Messianic Idea in Judaism and Other Essays on Jewish Spirituality* (New York: Schocken Books, 1971), 1–36.

11. Cf. Ibid., 8.

12. Cf. Ibid., 35, where Scholem cites the professor of theology Karl Bornhausen as the source of the phrase "wondrous certainty of pure interiority."

13. Ibid., 37.

14. Cf. Benjamin, "Theologisch-politisches Fragment," in *Gesammelte Schriften*, 2.1:204.

15. Ibid.

16. Ibid.

17. Cf. Benjamin, *Briefe*, 2:525–533, and Gerschom Sholem, *Walter Benjamin: Geschichte einer Freundschaft* (Frankfurt am Main: Suhrkamp, 1975), 196ff. *Correspondence of Walter Benjamin*, and Scholem, *Walter Benjamin: The Story of a Friendship* (Frankfurt am Main: Suhrkamp, 2001).

18. Scholem, "Zum Verständnis der messianischen Idee im Judentum," 74.

19. Cf. Josephus, *Contra Apionem* II, 165. Cf. also H. Cancik, "Theokratie und Priesterherrschaft. Die mosaische Verfassung bei Flavius Josephus, C. Apionem 2, 157–198," in *Relationstheorie und Politische Theologie*, vol. 3, *Theokratie*, ed. Jacob Taubes (München-Paderborn-Wein-Zürich: Schöningh, 1987), 65–77.

20. Scholem. "Zum Verständnis der messianischen Idee im Judentum," 74.

21. Cf. Josephus, *Bellum Judaicum*, II, 8 and *Antiquitates Judaicae*, XVIII, 1, 6.

22. Martin Buber *Zwei Glaubensweisen* (Zürich: Manesse, 1950). *Two Types of Faith* (New York: Macmillian, 1951).

23. Cf. H. J. Schoeps, *Paulus. Die Theologie des Apostels im Lichte der jüdischen Religionsgeschichte* (Tübingen: J.C.B. Mohr, 1959), 314. *Paul: The Theology of the Apostle in the Light of Jewish Religious History* (Philadelphia: Westminster Press, 1979).

24. Ibid., 146.

25. And, as I believe, really would have had a chance in the struggle, if they would not have been forsaken by the Jewish Diaspora and betrayed and vilified by the Pharisees and the rabbis, whose leading representative, Rabban Johanan ben Zakai plays "dead" in order to have himself brought out of the besieged Jerusalem in a casket by his closest students to Vespasian, the besieger of Jerusalem, to whom he flatteringly prophesies the imperial crown of Rome, and "arranges" with him that the rabbinical authority would remain guaranteed from then on).

26. A. von Harnack, *Marcion, das Evangelium vom fremden Gott: Eine Monographie zur Geschichte der Grundlegung der katholischen Kirchen* (Leipzig: J. G. Henrichs, 1921; repr. Darmstadt: Wissenschaftliche Buchgesellschaft, 1985). *Marcion: The Gospel of the Alien God* (Durham: Labyrinth Press, 1990).

27. Martin Buber, "Reden über Judentum," in *Werke*, vol. 3 (München-Heidelberg: Kösel, Lambert Schneider, 1964), 151.

28. Ibid., 152.

29. Von Harnack, *Marcion, das Evangelium vom fremden Gott*, 217.

30. Buber, "Reden über Judentum," in *Werke*, 3:152.

31. Bloch, *Geist der Utopie*, 330.

32. Ernst Bloch, *Das Prinzip Hoffnung* (1953; repr. Frankfurt am Main: Suhrkamp, 1959), 1499–1500. *The Principle of Hope* (Cambridge, MA: MIT Press, 1995).

33. Ibid., 1500.

34. Ernst Bloch, *Atheismus im Christentum: Zur Religion des Exodus und des Reichs* (Frankfurt am Main: Suhrkamp, 1968), 237ff. *Atheism in Christianity: The Religion of the Exodus and the Kingdom* (New York: Herder and Herder, 1972).

35. Cf. Benjamin, "Über den Begriff der Geschichte," in *Gesammelte Schriften*, 1.2:701.

36. Cf. Ibid., 695.

Seminar Notes on Walter Benjamin's "Theses on the Philosophy of History"

JACOB TAUBES

Translator's Introduction

The following text is the first English translation of seminar notes taken in a seminar on Walter Benjamin's "Theses on the Philosophy of History" given by Jacob Taubes in 1984 at the Freie Universität Berlin, where Taubes held the Chair for Jewish Studies and Hermeneutics.[1]

The notes were initially published in the German edition of Elettra Stimilli's documentation of Taubes's critical confrontation with Gershom Scholem's work on the phenomenon of Messianism and its history.[2] They cover the first seven sessions of Taubes's course on Benjamin, which took place from October 18 to December 6, 1984, before Taubes had to discontinue the seminar for medical reasons. (The course was then taken over by his student and assistant, Norbert Bolz.) Due to their character as seminar notes as well as the fact that they were not written down by a native speaker of German, the notes are fragmentary and occasionally border on unintelligibility. Frequent grammatical errors at times result in semantic ambiguities that cannot be resolved. Moreover, the scant editorial interventions by Stimilli in the German edition of these notes are in many instances unhelpful, and generally provide little support for the task of establishing the meaning of the text.[3] Any interpretative decisions that had to be made in the process of translating these notes are indicated in the endnotes.

Obvious grammatical errors that leave no doubt as to the intended meaning have been corrected. I also adjusted any odd and apparently random punctuation, if the result helped to clarify the text. When the text's ambiguity was found to be irresolvable, I have decided to preserve this ambiguity in my translation. In less obvious and uncontroversial instances where reasonable conjectures as to the notes' intended meaning seemed defensible, I "adjusted" my translation accordingly and indicated the basis for my conjecture in the footnotes. Rather than provide each of the problematic passages of the German original in their entirety, I limit myself to briefly pointing out the reasons for my interpretations, leaving it to the reader to compare the translation with Stimilli's edition, which is readily accessible. Minor editorial clarifications have been placed in square brackets.[4]

Although my translation is more heavily edited than the German version of the seminar notes, it was not my aim to smooth out the fragmentary, raw, and sometimes cumbersome character of the original notes; consequently the translation may yet be quite obscure at places.[5] The aim of this translation was to bring across the intended meaning of Taubes's commentary as closely as possible, even at the price of preserving—and perhaps, even, occasionally exacerbating—the linguistic and semantic shortcomings of the German original. If that intended meaning remained obscure in the original German, it was left obscure in the translation in as analogous a way as possible.

Despite their problematic literary character, the seminar notes provide some highly interesting insights into Taubes's reading of Benjamin's "Theses on the Philosophy of History," and his interpretation of Benjamin in general. Because of the premature end of Taubes's involvement in the seminar, the notes cover only the first seven of Benjamin's theses in detail. Nonetheless, in the spirit of Taubes's reading of the theses—according to which "each one of [them] is a complete unified whole in which the entirety of the *Theses* can be found" (session of December 6, 1984)—Taubes's interpretation may be said to be incomplete and complete at the same time. In keeping with his dialectical characterization of the individual theses relative to the series, Taubes frequently anticipates and alludes to the later ones in his discussion of the first seven theses. He refers to the first thesis as "the common denominator, which is subsequently elaborated in an ordered sequence in the various theses" (November 22, 1984). For Taubes, "[The first thesis] designates the program. Historical materialism needs to enlist the services of theology. This program, this 'enlisting-of-services' appears in ever new forms and facets [in the subsequent theses]" (December 6, 1984).

What is especially important to note in the context of the present volume is that Taubes opens his seminar by stating that "the turn from the theological to the materialist does not prove to be true," and "the basic motifs of Benjamin's thought are preserved while being transformed [in the 'Theses']" (October 18, 1984). In this way, Taubes takes a position against the tendency to downplay the importance of theology for Benjamin, as well as the tendency to downplay Benjamin's appropriation of historical materialism. Taubes's reading takes the side of neither Adorno nor Scholem. Taubes stresses that Benjamin's call to "enlist the services of theology" does not imply a rejection or "dissolution" of theology, but rather that the latter is to be "put to service *as* theology," that is, as being concerned with *redemption* (October 25, 1984).

Other intriguing aspects of Taubes's interpretation are his serious attention to the metaphysical presuppositions of Benjamin's model of the relationship of past and present, and its confrontation with Heidegger, as well as Taubes's emphasis on the fact that Benjamin's critique of historicism is motivated, at once, by political and epistemological concerns. Taubes aptly remarks that "the differences between Heidegger and Benjamin should not blind us to what they have in *common*" (November 1, 1984), a suggestion that Taubes likely would have pursued further had he been able to continue the seminar. Precisely in their rejection of a contemplatively minded historicism, the concerns of Benjamin and Heidegger converge, even though they have a very different kind of actualization of the past in mind, which they respectively seek to substitute for the aesthetic or antiquarian concern with "the way it really was," and the complacent belief in history as a history of progress.

In an original and suggestive reading, Taubes puts considerable stress on Benjamin's critique of the contemplative historian's "intellectual empathy" and the corresponding leisureliness of his activity as the "*organon*" of his knowledge, contrasting it with the historical materialist's encounter with the past "at a moment of danger" ("Thesis VI"). In a reading that exhibits traces of Taubes's studying with and study of Leo Strauss, Taubes sees Benjamin's critique of the historian's *acedia* ("Thesis VII") as a continuation of the Church Fathers'—especially Augustine's—critique of philosophy as the highest form of human life: "There is likely no passage in the works of Benjamin that is more Christian than *Thesis VII*" ("Leisure").

In his typical fashion, Taubes reconstructs "against whom" Benjamin wrote his theses, namely, against both contemplative historicism as well as the theory of continuous progress (even in its historical-materialist form)— antagonistic positions that Benjamin shares with the writers of the so-called conservative revolution—*and* against the conservative-revolutionary writers such as Ludwig Klages, Carl Schmitt, and Heidegger. At the same time, Taubes develops his reading in a constant, implicit and explicit confrontation with the various strands of Benjamin interpretation and appropriation. In his reading that rises beyond the politically charged opposition of a theological versus a materialist interpretation of Walter Benjamin, Taubes can be seen to anticipate some of the more balanced and sober scholarship of the last three decades, without falling into the trap of a scholarly neutrality that would fail to do justice to the urgency of Benjamin's final text.

> This document of Benjamin's—the last of his texts—treats
> and gathers all his theses under a new concept of history,
> which departs from and contrasts with both the historicist
> conception of history and the conception of history as
> determined by progress, and which teaches us to distinguish
> time that is historically fulfilled [*geschichtlich erfüllte*] from
> homogenous and empty time. The individual theses are going
> to serve as the basis for discussion in the seminar.
>
> J. Taubes, "'List of Courses with Course-Descriptions'
> Winter-Semester 1984/85," 11.

October 18, 1984

Legend of the Materialist Turn

The text—Benjamin's theses on the history of philosophy—is of particular interest because the turn from the theological to the materialist does not prove to be true. The basic motifs of Benjamin's thought are preserved while being transformed, i.e. [he has] recourse to earlier forms in order to achieve a new determination of the status of history. The theses can be read as an "epistemological" preface to the *Arcades Project*. If the epistemo-critical prologue to the book on baroque furnishes the framework of the form of the tragic drama, of the *Trauerspiel*, the theses on the philosophy of history furnish the framework for the unfinished *Arcades Project*.

Instruction/Identification of Method

From which accompanying texts do arguments proceed, when argument are made?

In each instance this is to be identified in Benjamin['s texts]/in the spirit of Benjamin himself.

Thesis I

The first thesis begins with a simile. The background to the simile is furnished by Edgar Allan Poe's *Maelzel's Chess Player*:

> "A system of mirrors created the illusion that this table was transparent from all sides."[6] (Thesis I)

The task of historical materialism is to make history transparent, to elucidate it. This claim, this task is rigorously executed in both the *Phenomenology of Spirit* (Hegel) and in *Capital* (Marx).

"Actually, a little hunchback who was an expert player sat inside and guided the puppet's hand by means of strings." (Ibid.)

Benjamin wants this image and finds it appropriate and accurate for the purpose of reflecting on philosophy.

"One can imagine a philosophical counterpart to this device." (Ibid.)

But how? Marxism's theory of history (historical materialism) is portrayed as the mere outward appearance, as the puppet. This puppet sits on a table, which is transparent from all sides. The strength of its theory is its transparency: yet Benjamin wants to expose this transparency as an illusion. [The theory is] transparent only by means of a system of mirrors which conceal the fact that the puppet itself is guided by means of strings. Guided by a little hunchback.[7] It is only after this has been recognized that historical materialism can or could do without any other concept of history, i.e., it could be a match for any such concept, "if it enlists the services of theology which nowadays, as we know, has become small and ugly and has to keep out of sight anyway" (ibid.).

Theology. What is Benjamin referring to here? What kind of experience does theology articulate?

Interpretative suggestion: to read the thesis from the perspective of its end.

Does not historical materialism's strength—[i.e.,] to think about, to reflect on history—derive from—[is it not] the still lingering effect [of]—German idealism (from Kant to Hegel)? Respectively from the "invisible hand." Kant taking over [this insight] from Adam Smith all the way to "absolute Spirit" (Hegel).[8]

How is historical materialism to be victorious, if it enlists the services of theology [*die Theologie*[9]]? Does it not in this way destroy what is most characteristic of it?

History is understood more profoundly (deeply) than nature: nature cannot be made, but history can.

Shortcoming of historical materialism: theology. Benjamin is concerned with the victory and with the defeat of historical materialism, although it is coherent.

What can still be expected or gained from theology, not in the sense of the theology of the church, in this age of profanization?[10] What does theology signify here? Did it not gratuitously cede ground to historical materialism: such as redemption/salvation, Dux (leader, ruler), millenarian kingdom? What does theology, what does Theology [*die Theologie*] mean here? Does Benjamin have images in mind?

"As is known"—at the beginning, as well as at the end of the thesis[11]—means: generally recognized. Historical materialism *ossifies* because it does not enlist the services of theology. There are powers at work in theology that are not even put to use yet.

Theology is for Benjamin messianism/the Messiah. It seems to be implausible, a dream, a myth. Historical materialism would have to enter into a pact with it. Historical materialism is *not* a Marxian expression, it is only in the second phase [of Marx's *Wirkungsgeschichte*] that the expression *historical materialism* is used to refer to the codified doctrine of Marxism (cf. Karl Kautsky among others). Historical materialism—here Benjamin stands in the tradition of the critics. [The tradition of] criticism of social democracy and the Third International, however, takes on a peculiar form with Benjamin: he wants to let historical materialism win *as* a thesis.

Not a recourse to theology, but rather utilization [*Indienstnahme*] of theology for a theory of history which, however, cannot be reduced to a theory of history, but rather is to be conceived from the perspective of an end: History is to be thought from the perspective of the end.

"As is known"—this means theology is in a state of retreat.

Which paradox is Benjamin demanding here? Who has constructed the automaton? Will the images, the experiences be utilized [*in den Dienst genommen*]? Who is holding whom to account, on whose behalf?[12] Questions upon questions—how could it be otherwise?

However, the first thesis is no redemption "as if" as Adorno understands it in the last section of his *Minima Moralia*.[13]

October 25, 1984

Interpretative procedure: The theses are *interwoven* and demand to be *read* accordingly.

What is the status of this black box? It is pointing toward a status that for Benjamin constitutes a weakness, or rather *its* weakness.

"As is known"—history follows a determined course: [history, according to] historical materialism, unwinds in an automatic fashion. The table of history is clear, or transparent on all sides. Advertised elements of historical materialism: as theory of history to make that theory transparent, or to shed light on it. Inversion of the image: that which is transparent is now directed.

The *metaphor of the game* is important: the theoretical position of historical materialism is supposed to win.

Theology—not inquired into at first—is what *can* come to historical materialism's aid, if the latter enlists its services.

Paradox: can historical science, which puts the emphasis on immanently reconstructing history gain from such a service, from such a utilization of theology? Is the project of [a science/theory of] history not being reduced *ad absurdum*? How could theology be of service to such a theory?

(1) Does Benjamin not mean that historical materialism succeeds in throwing light upon the *misty region* of theology, if the subtle nature of the superstructure (religion, etc.) was more comprehensible?—Taubes draws attention to the antiquated character of the base/superstructure scheme—This is not the case here!

(2) Theology is to be utilized [*in den Dienst genommen*] as theology, the latter is not to be dissolved. "Theology" signifies a particular tendency: REDEMPTION. A word that comes up in the overall context of historical materialism.

How Is Theology to Be Employed?

All subsequent theses are subordinated to this precept. Benjamin attempts to demonstrate this "enlisting of services [*in den Dienst nehmen*]" and attempts to develop a concept of theology that can go together with the radical immanence of historical materialism. [He does so] not by means of a theological treatise, but rather by questioning the immanence of history, by pointing out elements that are only noticeable while they "flit by" (Thesis V); [he does so] by pointing out that the driving elements [of history] develop possibilities, a dynamic, which otherwise remains paralyzed. Benjamin is concerned with resolving this paralysis. He does not employ direct theological examples, they are rather being built into the ethos that is constitutive of humanity (revolutionary process [*Gang*]).

(In the *Arcades Project* as well, Benjamin is cautious in drawing closer [*in der Annäherung*] to theology).

The end of the 1930s marks a fundamental problem: theology and/vs. historical materialism (the statements of Anders and Brecht are pointed out[14]).

The concern of the first thesis is opened up in the second thesis.

Thesis II

Interpretative procedure: A) read by itself, and B) how this "enlisting of services" transpires [in the second thesis].

". . . that our image of happiness is thoroughly colored by the time"[15] (Thesis II)

The idea of redemption resonates in the idea of happiness. Here, however, there is a leap.

Excursus 1: Theological-Political Fragment (1920/21)

Redemption and happiness are the central concepts of this fragment. Happiness is to be geared toward the "order of the profane."[16] The order of the profane effects the passing-away. This characteristic manner of expression [*Duktus*] remains constant throughout Benjamin's work.

What does Benjamin mean by "mystical conception of history"?

Our present is evanescent and there is another generation that cites what-is-past [*das Vergangene*]. We, as the ones who exist now [*Jetzt-Seiende*[17]] do not signify the (mystical) Now [*Nu*[18]]. This actuality [*Aktualität*[19]] [inherent] in what-is-past, or in the past, shows that the relation between past and present is not static. What-is-past is directed toward the future, toward the present, toward what is *expected*.

The difficulties lie for Benjamin in the concept of universal history and in the concept of actualization [*Aktualisierung*]. He can, however, uphold them, stand by them, preserve them under the key of the messianic. Here too Benjamin *carefully* introduces a *theologoumenon*. Redemption does not mean a final revolution at the end of history. Here the messianic is *distributed* across history and the generations.

Excursus 2: Lotze and Saint-Simon

If one reads the quote from Hermann Lotze in the context of another passage from Lotze's *Mikrokosmos: Ideen zur Naturgeschichte und Geschichte der Menschheit* (Leipzig 1909) [and] with a view to Benjamin's second thesis, especially with a view to the constellation weak messianic power/the weaker sex/wives and sisters, then the thesis approaches Saint-Simon's conception very closely, his conception in which the messianic figures as the feminine, woman as redeemer/redemption.

> "And, it is asked finally, is it not this unhistorical life that is actually lived by the greatest part of mankind? For the unrest and variety of revolutions and transformations, the meaning and connection of which we are seeking, is yet, when all is said, the history of the male sex alone; women move on through all this toil and struggle hardly even touched by its changing lights, ever presenting afresh in uniform fashion the grand and simple types in which the life of the human soul is manifested. Is their existence to count for nothing, or have we only for a moment forgotten its significance in scholastic zeal for the Idea of historical development?"[20]

(There are passages in the *Arcades Project* that go into the topic of the "female Messiah," la Mère[21])

The salvation of what-is-past is the task of the historiographer who *narrates* events. [The] comparison of the experience of happiness in the individual sphere and the collective sphere [*im Individuellen und Kollektiven*] is directly tied together [*verspannt*] *as* history.

Enlisting the services of theology is not a *theologoumenon*, but rather what is pronounced by theology, in a cautious manner [is a *theologoumenon*].[22]

What remains undecided: does the weak messianic sex signify transcendence, or is what is weak that which is messianic in human beings?

Contrasting delineation from the Saint-Simonian reading. "Weak" is read in the Paulinian sense: messianic in what is weak [*im Schwachen*] ([which] is also Lotze's reading).

The second thesis, like the third one, falls into the category of mystical description. Enlisting the services of theology proceeds in a secular manner. Without this procedure history would be condemned to a lack of coherent connectedness [*Zusammenhanglosigkeit*].

November 1, 1984

Thesis II

The second thesis is to be read/can be read as an implementation of [what is demanded in] the introduction: what is the state of historical materialism,[23] when it "enlists the services of theology."

The second thesis marks the peculiar form of theology: as weak, messianic power. The "proof" is no *theologoumenon*, rather [it consists in] references to our natural life; in happiness, in women's breathing, a frill[24] shines through [*deutet sich an*]: rather, where a frill shines through.[25] In these natural experiences something implicitly theological [*ein impliziertes Theologisches*] constitutes itself, which Benjamin then sums up under [the notion of] a "weak messianic power."

Thesis III

The third thesis differs from the second, in that here we are presented with a certain form of *narration* [*Erzählung*], which does not look like it has something to do with the "enlisting of the services" of theology, but which, in its simplicity, lets the entirety of the scheme of redemption flash up.

The simple form of the narration (of history) is that of the chronicler. The chronicler is the opposite of the constructor:

> "A chronicler who narrates events without distinguishing between major and minor ones acts in accordance with the following truth: nothing that has ever happened should be regarded as lost to history." (Thesis III)

This is the problem of historical narrative [*Geschichtserzählung*]—that it makes choices, that it is selective. Every utterance also makes manifest what is left *unsaid*. The lie is that which is not narrated. Nothing may be forgotten!

How is the transition made to the subsequent sentences of the thesis?

> "To be sure, only a redeemed mankind receives the fullness of its past—which is to say, only for a redeemed mankind has its past become citable in all its moments. Each moment it has lived becomes a *citation à l'ordre du jour*—and that day is Judgment Day." (Ibid.)

Redeemed from what? And what is the status of the past here? What is the status of the narrator? (A form of the narrator is introduced with the figure of the chronicler).

Is there such a thing as an arresting, a determination of the past? Or does this only happen *qua* narration, whereby the past becomes citable?

The chronicle is a *pre*-causal historical description. That what-is-past is past is already *to be blamed on consciousness*. Our finite, porous consciousness allows for events to fall through the cracks. The writing of history would be the mode in which to bring back to notice that which was pushed aside into what-is-past. This division of past/present/future is a derivative form. Benjamin does not lapse here into a kind of historicism. (Kittsteiner's thesis according to which Benjamin is not a historical materialist, but rather a *materialist historian*, according to which Benjamin's theory of history is not a historical materialism, but a "materialistic historicism"[26]—this thesis does *not* apply to Benjamin.)

The formula: historicism is equally close to God (Ranke),[27] anticipates a state of redemption. With Benjamin one is *in* this redeemed state, in the redeemed state of mankind. "Redeemed mankind" is also a liberation from the ways of being entangled [*Weisen der Verknüpfungen*].[28]

Interpretative Instruction: Reading Benjamin Like a pre-Socratic

Only at the end will all that is past be visible and transparent; here, of course, Benjamin is moving in a circle. Judgment day is not the spectacle at the end, but is rather possible in every complete memory [*Vollerinnerung*]. In/from this perspective, it is or becomes possible to understand Benjamin's rejection of a final condition: redemption is possible *anytime*. Judgment Day is built into time, which can abort [*abbrechen*]. This is the point of Benjamin's critique of the theological image, and of historical materialism as well, because for both Judgment Day is the spectacle at the end. This is different for Benjamin: Incorporation [*Hineinnahme*] of the idea of the end *into time itself.* That is to say: a punctiform, lightning-like breakthrough. Not a single day is excluded. The apocalyptic form is therefore embedded[29] in a *presentist time.*

While historical materialism, in its classic implementation or in its classic form, understands "time" as an *epochal* form, Benjamin's historical materialism will be subsumed [*gefasst*] under the revolutionary, in the sense of the *sudden*—this latter aspect is emphasized in Benjamin. Benjamin introduces a manner of thinking into historical materialism that is bound to blast it open. Benjamin's model is thus directed at action.

The third thesis intertwines and/or advocates a critique of theology just as/and a critique of historical materialism.[30]

Every narration anticipates the state of redemption in conceptual terms [*im Begriff*]. The transition to a redeemed humanity is not adventurous, because redeemed humanity is not set before an end. This presupposes or is based on the idea of the copresence of past, present and future, as in the divine mind. In principle, this idea does not have[31]—or rather it is not based on any human experience.

The case of man, and his fall,[32] is that time has cast [*gebannt*] itself into these three forms of experience.[33]

Every narration is also a salvation from the torrential past. What is forgotten is not forgotten *in itself*, it passes away though our forgetting. The narrator of history has taken on the function of Messiah.

With Benjamin, the historical perspective is at the same time "linked up" with a *metaphysical* perspective. The end is understood as present time. Revolution is thus not bound to a process of maturation: this has decisive epistemological consequences:

This understanding of time is based on [the idea] that presence can be broken through anytime, and on the process of narrating being granted a high status of salvation.[34]

The third thesis, read ontologically, and understood as an ontological thesis, marks the place from which Benjamin is speaking out: that the dissolution/its dissolution of time is already the case for it/is already its fall from grace [*ihr Fall ist*[35]]. Benjamin does not advocate a messianic futorologism, but rather a *messianic actualism*.

Benjamin's Shadow: Heidegger

The irritation (about Heidegger's work on Duns Scotus) as well as the proximity to Heidegger's distinction between qualitative and quantitative time—while these subjects [*Topoi*] are off [*schief*] in Heidegger—make for the fields/points where Benjamin makes contact with Heidegger.

One of the main differences consists in the presentation of time and history. While both, Heidegger as well as Benjamin, see history understood in terms of a sequence merely as the surface of history [*Historie*], while both experience the condensation of history in breakthroughs, in the sudden (rush, rashness), for Heidegger an original [*ursprüngliche*] humanity is in balance [*im Maß*]; for Benjamin, on the other hand, redeemed mankind is the measure [*das Maß*].

The differences between Heidegger and Benjamin should not blind us to what they have in *common*.

Differences between Heidegger and Benjamin: Being is to be interpreted with a view to a time that sublates [*aufhebt*] the sequences/sequence: past/present/future. This is read off from an idea of time, which is connected to life and the present instance [*Augenblick*]. From here, one can find the way to Proust: the distinction of two times by Proust. Metaphysical conceptions of time can be found in Benjamin's works on the philosophy of language.

The transformation becomes clear or is made most clearly in the case of the doctrine regarding theology. From this point, from the [perspective of] change, from the experience of the *"ordre du jour"* the service of theology can be enlisted.

"*Citation à l'ordre du jour*—and that day is Judgment Day" (Thesis III). Judgment Day, the threatening day; the danger is an elevated condition, into which the whole of life is condensed and in which it becomes visible.

The third thesis comprises the following constellation: chronicler/redeemed mankind/*citation a l'ordre du jour*/Judgment Day.

November 8, 1984

Review of Theses I–III

In the first thesis is elaborated/the problem is elaborated, what the conditions are, in which historical materialism can be a match for any theory of history, and [Benjamin] refers to theology, whose services are to be enlisted.[36]

The second and third theses were examples of how such an enlistment-of-services can occur. In the second thesis the *code-word of theology* entered the scene: weak messianic force.

The third thesis was the attempt to point out this weak messianic force by the example of the simple form of historical narrating: the chronicle. Precisely the nonconstructive manner of the chronicler does justice to the truth that nothing is lost for history.

The latter—that "nothing is lost"—is elaborated by means of the model of memory, which one could call a [*psycho*]*analytic* model. Even though what-is-past is present, it is covered over. Only upon redeemed mankind does what-is-past entirely devolve; in [psycho]analysis what-is-past is uncovered for someone who has detached himself from the drives, and it becomes citable. This citing does however involve a *threatening* aspect: Judgment Day is not only the day of happiness, but also of *annihilation*.

Preview of Theses IV–VIII

In Theses IV–VIII, Benjamin speaks about historical materialism itself, that is to say: how historical materialism itself, if understood, can interpret *itself*.

Thesis IV

The fourth thesis starts with an epigraph, which itself belongs to the problem of the utilization of theology:

> "Seek for food and clothing first, then the Kingdom of God shall be added unto you." (Hegel, 1807)

Hegel, in a letter to Knebel, dated August 30, 1807,[37] hence at the time of the *Phenomenology of Spirit* (1807), inverts a fundamental statement [*Grundwort*] of the Sermon on the Mount (Matthew, 5–7). The enlisting of the services of theology does not proceed *directly*, but is rather an enlisting of the services that has gone through the whole of history.

"Seek for food and clothing first" means to say[38] that first all material elements have to be taken care of, and only then/after that the spiritual ones. But this is not how the problem presents itself to historical materialism. The material and the spiritual aspects are *intertwined*. The spiritual is involved in the struggle for the material.

> "The class struggle, which is always present to a historian influenced by Marx, is a fight for the crude and material things without which no refined and spiritual things could exist." (Thesis IV)

According to Benjamin, the spiritual elements are present *in a different manner* in the class struggle than the bourgeois imagines them to be: as spoils, they go to the victor. They, the spiritual elements, are [present] in the subterranean ways that determine the material ways.

The attitudes Benjamin highlights make the struggle possible in the first place. Benjamin does not envisage a base/superstructure model. The kind of struggle that is the class struggle is fought by spiritual means: confidence, courage (cockiness), wit, humor, cunning. These latter are at work in the class struggle.

What does "they have retroactive force that retro-acts into the distance of time" mean?[39]

Only these present attitudes developed by the oppressed pry open the past.—In what manner?

It seems like two possibilities to appropriate the past or to act on it are developing. There is no nonpartisan history. The victor and the oppressed retro-act into the distance of time.—In what manner?

The victor retro-acts in the manner of consolidating a tradition by his victories. The oppressed does so by questioning the previous victories and prying open the tradition. The attitudes which are alive in the present class struggle—like confidence, courage, wit, and cunning among others—are not only ways to hold one's own in the now, but also ways of wresting what-is-past from the victorious form of tradition. Here Benjamin sees a *unity* of history, despite all change: that it is a history of the rulers. The ruling history is questioned *in principle* by the perspective from within the class struggle [*von der klassenkämpferischen Optik*].

> "As flowers turn toward the sun, by dint of a secret
> heliotropism the past strives to turn toward the sun which is
> rising in the sky of history." (Thesis IV)

There are some difficulties with this simile, which point toward a fundamental expression [*Grundwort*]: that of "secret agreement" (cf. Thesis II).

"Weak messianic force" also means the possibility of an end of history. The "secret agreement" between past generations and ours turns every presence of the now [*Jetzt-Zeit*] into a potentially messianic time. This is, for Benjamin, the secret agreement; this is that messianic force which every generation is endowed with. In a *new turn*, this "conspiracy-theory" also appears in the theology of class struggle.

How is it that—despite all the victories and victors of history—morale is not low, the struggle is still alive [and fought] with confidence? This leads Benjamin back to a natural tendency, a tendency that is inherent in history: heliotropism, [which Benjamin illustrates] with examples from nature itself. Just as in nature flowers, *naturalia*, align themselves toward the sun, so it seems as if in history what-has-been [*das Gewesene*] turns itself toward the sun. What does that mean? What does the transition from nature to history signify?

The past itself, what-has-been, turns itself toward the sun.

Sharp metaphors: sun, sky[40] of history.

[According to] Benjamin's esoteric doctrine, which is so sharply connected to the theory of class struggle, it appears that what what-is-past strives for is proliferating.[41]

Here, as in the second and third theses, what-is-past is not past, but present. In what manner is it present, and how is it covered over?

What-has-been appears to have a status in itself, which is only obsolete through being covered over. A status [of what-has-been], which is and appears present, is a metaphysical presupposition: [what-has-been] wants by itself to get to the surface.[42]

What does "sky of history" signify? Is it a casually pulled-out metaphor, or is it demanded by the matter at hand itself? Taking up Plato's simile of the sun: *methexis*?

There is a logic inherent in the first part of the fourth thesis: class struggle, struggle for the crude things without which there are no spiritual things. However, they exist differently in the victors. Benjamin takes the side of the oppressed, and brings the elements, the spiritual attitudes—confidence, cunning, courage, among others—into play, brings them into play as presentist attitudes, whereby the victory of the rulers is put into question.

However, this is problematic: in itself, there is no chance at all that the losers of history are capable of memory. So strongly is the weight of the victory of the rulers covered up by masks, in the form of a continuous anticipation [*Vorlauf*]; so strongly does Benjamin emphasize that something like memories, traces in the memory of human beings, are possible. And here Benjamin's recourse to *historical* heliotropism is correct. The heliotropism of the historical kind has strong metaphysical presuppositions in Benjamin: "sun" refers to Plato's parable of the cave; "sky" refers to the epistemo-critical prologue of the *Trauerspiel* book; "ideas as stars" (in the nightly sky) [function] here by heliotropism [as] a metaphor for the day. Thus, *here* a simile of sun and not a simile of stars is brought up. What-has-been itself—rather than an attitude or a human reaction—is said to have such a quality.

Benjamin's concept of origin is a transition of the Goethe's [concept of origin] into a historical concept.

Karl Marx

The Eighteenth Brumaire of Louis Bonaparte conserves Karl Marx's theory of history. Benjamin makes a correction of the Marxian metaphysical presuppositions of history. "The tradition of all dead generations weighs like a nightmare on the brains of the living,"[43] we read in Marx. Benjamin, on the other hand, presents what-is-past not as a nightmare, but rather as an element (cf. Thesis XIV), *where* what-is-past is charged with the presence of the now. Precisely what Marx rejects as "necromancy,"[44] is for Benjamin the guarantee that the revolution will happen.[45]

Ontology/Benjamin/Heidegger II

What does ontology mean here? Inquiring after the status of what-is-past. What-is-past is not past. Heidegger articulates history into past, present, and future: history becomes ontologized as historicity, which is always already prior to this articulation. In Benjamin, the ontologizing is not very conspicuous; while Heidegger freezes what has happened, in Benjamin's theory what has happened, what-has-been flashes up in a messianic theory.

(Attitude = subjective factor (cf. Simmel's concept).)

The transition from [the narration[46]] to the image is a transition that is a kind of correspondence: to the attitudes (subjective factor/sphere) like confidence, courage, cunning, among others, corresponds something in the objective sphere, namely heliotropism. The condition of possibility lies in what is subjective [*im Subjektiven*], the objective sphere has the possibility of what-has-been.[47]

The images remain empty, if they are not probed for their complex metaphysical presuppositions.

Is what-is-past that which is completed, or does it only become accessible in struggle? (*Ontologicum* signifies the idea "what is."[48]) What-is-past only devolves upon a redeemed mankind.

Difference to Heidegger with a View to Heliotropism

What does the last sentence signify?

> "A historical materialist must be able to detect this most inconspicuous of all transformations." (Thesis IV)

It is this nonapparent [transformation], which urges what is changed; it is this secret thing, by which the historical materialist is challenged, which he needs to be able to detect.[49]

Benjamin's mystical theory of correspondence, which is the basis of historical materialism if it were to understand itself—that is what the historical materialist must master.

November 15, 1984

What-has-been is not the past (Thesis IV). The theory of class struggle and historical materialism as well interpret history not merely as events, as consciously made by human beings (cf. Vico), but also as made behind their backs: a double level behind historical materialism (however *not* in the way presented by Benjamin in the *fourth* thesis).

The tendency of what-has-been is very *inconspicuous*: if it were to go unnoticed, the simile would not make sense. The tendency of what-has-been itself, this striving is a constitutive element, which Benjamin connects with the theory that what-has-been is not isolated [*abgeschieden*], but rather still has effects [*durchwirkt*[50]]; this element longs for salvation, Benjamin emphasizes. (It is superfluous to designate this as an ontological, as opposed to an *actualist* interpretation.)

Thesis V

This becomes easier to understand when considering the fifth thesis. In the latter it becomes clear that this substrate is not abstract, but is rather connected with the reality of the images.[51]

"The true image of the past *flits* by." (Thesis V)

That means the past changes, it is determined anew in every new present, which changes every moment.—If the past *flits* by, how is the past to be seized? How is the past given *anew*? [So] that it can be determined anew by the present? *Here*, Benjamin's "epistemology of the historical object" is on *full* display.

"The past can be seized only as an image which flashes up at the instant when it can be recognized and is never seen again." (Ibid.)

How is an image of the past attained?—Why is the past merely that *punctiform*? Why is the past, when seized, not determinate or pinned down?—What does "true picture of the past" signify?

"If the past is approached with a contemplative attitude, the images of the past are *false* images. However, if their deceptive character [*Scheincharakter*] is eliminated, the true image of the past shows itself or manifests itself. Opposing the concept of contemplation, Benjamin introduces the concept of realization [*Verwertung*]." (N. Bolz)

Because the past always changes in relation to the present, the image flits by, the image cannot be seized. It can only flash up, *flash up* in the *present instance*. That means the past is not dead potential, but is rather pulled violently *into* the present.

"The truth will not run away from us." (Ibid.)

Gottfried Keller's phrase means to say that if the truth is not knowable now, then it will be knowable *later*. However, truth is realized in the present [*vergegenwärtigt*] by *different presents*.—Are the ways of the present, in which the past is realized, of the same kind?

The past is no *depositum*, it does not exist apart from the relation toward it, apart from the present instance of its knowability.

What is wrong with historicism? What is wrong with the historicist[52] picture?

The "true picture" is not of the character of a copy [*Abbildcharacter*].

Is historicism distinguished from historical materialism in the presentation?[53]

Historical materialism has a normative character. For historicism, what is past is one *bloc*, whereas for Benjamin the construction of the past proceeds from the point of the present. Hence, history has an actualized function, an actualist point.

> "The 'now of knowability' signifies in Benjamin or is in Benjamin the 'now of readability.'[54] However, the paradox remains: the reading in the now, in the present instance." (N. Bolz)

The Problem of Correspondence

> "For every image of the past that is not recognized by the present as one of its own concerns threatens to disappear irretrievably."[55] (Thesis V)

Contrary to the historicist's view, according to which the past exists by virtue of the sources, we can know the past *only by virtue of a present*. This bridge (past—present) is problematic: only the past that exists in the present can be seized.

Benjamin has no model of appellation. The present must have an advantage [*ein plus* (sic!)] in/with the past, and stand in a constellation with it. Benjamin is concerned with attaining knowledge of the past, or with knowledge of history.—How can history be described, if the true image of the past cannot be seized?

The image or the image-character (of the past) offers itself, but it can be discarded by the present. It is dependent on what happens in the present. The past only exists, when it is *resurrected* as present.

> "*Claim* is to be understood, to be interpreted as a political category, which Benjamin applies to historical categories." (N. Bolz)

Actuality

Benjamin is against a certain interpretation of actualization. The form of actualization of [Stefan] George and/or other forms do not attain the thought, miss the target of the present and the past. Whereas Benjamin is skeptical in his appraisal of the possible forms of actualization:

> "The good tidings, which the historian of the past brings with throbbing heart may be spoken into a void the moment he opens his mouth." (Thesis V)

Benjamin [is] against "appellation" of history, of the past.

Whereas the historicist wants to *merely* determine the image of the past, Benjamin does not want to describe a determinate course or process of history. Benjamin attempts to take leave of [an] ontology that actualizes the ground, the archetypical configurations.

Antagonistic Positions/Opponents/Fascist Historiography

The opponents against whom Benjamin takes position, such as Klages, Jung, Heidegger, Schmitt, among others, are to be taken seriously. However, Benjamin stands in closer relation to fascist historiography than he does to that of historicism, i.e., Benjamin has willingly entered the fascist arena, in order to render it useless to Fascism.

> "It is necessary to enter the dangerous sphere of fascist theory, in order to render it useless to Fascism."[56]

Example: [Despite] all of Benjamin's criticism of Gundolf's book on Goethe, he nonetheless lets it be seen as the highest form of historiography at the time, or better: he recognizes its validity and gives it its due.[57]

L. Klages's "reality of the image, the images" and [the] "archetype" of C. G. Jung are employed for a revolutionary theory by Benjamin.

The *fragile form* of the construction of the historical object must be seen in the light of the constellation of an antagonistic position vis-à-vis Klages, Jung, Heidegger, Schmitt, among others (Theses VI–VIII are to be read from this point of view).

November 22, 1984

Status of the Theses/Text/How Are They to Be Read?

Problem: An unspoken presupposition was made, which was ignored until now. This unspoken presupposition relates to the way Benjamin's theses are to be read.

Can Benjamin's theses be read like a text, with a beginning/from the beginning to the end? Are these theses merely notes? Or is it possible to presuppose a syllogistic structure in Benjamin's text, according to which the theses succeed one another?

Is it not rather the case that the theses of Benjamin's theses are interwoven, and hence that the sequence of the theses is not arbitrary? Thus, the complexes of theses, which he treats, are not subject to an arbitrary sequence. The *first thesis* is the common denominator (enlisting the services of theology), which is subsequently elaborated *in an ordered sequence* [*in Folge*] in the various theses and [with a view to Benjamin's] various opponents.

Opponent I: Historicism

Is the way of proceeding of historicism different from Benjamin's way of proceeding?

The image of the past is fundamentally different: whereas for historicism what-is-past, the past in general, is a compound, Benjamin emphasizes the precarious way by means of which the past can be realized in the present. The past is no having: the past only breaks open in relation to the present; however, the present is itself a mobile having, rather than a static, determinate one. The historian, the "prophet turned backward" (Friedrich Schlegel), speaks into a void when he wants to seize what-is-past.

Thesis VI

The sixth thesis *exacerbates* the problem of historicism in a *twofold* way: (1) notably, here for the first time—a difference is made between the perspective of the rulers, which is condensed in the tradition, and a view which is animated by danger and misery;[58] and (2) what-is-past is made to depend on what we can read out of it, i.e., the past is not itself determinate, even as something that is past it can always be oppressed anew. And because this is so, Benjamin introduces a vocabulary at this point, which fully displays the enlistment of the services of theology (Thesis VI is one of the *key theses*).[59]

The present means of historical materialism do not suffice to save the dead.

Benjamin begins with a recourse to the famous Ranke passage: Ranke as the *princeps* of German historiography, who formulates the apotheosis (transfiguration, divinization) of historiography by designating the task to know "the way it really was." The emphasis is on the word *really*, that is the point. The historian is obliged by how it *really* was. For Ranke, this [word] *really* means precisely not to view the constellation from somewhere else; he means, rather, that *every epoch has its proper reality [Eigentlichkeit] in itself*. From there, the historian is able to reconstruct history, to reconstruct what-is-past, "in a just manner" (Ranke).

Against this—against an "objective presentation" (Ranke) of historiography—Benjamin posits the counter-thesis: memory, "to seize hold of a memory as it flashes up at a moment of danger."

What is the meaning of this recourse? Why should knowledge be denser, more precise, if it takes this thesis into consideration? Is the danger, the memory that flashes up at the moment of danger, a *better organon* of experience, or is a pacified situation, theoretical calmness, contemplative calmness, a better *organon*?

What is the tremendous new claim of a knowledge that is meant by danger?[60]

Does Benjamin draw conclusions from the perspective of the normal case or from that of the extreme case? The conditions of this exception are determined [*gefasst*] by Benjamin as the extreme case. That which shows itself in danger, shows itself without foresight, nonpredicting, without being influenced by theory; it breaks something open, something that is lost from sight in the theory of historical objectivity.

Benjamin believes in an immanent (immediate) knowledge of history. The crux here is: To render possible those elements for a historical method [needed] in order to get out of [the conception of an] *objective compound*.[61]

What happens is not in itself, but rather in the messianically fulfilled Now: only then does it become clear what was once intended and what happened.[62]

"Historical subject" means class, for Benjamin.

> "The Messiah comes not only as the redeemer, he comes as the subduer of antichrist." (Thesis VI)

This *theologumenon* is the central passage of the entire thesis: The Messiah comes not only as redeemer, but as the subduer of "what is." "What is," is the antichrist; the recitation of the view of the rulers is polished by historicism. The Messiah, from an apocalyptic perspective, only from this perspective alone can what-is-past be saved.[63]

The historiographer [*Geschichtsschreiber*] is *not* turned backward (in the language), positioned at the end, according to his intention. The opponent here is historicism. Historicism as the accomplice of Fascism: historicism takes over the language of the rulers.

> "even the dead will not be safe from the enemy if he wins.
> And this enemy has not ceased to be victorious." (Ibid.)

Although Benjamin does not believe in the resurrection of the dead, they can be buried once more. Hence, no doctrine of resurrection, but rather the *doctrine of the repeated burial of the past*.[64]

Either the dead are revived (again) (i.e., cited) or they are beaten (again). However, the process of beating is stronger and more forceful (the thesis is also directed against this: against the Frankfurt School of that time, which was untheological).

Does Benjamin insist on a rewriting of history?—After all, also Fascist, as well as Stalinist historiography undertook a rewriting of history (the exiled Trotsky was retroactively cut out of or retouched out of photographs, among other such cases—here too, the dead were beaten, killed for a second time).

> "Thesis VI [is] not an actuality-thesis[;] Benjamin refers to Proust's concept of memory, more is to be gained in the involuntary realization; further, he refers to psychoanalysis's doctrine/studies of hysteria (in the sense of incubation period), here the human being is healthy (from the looks of it, as the physicians say), latency drives hysteria to the fore." (N. Bolz)

"Time-bombs" (of memory) in hysteria.

(The complex: Proust/memory/doctrine of hysteria of psychoanalysis and its transposition[65] by Benjamin onto history ought to be more precisely determined)

In Thesis VI all levels of the theses converge. The dead depend on us, [it depends on us] whether they are hastily buried or whether they are resurrected. The past is *not* a dream.

Proust/Benjamin

The story of Madelaine (central figure, *Leitmotif* of Proust's *Recherche*), which is still licked, devoured, *consumed*, *distorted* by Proust scholars; for some, the *Leitmotif* becomes the motif of suffering [*Leidmotiv*]: in Proust it becomes a figure of failure, of insufficiency, which points toward a new stage of interpretation, toward the final stage.[66]

Proust, this/whose individual experience, is transposed[67] by Benjamin with an enormous effort onto collective history.

Construction/History/Presence of the Now

"History is the object of a construction." (Thesis XIV)

[A] construction by whom? History is the construction of the presence of the now (ibid.). Concentrated history has its *own proper* experience of time. Presence of the now means the past, or better: what-is-past only *now* has come into its own. The time of history is not a homogenous medium, but rather only concentrated time: presence of the now, to be thought only from the perspective of redemption. *Here* (Thesis XIV), however, [this is] meant in the spirit of class struggle [*klassenkämpferisch*].

Narrator/Chronicler

A symbol of genuine writing of history is the narrator. He does not differentiate between great and small things. In remaining *below the level* [*Unterschreitung*] [in terms] of presentation, the narrator or the chronicler wins out over the rulers' transgression [*Überschreitung*].

The dead mass of history is to be revived. Conditional resurrection of the dead.

Thesis VII

"To historians who wish to relive an era, Fustel de Coulanges recommends that they blot out everything about the later course of history." (Thesis VII)

What is so bad about this? This aspect of historicism is the target for the greatest or harshest of Benjamin's attacks: for him, this is exactly what historical materialism must break away from.

"Indolence of the heart, *acedia*," melancholia—does that make sense? Why does the gravest Christian sin come into play here: *acedia*? Because the historiographer who has fallen into *acedia* is unable to "kindle a spark of hope (in what-is-past)"; this [kind of] historiographer does not have the power to extract any meaning at all from the past.

Precisely the deepest intentions, such as intellectual empathy [*Einfühlung*], objectivity of history, giving each epoch its due, and others, are unmasked by Benjamin as constituting the *loci* of the Antichrist. These intentions belong to the infinite, universal acquiescence with "what is," the triumph of which is celebrated in historiography.

Here, in the most sublime form of hitherto existing historiography, Benjamin discerns acquiescence with the rulers. Benjamin attacks the prohibitions to think the presence of the now, because they are partly responsible, they transfigure consciousness.[68]

Benjamin consciously took the side of the rough and unsophisticated [*rauhbeinig*] form of historical materialism. Here, he saw a *new form* of historical articulation, as opposed to the *sublime form* of the historicists, like Simmel, Dilthey, and others, who stand opposed to the blasting of the presence of the now and the tension of the continuum of the past, of what-is-past, who want to prevent that blasting.

Benjamin's manner of presentation and confrontation of historicism is controversial and *roundabout.*

December 6, 1984

Each one of the theses is a complete unified whole [*Einheit*], in which the entirety of the theses can be found, however, needless to say, with moments of differentiation.

Historicism is *the* problem of the nineteenth century, against which historical materialism arises as a counterposition. In the last theses, the modern trait for which the consequences of historical materialism are treated as a main reason, becomes a subject of discussion.[69] The spiritual equipment of historical materialism has weakened Fascism.

The first thesis designates the program. Historical materialism needs to enlist the services of theology. This program, this "enlisting-of-services" appears in ever-new forms and facets: Benjamin not only charges historical materialism with this program, but he ascribes to historicism an antimessianic position. This culminates in ascribing to it *acedia*, melancholy, indolence of the heart, the gravest sin of the medieval catalog of vices, which Benjamin in an amazing turn of phrase imputes to historicism on account of its *intellectual empathy.*[70]

Fustel de Coulange, the Bachofen of the French, determined the French situation in the spirit of the *Restauration.*[71]

> "To historians who wish to relive an era, Fustel de Coulanges recommends that they blot out everything about the later course of history."

This means history is to be narrated as if what happens later did not vibrate back into its prehistory. Needless to say, this procedure—intellectual empathy—is not wrong in principle: if history is determined, fixed, with a view to a *telos*, one confuses the chances of an effect (not *telos*, but rather *teleo*).

Historicism as a whole is a renunciation of the theological and teleological historiography of the Middle Ages, which is triumphant in Hegel: if history is written with a view to a goal/*telos*, all epochs are merely preludes.[72] That was what was genuine about historicism, to break free from the corset of the *teleo*.

Benjamin wants to restore the construction of a philosophy of history under exacerbated conditions. What particularly interests him about historical materialism, is (a) the reference to what happens at the base, and (b) historical materialism as an heir that continues the theological and philosophical heritage.

Progress, it has been said, is an overextended, secularized version of the end of history. Not according to the form, but when one speaks of progresses, when suddenly progress is an impersonal (=self) force working through everything (through constellations like an epoch).[73]

History, the *singulare tantum*. History itself is charged with being a subject. To charge things mythically is an invention of the eighteenth century.[74]

Revolution

> The history of European revolutions is the history of the turning away from the Ptolemaic Kyrios Christos cult, from the charismatic Christianity of the Middle Ages. The word revolution is found in the writings of Copernicus and Galileo, the fathers of the modern picture of the world. Because of them, mankind living in the modern age experiences his historical experience as *revolution*. In the main work of Copernicus, dating from 1543, and even earlier in Dante, revolution means the rotation of heavenly bodies and heavenly worlds. The generation following Dante is the first to apply the concept of rotating heavenly bodies to events in the small Italian city-states. The perennial changes in the constitution of these small states appear to stage the drama of the world. Ever since Galileo and his contemporaries Rohan and Hobbes defined man as a speck of dust on the planet and ejected him from the center of the cosmos, we dare to refer to the pronounced upheavals of the great empires as revolutions.[75]

Progress becomes a mythical subject, just like the concept of revolution, the rotation of heavenly bodies, which is not determined by events, but rather becomes a subject. Progress is a term of the eschatological tradition (that was the opinion!). However, Benjamin is one of those within the apocalyptic tradition who speak of discontinuity: this is not based on thinking in terms of transition, but rather history and historical time come to an end with the apocalypse. Benjamin belongs to those who want to determine the apocalyptic as a shocking end of all historical existence, an end that opens the reign of a new dispensation, which is beyond any idea of world [*Vorstellung von Welt*]. Hence, for theological, historical, and actual [*aktuelle*] reasons and out of insight into his present, Benjamin is interested (in) understanding the concept of progress as a bourgeois concept that has nothing to do with (a) religious, theological, messianic, apocalyptic concepts, and (b) with historical materialism.

Everything is lost for Benjamin, if you don't understand the *concerns* as primary. That seems to be a fundamental theme: being a concern (however separated from Marx himself). Benjamin interprets Marx in an anarchistic, Blanquist[76] form. Benjamin forces the meaning of Marx. Benjamin's concern has been misjudged by Rolf Tiedemann, Hans Heinz Holz, and Heinz-Dieter Kittsteiner. Benjamin collides with the primary texts of Marxism.

Historicism

Historicism is based on one genuine *concern*: To pronounce history to be a construct and to see the [center of] gravity *in* the [respective] epoch. All epochs are equal to god,[77] God-like (Ranke against Hegel). This is the enemy Benjamin targets from Thesis III onward (historicism).

How does Benjamin proceed? What does he demonstrate? How does he proceed to ascribe historicism as an attitude to feeling?[78]

Benjamin unmasks the *organon* of historicism, *intellectual empathy*. In itself, intellectual sympathy, in the way of Fustel de Coulange or Dilthey, is not a bad *organon*. However, Benjamin detects something almost bordering on criminal here. *Intellectual empathy* is *acquiescence* with *what rules*, what becomes *visible*.

Present Instance [*Augenblick*]

One can imagine danger as *organon* of historical knowledge in Paulinian terms: Constellation of all that is past with the *point-of-now* [*Jetztpunkt*].

Intellectual sympathy, the *organon* of historical knowledge of historicism, is the exact opposite: the moment of calmness and the (romantic) leisurely roaming around in a prescinded past.

The *fundamental* difference is thus in the *organon* of knowledge. The background for this is the *malaise* that was already brought up by Nietzsche; [brought up] vis-à-vis the historian, who is an idler, and can afford [to be idle] again and again, as "an idler in the garden of knowledge." What Benjamin prevents by means of historical materialism, is the concentration [*Konzentrat*] of history. The messianic community is *not without history*, all that is past pushes toward a *Now*, is given in a *permanent state of emergency*.

Historicism has time, what-is-past, or, as Gottfried Keller has it, "the truth will not run away from us" (cf. Thesis V).

Intellectual empathy is not neutral. Intellectual empathy is itself a mode of leisure. Like things are known by like things, leisure is known by leisure. It is the leisure of intellectual empathy, which makes intellectual empathy the *organon* of the rulers; it overlooks that even the highest form (leisure), culture, is not only the expression of the effort of great spirits, but also of the drudgery of their anonymous slaves.

This inexplicit perspective of history or of culture has been brought out most ruthlessly and most truly by Nietzsche. Culture is leisure. [The] price [to be paid for] this leisure: slavery. Nietzsche affirmed this price, as opposed to Jacob Burckhardt, who did not sufficiently expose this issue.

The struggle for cultural history, as the highest form of historical knowledge was represented in Benjamin's time and before by sublime fascist theoreticians, especially by Christoph Steding in his book *Das Reich und die innere Krankheit Europas* (Hamburg 1938/1940). Cultural history as the history of leisure. Whereas Benjamin posits historical materialism as the antipode to the history of leisure, Steding posits political history.

Steding points out that cultural history [forms] a *neutralized* geographical belt between Basel and Amsterdam: in Basel, Burckhardt and Bachofen; in Amsterdam: Johan Huizinga. Steding, who is praised by Carl Schmitt,[79] argues that it is those historians from Jakob Burckhardt to Johan Huizinga, who poison and disempower the *Reich*, and who cut history down to cultural history. Benjamin is the counterposition to Steding, his exact opposite: power, drudgery, and suffering are present even in cultural history, even though they are not visible.

Benjamin wants to wrest its insights from fascism and enlist their services in antifascist perspectives. Benjamin is not a reader of progressive literature. However, he undertakes an enormous, sublime reading of the right: De Maistre, Baudelaire. Benjamin attempts to wrest those powers that had the greatest evidence from fascism as an epochal movement.

Benjamin had more power than Ernest Bloch; the latter regarded fascism as a fraud.[80]

What is scandalous about the text, what is—as attitude, as burden—the basis of historicism, is the mythical conception of history, i.e., that only like things are understood by like things.

Leisure

For Plato and Aristotle, the philosopher is someone who understands the theoretical life to be the highest life. The philosopher thus understood has an interest in the possibility of philosophy. And philosophy is possible only if leisure is possible. *The philosopher is a partisan of leisure.*

The profound objection of the Christian tradition: that salvation—that the highest state as a human way of life—is in principle accessible to *all* human beings. Hence, leisure and the resulting life of theory cannot be the highest human way of life. There is likely no passage in the works of Benjamin that is more Christian than Thesis VII. *Leisure,* or idleness, *acedia,* melancholy, as the *genealogy* of the truest, most innocent form of *historicism.* Benjamin rejected this society that is based on *leisure,* on culture, as a matter of principle.

Benjamin denounces leisure as indolence of the heart. The price of this indolence is to be denied to take possession of the genuine historical image, which [is accessible] only fleetingly at the moment of danger (cf. Theses V and VI).[81]

This genealogy cannot be surpassed in its negativity. Benjamin mobilizes the heaviest artillery in order to vanquish historicism. The most shameful acts of the historicists are, in accordance with Augustine, their pagan *virtus.* On the surface, historicism does not yield what Benjamin demands from it here. In historicism, Benjamin sees the culmination [of nineteenth-century culture], he sees that the perspective of this culture is fundamentally historical. Hence, Benjamin is hoping to have [found] an *organon* in historical materialism, which runs counter to historicism. For Benjamin, there are two configurations here, configurations of how the old and the new as perspectives present themselves in principle. *At this point* the future of society will be *decided.*

What is the place of historicism in the theses, in the "theses on the philosophy of history"? For example, Thesis XVII: that historicism is the peak of universal history. Are we supposed to read only particular history? What is wrong with universal history?

Here it becomes clear what the difference is. Historicism has the sense of justice of a teleological sense. What Benjamin needs to develop, step by step, is an opposition to what is plausible in historicism.

The messianic history of Benjamin must defend itself against (a) the justice of historicism, and against (b) intellectual sympathy as natural *organon*, (c) against [the] standstill [of the *status quo*] with the standstill of the messianic; (d) against universal history, which is false and must be differentiated from genuine history. Not the universal as such is false, but rather universal, homogenous time.

Summary/Notes: Historicism as the antipode of a *messianic reading of history*. Augustine's critique of the Stoics and the eternal return. [The imputation of] *acedia* is the *non plus ultra* of the unmasking of historicism.

Taubes is very ill: N. Bolz "substitutes" for Taubes.

Translated by Kaspar Bulling

Notes

1. The notes were taken by Josef R. Lawitschka, a student of Taubes's, who later published a dissertation on the historical thought of Franz Rosenzweig and Isaac Breuer.

2. E. Stimilli, ed., *Jacob Taubes—Der Preis des Messianismus: Briefe von Jacob Taubes an Gershom Scholem und andere Materialien* (Würzburg: Königshausen und Neumann, 2006), 67–92.

3. Where these editorial interventions seemed appropriate and helpful to me, they have been taken over without indication. Where they did not seem to me to contribute to elucidating the text, they were silently ignored.

4. All insertions of square brackets ([ ]) are mine. Where Stimilli had amended the notes with square brackets in her edition, these have either been silently taken over or ignored, as indicated in note 3.

5. The text published by Stimilli has barely been edited at all, much to the detriment of its readability. Unfortunately, Stimilli did not make the original notes by Josef R. Lawitschka—which are in her possession—available for this translation.

6. [For the sake of familiarity, the quotations from Benjamin's text are largely based on Harry Zohn's translation of the text in *Illuminations*. However, I frequently made slight and occasionally more substantial corrections to Zohn's translation where his lack of literalness was seen as an obstacle for understanding Taubes's commentary.—Trans.]

7. Cf. "Das bucklige Männlein," in Clemens Brentano, *Sämtliche Werke und Briefe*, vol. 8 (Stuttgart: Kohlhammer, 1977), 290–291. [This and all of the following endnotes contain references by Taubes, which in the German edition of these notes are provided in brackets within the text. For the sake of

readability, I have moved them to endnotes. A note on source references: For sources and references that have been translated into English, I provide the published translations provided that I was able to track them down. For sources that have not been translated into English, or for which the edition Taubes is referring to was not accessible to me, I provided Taubes's original reference.—Trans.]

8. For "invisible hand," cf. Heinz-Dieter Kittsteiner, *Naturabsicht und Unsichtbare Hand. Zur Kritik des geschichtsphilosophischen Denkens* (Frankfurt am Main/Berlin/Wien: Ullstein, 1980).

9. In the notes, the definite article *die* in *die Theologie* is underlined (italicized) for emphasis, drawing attention to the problem *what kind* of theology Benjamin is referring to when he simply speaks of "theology" as if there was just one theology and as if it was generally understood and agreed upon what it is.

10. Literally, the text reads: "What can theology, not in the sense of the theology of the church, still expect or gain in this age of profanization?" However, the context strongly suggests that the German "seitens der Theologie" is here simply misused and is intended to mean "von der Theologie."

11. At the beginning of the second thesis the German *bekanntlich*—rendered here as "as is known"—is translated by Zohn as "the story is told"; at the end of the thesis, he uses "as we know."

12. The German is extremely obscure here. The phrase, "*Wer hat wen von wem am Wickel?*" has no obvious meaning, and the present rendering is only one possible interpretation of what it may mean.

13. Cf. Theodor W. Adorno, *Minima Moralia: Reflections from Damaged Life*, trans E. F. N. Jephcott (London: Verso, 1978), 247. Cf. also Norbert Bolz, "Erlösung als ob," in *Religionstheorie und Politische Theologie*, vol. 2, *Gnosis und Politik*, ed. J. Taubes (München: Fink, 1984), 264–289.

14. Cf. Hubert Cancick, ed. *Religions- und Geistesgeschichte der Weimarer Republik* (Düsseldorf: Patmos, 1982).

15. In the notes, the quote breaks off here. In Benjamin's text, it continues as follows: "by the time to which the course of our existence happened to assign us."

16. The notes have "*Glück hat sich an der Ordnung des Profanen auszu-richten.*" The German original of Benjamin's fragment states: "Die Ordnung des Profanen hat sich *auf*zurichten an der Idee des Glücks." This is translated as: "The order of the profane should be erected on the idea of happiness." The latter is a questionable translation; the German seems closer to "the order of the profane is to be edified by the idea of happiness." Or at least the latter meaning is also connoted. However the case may be, the point is to draw attention to the difficulty of trying to make sense of the text of the notes. What can it mean that "happiness is to be geared toward"—or perhaps "happiness is to be aligned with"—"the order of the profane"? It seems likely that Lawitschka could not follow Taubes's elaborations here.

17. The notes have "Jetzt-Seinige," which I take to be a typo or transcription error as it it makes no sense.

18. The German is extremely obscure here. In present-day German, the term *Nu* is only used in the combination *im Nu* which means something like "very quickly," "right away," or "instantaneously." The Grimm dictionary has as one of its meanings, which was used, among others, by the German mystic Meister Eckhart, "the quickly vanishing present, the short present life as opposed to eternity" ("*die schnell hinschwindende Gegenwart, das gegenwärtige kurze Leben im Gegensatz zur Ewigkeit*"; Jacob and Wilhelm Grimm, *Deutsches Wörterbuch*, vol. 13, columns 993–996).

19. This term connotes above all current, present, contemporary relevance or import.

20. Hermann Lotze, *Microcosmus: An Essay Concerning Man and His Relation to the World*, trans. E. Hamilton and E. E. Constance Jones (Edinburgh: T. and T. Clark, 1885).

21. Cf. Walter Benjamin, *Das Passagen-Werk*, in *Gesammelte Schriften*, vol. 5.2 (Frankfurt am Main: Suhrkamp 1982), 737–743.

22. The German is quite ambiguous here.

23. The German construction connotes something like: "How is historical materialism doing?"

24. Cf. *Passagen-Werk*, N3,2.

25. The sentence in the German is grammatically incoherent. I read a semicolon instead of a comma after "Leben" and read "dem" instead of "das Atmen der Frauen."

26. Cf. H. D. Kittsteiner, Walter Benjamins Historismus, unpublished manuscript, 21; lecture given during the "Arcades" Colloquium, Berlin, June 1–3, 1983. [An expanded version of Kittsteiner's text was published in N. Bolz and B. Witte, *Passagen: Walter Benjamin's Urgeschichte des neunzehnten Jahrhunderts* (Munich: Wilhelm Fink, 1984), 163–197. Shortly after, Kittsteiner's text was translated into English by Jonathan Monroe and Irving Wohlfarth and published in the journal *New German Critique*. See H. D. Kittsteiner, "Walter Benjamin's Historicism," *New German Critique*, no. 39 (Autumn 1986): 179–215.—Trans.]

27. This is what the notes say. It is obviously shorthand for Ranke's dictum that all historical epochs are equally "immediate before God." See Leopold von Ranke, *Über die Epochen der neueren Geschichte* (Darmstadt: Wissenschaftliche Buchgesellschaft, 1954), 7.

28. The entire paragraph is rather obscure in the German notes.

29. Reading "in . . . *eingelegt*" instead of "*angelegt*."

30. This is an attempt at as literal a translation of a highly condensed statement as possible. I suppose what is intended is the following: "In the third thesis the critiques of theology as well as of historical materialism are intertwined, and that thesis advocates (or: takes a stand for) both these critiques."

31. The formulation suddenly breaks off here, but we can conjecture that Taubes meant "does not have a human experience as its basis—."

32. The German reads: *"Der Fall des Menschen, im doppelten Sinne."* In German, *Fall* can mean both "[the] case [of]" and "[the] fall [from grace]."

33. Cf. J. Taubes, "Von Fall zu Fall. Erkenntnistheoretische Reflexionen zur Geschichte vom Sündenfall," in *Poetik und Hermeneutik*, vol. 9, *Text und Applikation*, ed. Manfred Fuhrmann (Munich: Fink, 1981), 111–116.

34. The German is grammatically incoherent here. I drop the second *dem* and I take it that there *gedacht* or *vorgestellt* or a similar participle (rendered as "idea" in square brackets here) is missing from the construction *"durchbrechbar . . . ist."* This seems to me the only way to make sense of this sentence.

35. Here, Taubes seems to play on the ambiguity of the German word *Fall* again; see note 32.

36. The German is once more grammatically incoherent here, but the intended meaning seems to be clear.

37. Cf. K. A. Varnhagen von Ense and Th. Mundt, ed., *K. L. von Knebel's Nachlaß und Briefwechsel*, vol. 2 (Leipzig 1849), 446.

38. The German here reads *"ist von der Art,"* which means "is of such a kind," which is superfluously strange in both English and German.

39. The "into the distance of time" is for some reason omitted in the translation by Zohn, which has simply "has retroactive force" for *"wirken in die Ferne der Zeit zurück."*

40. The German *Himmel*, of course, can mean both "sky" and "heaven."

41. The German text is not coherent here and is further confused by the editor's intervention. I decided to drop the first *sich* and to add the opening "[According to]" to make sense of the paragraph.

42. The paragraph is very obscure in German as well. I take the passage to mean that what-has-been by itself (or independently of any present "actualization") has an ontological or metaphysical property (or status) that connects it to the present, that makes it "want by itself to get to the surface" in the present.

43. Karl Marx, *The Eighteenth Brumaire of Louis Bonaparte*, chap. 1.

44. Ibid.

45. On the *Eighteenth Brumaire*, cf. W. Fietkau, *Schwanengesang auf 1848—Ein Rendezvous am Louvre: Baudelaire, Marx, Proudhon und Victor Hugo* (Reinbek: Rowohlt, 1978), 125–233.

46. The German edition of the notes conjectures *Diskretion* here for the obvious *lacuna* in the text, which I take to intend to mean *Deskription* (description): the Italian is *descrizione*, so it seems that the editor was confused about the German and the Italian. Her conjecture seems in principle not unfitting, though: what is missing is something that contrasts with Benjamin's notion of the "dialectical image." I chose "narration" as contrast, but "description" may fit as well. The problem with this conjecture is that it seems that "image" might refer here not

to Benjamin's notion of a "dialectical image," but rather to the "image" or simile of heliotropism. It is impossible to make a responsible decision without seeing the manuscript of the notes.

47. The entire paragraph is rather obscure in German, but I take the last sentence to mean that the "subjective" attitudes of those fighting the class struggle in the present is the condition of possibility for the "objective" potential or "possibility" of actualization of what-has-been to be realized.

48. This must not be taken to be connected to the expression "what-is-past" here. The latter is simply my translation for *das Vergangene* in contrast to *die Vergangenheit* (the past).

49. I take it that *worauf* is missing before "sich verstehen muss." Then the commentary corresponds closely and meaningfully to the passage it comments on, and the sentence is more meaningfully connected to the next. I have chosen to change Zohn's "must be aware of" into "must be able to detect" in order to render the German "*sich auf etwas verstehen*"; the German expression connotes a skill or competence or ability, something that is completely lost in Zohn's translation. The "master" at the end of the next sentence is a translation of the same "*sich auf etwas verstehen*"—in this case, Benjamin's mystical theory of correspondence.

50. *Durchwirkt* seems to be employed here as a conjugation of the verb *durchwirken*, as in "*das Gewesene wirkt durch die Zeit*"; it seems to signify a "working-through-time" or "across time" of what-has-been. Alternatively, one could read *durchwirkt* as an adjective, in the sense of "*durchwirkt mit Jetzt-Zeit*," or "enwrought with presence of the Now." Then the last clause would be "but rather enwrought [with presence of the Now]."

51. This is also the title of a chapter in Ludwig Klages, *Der Geist als Widersacher der Seele* (Bonn: Bouvier, 1972), 801f. [The title Taubes is referring to is "Die Wirklichkeit der Bilder" (The Reality of Images).—Trans.]

52. The German text has *historischen* (historical), but the context strongly suggests that what is meant is *historistischen*.

53. It is unclear whether Taubes means to raise the question if historicism is distinguished from historical materialism in Benjamin's presentation, or if the two are different in how they present history. This ambiguity does not come out as much in the translation.

54. Cf. Walter Benjamin, *Passagen-Werk*, in *Gesammelte Schriften*, vol. 5.1 (Frankfurt am Main: Surhkamp 1982), 577.

55. The *Illuminations* translation is not very literal, but a strictly literal translation is simply not achievable here. This poses problems for fully understanding some of Taubes's commentary. See also note 62 below.

56. J. Taubes, quoted in *Romantische Utopie—Utopische Romantik*, ed. G. Dischner and R. Faber (Hildesheim: Gerstenberg Verlag, 1979), 37.

57. On Gundolf, cf. Benjamin, "Goethes Wahlverwandschaften," in *Gesammelte Schriften*, vol. 1.1 (Frankfurt am Main: Suhrkamp, 1972), 158–167; and "Bemerkungen über Gundolf: Goethe," in *Gesammelte Schriften*, vol. 1.3

(Frankfurt am Main: Suhrkamp 1974), 826–828; cf. also W. Benjamin, *Briefe*, vol. 1 (Frankfurt am Main: Suhrkamp 1966), 181, 250, 264, 266, 284, 423; and *Briefe*, vol. 2 (Frankfurt am Main: Suhrkamp 1966), 523.

58. The German is very obscure here, but this strikes me as the only sensible solution.

59. Again, this is an interpretation of a borderline meaningless sentence in the original notes.

60. This is a literal translation of the German. It appears that what Taubes meant to say was: "What is . . . the claim . . . of a knowledge that understands itself as becoming available at the moment of danger."

61. This, too, is an interpretation of Taubes's most likely intended meaning based on an obviously incomplete sentence in the German notes.

62. The relation of this commentary to the sixth thesis becomes fully comprehensible only on the basis of the literal meaning of the German.

63. The sentence is equally incomplete in the German notes. It is not obvious how it should be completed.

64. Cf. "Letter from Horkheimer dated 16 March 1937," in *Gesammelte Schriften*, vol. 5.1 (Frankfurt am Main: Suhrkamp 1982), 588f: "The affirmation of open-endedness is idealistic, if completion is not included in it. The injustice of the past has happened and is completed. *Those who were slain are really slain* . . . , thus one must believe in Judgment Day." Cf. also "Letter from Benjamin to Horkheimer dated 28 March 1937," in *Gesammelte Schriften*, vol. 3.2 (Frankfurt am Main: Suhrkamp, 1980), 1338.

65. Substituting *Transposition* for *Transformation*. This way the sentence makes much more sense, both grammatically and semantically.

66. The sentence is as incomplete in the German notes. Cf. also Gilles Deleuze, *Proust und die Zeichen* (Frankfurt am Main: Ullstein, 1978), 14.

67. Again, *transformiert* is replaced by *transponiert*.

68. The German notes are rather obscure here. This appears to be the most likely meaning intended by Taubes.

69. Again, this is the best solution for a very obscure and incomplete passage in the German notes.

70. Regarding the last two sentences, see the previous two notes.

71. Cf. Fustel de Coulanges, *The Ancient City* (1864).

72. The German notes have *Vorgaben* here, which seems to make no sense in this context, so another expression based on the prefix *Vor-* that fits the context (*Vorspiel*) was chosen. Others would work just as well, for instance *Vorläufer* (precursors/forerunners).

73. Again, the notes are very confusing and incomplete here.

74. Cf. Marx, *German Ideology*.

75. J. Taubes, *Occidental Eschatology* (Stanford, CA: Stanford University Press, 2009), 88. [The translation has been slightly amended.—Trans.]

76. Cf. *Thesis XII*.

77. As to the precise wording of Ranke's *dictum*, see note 27 above.

78. The German is nonsensical here, and it is very difficult to conjecture what Taubes may have meant. The present rendering is as literal as possible while providing a *modicum* of intelligibility.

79. Cf. the review by C. Schmitt, "Neutralität und Neutralisierungen," in Carl Schmitt, *Positionen und Begriffe* (Hamburg: Hanseatische Verlagsanstalt, 1940), 271ff.

80. Cf. E. Bloch, *Heritage of Our Times*, trans. N. Plaice (Oxford: Polity Press, 2009).

81. Replacing *verzagt* (disheartened), with "*bleibt . . . versagt* [denied]." The whole sentence is quasi nonsensical in the original notes, and the present rendering is based on several conjectures.

Dislocated Messianism: Modernity, Marxism, and Violence

On Benjamin's *Baudelaire*

GIORGIO AGAMBEN

Walter Benjamin's *Charles Baudelaire, A Poet of the Age of Advanced Capitalism* is a special book, not only because of its unusual form, but also because of its somewhat adventurous history, or rather, prehistory, which is inseparable, at least for me, from its existence in the form of a printed document.

In 1981, I was in Paris, searching for the traces of the famous manuscript that, according to the testimony of Lisa Fittko—the woman who had guided Benjamin in the attempt to flee from occupied France to Spain that ultimately cost him his life—Benjamin had kept by his side in a black leather-bound folder.

For this reason I had looked through the correspondence of George Bataille, which was and still is in the Department of Manuscripts at the Bibliothèque nationale de France. Imagine my surprise and joy when I came across a letter addressed from Bataille to Jean Bruno, then a librarian at the Bibliothèque, in which he called attention to unspecified manuscripts of Benjamin's that he had been entrusted with. Alongside the letter, an annotation of Bruno's read: "These manuscripts are now in the B.N." The date of the letter differed from the date of the annotation and both were dated after 1947, the year when Bataille had submitted the manuscripts in his possession to Pierre Missac, who had them sent to Adorno.

I rushed to the librarian of the manuscript room and asked her if she knew where to find the manuscripts in question. She strongly denied that the Bibliothèque possessed any of Benjamin's manuscripts, but faced with the evidence of the annotation, she agreed to telephone Bruno, who had already retired in the meantime. Bruno did not remember precisely the manuscripts in question, but he asserted without reservation that if he had written that the manuscripts were at the Bibliothèque, then it must be true.

Thus the research on the part of the manuscript librarians began and a month later I received a laconic message informing me that the manuscripts had been found and that I could consult them. I then learned that the manuscripts in question had been deposited at, but not donated to, the Bibliothèque by Bataille's widow and that the Bibliothèque did not catalogue manuscripts that it did not own. Then I was led into a room in which a wooden cabinet held the manuscripts on deposit, among which there appeared to be other manuscripts of important authors that are perhaps still waiting to be catalogued.

Whatever the case may be, it was not without emotion that I received from the librarian five yellow envelopes filled with Benjamin's manuscripts, some of them typewritten, but the greater part lined with the minute calligraphy that was familiar to me. This was not the first time that I had been captivated to discover some pages of Benjamin's. When you work on an author, and bury yourself in his thought, work, and life, some curious phenomena can occur that might seem to be the result of magic, but that I believe can be categorized as what Giordano Bruno called "natural magic," which he conceived of as a particular material science.

I mean to say that if you truly identify with the mind of an author, pondering and studying his works and words with philological rigor, if, as in my case, you have also frequented the places where he lived and spoken with the people who knew him, if you enter, therefore, with him into a contact that is, so to speak, material, certain unexpected correspondences can come out of that (in the esoteric sense that the term *correspondance* has in Baudelaire, in the sonnet that Benjamin was to carefully comment on). A correspondence of this kind had happened in Rome some years earlier when I had discovered that about three hundred feet from my house (I then lived around the Campo dei Fiori) lived Herbert Blumenthal Belmore, who had been among Benjamin's best friends during the years of the Berlin youth movement, that is, between 1914 and 1916. This gentleman, with whom Benjamin had abruptly broken off relations, had kept a great number of Benjamin's letters and manuscripts, which he entrusted to me and which are still in my possession. And the most curious thing was that, while he showed me the manuscripts that he had faithfully preserved, he openly confessed to me at the same time his hatred for their author, whom he had not seen for more than sixty years and who had been dead for forty. With one of the abrupt reversals that Baudelaire was familiar with, wounded love had been converted into hatred.

Anyway, back to the Paris manuscripts. Their discovery was important, because they allowed us to look at Benjamin's work of his last three years, from 1937 to his death in 1940, in a new way. One of the envelopes, in fact, contained a series of manuscripts that referred to the book on Baudelaire to which Benjamin, interrupting his work on the *Arcades Project* [*Passagenarbeit*], had devoted his utmost effort.

In March 1937, Benjamin, who had just finished the draft of his study on Fuchs, proposed to the Institut für Sozialforschung three possible subjects for his next work. The first is a study on Klages and Jung, intended to clarify some methodological aspects of his work on the *Pariser Passagen*, on which he had been working for years; the second is a "comparison between the bourgeois and materialist exposition of historiography," which like the first was to contribute to establishing the conceptual structure of the book; "finally, in case you do not feel up to really approving this way of proceeding, . . . I would propose to you then, entering *in medias res*, to expect the draft of the chapter on Baudelaire."[1] Having rejected the first proposal, which would have implied, within the Institute, a heated debate with Erich Fromm over psychoanalysis, and the second, because it risked overlapping with themes already treated in "Fuchs," it is on the third project that Horkheimer's attention lingered: "a materialistic article on Baudelaire has long been a desideratum. I would be extraordinarily grateful to you, if you could truly decide to write this chapter of your book first thing."[2]

A few months later, having overcome the difficulties of a change of residence, Benjamin set himself to work.

In this phase, the project appeared, for both its clients and its author, as an advance draft of a chapter of his book on *Paris, Capital of the Nineteenth Century* (*Passagenarbeit*, or *Pariser Passagen* as it was informally designated in conversations or letters to friends). The *exposé* composed in May 1935 to present the *Passagen* to the friends of the Institut (then still at Geneva as *Société internationale de recherches sociales*), contained a section (the fifth, which bears the title *Baudelaire, or the Streets of Paris*) that gives an idea of the themes originally envisioned for the chapter. However, while the work of research and articulation of the materials proceeded, Benjamin realized that the projected "chapter" was acquiring an importance and breadth in part already foreseen. On April 16, 1938, in a letter to Horkheimer, while he was engaged in a schematization [*Schematisierung*] of the work in three parts, he presents the work in these terms:

The result is that the treatise is becoming more voluminous and the essential motifs of the *Passagen* are converging in it. This is due both to the nature of the subject and to the fact that this chapter, conceived as one of the central chapters of the book, has instead been written first. I already foresaw this tendency of *Baudelaire* to configure itself as a sort of miniature model [*Miniaturmodell*] of the book in conversations with Teddie. Since San Remo, this has been confirmed to a greater degree than I had thought. . . . Mr. Pollock has asked me to communicate to you with regard to the above, because originally you would have expected a manuscript of the usual dimensions. I knew it, but I thought that for once it would have been better if one of my studies might have assumed the dimensions of a work of a certain bulk. Still, today I hope that there will not be any decisive objections in principle; in fact I truly would not know how to treat the fundamental aspects of the problem in thirty or forty pages. I imagine instead a maximum length—I'm referring to the pages of the manuscript—equal to triple that, and a minimum equal to around double. (*GB*, 6:64–65)

It is necessary to underline the peculiar status that the qualification as "miniature model" attributes to *Baudelaire* at this point. It establishes between the part and the whole a paradoxical relation, in which, if the whole contains itself so to speak *en abîme*, the part extends to incorporate the whole, acting as a factor of erosion and of a progressive emptying out of the comprehensive work. Again in a letter to Scholem on July 9, while he was in Danimarca with Brecht, Benjamin presents the study as a "more precise model of the *Passagenarbeit*, which puts in motion the entire bulk of thinkers and studies of the last few years" (*GB*, 6:131); and, a few days earlier, writing to Pollack, he speaks of the work in progress as a "concentrated form [*Extract*]" of the *Pariser Passagen*, which "will make possible a perspectivally articulated glance into the depths of the nineteenth century" (*GB*, 6:133).

A month later, after having moved on to a new organization of the materials and the structure of the work, Benjamin is forced to admit that the "miniature model" has by now become an autonomous book, which is extending to encompass in itself a considerable part of the materials and themes envisioned for the *Passagen*:

I have communicated to Mr. Horkheimer that his impulse toward *Baudelaire* has become, as it probably would have been for any reelaboration of material already accumulated by me for such a long time, the impulse toward a book. I have sought to confront myself

with the necessities inherent in the thing itself, which have led to
this result that had not originally been taken into consideration. . . .
This book is not identical to the *Pariser Passagen*. It contains, however, not only a considerable part of the materials that I had collected for the latter, but also a quantity of contents of a philosophical
character. (*GB*, 6:158–159)

On August 3, in a letter in which the triadic structure of the book was
further specified, its growing weight in the economy of Benjamin's critical
laboratory was also newly emphasized:

That "Baudelaire" would have had to be treated separately with respect
to the context of the studies and reflections for the *Pariser Passagen*
was obvious . . . The fundamental categories of the *Passagen*, which
converge in the determination of the character of the commodity
fetish, enter fully into play in "Baudelaire." Nevertheless their development, as much as one wants to limit it, exceeds the confines of
one study. (*GB*, 6:149)

On September 28, in the letter to Horkheimer that accompanies the
shipment of the final part of the work (corresponding to the second of the
three sections envisioned, which bears the title: *Das Paris des Second Empire bei Baudelaire*), we can see more clearly both the autonomous character of the book and, at the same time, the close relationship that ties it to
the *Passagenarbeit*:

The book proposes to present, I hope in definitive form, certain decisive philosophical elements of the project of the *Passagen*. If, beyond the original project, there was a subject that offered optimal
possibilities, this was undoubtedly Baudelaire. Consequently essential materials and constructive elements of the *Passagen* have oriented
themselves spontaneously around to this subject. (*GB*, 6:162)

But the fact that, in this way, the Baudelaire "chapter" is in reality
functioning as a principle of disaggregation for the entire structural unity
of the book on Paris, is implied by Benjamin himself a little further down:
"The evolution that the chapter on Baudelaire of the *Passagen* is about to
undertake, I would see being reserved for two other chapters of the *Passagen*:
the one on Grandville and the one on Haussmann" (*GB*, 6:163).

The unfavorable welcome of the study on the part of the Institut für
Sozialforschung and the dense correspondence with Adorno that followed
open a new phase in the evolution of the work. Despite the discomfort
("the isolation in which I live and, at the same time, work, produces an

abnormal dependence on the welcome that is found by what I do" [*GB*, 6:217]), Benjamin immediately projects a revision of the second chapter of the study ("The *Flâneur*") and proceeds to a partial re-elaboration of the material according to new categories. On June 26, in a letter to Gretel Adorno, he realizes that the new draft marks a further step forward in the importance of *Baudelaire* in the whole of his production: "In no previous work have I acquired such a certainty of the vanishing point in which (as always, as it now seems to me) all my reflections, which begin from divergent points, coincide" (*GB*, 6:308).

The new partial draft (which corresponds to the second chapter of the previous draft and thus covers the central section of the second part of the entire book) is finished at the end of July 1939 and, this time, received enthusiastically by his friends in New York. That the book is now, even more than the *Passagen*, firmly at the center of Benjamin's theoretical labor is proven by the fact that the "Theses on the Concept of History," probably composed in the early months of 1940, could be presented by their author not so much as an autonomous text, but rather as "a theoretical armature for the second study on Baudelaire" (*GB*, 6:400); "to the extent that they have the character of an experiment," he writes a month later to Gretel Adorno, "they function, not only from the methodological point of view, as a preparation for the continuation of *Baudelaire*" (*GB*, 6:436).

From a "miniature model" of the book on Paris, *Baudelaire* has now become the place where the project of a "protohistory of the nineteenth century"—that had initially been assigned to the *Passagen*—has found perhaps its most advanced realization, in which all the motifs of Benjamin's thought seem to converge. The last mention of the work is in a letter of May 7, 1940 (*GB*, 6:444), a few weeks before the flight from Paris that will take Benjamin first to Lourdes and Marseilles, and then, after the clandestine crossing of the French-Spanish border, to his death at Port-Bou on September 26, 1940.

The *Passagen*—or rather, the collection of cards and materials that constituted its documentary basis (because today we know that what the editors have presented as a book is only Benjamin's card-index)—were published by Rolf Tiedemann in 1982, as volume 5 of the *Gesammelte Schriften*. The two parts of the book on Baudelaire that had reached the draft phrase were instead published in volume 1 of the *Gesammelte Schriften*, that is, the first draft of the second of the three envisioned parts (*Das Paris des Second Empire bei Baudelaire*) and the new draft of the central section of the same (*Über einige Motive bei Baudelaire*); to these have been added the collection of *Zentralpark* notes, more additional materials of a various nature published in the *Anmerkungen* [Annotations] to volume 1 (*GS*, 1.3:1137–1188). No attempt at a reconstruction of the book had been undertaken, nor at that stage of the edition (1974), did it appear to be possible.

The situation changed radically in 1981 with the discovery of the manuscripts in the Bibliothèque. One of the envelopes (catalogued by the discoverer as the fifth) contained a collection of cards and notes that referred in various ways to the work on Baudelaire and that (integrated with a few other manuscripts found immediately after with their help) permit us not only to reconstruct the structure of the book with a sufficient approximation, but also to shed light to an unanticipated degree both on the genesis and evolution of the work and, more generally, on the entire method of labor in Benjamin's final workshop. Tiedemann, undoubtedly the greatest connoisseur of Benjamin's manuscripts, while publishing a selection of the Paris Manuscripts in *Gesammelte Schriften*, wrote: "if [such manuscripts] had been accessible to the editor at the time, it would have been possible, in this case [namely, for the book on Baudelaire] . . . to offer at least the model of a historical-critical edition of Benjamin's tests, even if it would have meant shattering the limits of the present edition" (*GS*, 7.2:736).

The present volume [Agamben's Italian edition of Benjamin's *Baudelaire*] is an attempt to offer not such a historical-critical edition (which, in translation, is obviously not thinkable), but a historical-genetic edition that, on the basis of all the documentation available today, allows us to follow to an exceptionally rich and articulated degree the genesis and development, in the various phases of its drafting, of the "work in progress" that constitutes, in a certain sense, the *summa* of Benjamin's late production.[3]

I underline the expression *work in progress* not only because this book is one of the rare occasions where one can succeed in following and displaying the genesis of a work in its movement from the first conception and the rearranging of the card-file up to the book. But I also emphasize it because this work allows us to reflect in an exemplary way on what *work in progress* signifies—that is, to ask the question: Toward where does the work in progress proceed, where is it going? Or put otherwise, what is an incomplete work and how does it differ from a completed work?

We are accustomed to distinguish clearly between these two concepts and certainly in common editorial practice the distinction seems to be self-evident. But things are not always that simple. There are works that present themselves as incomplete, but that the author has decided to publish as such. This is the case with Pasolini's *Petrolio*, which is certainly not easy to classify among completed works or incomplete works. And if one goes back in time, one often encounters works, and not only literary ones, that have been completed, one says, by other authors (think of the *Roman de la Rose*, begun, one says, by one author, Guillaume de Lorris, and finished by another, Jean de Meun, or Bellini's *Festino degli dei* which is said to have been completed by Titian—but what sense does the word "completed" have here?).

Just as difficult is the distinction between completed and incomplete for posthumous works, as the works of Benjamin are for the most part. Here the decision is often made by the publisher and not always according to philological criteria.

The fact is that every work is in some way a work in progress, a work on the way: but on the way toward where and toward what? One too easily takes it for granted that the work is in progress toward its completed form, which is reached or missed as the case may be, as if the way was always necessarily direct between a middle and an end. But certain works—and perhaps all works of a certain weight—are destined to remain always on the way, and on the way toward themselves, and this does not necessarily imply an end, indeed at times it can exclude it. As Aristotle said of nature, every work is a *hodos*, a way toward itself.

In this sense, a work never stops keeping itself on the way toward itself: what happens is that, for reasons that can be the most varied, at a certain point the author *abandons* the work, as Giacometti said of his paintings. And this abandonment does not necessarily coincide with anything that could legitimately be considered as finished—even if the adjective *non-finished* does not seem adequate either.

Here I would like to call your attention to a singular fact, which shows that even textual criticism and philology—that is, the so-called ecdotic sciences, which relate to the editing of texts—are beginning to realize this truth. You know that in the tradition of philology, the philologist's labor consisted in examining the manuscripts or existing editions of a certain work, in order to arrive at the constitution of a text, called critical, that was presented as the most authentic possible. So, in the fifties, the Beissner edition of the hymns of Hölderlin produced one unique critical text where the manuscripts presented many drafts of the same hymn. But a few decades later in the Sattler edition, there was no longer one unique hymn, but three, five, or even six hymns that were considered no longer as drafts or variants but as poems that were in some way autonomous and with regard to which it does not make sense to ask oneself whether they are complete or incomplete.

This perhaps corresponds to the crisis that the concept of work is undergoing in our time, a crisis in which so-called contemporary art plays a certain role in a way that is not properly responsible. But this is not the place to put forward this problem, which is certainly decisive. What matters to me is rather to signal to you the peculiarity of this edition that, perhaps for the first time with such precision, has sought to follow the way of a work toward itself.

The occasion was all the more precious inasmuch as Benjamin, who often discusses the theoretical presuppositions of his work with his friends in minute detail, seems by contrast to jealously keep the secret of the so-called material processes of his own production, which have thus wound up assuming in the eyes of his critics and friends a legendary aura of esoterism. Precisely insofar as it allows us to follow the process of its genesis and development in all its phases and in an extremely well-articulated way, the book on Baudelaire, exploding this myth, presents us instead, in its becoming, the model of a materialist writing as Benjamin understood it, in which not only does the theory illuminate the material processes of creation, but the latter also sheds a new light on the theory.

Benjamin distinguishes early on between documentation and construction in his work. Espagne and Werner, who have called attention to this distinction, rightly observe that it is not to be understood as a "chronological division between two phases of work, but as a systematic distinction between two fundamentally different modes of work that, from the chronological point of view, sometimes run in parallel."[4] The fact is that Benjamin grasped with perfect clarity the Marxian distinction between mode of research (*Forschungsweise*) and mode of exposition (*Darstellungsweise*), which he explicitly cites in section N of the *Passagen*:

> Research must appropriate to itself material in the particulars, must analyze their different forms of development [*Entwicklungsformen*], and track down the internal link [*inneres Band*]. Only after this work has been completed can the real movement be represented in a suitable manner. If this succeeds, if the life of the material [*das Leben des Stoffs*] now presents itself as ideally reflected, it can seem that one has to do with an a priori construction. (*GS*, 5.1:581)

It is necessary to reflect on the implications of this passage for a correct analysis of the processes of intellectual labor: the material, which research collects, is not something inert, but something living, which already contains in itself forms of development and an internal bond. The task of research is that of bringing to light these forms and this link, in a way that allows the very life of the material to appear at the end as an a priori construction. When in a letter to Gretel Adorno of October 9, 1935, Benjamin writes of having pushed himself lately "to a decisive point in the graduated network of the construction that is so to speak cut by that of documentation" (*GB*, 6:170–171), he is expressing in a more figurative way the clear distinction and, at the same time, the intimate interpenetration of documentation and construction, mode of research and mode of exposition. In terms of the relationship between documentation and construction, something happens here that is similar to what Benjamin describes in the encounter between past and present in the "now of knowability" (*Jetzt der Erkennbarkeit,* one of Benjamin's most secret concepts, which he himself admitted to "having fashioned in a very esoteric way" [*GB*, 6:171], but which becomes perfectly transparent from this perspective):

> The historical index of images means, in fact, not only that they belong to a determinate epoch, but above all that they attain legibility only in a determinate epoch. And precisely this having attained "legibility" is a determinate critical point of movement within it. Every present is determined by the images that are synchronous with it: every Now [*Jetzt*] is the Now of a determinate knowability. In this Now, the truth is laden with time to the point of shattering. . . . It is not that the past throws its light on the present or the present on the past, but the image is that in which what has been is united in a lightning flash with the Now in a constellation. In other words: the image is the dialectic at a standstill. (*GS*, 5.1:577–578)

In this case more than anywhere, the concrete analysis of Benjamin's productive process allows us to clarify fundamental categories of his theory of knowledge: just as the constructive moment is not imposed a posteriori on the material of documentary research, but rises up out of its own interior movement which unfolds in the various phases up to the final draft, so also is contemporaneity (*Jetztzeit*) not something that can be situated chronologically only in the present, but the constellation in which what has been is united in a lightning flash with the Now and a determinate historical fact is polarized into its pre- and post-history (cf. *GS*, 5.1:69; N7a,1).

A chance event that was probably unique in the history of historical-philosophical literature (and thus certainly in the work of Benjamin) has made it possible, thanks to the Paris manuscripts (particularly the *Lists* and the *Blue Papers*, respectively sections 2.7 and 3.3 of the Italian edition of *Baudelaire*), to follow at close range the "internal movement" by means of which documentation, in its development toward the draft, intersects with the "graduated network" of construction.

It is as if, beyond possessing the card-index of an author (in this case, the "Annotations and Materials" section of the book on Paris) and the work that results from it (or, rather, part of it), we can, thanks to a miracle of animation, observe the card-index as it moves and arranges itself toward the draft, laying bare its internal lines of development. And this movement of the material is not theoretically neutral, but is accompanied (without it being possible to decide to what extent theoretical reflections are putting the card-index in motion or, conversely, the life of the material is secreting the pearl of theory) by an imposing production of fragments of a philosophical-methodological character (of which *Zentralpark* is the most remarkable concretion and which, symptomatically, is always interposed by metatextual notations on the order and disposition of the texts).

The phase that classical rhetoric, situating it between *inventio* (today we would say the discovery of the subject and its documentation) and *elocutio* (corresponding to the exposition or draft), called *dispositio* and that Cicero defined as *rerum inventarum in ordinem distributio* [the distribution of invented things in order], thus emerges in the foreground in Benjamin's creative process, in striking contrast with the privilege accorded by modern authors to the phase of exposition, but with characteristics that are so strange that one can rightly speak of a "dialectico-Benjaminian disposition."[5]

This also allows us to situate in the proper perspective the "literary montage" that Benjamin once identifies with the most proper method of his work (*GS*, 5.1:574). It is not so much a matter, as Adorno maintains, of "allowing meanings to appear solely by means of a shocking montage [*schokhafte Montage*] of the materials" and of writing a work "composed only of citations,"[6] so much as rather—by means of making *dispositio* the center of the compositional process—of allowing the forms of development and the internal bond contained in the philological materials to lead to the draft solely through their construction. From this point of view, as Tiedemann suggests, the book on Baudelaire certainly allows us to imagine "what the draft [of the *Passagen*], which Benjamin never reached, would have looked like" (*GS*, 5.2:1073).

More generally, the whole methodological dispute with Adorno in the exchange of letters that followed the first draft of *Baudelaire* is illuminated once one clearly has in mind (as this edition permits one to do) Benjamin's compositional method and the concept of construction implicit in it. Against his friend who reproved him for having omitted mediation through theory and of thus having remained entangled in a "dismayed exposition of pure facticity" (*GS*, 1.3:1098), Benjamin holds firm to the necessity of what he defines as a "methodological precaution" implicit in construction:

> I mean to say that speculation can take its necessarily reckless flight with some prospect of success only if, instead of putting on the wax wings of the esoteric, it seeks its source of strength solely in construction. Construction required that the second part of the book be formed essentially from philological materials. Therefore it is less a matter of an "ascetic discipline" than of a methodological precaution. . . . When you speak of a "dismayed exposition of facticity," you are characterizing in this way the genuine philological attitude. This must be dropped in construction not only for love of its results, but as such. . . . The appearance of narrow facticity, which adheres to philological research and casts its spell on the researcher, vanishes to the degree that the object is constructed in an historical perspective. The lines of flight of this construction converge in their own historical experience. With this the object is constructed as a monad. In the monad that which, as textual evidence, lay idle in mythic rigidity, becomes living. (*GS*, 1.3:1103–1104)

The reference to Leibniz's concept of the monad is to be understood literally here. That the monad has no windows "through which anything can enter into it or come out of it" implies that its transformations "proceed from an internal principle."[7] On the other hand, because its nature is "representative," each monad represents, along with the entire universe, also "the body that has been assigned to it in particular."[8] That the philological evidence of documentation presents itself in construction as a monad means, then, that it has no need, in order to be able to be interpreted, of the mediating influence of theory; on the contrary, only if the intertwining of documentation and construction has been pushed to the end will the work then be able to "be struck, not to say shaken, by interpretation" (*GS*, 1.3:1104).

There is, in Benjamin's method, something like a renewal of the medieval doctrine according to which the material already contains the forms within itself, is already full of form in an "inchoative" and potential state, and knowledge consists in nothing other than in bringing to light (*eductio*) these forms hidden (*inditae*) in the material. What to Adorno up to the end seemed like an adialectical residue is instead a profound constructive adherence to this "form that flows" (*forma fluens*, as the medievals said) in the material itself. The vanishing point toward which the constructive becoming of this form-material is converging is not, however, as in the medieval theologians, the divine intellect, but "our own historical experience."

Here one sees, in action so to speak, the conception of philology as mystical practice, which the young Benjamin discussed with Scholem. As in every mystical experience, the philologist had to lower himself body and soul into opacity and into the mists of the investigation of regests and documents, of archives and glosses, of palimpsests and variants. But this practice, in which the risk of losing one's way is constant, is also a contact with the material, from which the forms seem to emerge in a sort of divinatory illumination and in which, as in the astonishing theorem of a medieval philosopher condemned for this reason as a heretic, "the mind, God, and the material are the same thing" (*mens, Deus, et Yle idem sunt*).

I want to conclude—but in reality one never concludes, one abandons, as Giacometti said of his paintings—with what is for me the riskiest but also the most vital center in the adventure that was the reconstruction of this book that—like every "work in progress"—remains properly interminable.

I am referring to the surprising fact that the reconstruction of the genesis and development of the book goes hand in hand with the delineation of the image of Baudelaire's poetry that Benjamin had in mind—so that the subject matter is revealed to be indiscernible from the way in which the book was formed. It was as if the very becoming of this work in progress—the slow, detailed, tenacious procedure of its construction, in which, as we have seen, the *form* of the draft seems to spring from the very assembly (*montaggio*) of the research *materials*—repeated and almost mimicked Baudelaire's strategy in his fatal duel with his time, the age of advanced capitalism.

To the experience of *choc*, which according to Benjamin stands at the center of Baudelaire's poetry, corresponds in Benjamin what Adorno perhaps improperly called the "shocking montage" of the materials; to the poetic experience of the loss and recovery of the aura, there corresponds in the book the glance of the researcher who, while he observes the fragments that he is patiently assembling, feels in the same way that he is being looked at by them and succeeds in providing them with the capacity to return his glance—which is, as you know, the definition that Benjamin, in an important fragment published here for the first time, gives of the aura.

Benjamin—who in the reading room of the Bibliothèque nationale feels himself confusing the rustle of the pages of books with those of the leaves painted on the arches of the vault or in their *flâneries* along the streets of old Paris and seeks to decipher the signs of the time—is engaged in the same deadly conflict that Baudelaire fought with his time.

I believe that the reader who enters the labyrinth of this book—which, if I have succeeded in showing it as truly "in progress," that is, on the way toward itself, is a living, throbbing thing—should finally encounter a Minotaur who is a curious monster, half Baudelaire and half Benjamin, half poet and half critic. And this is surely the most surprising experience— this hybrid monster coincides in the end perfectly with the very structure of the book that the reader has in his hands. It is also a hybrid of material and form, research and draft, reading and writing.

Translated by Adam Kotsko

Notes

The text of this unpublished lecture, given by Giorgio Agamben in 2013 in Rome, contains parts of the introduction to the author's Italian edition of Benjamin's posthumous book. All translations from Benjamin's correspondence are based on those provided by the author and the original German text.

1. Walter Benjamin, *Gesammelte Briefe*, 6 vols., ed. Christoph Gödde and Henri Lonitz (Frankfurt am Main: Suhrkamp, 1995–2000), 5:489–490. Hereafter cited in text as *GB*.

2. Walter Benjamin, *Gesammelte Schriften*, 7 vols., ed. Rolf Tiedemann (Frankfurt am Main: Suhrkamp, 1974–1989), 5.2:1158–59. Hereafter cited in text as *GS*.

3. The expression "work in progress" appears in English in Agamben's original text.

4. Michel Espagne and Michael Werner, "Vom Passagen-Projekt zum "Baudelaire." Neue Handschriften zum Spätwerk Walter Benjamins," in *Deutsche Vierteljahrsschrift für Literaturwissenschaft und Geistesgeschichte* 58 (1984): 602.

5. Pierre Missac, "Dispositio dialectico-Benjaminiana," in *Walter Benjamin et Paris*, ed. Heinz Weismann (Paris: Cerf, 1986), 689–706.

6. Theodor W. Adorno, *Über Walter Benjamin*, ed. R. Tiedemann (Frankfurt am Main: Suhrkamp, 1970), 22.

7. Gottfried Leibniz, *The Monadology*, §7 and §11.

8. Ibid., §62.

On Vanishing and Fulfillment

ELI FRIEDLANDER

In various places in Benjamin's writing the divine is identified in the total passing away and disappearance of the phenomenal. Probably the most famous case for such annihilative characterization of the divine occurs in the essay "Critique of Violence." Yet, the account of divine violence in that essay, with its intimation of active destruction, tempts one to construe the moment of disappearance in terms of catastrophic effects wrought by God on the physical world, on the model of a force that makes visible changes in reality. This problematic figuration of the catastrophic in Benjamin's vision of history might hide a broader and more pervasive "logic" of *redemptive* vanishing and dissolution. One of the clearest formulations of this duality of vanishing and fulfillment is found in the "Theological-Political Fragment" in which Benjamin states that "nature is Messianic by reason of its eternal and total passing away."[1] Such a notoriously difficult statement is quoted here at the outset only to suggest how this essay can be seen as laying out a direction for its interpretation.

I will argue that in order to properly grasp the relation of the annihilative and the redemptive, it is necessary, first and foremost, to understand these as pertaining to the dimension of meaning or to Benjamin's conception of language as such. This, for sure, does not preclude the dimension of human action, but rather seeks to relate its highest possibilities with the most articulate, most existent, or actualized state of meaning. To underscore this matter it is best to read Benjamin's account of divine violence against the background of some of the essays composed in the same period. I will therefore begin by considering briefly Benjamin's early essays on language translation and criticism to trace in them the internal relation of actualization and destruction as possibilities of meaning.

On Vanishing and Fulfillment in Meaning

In the essay "On Language as such and on the Language of Man," the relation of the logic of fulfillment and that of vanishing can be discerned initially with regard to the disappearance of the subject from the world in the realization of the task of naming the world. Indeed, if one follows the broad lines of Benjamin's formulation of his view of language in terms of the narrative of creation, the Edenic condition, and the Fall, it is clear that man is not viewed as having a specific essence of his own. Adam's task is to continue or fulfill creation by naming the world. Whereas natural beings are understood as created by the divine word—as containing so to speak, the possibility and tendency of expression inherent to this act of creation—in man, language is set free to give expression to all of created nature. Thus the fundamental position of a subject in language should be understood together with the sense that man is realized by fulfilling the task of creation in naming beings. One might say, that man is realized as subject by naming the world. But this means in turn that it is only the unity of the world articulated in meaning that will be the realization of man's highest capacity. It is a condition in which the meaning of the world as a whole is that through which the position of a human subject is realized. In other words there is a sense in which what is expressed here is the willingness to disappear as an individual subject positioned *in* experience, or in the world, in favor of the emergence of a significant world.[2]

To speak of man's capacity to realize meaning in terms of the world as whole, further implies that fulfillment cannot be contained in the living unity of *a* being in the world. This understanding is, I take it, at the basis of Benjamin's characterization of revelation in that early essay. Revelation is not a manifestation *in* the world. Revelation must be assessed at the level of the very existence of language. It is not a specific meaningful manifestation that is intrinsically above all phenomena. It is absolute communication, that is, communication that goes through all the orders of being, correlative with the total articulation of the world in meaning. Revelation is having the world itself totally articulated or realized in meaning. It is the reason that Benjamin argues that the only sphere from which the unsayable is totally absent is that of revelation. But this is also the condition in which partial seemingly self-sufficient substantial unities come to be seen as partaking in the uniqueness of a world. In other words, full realization of the tendency of expression inherent in nature is seen to involve language as a whole.

I take this to be the point of the image of the flow of communication closing the essay:

> The language of an entity is the medium in which its mental being is communicated. The uninterrupted flow of this communication runs through the whole of nature, from the lowest forms of existence to man and from man to God. Man communicated himself to God through name, which he gives to nature. . . . The language of nature is comparable to a secret password that each sentry passes to the next in his own language, but the meaning of the password is the sentry's language itself. All higher language is a translation of lower ones, until in ultimate clarity the word of God unfolds, which is the unity of this movement made up of language. (*SW* 1:74)

Revelation is "the unity of movement made up of language" and correlative with establishing a continuity of meaning between the different orders of beings in language. Note that Benjamin calls this communication a *flow*. The flow is the communication of of a force, revealed in establishing a continuity between different orders of beings. It is not a force of nature that is limited to a certain ontological domain, or order of beings, but rather a force that runs through the different orders of creation, or that is shown to be present when the phenomenal is presented as a hierarchy or order of beings in language.

The characterization of revelation in relation to the whole that is a world, should not lead us to conclude that fulfillment cannot be recognized in the singular and the finite. This is where Benjamin's thinking must be understood as monadological in nature. Indeed the totality can be fragmentarily refracted in the singular, for instance, in the work of art or, more precisely, in its afterlife. One of the possibilities to work constructively toward that condition of the dissolution of conditional meaningful unities in favor of the realization of meaning as such, as it is refracted in the singularity of the work of art is elaborated in his essay "The Task of the Translator." Although concerned with the particular poetic work, translation, in relating the language of the original and the language of the translation, presents something pertaining to language as a whole or to what Benjamin calls language as such, or the pure language.

Translation, as Benjamin understands it, is the vanishing of the local unity of sense in favor of relationships of meaning that cannot be localized ("a translation touches the original lightly and only at the infinitely small point of the sense" [*SW*, 1:261]). Translation properly understood is the movement from intentional language to the intentionless, from the specific intentional context to the articulation of meaning by the measure of language as a whole. Consider how, for Benjamin, a way of meaning in the original is *echoed* in the field of language as a whole in the translation: "the intention of the [poet] is never directed toward the language as such, at its totality, but is aimed solely and immediately at specific linguistic contextual aspects. . . . The intention of a translation . . . [is] language as a whole, taking an individual work in an alien language as a point of departure" (*SW*, 1:259). The original has a specific intention, a poetic context. In the translation, however, that specific context is echoed in the linguistic forest, and there is no limit on what part of language needs to be brought to bear in order to reproduce the ways of meaning. The pure language, made manifest fragmentarily in translations is thus expressionless because expression requires *specific* unified manifestations: "In this pure Language . . . all information, all sense, and all intention finally encounter a stratum in which they are destined to be extinguished" (*SW*, 1:261).[3]

I would like to suggest a third register in which one can conceive of the dissolution of sense in relation to actualization, namely Benjamin's early work on romanticism. The work of dissolution is most evident in Benjamin's description of the effects of criticism on the work of art. Criticism realizes the work by dissolving its individuality in the medium of the idea of art. That medium is itself constituted by criticism, as a continuum of the different forms of art: "In this medium all the presentational forms hang constantly together, interpenetrate one another, and merge into the unity of the absolute art form, which is identical with the idea of art. Thus the romantic idea of the unity of art lies in the idea of a continuum of forms" (*SW*, 1:165). In criticism there is both an intensification of meaning, or relatedness, and a dissolution of individuality. When things hang together, their own identity is problematized to the extreme.

But the standpoint of actualization in the dissertation is not identified solely by way of the romantic idea of criticism. It is counterbalanced, in the epilogue, by another moment, traced to Goethe's conception of the ideal. I hint here at this complex moment, for it will be of importance in my discussion of divine violence: The formal, or methodical dissolution of romantic criticism cannot be the mode of realization since it has no end. It requires the moment of critical violence which Benjamin identifies with the expressionless. The expressionless is not identified in the dissolution of individual intention or expression, but in an arrest or discontinuity that seals or completes. It is the shattering of the semblance that made the finite appear to have possibilities of completeness internal to it, that is, to appear self-sufficient. It is the ultimate judgment in which the finite is reduced to what it is in truth, fully actualized and shown as lacking, as merely a fragment, albeit a fragment of the maximal reality which is the ideal. Such a shattering is the sobering and striking actualization of the finite that presents its core of reality, or presents it as partaking in the highest reality.[4]

Pure Means and Realization as Dissolution

Before tackling the difficult notion of divine violence, I would like to consider an example of the relation of vanishing, or dissolution and fulfillment, taken from an earlier moment of Benjamin's essay "Critique of Violence," namely the nonviolent resolution of conflict through pure means. I will begin by explicating the notion of *pure means*, and then turn to its subjective preconditions and to its grounding in language.

Pure means "are never those of direct solutions but always of indirect solutions" (*SW*, 1:244). The sphere of means or technique at its purest is not to be identified with the instrumental put at the service of justified ends or purposes. Pure means are not means to pure ends. Rather, pure means would in the first place be defined by the possibility of remaining *solely* with means, to be purely instrumental. But what can pure instrumentality without end eventuate in, if it is not directed by some concept of *achievement*? How can it be valuable in achieving nothing? That is, how does one understand fulfillment while getting away from a concept of achievement that is wedded to the articulation of an end.

Instrumentality without end should not be confused with essential incompletion. One might be tempted to conceive of what it is to remain in the sphere of means, in terms of some form of purposiveness without purpose. But this would be precisely falling into the kind of problematic aestheticization of the political that Carl Schmitt identifies in parliamentarianism, and which he calls "political romanticism." There is completion that is not achievement, and that cannot be articulated in the form of an end. It has the form of complete disappearance. What remains open to pure means, then is to have solution be the dissolution of conflict, its disappearance, rather than bringing about the victory (whether in some sense justified or not) of one side over the other. I note that justice is conceived in relation to the purity of ends (or to what will replace ends in the idea of a pure terminal state). Thus with pure means, one is not quite in the realm of morality, or one is not concerned with doing justice, but rather with a mode of activity that can at most identify resolution with dissolution.

Benjamin's understanding of the importance of such disappearance of conflict can initially be considered in the case of conflicts between private persons over matters of property, where, for example, a prolongation of conflict would be detrimental to both sides. The dissolution of the conflict would be imperative out of "the fear of mutual disadvantages that threatens to arise from violent confrontation, whatever the outcome might be."[5] But this perspective might only take us so far as to explain some motivation for a settlement of the conflict, which would be equally nondetrimental, or equally beneficial to both parties. That is, it would remain in the sphere of a calculation of interests and thereby, while settling the conflict would not give us the proper perspective on the possibility of its dissolution or disappearance.

But Benjamin notes that something further is at stake when one conceives of the matter in relation to conflicts between nations, that is when addressing such conflicts from the standpoint of history: "It is different when classes and nations are in conflict, *since the higher orders that threaten to overwhelm equally victor and vanquished are hidden from the feeling of most, and from the intelligence of almost all* . . . such higher orders and the common interests corresponding to them . . . constitute the most enduring motive for a policy of pure means" (*SW*, 1:245; emphasis added). Benjamin refrains in that moment of the essay from explicating what these higher orders are, but one might identify them with the way in which both victor and defeated are equally caught up in fate. In other words, the possibility and importance of pure means is to be recognized in relation to a sense of the pervasiveness of what Benjamin calls in that essay "mythical violence," a notion I will elaborate shortly.

One example Benjamin gives of the use of pure means is the technique of the conference. Diplomacy is activity through pure means and demands such virtues as "courtesy [or politeness], sympathy, peaceableness, trust." I want to briefly focus on courtesy or politeness [*Höflichkeit*] as an example of such subjective virtues, before considering their objective preconditions, the real basis for the methodical deployment of pure means in language or meaning.

In a text entitled "Ibizan Sequence," written between April and May 1932, Benjamin considers the role of politeness as mediator. The text opens with a remark that in human affair conflicts of interests (or conflicts for survival) often leave unheeded various ethical demands. The truly ethical, one might say, has in human affairs, no force in bringing about the end of a conflict. The situation, in these cases, might for sure present itself as a conflict of duties, as though the two sides represent irreconcilable ethical demands. But these will most likely be moralistic garbs of interests belonging to the struggle for existence. In such cases one is in need of a mediator that neither belongs to morality nor to the sphere of interests. That is, one needs to transform and incorporate ethical virtues in such a way that they come to bear on the dissolution of the conflict (which, again, is not the same as doing justice): "The true mediator, the product of the conflict between morality and the struggle for existence, is politeness" (*SW*, 2:586).

One might object that politeness is too little. Instead of morals one gets mere manners. Moreover, that is it precisely what would allow people to cover up with a beautiful veneer the ruthlessness of their behavior and the unrestrained rule of interest. And it can indeed be nothing but beautiful appearance. But, for Benjamin there is also another way to conceive of the matter. Politeness draws its force from the grounding of conflict in an abstract view of adversarial positions. One might say that abstractness allows one to get a hold on one's adversary, that is, to pin him down *as* an adversary. Therefore, all such abstract articulation of the situation remains within the sphere of the conflictual—it provides plenty of opportunities for impoliteness masquerading as honor or authenticity, according to Benjamin.

Politeness allows the expansion of the conflict beyond any of the conventional ways in which it is played out. There is something unintuitive about the dissolution of conflict being based on boundlessly expanding it, that is, expanding it beyond any of the rules and conventions through which it is played. One might even argue that certain conventions associated with engaging in conflict are essential so as not to have its effects cause harm indistinguishably (thus the idea of conducting war with certain rules that protect the civilian population). To take another example: a duel is a situation in which conflict is conducted according to the strictest conventions. The conventions are like "the lists of a jousting tournament" (*SW*, 2:586).

It is therefore important to note that this idea of doing away with the bounds of the conflict does not mean doing away with it, as it would be encouraging one to view others out of sympathy, that is, over and above what they are as adversaries. It is rather making the conflict all pervasive. But as Benjamin thinks of it, it becomes a precondition for the entrance of powers and instances that the abstract standpoint has disallowed. The conflict cannot be dissolved as long as it is set in abstract terms, it must seep toward details and singularities, which are precisely the places in which politeness has power or comes to its own: "an alert openness to the extreme, the comic, the private and the surprising aspects in a situation is the advanced school of politeness" (*SW*, 2:588).

Expanding the conflict into surroundings and bringing in the articulations of details by means of the myriad of ways politeness has of avoiding straightforward confrontation also allows to reposition the components of the situation in a different order, thus disengaging them from their seemingly unmovable position in the conflict. Benjamin describes this as though moving from an adversarial game of cards to a game of solitary, or, as it is called in German, patience. In order to get from the confrontational character of a situation to the condition in which everything unfolds according to a simple order, one needs patience for sure. If indeed politeness is a form of mediation, that allows one to transform the so-called ethical stance, by translating the intransigent rage of moralism into manners, the only virtue which is incorporated into politeness, as it were, would be patience. It is only patience that "politeness adopts without modification." I will not go into the question of the way patience points to the role of time in fulfillment apart from an end, but only warn against conceiving of the situation as one of eternal postponement.

At this point, I would like to return to the objective presuppositions that underlie the possibility of dissolution of conflict. In discussing the form of the conference in "Critique of Violence," Benjamin notes further that the conference is a technique in which "there is no sanction to lying." Subjectively speaking this means that such technique is not taking up a moral stance or judgment. It avoids moralism. But objectively speaking, this is taken by Benjamin to signal that "there is a sphere of human agreement that is nonviolent to the extent that it is wholly inaccessible to violence: the proper sphere of "understanding language" (*SW*, 1:245). Ultimately, the possibility of pure means points to the sphere of language. It is in language that pure means allow the formation of not only a status quo, modus vivendi, or middle ground, but truly a medium of dissolution.

Lying can be encompassed by language. This is not so just because the liar expresses himself in language, and thus can be understood as much as the person who says what is right. Moreover, it is not just that lying can be encompassed as part of our view of human nature. This would be nothing surprising. Rather, the way in which lying can be encompassed in language points to something deeper, namely to a distinction that is to be drawn between fulfillment in meaning on the one hand, and correctness, which is an aim of knowledge, on the other. From the standpoint of fulfillment which is not the realization of an aim, lies can be encompassed, and their violence neutralized, in presenting what is higher.

Let me try to clarify what is at issue by referring to another, related example of the indirectness of pure means in language, in Benjamin's use of the method of quotation, whose principle is described in the "Epistemo-Critical Preface" of *The Origin of German Tragic Drama*. It is in considering the form of the medieval treatise, which Benjamin takes as a model for his own writing that he considers the authority of quotation in contrast to other models of authoritative expression to which philosophy has availed itself—such as the "*coercive* proof in mathematics,"[6] or the all-encompassing power of the systematic. In the treatise, Benjamin writes, the only mode of authority allowed is that of methodical quoting. This is indeed a method of pure means, that is, essential indirectness: "Its method is essentially presentation. Method is a digression. Presentation as digression—such is the methodological nature of the treatise." In presentation by way of quotation, one precisely overcomes the polarity of judgment as correct or incorrect (*richtig und falsch*) in language. For what is incorrect in its original context of assertion may be as valuable as what is correct, when used as quotation material for the presentation of a higher configuration of truth (*Wahrheit*).[7]

As becomes evident in the task Benjamin set himself in his later work on the Paris of the Second Empire, the method of quotation deployed in the *Arcades Project*, would allow expressions of illusion, self-deception, fancies, dreams, as well as lies, to be assumed, taken up, and put on a par with what is correct, factually speaking, in presenting the face of necessity in history. This is not because such realms of semblance can be placed in their proper context of facts, but rather because they can be assumed and partake in the presentation of a higher order of truth.

Truth in that latter sense is not opposed by lies, but rather by a demonic principle that perverts the spirit of language. Whereas lies can be encompassed and dissolved by a methodical application of pure means, this other pernicious semblance, which has a far deeper metaphysical ground, must be *eradicated*. To clarify what this mode of semblance is consider that quotation used *methodically*—that is, throughout or boundlessly as the only mode of authority—tends to forego the *I* dimension of judgment, that is, the *authority* of the first person. This suggests that, if there is something that will resist this method, it is the principle of subjectivity, or the power of the *I*.[8]

A hint of this deeper problem may be found in Benjamin's remarks on the paradox of the Cretan or liar's paradox. First, Benjamin emphasizes that it is essentially a paradox that must be formulated in the first person. That is, it is not something that can be put in the reflexive yet impersonal form "this sentence is false," where *this* supposedly is self-referential. Secondly, this would mean that for him the liar's paradox is not a problem of the realm of meaning. Indeed, the paradox cannot be dismissed as meaningless. It is not to be dismissed by considering logic alone. It has a source that is ontologically distinct from the sphere of language: This source is the *I*'s relation to language. Finally, Benjamin formulates the paradox, in all its force, not in terms of a single assertion, but of the *I*'s relation to all of his assertions, that is to a principle of deception that pervades the *I*'s use of language. (Benjamin compares it to Descartes's evil demon).

In other words, the way in which the liar's paradox does not reduce to incoherence, shows that, ontologically speaking, the semblance it presents has a reality. As Benjamin puts it: "it is an appearance that cannot be resolved in the truth—it can only be destroyed by it" (*SW*, 1:211). It manifests what it is for the *I* to arrogate to himself an authority that can only belong to language itself, the power of language. This is not merely egoistic lying, that is, lying in order to achieve various purposes. The metaphysical problem of the relation of the *I* to language is not lying, but a principle of deception that goes to the root of the spiritual character of evil. The authority of subjectivity is demonic; it exhibits itself as always triumphant or never wrong.

The full elaboration of this problem of the relation of subjectivity and mastery over meaning is given in the final pages of Benjamin's *The Origin of German Tragic Drama*, in what might be called the recognition of the satanic character of the allegorist. The allegorist is revealed as the embodiment of the power that the *I* seeks to monopolize for himself, the power of language. This absolutizing of subjectivity is revealed as an empty play of mirrors, which masters only a dead world of objects. Subjectivity comes to nothing.

Divine Violence and the Afterlife of Meaning

Bearing in mind the various elaborations of disappearance and realization in meaning, I want to reconsider the annihilating character of divine violence, which I raised in the introduction to this essay. The notion of divine violence is elaborated by way of a complex contrast with that of mythical violence. Both divine violence and mythical violence problematize to the extreme the means-end structure of action. In the case of mythical violence, the key to this is to be sought in Benjamin's understanding of the character of its *manifestation*.

"Mythical violence in its archetypal form is a mere manifestation of the gods" (*SW*, 1:248); Benjamin exemplifies initially how one is to understand such a nonmediate manifestation of violence by considering the familiar case of an outburst of anger. Anger has an intensive manifestation. It is not as if the outburst is the external expression of a distinct inner mental state of anger. The outburst *is* intensely manifest anger. An outburst of anger may be related to an occurrence that lies in the past but the person does not take the past as a *reason* for now manifesting anger. Nor does it mean that the outburst of anger is merely *caused* by what occurred in the past. The precipitation of the violent outburst may be occasioned by the smallest and insignificant event. Moreover, such an outburst of anger may establish a new mode of behavior of those affected by it, without *aiming* at these effects. For instance, an outburst of anger may draw a line not to be crossed, without it being in any way the intention of the angry person, nor a reason for the expression of anger.

More generally, one wants to find a way to relate the notion of intensive manifestation to that of force and distinguish it from the presence in experience of such conditional structure, as that of cause and effect or of willing expressed through the relation of means and ends. To clarify, consider Kant's distinction between the quantity and quality in the mathematical principles of experience in the *Critique of Pure Reason*. The former are principles of extensive magnitude, whereas the latter define the behavior of intensive magnitudes. An extensive magnitude, such as length, is one whose parts are external to one another and thus can be summed up (or subtracted by taking away an identifiable part), whereas changes of intensive magnitude involve continuous increase or decrease of degree of one and the same quality. A simple example of the latter is a phenomenal quality such as the presence of color in the visual field. It can increase or decrease in degrees of intensity. Importantly, the distinction between degrees of intensity is correlative with the presence of a *force* that, Kant would argue, underlies such qualitative transformation.

To further draw the connection of this idea of intensive manifestation to that of *unlimited* force, consider that the problem of intensive magnitudes has been the locus of a reevaluation of the Kantian understanding of the "relation" of the thing in itself and experience. For Hermann Cohen, for instance, the identification of the intensive with qualities of the given in experience precisely touches on a problematic moment of Kant's idealism, namely the way in which the passive material of sensation is supposedly left out of the articulation of form whose source is the activity of the transcendental subject. Cohen approaches this problem through a reinterpretation of Kant's "Anticipations of Perceptions." In them Kant considers the principle of experience corresponding to the schema of the category of reality. The real in sensation is understood as that which corresponds to the possibility of intensive change in a quality in sensation from any given degree to zero. Cohen sees in that a danger of founding empirical reality on the ground of the sensuous given. He thus wishes to start from a principle of pure thinking, which would provide the explanatory ground for the change of intensity in sensation. Since these changes form an infinite continuum of degrees of quality, they must be based on the possibility of a pure thought of the infinitely small. It is this which science, primarily mathematical physics, has come to realize in the concept of the infinitesimal. The key for Cohen of the translatability of the qualitative intensive into the extensive character of universal law would be the notion of the infinitesimal introduced into mathematical physics.

In his "On the Program of the Coming Philosophy," written after reading Cohen's *Kant's Theory of Experience*, Benjamin raises the question of how to address the problem of the matter of sensation in Kant's idealism. But, contrary to the direction of Cohen's solution, Benjamin, seeks a method to think through the intensive character of experience without reducing it to the mathematical. This demands in the first place conceiving of intensive manifestation not merely with respect to given phenomenal qualities, but rather in terms of meaning. It also requires conceiving of instances in which intensive manifestation in meaning reveal a force that, in itself does not belong to the phenomenal. In other words, it would hold that the existence of a force that is infinite in character and does not *belong* to the order of regularities of experience *can* be meaningfully manifest in intensive terms. This separates fundamentally such manifestation of unlimited or unconditioned force from the causal order, and, of interest here, from the structure of a will that is causally effective through ends.

To return to Benjamin's account in "Critique of Violence," note that the paradigm of such an unlimited force—manifest in the intensification of meaning, and moreover closely related to the nature of mythic violence—is to be found in tragedy. The tragic is the manifestation of an unlimited force in the finite as a horrifying precision of meaning. It is as though a vast field of meaning, a series of unrelated events, from the standpoint of practical reasons and the successive order of causality, come together in the intensive and concentrated moment of recognition of the tragic hero.[9]

Such a manifestation of violence does not have the structure of will. It is the manifestation of the *existence* of the Gods. As Benjamin puts it, "Not a means to their ends, scarcely a manifestation of their will, but primarily a manifestation of their existence" (*SW*, 1:248). It follows that strictly speaking one is not to conceive of such a manifestation through the register of punishment (although it does involve the concept of retribution). Rather, mythical violence establishes a *boundary line*. It is, one might say, the coming to experience or to visibility in and through suffering of the very limit or the division of the finite and the infinite.[10]

At this point I wish to set divine violence against mythical violence and explicate the series of distinctions that Benjamin makes between the two: "If mythic violence is lawmaking, divine violence is law-destroying; if the former sets boundaries, the latter boundlessly destroys them; if mythic violence brings at once guilt and retribution, divine violence only purifies [*entsühnt*]; if the former threatens, the latter strikes; if the former is bloody, the latter is lethal without spilling blood" (*SW*, 1:250).

The manifestation of mythical violence draws a boundary. It has visibility and distinction over and above everything in experience. Divine violence is boundless insofar as the destruction it assumes affects the phenomenal equally. It does not have the character of the miraculous, or is not manifest in the intrusion of some infinite order into the finite order of experience. Insofar as one remains within the phenomenal, divine violence is *inconspicuous*. Put differently, it is not a violence to which one can attribute *specific* destructive effects. Rather, if at all, it is one that can be presented by taking up the destruction that belongs to the phenomenal *as such*.

It would therefore further be wrong to say that divine violence indicates how God destroys, or annihilates, as though destruction is willed by God as punishment or retribution. Divine violence does not cause destruction, but rather *assumes* destruction in the world. This is the sense in which "[mythical violence] demands sacrifice; [divine violence] assumes it." Within the context of my earlier account of the encompassing of lying in language, one can say divine violence assumes the destruction of the phenomenal. This assumption of destruction is the purifying capacity of divine violence.

The character of this purifying capacity of divine violence can be further clarified by thinking of its contrast with mythical violence in relation to the notion life. "Mythic violence is bloody violence over mere life for its own sake, divine violence is pure violence over all life for the sake of the living" (*SW*, 1:250). The phrase to clarify here is "mere life" and its distinction from "all life" pertaining to "the living." *Mere life* denotes a natural dimension of existence, yet it cannot be grasped insofar as one thinks of life only in terms of the individual living being and his or her internal organization. Neither is it assessed in terms of *forms* of life in common, nor is it merely what remains of the human being, when he or she is expelled from life in common.

Mere life is the natural condition of the living partaking in a *field* that has an inner cohesion whose "logic" is neither merely biological nor merely social. It has the necessity of fate.[11] The relation of life and fate is at the heart of Benjamin's account of mythic violence. Mere life is that field of life whose lack of articulation, whose internal ambiguity, makes the living guilty before any specific offense. It is the condition of indeterminacy of the field of meaningful human existence which can be brought out even in considering life in nineteenth-century Paris. (One of the central tasks of Benjamin's Arcades project is to present modern life as such a field in which fate reigns.)

One must carefully distinguish the character of guilt of mere natural life (*blossen natürlichen Lebens*) from guilt traced to and attributable on the basis of the actions of the living. The living beings are committed to the destructive logic of that field of fate. They are not personally guilty, insofar as the guilt of such a field of life unfolds the consequences of the meaning of their actions, far beyond anything individuals can control, intend, or expect through their actions. This importantly implies that the guilt of mere life is not identical to individual guilt associated with the infringement of law. The individual living beings can be innocent insofar as their actions go, as well as made guilty by the character of life itself. One of the problematic features of law is that it transforms the guilt that belongs to mere life into an individual guilt, which the law can recognize, judge, and apportion punishment accordingly. Law thereby takes it upon itself to rule over what belongs to manifestations of mythical violence.

Taking into account the dimension of divine violence would be the key to conceiving the possibility of a realization of life which is at the same time a release from law and its perverse association with the cursedness of life manifest in mythical violence. That release from law is not something that can be achieved by the purposive striving of the living, by an anarchic activity or, even by a coordinated passivity, which refuses all bargaining and threat, such as the general strike. But it is not thereby to be identified with a reduction of the human to an existence apart from meaning. Rather it denotes the highest articulation of meaning, which encompasses the space of existence of the living. The problem raised therefore by the purifying character of divine violence is how to articulate life in such a way that a decisive meaningful configuration of it would emerge, an *order of life* apart from law.

The bloody nature of mythical violence is, one might say, a figuration of the impossibility of holding on to the integrity of individual life in a field of fate. It is the mark of the essential breach of the unity of purposive individual life by such violence. Mythical violence destroys life or demands sacrifice as part of its logic or order. But, just as the relation of life and fate is not recognized by remaining with the unity of the individual life, there would be, according to Benjamin, ways of recognizing how the destruction of such life is encompassed in a higher life.

Life, as Benjamin insists, is a term that is used ambiguously "with reference to two distinct spheres" (*SW*, 1:251). The higher sphere of life is manifest only when one sees life to encompass and be present in earthly life, as well as afterlife. There is life "which is identically present in earthly life, death, and afterlife" (*SW*, 1:251).[12] Mere life cannot encompass any such notions, for they only arise in relation to the actualization of life, that is, in relation to the possibility of purifying or redeeming the guilt of mere life. It is in that sense that divine violence is "pure violence over *all life (alles Leben) for the sake of the living*" (*SW*, 1:250). Indeed, one can conceive of divine violence as assuming sacrifice or destruction, precisely by understanding its "scope" to involve afterlife. It is also the reason Benjamin calls it bloodless.

It is only the articulation of the meaning of existence in the afterlife that allows one to recognize the higher life identified with divine violence. That this is a work of meaning, is further clarified if one properly understands the relation between life and purposiveness:

> The relation between life and purposiveness, seemingly obvious yet almost beyond the grasp of the intellect, reveals itself only if the ultimate purpose toward which all the individual purposiveness of life tends is sought not in its own sphere but in a higher one. All purposeful manifestations of life, including their very purposiveness, in the final analysis have their end not in life but in the expression of its nature, in the representation of its significance. (*SW*, 1:255)

The careful formulation that Benjamin gives makes clear that he wishes to distinguish that which living beings can achieve as an end, by actualizing their individual capacities from that which is the realization of the significance of life and cannot be identified with the aim of individual purposiveness. The realization is significance is better called a terminus of life rather than an end. Divine violence is not manifestation but revelation—the actualization of meaning—and its medium is language. Language as such, for Benjamin, is not a capacity of the human being. Language or meaning, as Benjamin understands it, is the medium of purification of the living.

Divine violence can only be recognized, or presented, in a human gaze that encompasses the destruction of human edifices, that is in the unity that holds together life and afterlife. It is therefore, from a human standpoint, a matter of the presentation of history. Indeed, Benjamin states that "in the final analysis, the range of life must be determined by the standpoint of history rather than that of nature, least of all by such tenuous factors as sensation and soul" (*SW*, 1:255). Thus, toward the end of the essay, Benjamin claims that the "critique of violence is the philosophy of its history." He further clarifies this by adding "the 'philosophy' of this history because only the idea of its development makes possible a critical, discriminating, and decisive approach to tis temporal data" (*SW*, 1:251). I note that the use of the term *idea*, which is to be taken in its Kantian as well as Platonic connotations, suggests a gulf between any given experiential unity and the presentation of the truth of the matter. Only in assuming the destruction of the lawful unities of experience can the idea be presented in history. Relying on Benjamin's work at the time on the *The Origin of German Tragic Drama*, one can argue that an idea can be recognized only in a construction out of phenomena. It is an order, or is essentially composed. In that construction, phenomena are purified or redeemed in taking part in the presentation of the idea.

In other words, the question of realizing the presence of divine violence is tantamount to the problem of the presentation of history. This presentation has two sides: On the one hand, it involves taking up the destruction of the phenomenal, that which has been severed from its life world in the afterlife of meaning. On the other hand, the purifying moment or the redeeming moment is that through which the material of life is brought together so as to present in that construction a higher configuration of truth.[13]

So as to recognize the *force* of such a configuration in relation to the manifest image of history, consider how Benjamin argues that mythical violence is taken up by law-instating violence, that is, arrogated by the latter as its own power. Law-instating is a form of hubris, which takes the unlimited mythical force and turns it into legal power over the living. It leads of its own dynamics (that is by means of its compromising internal relation to law preserving violence), to its demise, and therefore to a new moment of law-instating. This cycle brings out how mythical violence essentially has no end. Or it is violence that belongs to the field of life insofar as it has not undergone the highest articulation, insofar as it is caught up in fate, in the eternal return of torments. The manifestation of mythical violence in time is the form that primal history takes as eternal return, and against which the true historical picture of the past is set.

Divine violence must be conceived as a terminal moment that releases from this cycle of eternal return. In that sense it has the highest force. Divine violence strikes. It is the striking, that is the *arresting* of the cycle of fate, what is "able to call a halt to mythic violence" (*SW*, 1:249). I have already argued why the striking character of divine violence should in no way be seen as violence that is unleashed on the living catastrophically, indiscriminately, causing total annihilation. But, taking divine violence to be terminal or to have an arresting character also explains why Benjamin conceives of it as free of threat. This again can be mistakenly taken to be violence that is cruel since it strikes without warning. But the concept of warning and threat belongs to the phenomenal in time, not to the recognition of history as a terminal moment.

Consider that mythical violence is threatening in its being both ambiguous and inescapable. These two characteristics might appear to be contradictory; but properly understood, ambiguity of meaning, or tragic irony, is precisely the way in which the inescapable violence—that is, violence that belongs to an other, unlimited order—manifests itself in the order of succession of empirical events.[14] Threat rests on essential ambiguity, which is the other side of the excessive precision of meaning with which mythical violence bursts upon the living. Divine violence is free of threat insofar as it is identified with the highest actualization of meaning.

There still remains the question of how to interpret the last paragraphs of the essay in which Benjamin seems to relate the manifestations of divine violence to human violence.[15] Here it is necessary to stress the way that the work of construction, understood as a philosophical task, is necessary to make recognizable the redeeming character of divine violence. This should be a presupposition of all attempts to relate the divine violence immediately to historical phenomena. In other words, there would be no way to point to a certain event or phenomenon and argue whether it is or is not a manifestation of divine violence. There is always a prior necessity of configuring historical content as an order by way of construction, to make visible the lines of force that encompass life, death, and afterlife in meaning. No specific form of directed force can be identified in itself as a manifestation of divine violence.

The purifying capacity of divine violence is not readily visible. There is nothing in the character of the individual phenomena that will decide whether they can be part of the recognition of divine violence. This is the reason that Benjamin refers toward the end of the essay to the comparison between true war and a crowd passing judgment and punishment on a criminal. A war is planned and has justified aims; a crowd judging a criminal is almost like a collective outburst of anger. They are thus opposed in their phenomenal characterizations as types of destructive behavior of humankind. Since they can both partake in the presentation of divine violence, neither one of these phenomena allows us to decide on the basis of their phenomenal characteristics how they are part of it.

The last line of the essay condenses the different themes touched upon in its final paragraphs: "Divine violence, which is the sign and the seal, but never the means, of sacred execution [*Vollstreckung*], may be called sovereign violence" (*SW*, 1:252; translation modified). In interpreting this concluding image one should refer back to Benjamin's distinction between the mark, which appears in a medium, and the sign, which is imprinted on a background.[16] Divine violence is both mark and sign. It is

mark insofar as it is revelation in and through the medium of the phenomenal (rather than *within* the phenomenal). The presentation of divine
violence as an arrest has also the structure of a sign, an imprint on the
ground of the destruction of the phenomenal. Being a seal, it presents a
terminal moment. Benjamin uses the term *insignium*, which I here read as
emblem, namely something that, just like the seal, is often associated with
sovereignty. It is moreover something that takes the form of an image, or
a certain graphic configuration. It is the striking presence of that order
which can be identified as a mode of the original image—the archetype.
In other words this is the sovereignty recognized in holding together the
destruction of the phenomenal as a constellation, or as Benjamin would
call it later, a dialectical image.[17]

Notes

1. Walter Benjamin, "Theological-Political Fragment," in *Selected Writings*,
4 vols., ed. Marcus Bullock, Howard Eiland, and Michael Jennings (Cambridge:
Harvard University Press, 1996–2003), 3:360. Hereafter cited as *SW*.

2. The Fall—understood as a predicament of language, the replacement of
naming by judgment as the fundamental mode of relating to the world in
language—poses a problem not only in man's relation to nature, but also in
the recognition of man's own spiritual unity. From an understanding of value
correlative with having a significant world altogether, after the Fall, value
becomes a matter of will and the ethical will is identified in terms of
meaningful principles distinguishing good from evil. This would be a way to
reify subjectivity, to identify the metaphysical subject through the
characterization of the lawfulness or unlawfulness of the actions willed. Yet, if
one properly understands the position of a subject, guilt precedes law and is
characterized by the abandonment of naming, by the very questioning in terms
of the polarity of good and evil. Overcoming law in one's relation to the world
and in one's sense as a subject, standing beyond good and evil would mean
finding a perspective that does not locate value in identifying one state of affairs
over another. It will problematize the understanding of the ethical in relation to
the realm of law (whether established or still to come). But it might also
demand, in turn, a willingness to disappear as a subject.

3. The case of the destructive power of translation is good to bear in mind
when we articulate the character of divine violence, because with translation,
we have no temptation to figure such a destruction of living unities of meaning
as a catastrophic unleashing of a force as it were striking from the outside. It is
painstakingly slow, precise, and uninspired work.

4. The relation between realization and disappearance can be further
recognized in many of Benjamin's essays. In his essay on Goethe's *Elective
Affinities*, Benjamin emphasizes that the mythical themes of the novel are
countered by redemptive themes in the novella. The lingering of the characters

of the novel is counterbalanced by the readiness for disappearance identified with the promise of bliss of the characters in the novella with such an understanding: "Whereas the characters of the novel linger more weakly and more mutely, though fully life-sized in the gaze of the reader, the united couple of the novella disappears under the arch of a final rhetorical question, in the perspective, so to speak of infinite distance. In the readiness for disappearance is it not bliss that is hinted at" (*SW*, 1:333).

Consider further how this works in the essay on Proust: Voluntary memory is that which encompasses unities of meaning (on what one can be conscious of). One might at first think that what Benjamin wishes is to identify the power of the involuntary memory with the accidental which in its smallness escaped the unity of consciousness. But this is only half of the truth. The point is how this contingency gives rise to a whole interconnection of experience in which everything becomes equally valuable (or forms the texture of experience). That is, what one gets is precisely the dissolution of the directed, intentional memory, in a space that is undifferentiated, in the weave of the ordinary. Benjamin has a powerful figure to characterize this movement of writing, the image of the sock, which also appears in *Berlin Childhood around 1900*. What matters for me in this image, for the present purpose, is the way the attraction of a specific meaning, of that which appears more valuable than the rest, the present, is dissolved in the undifferentiated weave of meaning.

5. Benjamin, "Critique of Violence," in *Selected Writings*, 1:245.

6. Walter Benjamin, *The Origin of German Tragic Drama*, trans. J. Osborne (London: NLB, 1977), 28; emphasis added.

7. I note that quoting has a destructive character and, in detaching language from the original context of assertion, also an equalizing effect or it tends toward abolishing the value distinction between major and minor.

8. In "On Language as such and on the Language of Man" (*Selected Writings*, 1:62–74) Benjamin criticizes the bourgeois conception of language, which conceives of language as essentially a matter of communicating a factual subject matter from one speaker to another. This is the consideration of language as means but in no way as pure means. For then language is a means to further interest, as though the property of a subject who uses it for his or her purposes. But this is very different from what is at issue in the appropriation of the power of language by the *I*. What one seeks is a mode in which the subject takes itself to appropriate power that can only belong to language.

9. The consideration of tragedy is particularly important as an articulation of the field of myth, fate, and guilt. The tragic hero concentrates something that pertains to conditions of existence onto a visible course of occurrences in the world; he takes up and makes visible these limiting conditions of the whole as a recognizable event. This is indeed in part why the tragic hero is representative and his suffering serves to establish a new law for the community.

The comic hero, by contrast, is a person of character. Having character, as Benjamin understands it, is not manifested in extraordinary events. It is something that is best brought out by describing the world of the person of character: each and every one of the person's dealings with his or her environment colors it in terms of his character. There is an equality, nothing so to speak stands out (he or she is always equally destructive, equally mischievous, or equally naïve.) This is why Benjamin describes the effects of character as though lighting up the surroundings of the person. His spirit is not localizable. One can also say that there is anonymity in character insofar as it is not a localizable subject that can be named. A character is a type for whom individuality is dissolved in the space of the world opened through his presence. True innocence, understood in spiritual terms, demands the anonymity of character. (This innocence of character can be compared to the vanishing of the subject in naming the world I discussed earlier. Character would be a way of refiguring natural innocence. This is why Benjamin insists that it is not a moral notion, or it stands beyond good and evil.)

This extreme disappearance of individuality in the world opened by a type or character should be contrasted with Benjamin's understanding of the tragic as an extreme manifestation of the paradox of individuation through the localization of the condition pertaining to the world in the tragic hero. The movement of the tragic is the opposite of dissolution. It is the internalization of limits in a particular place in the world, in the figure of the hero. The dissolution of individuality in comedy is the sense that the hold of fate can always be avoided. There will be no event that can be decisive for the sense of life as a whole. Nothing is unavoidable in meaning. The ever-present dissolution in the medium of meaning presents a world free of tragedy. Tragedy is a view of the world in which there is essential conflict. Benjamin also thinks of it as a manifestation of the force of the word. Here one encounters the *eternal inflexibility of the spoken word*.

10. It is not a boundary line that humans can cross. Yet, the drawing of a boundary by mythical violence can be taken up by law and turned into an interdiction or a division in which the two sides are possibilities for human action. This would be how the violence of law-instating arrogates what properly belongs to the manifestation of mythical violence. For more details, see my "Assuming Violence: A Commentary on Walter Benjamin's 'Critique of Violence,'" in *boundary 2* 42, no. 4 (November 2015).

11. "Nature is not something that belongs especially to every individual body. Rather it relates to the singularity of the body as the different currents that flow into the sea relate to each drop of water. Countless such drops are carried along by the same current. In like fashion, nature is the same, not indeed in all human beings but in a great many of them. Moreover, this nature is not just alike; it is in the full sense identical, one and the same" (*SW*, 1:395) This makes clear that the idea of natural life is one that essentially is not encompassed in the individual.

12. This standpoint is also what Benjamin calls existence (*Dasein*). This notion of existence, central to Benjamin's understanding of divine violence, is

initially developed in relation to the way one is to understand the relation of philosophy's questioning to the total realization of meaning in a metaphysics of experience. Thus in "On the Program of the Coming Philosophy," Benjamin distinguishes the intentional unities of experience, which are investigated by philosophy and constitute philosophy's knowledge, from their unattainable integral which is existence: "Indeed, it must be said that philosophy in its questionings can never hit upon the unity of existence, but only upon new unities of various conformities to laws, whose integral is existence" (*SW*, 1:109). Existence is utter actuality. Whatever reality one can articulate from one's finite standpoint will appear to be partaking in the ideal, that is to be a part or fragment of that whole.

13. A hint at the relation of realization and disappearance in divine force can be gleaned from the choice Benjamin makes to exemplify the immediate manifestation of divine force: the story of Korah and his clan. The specificity of this example has not been brought out enough. In particular, one should note that Korah challenges the authority of Moses and Aaron in the name of equality. All are equally holy. This claim of equivalence is something that cannot be dismissed as merely blasphemous or merely rebellious. Indeed, in an important sense there is no way to identify a place in the world that is higher or more intrinsically valuable than another. It is only in relation to the whole that the highest value can be revealed. It is in this context that one should distinguish the fate of Korah and his clan from punishment or even from the manifestation characteristic of mythical force (as in the story of Niobe). The complete and utter disappearance of Korah and his clan also has a dimension of realization. As though it expresses what it means to realize equality of value in the world: It is to vanish as an individual without a trace.

14. This should be clearly distinguished from the threat of retribution, which is one of the justifications for punishment within the legal system. For the latter is precisely open to calculation which would justify taking the chance of infringing the law and hoping to avoid punishment. The threatening ambiguity of mythical violence is precisely incalculable and inescapable. The law might be seen to draw its power from mythical violence for instance in cases where there is no way to proportionally calculate punishment that would be apportioned for a particular offense, that is in cases where the death penalty can be the punishment for a slight offense against property.

15. I leave open the question of the character and possibility of relating revolutionary violence and divine violence. Benjamin writes that "the existence of violence outside the law, as pure immediate violence, . . . furnishes proof that revolutionary violence, the highest manifestation of unalloyed violence by man, is possible, and shows in what name" (*SW*, 1:252; translation modified). This problem is identical in its scope with understanding Benjamin's Copernican revolution of history, with its sense that history revolves around politics.

16. See in particular the fragment "On Painting, or Signs and Marks," in *Selected Writings*, 1:83–86.

17. In a fragment entitled "Language and Logic," which is probably a draft from the "Epistemo-Critical Preface" of *The Origin of the German Tragic Drama* book, the relation between sovereign power and ruling and the relation between multiplicity and unity characteristic of the manifestation of a systematic unity of essences is made very clear: "In the sphere of essences, the higher does not devour the lower: Instead, it rules over it. This explains why the regional separation between them, their disparateness, remains as irreducible as the gulf between monarch and people. . . . The essential unity reigns over a multiplicity of essences in which it manifests itself, but from which it always remains distinct" (*SW*, 1:273).

Rhythms of the Living, Conditions of Critique
On Judith Butler's Reading of Walter Benjamin's "Critique of Violence"

ASTRID DEUBER-MANKOWSKY

In her reading of Walter Benjamin's "Critique of Violence," Judith Butler provides a persuasive interpretation of the critical resources Benjamin mobilizes. She points out that Benjamin draws on an alternative Jewish tradition of understanding the commandment "Thou shall not kill." In her analysis, the commandment is opposed to a principle of guilt and hence can become the basis for a critique of legal violence. Moreover, according to Butler, the commandment, as Benjamin conceives of it, constitutes the condition for a theory of responsibility that would be fundamentally concerned with the ongoing struggle with nonviolence. Benjamin's controversial distinction between fate and divine violence culminates in the demand to oppose the kind of violence that strikes the "soul of the living"—which means, as Butler points out, the violence of positive law.

Butler connects her interest in Jewish philosophy to a critique of Israel's Zionist politics, its politics of settlement and occupation, and its wars against the Palestinians. As she once put it, what matters for her is a public critique of state violence.[1] She thus starts from the premise—and this is crucial for the philosophical implications of her critique, a critique that is not merely political—that the critique of state violence as an ethical demand derives from the framing conditions of Jewish thought itself, whether it is religious or not.[2] Butler supports the claim that in this context Jewish thought is not tied to belief in and observance of the commandments with the thesis—central to her interest in a Jewish critique of state violence—that a religion can function as a matrix for a particular subject-formation, a reference system of particular values, and a basis for a particular kind of belonging and embodied social practices.³ As a result, "secularization," she notes, "will be one way that Jewish life continues as Jewish."⁴

With respect to this thesis and her reading of Benjamin's remarks on the critique of violence, I will support and then expand upon the claim that Benjamin's reflections should be understood in connection with an attempt to think human agency through Jewish interpretive practices concerning the command "Thou shalt not kill."⁵ As can be shown with reference to Hermann Cohen's philosophy of religion,⁶ this form of agency can be characterized, first, as conditioned by temporality and thus by the contingency of human existence and, second, as a form of agency that abrogates the principle that punishment stands in a determinate causal relationship to guilt [Schuld], a principle governing, for instance, the state violence Benjamin criticized. Benjamin's reflections on the critique of violence arose, as is seldom noted, in the tension between his reference to Jewish traditions of thought and his critical confrontation with Max Weber's secularization thesis.⁷ Put more strongly: in his reflections on the critique of violence, Benjamin proposes—along with a critique of the violence of the state that makes reference to Jewish sources—a form of cosmopolitanism, which likewise makes use of Jewish sources, and whose method, as he writes, would "be called nihilism."⁸ Benjamin follows Max Weber's thesis that the spirit of capitalism derives from the Protestant ethic. Unlike Weber, who understood the relationship between Christianity and capitalism as *genealogical* and who defined capitalism as a secular phenomenon, Benjamin interprets the relation between capitalism and Christianity as *parasitical* and claims that capitalism is a "purely cultic religion"⁹ whose originality consists in this cult's not containing a principle of atonement but, instead, creating universal guilt.¹⁰ Consequently, the possibility of the quest of free humanity for happiness appears, from this perspective, as incompatible not only with capitalism but also with the belief in a form of secularization that would merely conceal the religious character of capitalism.¹¹ Benjamin adheres to the designation of capitalism as a religion not least because it allows him to formulate and consider the position of "individuals who were irreligious or had other beliefs" and thereby assume a standpoint that, if not external, is nevertheless one of critique.¹² At the same time, Jewish messianism—with its concepts of fulfilled time, hope, and postponement, turning [Umkehr] and remembrance—becomes a point of reference not only for the critique of capitalist modernity but also of state violence.

Finally, I conclude by examining the connection that Butler establishes between the conditions of critique, the critique of violence, and "the apprehension of life's value." From Benjamin's hint in the "Theological-Political Fragment" that "the spiritual *restitutio integrum*, which introduces immortality corresponds to a worldly restitution that leads to an eternity of downfall,"[13] Butler infers that the soul of the living is revealed in the rhythm—and by implication in the eternity—of the transience of life. In consequence, she transposes divine violence, as eternally enduring destruction, into life itself. But is this interpretation of divine violence—an interpretation that refers so completely to the worldly order that the divine is finally entirely realized within it—still compatible with Benjamin's concept of critique and his references to transcendence—however unattainable it might be—in concepts such as turning [*Umkehr*], deferral, hope, justice, history, or even destruction in the name of the living?

In What Sense Can Benjamin's Critique of Violence Be Considered as a Jewish Critique?

Walter Benjamin wrote "Critique of Violence" around New Year 1921 for the *Weißen Blätter*, edited by Emil Lederer.[14] The essay was published in August 1921 in the well-known journal, *Archiv für Sozialwissenschaft und Sozialpolitik*, founded by Max Weber and Werner Sombart in 1904 and edited by Lederer in 1921. Benjamin's essay seemed to the editor to be too long and difficult for the *Weißen Blätter*;[15] indeed, as Scholem recalled, it made a "very strange" impression in the context of the contributions to the *Archiv für Sozialwissenschaft und Sozialpolitik*.[16]

Benjamin had begun to reflect on politics and on the relationship among politics, critique, and violence when he made the acquaintance of Ernst Bloch in Switzerland in the spring of 1919. Benjamin not only incorporated these political considerations in "Critique of Violence," but also treated the investigation of aesthetic questions and the relationships among art, critique, and cognition, which he had treated in his dissertation, *The Concept of Criticism in German Romanticism* (1919), among other works, as well as his uninterrupted engagement with questions of Judaism. His engagement with Judaism also left its mark on his treatment of Max Weber's socioreligious methods. His idiosyncratic critique of the Weberian thesis that the "spirit of modern capitalism" represents a rationalization of Protestant ethics and that capitalism is therefore to be regarded as the overcoming of religion was not the least important reason that his reflection on the critique of violence seemed so strange in the context of the contributions to the *Archiv für Sozialwissenschaft und Sozialpolitik*. Capitalism—as Benjamin also wrote in 1921 in his short note entitled "Capitalism as Religion"—is not, as Weber thought, a "formation conditioned by religion" but a "purely cultic religion." Furthermore, capitalism is "the first instance of a cult that creates guilt [*Schuld*] not atonement."[17] Here Benjamin plays on the ambiguity in the concept of *Schuld* [guilt or debt] to make clear, on the one hand, the connection between the economic and the symbolic order, and, on the other hand, the fact that the obverse of the rationality of capitalism is the return and intensification of mythical relations of violence.

According to Butler, Benjamin's critique of violence can be termed "justifiably Jewish," because some of the "critical resources Benjamin brings to bear" are based on Jewish tradition.[18] This first of all concerns the reading of the commandment "Thou shalt not kill," which Benjamin, with reference to Jewish sources, does not interpret as a "criterion for judgment" but as a "guideline for action."[19] Benjamin takes as his point of departure the discussion of legitimate self-defense [*Notwehr*] found in some Jewish writings. On the basis of his reflections, he concludes that disregarding the commandment in individual cases means that the person or community that acts must take responsibility for wrestling "in solitude" with the commandment.[20] The connection between commandment and personal responsibility is thus central for Benjamin's critique of violence, because through it the causal—and thereby quasi-fatalistic—link of judgment and guilt is broken or made breakable. Alongside the legal principle of guilt, the ethical principle of a responsibility that releases the question of debt and guilt from the domain of jurisdiction enters. The question of debt and guilt can be dissociated from the domain of jurisdiction through its transfer to the realm of reconciliation. This realm of reconciliation consists of a transcendent authority and a solitary subject or community that allows for a critical stance toward legal authority and permits a reconciliation of the acting person or community with herself and with her actions or deeds.

Guilt-Making Violence

Benjamin refers here to an idea which Hermann Cohen had outlined in the *Ethics of the Pure Will* and then developed and explored in detail in chapter 11 of his *Religion of Reason out of the Sources of Judaism*, published posthumously in 1919.[21] Benjamin quotes Cohen's remark in the *Ethics of the Pure Will* that in myth it is "the orders themselves that seem to occasion and bring about this breaking-away, this defection."[22] As Cohen then explains, in sections entitled "The Interest of Myth in Evil" and "Fate and Guilt," it is characteristic of myth that it turns "the problem of freedom in self-determination" into "the question, or, better, the interest in, the generation of evil."[23] This means that freedom can only be conceived of as self-overcoming and, in consequence, only in connection with guilt. Freedom appears in the realm of myth as the chaff [*Abfall*] of fate. In Cohen's formulation, "evil turns . . . into guilt. And guilt becomes fate [*Verhängnis*]."[24]

This order, defined by Cohen as "mythic," displays the same structure as that which Butler—drawing on Walter Benjamin's description of Niobe in "Critique of Violence"—describes as a reference frame for subject-formation. According to Butler, it is the case that "to be a subject . . . is to take responsibility for a violence that precedes the subject and whose operation is occluded by the subject who comes to derive the violence she suffers from her own acts."[25] The centrality of Benjamin's reference to Cohen's analysis of the mythic order to the "Critique of Violence" is, for instance, shown by Benjamin's use of the same quotation from the *Ethics of the Pure Will* in his famous essay "Franz Kafka: On the Tenth Anniversary of His Death" (1934) in order to describe the particular violence that determines the world in the novel *The Trial*.[26] As is the case for Niobe, the figures in *The Trial* are antecedently condemned to guilt by the order in which they live. It is this insight into the constitutive connection between order and guilt that Benjamin designates, following Cohen, as "inescapable." The jurisdiction whose trial rules against K in the novel thus refers back, as Benjamin establishes, to a "pre-world" in which "the written law is contained in law books, but these are secret; by basing itself on them, the pre-world exerts its rule all the more boundlessly."[27]

In her congenial interpretation of Niobe, Butler vividly exposes this pre-worldy structure of violence in which the subject is brought under a jurisdiction that only posits its laws in the act of punishment. Niobe is punished because, as the mother of fourteen children, she boasted of being more fertile than the goddess of fertility, Lethe, who had only two children, Apollo and Artemis. In consequence, the enraged Lethe had Apollo and Artemis first murder all seven sons and then all seven daughters with bow and arrow. Niobe herself was transformed into a stone by the gods but, even as a stone, never ceased crying over her children. Now, as Butler convincingly demonstrates, the mythic violence to which Niobe is exposed is characterized by her being punished despite not transgressing any existing law: through her hybrid speech-act, she challenges fate all the more, and Artemis and Apollo become the medium through which fate is instituted as law. Benjamin introduces the example of Niobe in "Critique of Violence" as an instance of the manifestation of *immediate mythic violence*, which he then distinguishes from *pure divine violence*. The mythic manifestation of violence is the expression of an affect, which manifests nothing more and nothing other than the mere *existence* [*Dasein*] of the gods and thus their superior power with regard to human beings. Niobe, transformed into a stone, appears, Benjamin writes, "as an eternally mute bearer of guilt and as a boundary stone on the border between men and gods."[28]

One of the most contested theses in Benjamin's "Critique of Violence" is his claim that the mythic manifestation of violence he describes refers back to a problematic of legal violence [Rechtsgewalt]—more precisely to a problematic of the violence that establishes law [rechtsetzende Gewalt]: in analogy with mythical violence, the establishment of legal violence has a twofold function: on the one hand, violence serves as a means for establishing law, but, on the other hand, this violent establishment serves as a manifestation of the power of law and in turn legitimates that power by maintaining violence in an institutionalized, law-preserving form. This has the consequence that law-maintaining violence, no less than mythic violence, becomes a manifestation of itself. The establishment of law [Rechtsetzung] is, as Benjamin sharpens the point, nothing other than the establishment of violence [Machtsetzung].[29] For Benjamin, mythic violence is primarily distinguished by performative self-referentiality and the absence of justice. He cites Anatole France's famous line that laws equally forbid the poor and the rich from sleeping under bridges in order to illustrate the ambiguity of laws which may not be transgressed and which, from this perspective, recall Niobe's fate far more than they recall a state under the rule of law [Rechtstaat]. Benjamin—who in the first sentence of his essay declares that the task of a critique of violence can be summarized as "expounding its relation to law and justice"[30]—correctly derives from the insight that the law-establishing violence is identical with the mythic manifestation of violence the demand for its destruction to become a task—or, as Butler argues, an ethical demand. One could put the point more strongly and say that for Benjamin the possibility of an ethical demand and the possibility of justice itself depend on the destruction of the mythic manifestation of violence. As he formulates it in the second sentence of the "Critique of Violence," "a cause, however effective, becomes violent, in the precise sense of the word, only when it enters into ethical relations."[31] This means that there is violence in the strict sense only when a cause does not act as a natural law in the scientific sense.

Divine, Destructive Violence

Mythic and law-establishing violence condemns as guilty, as the example of Niobe shows, and thereby destroys precisely the space for free play that is a precondition for the possibility of self-alteration and freedom. In consequence, law is not identical with justice; nor is the institution of justice—and here we encounter another contentious thesis of Benjamin's—free of violence. For Benjamin does not answer the question of how the mythic manifestation of violence can be overcome by turning to reason or the rational will; instead, he refers to a further Jewish source—the Bible—and binds the possibility of justice, and thereby also the possibility of a critique of violence itself, to the (law-)destroying force of divine violence. The implication Benjamin draws is, in fact, shocking at first glance—all the more so because he connects it with the divine judgment upon Korah's company in the Bible, contrasting this to the mythic guilt of Niobe. Korah's company consisted of a part of the Jewish elite who rebelled against Moses and Aaron's claim to be closest to God and to represent his will and bring forth his laws. Thereupon Moses asked God for help. God caused the rebellious families to disappear into the earth in a single stroke. The Bible speaks of a "rebellion [*Aufruhr*] against the Lord" and of Korah's company having "provoked the Lord." In addition, Moses emphasizes that one can recognize in the novel manner in which God annihilated Korah's company alive that his God is the only God (Numbers 16:30). It is decisive for Benjamin that, in the case of Korah's company, it is a matter of the "privileged,"[32] that the violence comes without threat, and that it is, as he writes, unmistakably expiating. But how can it be unmistakably expiating? This claim can only be reconstructed when one recalls and takes into account the fact that, as is said in Numbers 26:11, Korah's children did not die. If the children are saved, then they do not, like Niobe's children, have to make amends for the guilt of their parents, and this, in turn, is a sign that with the destruction of Korah's company a legal system resting on prerogatives and guilt is destroyed.[33] "Pure divine violence" is, as Benjamin states immediately afterward, "pure violence [*Gewalt*] over all that lives for the sake of the living."[34]

Butler follows Benjamin's analyses and also concurs with him in the identification of the mythic manifestation of violence with the violence of the state ruled by law. Now, this may seem astonishing at first glance but a closer look reveals otherwise. For, in fact, astonishing parallels emerge between Butler's analysis and critique of subject-formation within the frame of the heteronormative matrix she identifies and Benjamin's illustration of the effects of mythic violence in the example of Niobe. The very title of chapter 5 of *The Psychic Life of Power: Theories in Subjection*, "Melancholy Gender / Refused Identification," recalls Niobe and at the same time refers to the problem that has concerned Butler in varying guises since *Gender Trouble*: How is an interruption of this genealogy of violence possible? How can the subject that has emerged out of relations of violence withdraw from them, oppose them, refuse an identification with them? "Law," as Butler summarizes Benjamin's critique of violence, "thus petrifies the subject, arresting life in the moment of guilt."[35] It is the same legal order which, as Butler demonstrates in *The Psychic Life of Power*, makes homosexual desire into "a source of guilt"[36] and which, as she explains in the introduction to *Bodies That Matter: On the Discursive Limits of "Sex,"* produces a "domain of abject beings." "The abject" designates, as Butler explains there, "those 'unlivable' and 'uninhabitable' zones of social life which are nevertheless densely populated by those who do not enjoy the states of the subject, but those whose living under the sign of 'unlivable' is required to circumscribe the domain of the subject."[37]

Butler shares with Benjamin, first, the view that the critique of violence is directed against the denunciation of human life as conditioned; second, a conception of the question of justice as culminating in that of how one can do justice to the weaknesses—or to cite the title of another one of Butler's books, to the "precariousness" and temporality—of human life.[38] Benjamin refers here, as I will show next, to an interpretation of Jewish monotheism based in the ideas of Enlightenment philosophy and grounded in the works of Hermann Cohen. The question is whether Butler also follows him in this regard.

Critique of the Death Penalty and of Legal Violence

For Cohen, the generation of the concept of the concrete individual who is in a position to oppose the compulsion [*Zwang*] of the guilt-prescribing law is linked, on the one hand, with the subjective recognition by the very individual who has become guilty of his capacity for guilt and, on the other, with the individual's reconciliation with his weakness, which, for Cohen, is only conceivable as the "correlation of God and man" and thus as something that takes place in the realm of religion.[39]

The justification which Cohen gives for the dependence of the ethical demand of a critique of violence on religion is strictly epistemological: he argues that, since ethics claims universality for its assertions, for ethics man can be "only a point to which it relates its problems, as for science also he is only a particular case of its general laws."[40] The concrete individual that addresses itself as an I does not, however, think of itself as such a case, as he explains, but as "isolated, as absolute," as singular.[41]

A liberation from perpetual guilt is consequently only possible through a "turning-away" [*Umkehr*], which he interprets, following the Prophet Ezekiel, as *teshuva*, repentance. Guilt is transformed into personal sin in the correlation with God in which the social individual for the first time becomes a concrete singular individual. The overcoming of the guilt-making order of myth is, for Cohen as well as for Benjamin, first linked to the recognition of the concrete and singular existence of the individual. Second—and this distinguishes the Cohenian concept of the individual who addresses herself as "I" from the Kantian concept of the moral subject—the recognition of the individual who is responsible for herself and for her deeds is bound to the recognition of the temporality of human life.

As a result, Cohen interprets this turning [*Umkehr*] as, at the same time, a turning *away* from death and from the death penalty and as a turning *toward* life.[42] The centrality of the concept of turning around for Cohen's critical philosophy is shown by the fact that it encompasses not only the individual but, in a certain sense, also God himself. The essence of God, as Cohen explains, has itself changed in Ezekiel's prophecy, after which the saying that "the fathers eat sour grapes and the children's teeth are set on edge" (Ezek. 18:2) is no longer valid. Cohen writes: "Punishment is not the infallible sign of his rule, but rather the pleasure he has in the sinner's turning away from his ways. God, therefore, has no pleasure in his death, but rather in his life."[43] As is clear, Benjamin is not the first for whom the Jewish God is the God of forgiveness.[44]

The life in which the Jewish God takes pleasure—and this brings us back to Benjamin's reflections in "Critique of Violence" and to Butler's commentary on that difficult text—is mutable and temporally conditioned life. Along with lending meaning to the event of turning-back, Cohen performs a reevaluation of vulnerable and precarious life.[45]

Cohen justifies his demand for a strict separation of punishment and guilt, on the one hand, from punishment and condemnation, on the other, on the grounds that: "The causal nexus of the actions, deeds, and events of a single human being is not known to us under the methodological form of science [*Wissen*] for a single moment of her existence."[46] From this methodologically conditioned limit of knowledge, he derives the limits of legal judgment that are required for an ethical state ruled by law. These refer, on the one hand, to the question of guilt and, on the other, to life. Cohen declares the death penalty to be incompatible with an ethical state under the rule of law on the grounds that punishment is never permitted "to exceed the limit of self-preservation";[47] he turns against the notion that the task of the judge is to condemn [*Verurteilung*] the perpetrator on the basis of the argument that the judge cannot determine the guilt of the perpetrator but only the extent of the contractual break which the perpetrator has committed as a citizen against the state. For Cohen, as becomes clear here, there exists no incompatibility among law, religion, enlightenment, and justice. Instead, the critique of reason and the critique of mythic violence themselves make reference to the religion of reason that Cohen reconstructs out of the sources of Jewish monotheism. Butler would have good grounds for calling upon Cohen to support her thesis that a critique of state violence as an ethical demand derives from the framing conditions of Jewish thought itself. Of course it must at the same time be emphasized that Cohen's critique of state violence is directed not toward the destruction or the replacement of the legal order with a new law but, as has been shown, toward the differentiation of punishment and guilt, the elimination of the death penalty, and the foundation of a state under the rule of law on the basis of a contract rather than on that of an ethnic community [*Volksgemeinschaft*].

The Critique of Capitalism

While the critical idealist and ethical socialist Hermann Cohen was concerned with the formulation of an ideal state under the rule of law [*Rechtsstaat*], Walter Benjamin, fifty years younger and writing against the backdrop of the uprisings and crises of the Weimar Republic, was concerned with the critique of state violence—a kind of violence that, in his eyes, could be legitimated neither on ethical grounds nor on those of a state under the rule of law. Unlike Cohen, Benjamin, in "Critique of Violence," starts from the imbrication of law and the state with capitalism, imperialism, and war.[48] In the note "Capitalism as Religion," as I mentioned at the start, he describes capitalism as a "purely cultic religion."[49] As is widely known, Weber tried to explain the irrationalism of the capitalist conduct of life through secularized man's emotional tie to his profession. Not so Benjamin: in the moments diagnosed by Weber as irrationalism, he saw the continuity of the religious within capitalism.

His argument is just as simple as it is pragmatic: "Capitalism serves essentially to allay the same anxieties, torments, and disturbances to which the so-called religions offered answers."[50] In this regard—and that is perhaps the remark of Benjamin's richest in consequences—as "an essentially religious phenomenon," capitalism remains simultaneously linked to the history of Christianity so that, he continues, "Christianity's history is essentially that of its parasite—that is to say, of capitalism."[51] With this, Benjamin follows—I would like to stress—Weber's analysis in every regard. According to this analysis, the historical and religious process of the demystification of the world and of the formation of the capitalist way of life corresponds to the doctrines of predestination and of the Calvinist theory of grace. In particular, he joins Weber in drawing the consequences which this—according to Weber—"harsh doctrine of the absolute re-moteness of God and of the worthlessness of all creatures" has for the conduct of life of its believers:[52] "inner isolation of man,"[53] loneliness and inconsolability, the "fundamental rejection of every kind of culture of the senses."[54] Benjamin follows, nearly word-for-word, the subsequent passage in which Weber depicts the "pathos of the doctrine's inhumanity," which states that "all of creation is separated from God by an unbridgeable gulf":[55] "In what was for the man of the age of the Reformation the most important thing in life, his eternal salvation, he was forced to follow his path alone to meet his destiny, which had been decreed to him from eter-nity. No one could help him."[56] For Benjamin this means, when posed in relation to the religious movement of capitalism that he sees Nietzsche as formulating for the first time in the nineteenth century: "God's transcen-dence is at an end. But he is not dead; he has been incorporated into human existence. This passage of the planet 'Human' through the house of de-spair in the absolute loneliness of his trajectory is the ethos that Nietzsche defined. This man is the superman, the first to recognize the religion of capitalism and to begin to bring it to fulfillment."[57] Ignoring Nietzsche's own sharp critique of Christianity, Benjamin locates the ethos of his philoso-phy in the tradition of the Protestant secularization of asceticism and in-terprets it in its continuance as a "paradigm of capitalist religious thought."[58] For Benjamin, the decisive criterion is that "the idea of the superman transposes the apocalyptic 'leap' . . . into an apparently steady, though in the final instance explosive and discontinuous intensification."[59] Benjamin is playing here on an idea that heaven could be broken open by an "intensi-fied humanity"[60]—an allusion to the Biblical *ecce homo*, the God become human. According to this example, for Benjamin, the superman must grow up through the heavens without being given the possibility of return [*Umkehr*], of cleansing, or of atonement.

Benjamin's reference to Weber's study of the history of religion be-comes particularly apparent where it is concerned with the depiction of the religious exaggeration of work as its central consequence.[61] One could read the sentences in which Weber describes the process through which "intense worldly activity" became the "predominant means" to obtain the certainty of grace[62]—and in which, at the same time, good deeds be-came "technical means, not of purchasing salvation, but of getting rid of the fear of damnation"[63]—as a direct illustration of Benjamin's remark that "capitalism is the celebration of a cult *sans rêve et sans merci*."[64] This cult—without ceasefire and grace, which, for Benjamin, knows no "weekday" and thus no day,[65] which would not be a feast day, on which, to put it differently, one would not work—is none other than the secularization of asceticism through the cult of work, so vividly described by Weber. When, in his fragment, Benjamin describes capitalism as a cultic religion, this is not based on the fetish character of the commodity, as one might easily suppose, but instead upon the "sanctification of life" through the fulfillment one's duty and the systematization of the ethical conduct of life, which, as Weber laconically formulates it, "almost takes on the character of a business enterprise."[66] It becomes clear in Benjamin's description that capitalism—in the very complexities of its organizational structure—represents an intensification of the mythic manifestation of violence, of unhappiness and of heteronomous rule.

Although Benjamin sees in capitalism an "extension of despair to a state of world religion"—and despite capitalism's "historically unprecedented" aspect, which consists in being "not the reform of existence but its complete destruction"[67]—he nevertheless does not foretell a doomsday narrative [*Verfallsgeschichte*] for us. But how is it possible to overcome these mythic relations of violence? How can opposition and the reevaluation of human life be possible under the condition of such an intensification of the relations of violence?

I think that Butler is right to point out that Benjamin's critique of violence can only be explained with reference to his concept of the messianic.[68] But what does this concept of the messianic look like? How does Butler interpret it? And how far does she follow not only Benjamin's critique of violence but also his concept of the messianic?

Messianism and the Soul of the Living

Butler uses Benjamin's "Theological-Political Fragment," also composed in 1921, to introduce her interpretation of the messianic and Benjamin's concept of the "soul of the living." Benjamin begins the "Theological-Political Fragment" with the statement that nothing historical can relate to the messianic on its own. He thereby refuses all attempts to incorporate the messianic into an intra-historical teleology or to functionalize it politically. The concept of the messianic nevertheless possesses an important meaning for Benjamin's concept of the political: it constitutes the unapproachable, inaccessible, and unrepresentable counter-pole to the mythic, performative manifestation of violence and, as such, it sets out the task of a world politics whose method, as Benjamin writes, "must be called nihilism."[69] In his more detailed descriptions of this "method of nihilism," Benjamin is unmistakably oriented by the concept of destructive, divine violence as it is described in the "Critique of Violence." This method is directed, first, against mythic violence and the making-guilty of mere life. Second, it fulfills this task not by answering violence with violence but, to use a formulation of Butler's, by fighting for the absence of violence, and, third, it orients itself toward a reconciliation with the transitoriness of life. To summarize, the method of nihilism is directed toward the "idea of happiness."[70] But the idea of happiness is realized, for Benjamin, in the "quest of free humanity for happiness." This formulation once again makes clear that Benjamin holds firmly to the idea of enlightenment—world politics is nothing other than cosmopolitanism—and that he links the idea of enlightenment to the idea of Jewish monotheism. Even if, as he writes at the beginning of the essay, nothing historical can on its own relate itself to the messianic, the philosophy of history is nonetheless also conditioned, for Benjamin, by a mystical conception of history in which the messianic and humanity's quest for happiness refer to each other in countervailing tendencies. He describes this diagram of forces filled with tension in the following image:

> If one arrow points to the goal toward which the secular dynamic acts, and another marks the direction of messianic intensity, then certainly the quest of free humanity for happiness runs counter to the messianic direction. But just as a force, by virtue of the path it is moving along, can augment another force on the opposite path, so the secular order—because of its nature as secular—promotes the coming of the Messianic Kingdom.[71]

The formulation "quest of free humanity for happiness" plays no greater role in Butler's interpretation of Benjamin's idea of the messianic than does his concept of "world politics." She focuses her reading on Benjamin's distinction between mere life and the soul of the living and asks, against this backdrop, what worth life has after the soul is destroyed.[72] Butler sticks to the example of Niobe, which serves for her as the preeminent case of a subject who is constituted by structures of violence. Her interpretation of the messianic is oriented by the question of how a subject constituted by violence could pursue or even postulate the ethical demand for nonviolence.[73] Those who are familiar with Butler's work know that this question has not only been central for her thought from the time of her Adorno lectures in 2002, which were published in a German edition under the title *Critique of Ethical Violence*, but that it extends back to *Gender Trouble* and the question formulated there of the possibility of destroying the matrix of heteronormativity, which represents a no less guilt-inducing cult than does capitalism.

What role does the messianic play in Judith Butler's reading of the "Theological-Political Fragment"? It is central to her reading of the messianic that she links it with the concept of destruction. First, she interprets destructive divine violence as a destruction that goes on eternally, which "is already at work as the presupposition of positive law and, indeed, life itself."[74] From the divinity of violence, Judith Butler then derives the sacredness of life; she determines this concept of the sacred, for its part, through the concept of destruction: the concept of the sacred accordingly means nothing other than "that destruction can have no end and that it is redeemed neither by lawmaking nor by a teleological history."[75] Destruction is, she continues, "at once the anarchistic moment in which the appropriation of the commandment takes place *and* the strike against the positive legal system that shackles its subjects in lifeless guilt."[76]

The sacred interpreted as eternal destruction becomes, in Butler's reading, an immanent moment of life itself, of its hidden and repressed or forgotten meaning. As such, the form and the function which she ascribes to Benjamin's concept of the sacred recalls the form and function which the concept of iterability, borrowed from Derrida, possesses in her critique of violence. Iterability, as she writes in "The Claim of Non-Violence," "is crucial for understanding why norms do not act in deterministic ways."[77] Opposition to guilt-inducing legal violence is, as she explains, to be understood as a break that is nothing other than "a series of significant shifts that follow from the iterable structure of the norm."[78]

The Claim of Redemption and the Idea of Happiness

Butler's interpretation of the messianic begins with Benjamin's assertion that in happiness everything earthly seeks its downfall.[79] She shows that this downfall would not occur only once. Instead, it would be characterized by a temporal duration and a structure of repetition; from this temporality of destruction, she further concludes that downfall is a part of life itself. In fact, she goes a step further, contending that the eternal downfall "may well constitute what is sacred in life, that which is meant by 'the soul of the living.'"[80] According to Butler, "The messianic occurs precisely at this juncture, where downfall appears as eternal."[81]

Now, how does Butler interpret Benjamin's assertion that "the rhythm of this eternally transient worldly existence, transient in its totality, in its spatial but also in its temporal totality, the rhythm of messianic nature, is happiness"?[82] She interprets this assertion dialectically: "Indeed the rhythmic dimension of suffering becomes the basis of the paradoxical form of happiness with which it is twinned."[83]

This dialectic recalls not only Hegel but also a very specific passage in Butler's writings in which she confesses that she holds "a form of vitalism" that "persists even in despair."[84] Butler encountered this vitalism, as she writes in this highly personal text, through her reading of Spinoza and his concept of conatus. This vitalism was furthered, as she writes, in Hegel's dialectic: "Spinoza's insistence that the desire for life can be found nascent in the emotions of despair led to the more dramatic Hegelian claim that 'tarrying with the negative' can produce a conversion of the negative into being, that something affirmative can actually come of the experiences of individual and collective devastation even in their indisputable irreversibility."[85] It appears to me that this Hegelian dialectic also constitutes the reference point for Judith Butler's reading of Benjamin's concept of the "soul of the living" and of his concept of the messianic.

As emerges clearly from the passage cited, the question of the living and a particular trust in the self-healing powers of life are grounded in Butler's politics of the performative. She underlines this particular relationship between the poststructuralist conception of the norm and the rhythm of the living when she writes: "To say that the norm is iterable is precisely not to accept a structuralist account of the norm, but to affirm something about the continuing life of poststructuralism, a preoccupation with notions such as *living on, carrying on, carrying over, continuing,* that form the temporal task of the body."[86]

I think that Benjamin's demands of life extended further than merely surviving and living on when he created an "image of happiness" that is "thoroughly colored by the time to which the course of our own existence has assigned us" and when he concluded from this that the "idea of happiness is indissolubly bound up with the idea of redemption."[87] Benjamin firmly adhered to the image of happiness and to the image of a free humanity pursuing happiness until the end of his life. In "On the Concept of History," he linked the idea of happiness and of redemption with the past and, from the perspective of the past, designated each existing generation as the expected one. This existing generation, consequently, is the one which is endowed with a "weak messianic power,"[88] to redeem the past and to write history anew. In order to formulate this idea of happiness and of the weak messianic power with regard to the writing of history, Benjamin also makes use of philosophical interpretations of the Jewish tradition, as Butler has demonstrated in the development of the critique of state violence. Indeed, for him, perhaps the one cannot be thought without the other.

Translated by Catharine Diehl

Notes

1. Judith Butler, "Is Judaism Zionism?," in *The Power of Religion in the Public Sphere*, ed. Eduardo Mendieta and Jonathan Vanatwerpen (New York: Columbia University Press, 2011), 73.

2. Ibid.

3. Ibid., 72.

4. Ibid.

5. Judith Butler, "Sacred Life in Benjamin's 'Critique of Violence,'" in *Political Theologies: Public Religions in a Post-Secular World*, ed. Hent de Vries and Lawrence E. Sullivan (New York: Fordham University Press, 2006), 213.

6. According to the subtitle of the posthumously published *Religion of Reason out of the Sources of Judaism*. See Hermann Cohen, *Religion of Reason out of the Sources of Judaism*, trans. Simon Kaplan (Athens, GA: Scholars Press, 1995).

7. In 2003, Dirk Baecker devoted an entire essay collection to Benjamin's fragment; however, most of the contributions did not seriously pursue questions concerning the meaning of the difference between Judaism and Christianity in Benjamin's critique of Weber's secularization thesis. Cf. Dirk Baecker, "Einleitung," in *Kapitalismus als Religion*, ed. Dirk Baecker (Berlin: Kulturverlag Kadmos, 2003), 7–17. An exception is provided by Werner Hamacher's contribution, "Schuldgeschichte. Benjamins Skizze 'Kapitalismus als Religion,'" 77–121 (translated by Kirk Wetters as "Guilt History: Benjamin's Sketch 'Capitalism as Religion,'" *diacritics* 32, nos. 3–4 (2002): 81–106), which, in the context of the concept of turning [*Umkehr*] not only explicitly refers to the connection between Benjamin's fragment and Hermann Cohen but also explores this connection in more depth. At important places in his contribution, "Schwarzer Freitag: Die Diabolik der Erlösung und die Symbolik des Gildes," 121–144, Joachim von Soosten, a theologian from Bochum, also discusses Benjamin's thesis that capitalism is a parasite of Christianity.

8. Walter Benjamin, "Theological-Political Fragment," in *Selected Writings*, 4 vols. ed. Michael W. Jennings, Howard Eiland, and Gary Smith (Cambridge, MA: Harvard University Press, 1996–2003), 3:306. [Standard translations have been used where available, occasionally with modifications. Trans.]

9. Benjamin, "Capitalism as Religion," in *Selected Writings*, 1:288.

10. Ibid.

11. This formulation comes from Benjamin, "Theological-Political Fragment," *Selected Writings*, 3:305.

12. Benjamin, "Capitalism as Religion," in *Selected Writings*, 3:290.

13. Benjamin, "Theological-Political Fragment," *Selected Writings*, 3:305–306.

14. Emil Lederer was a professor of political economy and finance at the University of Heidelberg between 1918 and 1931; he had studied law and economics in Vienna, was a social democrat, and was an important

influence on the new field of sociology through his interdisciplinary works on the sociology of employees. Benjamin was often in Heidelberg in 1921 and also participated in Marianne Weber's evening discussions on sociology; he was friends with the younger brother of Max Weber, Alfred Weber, who died in 1920; he knew the young sociologist Kurt Mannheim, and was in contact with Ernst Bloch and Georg Lukács. Benjamin had begun to reflect on politics and on the relationship between politics, critique, and violence after becoming acquainted with Bloch in Switzerland in the spring of 1919.

15. See Walter Benjamin, *Gesammelte Briefe*, vol. 2, ed. Christoph Godde and Henri Lonitz (Frankfurt am Main: Suhrkamp, 1996), 138.

16. Gershom Scholem, *Walter Benjamin: Die Geschichte einer Freundschaft* (Frankfurt am Main: Suhrkamp, 1975), 119.

17. Benjamin, *Selected Writings*, 1:288..

18. Butler, *Sacred Life*, 205.

19. Benjamin, "Critique of Violence," in *Selected Writings*, 1:250.

20. Ibid.

21. Benjamin mentioned the book immediately after its publication in a letter to Scholem, from which it can be concluded that he had read it at least in part.

22. Hermann Cohen, *Ethik des reinen Willens*, in *Werke*, ed. Helmut Holzhey et al. (Hildesheim: Olms, 1977), 7:362. Quoted in Benjamin, "Critique of Violence," in *Selected Writings*, 1:249.

23. Cohen, *Ethik des reinen Willens*, 361.

24. Ibid., 363.

25. Butler, *Sacred Life*, 208.

26. Walter Benjamin, "Franz Kafka" in *Selected Writings*, 2:797.

27. Ibid.

28. Benjamin, "Critique of Violence," in *Selected Writings*, 1:248.

29. Ibid., 1:249.

30. Ibid., 1:236.

31. Ibid.

32. Ibid., 1:250.

33. There is a group of Psalms that are given the title of the children of Korah (Pss. 42, 44–49, 84, 85, 87, 88). In the medieval Jewish tradition one finds in Rashi (1040–1105) the commentary that the sons of Korah sang these Psalms when everyone around them was consumed by the earth but they were saved.

34. Benjamin, "Critique of Violence," in *Selected Writings*, 1:250.

35. Butler, *Sacred Life*, 208.

36. Judith Butler, *The Psychic Life of Power: Theories in Subjection* (Stanford, CA: Stanford University Press, 1997), 140.

37. Judith Butler, *Bodies that Matter: On the Discursive Limits of "Sex"* (New York: Routledge, 1993), 3.

38. One should refer here to Butler's concept of the "post-sovereign subject." In contrast to the sovereign subject, this subject "acts precisely to the extent that he or she is constituted as an actor and, hence, operating within a linguistic field." *Excitable Speech: A Politics of the Performative* (New York: Routledge, 1997), 15. This linguistic field, as Butler underlines, is limited by constraints that nevertheless open up possibilities. Vulnerability becomes a condition for placing oneself in relation to the other.

39. Hermann Cohen, *Religion of Reason*, 168.

40. Ibid.

41. Ibid.

42. Ibid., 193.

43. Ibid.

44. Judith Butler rightly observes that Benjamin's Jewish God is not the vengeful or harsh God of the laws, as he is often depicted from a Christian perspective, particularly in the Pauline tradition, but, rather, a God of reconciliation. Butler, *Precarious Life* (London: Verso, 2006), 210.

45. Cohen, *Religion of Reason*, 206–207.

46. Cohen, *Ethik des reinen Willens*, 381.

47. Ibid., 382.

48. In 1921, the Weimar Republic existed against the shadow of World War I and the failed November Revolution, the material battles [*Materialschlachten*], and the many dead and wounded. There were massive economic problems, including a hyperinflation that led to the brutally suppressed uprisings that shook the Republic to its core.

49. Benjamin, "Capitalism as Religion," in *Selected Writings*, 1:288.

50. Ibid.

51. Benjamin, "Capitalism as Religion," in *Selected Writings*, 1:288–289.

52. Max Weber, *The Protestant Ethic and the Spirit of Capitalism*, trans. Talcott Parsons (New York: Charles Scribner's Sons, 1930), 105.

53. Ibid.

54. Ibid., 103.

55. Ibid., 105.

56. Ibid., 104.

57. Benjamin, "Capitalism as Religion," in *Selected Writings*, 1:289.

58. Ibid.

59. Ibid.

60. Ibid.

61. Weber, *Protestant Ethic*, 108. Michael Löwy also points to this. See Löwy, "Capitalism as Religion: Walter Benjamin and Max Weber," *Historical Materialism* 17 (2009): 64.

62. Weber, *Protestant Ethic*, 112.

63. Ibid., 115.

64. Benjamin, "Capitalism as Religion," in *Selected Writings*, 1:288.

65. Ibid.

66. Weber, *Protestant Ethic*, 124.

67. Benjamin, "Capitalism as Religion," in *Selected Writings*, 1:289.

68. Butler, *Sacred Life*, 204

69. Benjamin, "Theological-Political Fragment," in *Selected Writings*, 3:306.

70. Ibid., 3:305.

71. Ibid.

72. Butler, *Sacred Life*, 210.

73. Cf. Judith Butler, "The Claims of Non-Violence," in *Frames of War: When is Life Grievable* (London: Verso, 2010), 165–184.

74. Butler, *Sacred Life*, 215.

75. Ibid.

76. Ibid.

77. Butler, "Claims of Non-Violence," 168.

78. Ibid., 169.

79. Benjamin, "Theological-Political Fragment," in *Selected Writings*, 3:305.

80. Butler, *Sacred Life*, 215.

81. Ibid., 216.

82. Benjamin, "Theological-Political Fragment," in *Selected Writings*, 3:306.

83. Butler, *Sacred Life*, 216.

84. Judith Butler, "Can the 'Other' of Philosophy Speak?," in *Undoing Gender* (New York: Routledge, 2004), 235.

85. Ibid.

86. Butler, "Claim of Non-Violence," 169.

87. Benjamin, "On the Concept of History," in *Selected Writings*, 4:389.

88. Ibid.

One Time Traverses Another
Benjamin's "Theological-Political Fragment"

JUDITH BUTLER

Benjamin's "Theological-Political Fragment" opens up several questions about the status of religion in Benjamin's work. Two questions tend to emerge when I teach this short text. One of them is whether Benjamin understands the divine as a purely immanent feature of the world. The second has to do with the notion of the "rhythm of transience" that appears in the text and, simply put, whether the rhythm of transience is itself transient—that is, it comes and goes but not in a regular or law-like way—or whether that transience comes and goes in a rhythmic way, suggesting that the rhythmic is not at all transient, instead it repeats regularly, as living things come and go. This last question is connected to the first, since if transience is the marker of the this-worldly, then it would seem that the rhythms of transience would be equally this-worldly. But that conclusion is not so easily arrived at. What becomes surprising as we read along is that Benjamin identifies a certain happiness with this rhythm of transience. So is that happiness this-worldly or otherworldly, or is it some kind of crossing of two temporalities that we might be able to think about in an interesting way.

Astrid Deuber-Mankowsky's essay in this volume, "Rhythms of the Living: Conditions of Critique," is a rich and provocative text that raises several questions. At issue is the relation between the practice of critique and Benjamin's specific critique of violence, and at least some of his remarks on the messianic. Deuber-Mankowsky's own scholarship forms the basis for her remarks on the similarities between Benjamin's ideas on guilt and fate and those of Hermann Cohen. In addition, she argues that Benjamin's essay "Capitalism as Religion" foregrounds Benjamin's reading of capitalism as a "purely cultic" religion whose task it is to establish universal guilt. Accordingly, she situates Benjamin's idea of the messianic, and my own reading of the messianic promise of an expiation from guilt, as part of the critique of both capitalism and legal violence.[1]

In this essay, I would like to concentrate on one claim that Deuber-Mankowsky makes in the course of her argument and mark my regret that I cannot respond to all of the important ideas raised by her essay. That query emerges in the context of considering my reading of the reference to "the soul of the living" in "Critique of Violence" in relation to the "Theological-Political Fragment." In two separate textual instances, Deuber-Mankowsky argues that I incorporate the divine into life itself and, in so doing, make the divine into a purely immanent feature of the world. Her view is that I understand the rhythm of transience as this-worldly, and so make the incessant destructiveness characteristic of *downfall* (*Untergang*) into the larger framework within which divine violence might be understood as an instance. At stake is whether what makes a particular kind of violence "divine" is the same as what makes a particular understanding of "downfall" eternal.

So is the divine a purely immanent feature of the world? If in my earlier work I understood the rhythm of transience as this-worldly, did I also then establish the incessant destructiveness characteristic of downfall as the encompassing framework within which divine violence might be understood? At stake is whether what makes a particular kind of violence divine is the same as what makes a particular understanding of downfall eternal. If the divine is destructiveness, does it follow that violence and downfall, or even violent downfall of this or that regime or some other existing state of affairs, is a certain action of the divine, the divine in action?

Although it may not seem immediately related, I want to suggest that this last set of questions is related to a broader theological one, namely, whether the messianic can appear or reveal itself in history. In my reading of Benjamin, the messianic does not, and cannot, follow the trajectory of revelation. Rather, it is figured time and again in Benjamin's work as the traversal of one temporal modality in and through another. In the "Theological-Political Fragment," for instance, the messianic figures the failure of the historical to signify the divine (which is one reason why the messiah cannot be a historical instantiation of the divine); the messianic, understood not as a human figure, becomes the recurrent and rhythmic downfall or going under that characterizes the transience of all living things. The eternal thus traverses the transient without exactly becoming transient and losing its status as the eternal. In the "Theses on the Philosophy of History" (1940), it is the history of the oppressed that flashes up within present time, disrupting its continuity and contesting its progressive claim. In each case, we have to understand how one time traverses another, without precisely that first time becoming absorbed and contained in or by the time traversed. And although the focus changes in the twenty-one-year interval between these two pieces from eternity to the history of the oppressed, both modalities are referred to as messianic, meaning a traversal or a breaking through of one time in another.

The idea of eternal downfall in Benjamin does not serve a view of the divine as immanent. Indeed, the very distinction between immanence and transcendence is confounded by the "Theological-Political Fragment," so it makes little sense to seek recourse to the distinction to apprehend what is happening there. The immanent is itself broken up or traversed by what is eternal, which means that the eternal is both a feature of immanence and yet irreducible to it—it can be in it or of it without being fully encompassed by it. Indeed, the formulation that Benjamin supplies suggests that not only is *this* life transient, but that all life is transient, and that transience is that which recurs in this life and in all other lives or living processes. As you can see, we just arrived at quite a generalization: the recurrence of transience is not itself transient; in other words, there is no condition under which a living being is not brought under the recurrent sway of transience; we lose others and things, and invariably our own lives are lost to others, and this business of losing does not leave us alone as long as we are still living.

So let us remain, if we can, with this thought: if the recurrent character of transience is eternal, meaning that it has no beginning and no end, then the recurrence itself is not transient. And yet, if we can only understand recurrence as a feature of transience, then there is no recurrence itself. However, the particular form of recurrence that characterizes transience requires the multiplicity of transient beings or processes in duration, since without that multiplicity and duration, there would be no recurrence (or reiteration) and so no punctual condition for what Benjamin calls the rhythm of transience. That rhythm seems to inform and exceed all things transient, and that situation does not cease happening (or, rather, it would cease only with the destruction of all things transient, that is, when all transience has ceased, so as long as there is transience, there is this rhythm).

If transience, however, is what characterizes the time of *this* life, and of all life or living processes, then a principle or a movement that is eternal or nontransient traverses this time of the living. I use the term *traverse* to characterize the radical alterity of this eternity to transient life; eternity characterizes the recurrence of transience, and so informs all transient things; and yet, it is not reducible to the transience of any of those things. Indeed, the problem with which we must come to terms is the following: how can the eternal characterize the recurrent character of transience while not being the same as the transience it characterizes. We might say that there is no instance of transience that cannot be understood as a recurrent moment of transience, and this would clearly lead to the conclusion that any given transient life is but an instance or permutation of a recurrent transience, even an eternally recurrent transience. *This* loss is thus one of an infinite number of recurring losses, but there is no one loss or dying away in which every particular loss participates—loss cannot take the form of a Form. We are asked to understand this process of transience or downfall as a rhythmic recurrence. If any particular process that dies away (or any particular dying away) fails to exhaust the recurrent process of dying away, neither is it possible to say that whatever role the eternal plays in transience is itself transient, and that the eternal is but an instance of the transient and, hence, itself transient. The eternal recurrence of the transient is itself not transient; even as we must understand this eternal recurrence as specifically characterizing the transience, it is neither absorbed nor defeated by the transience that it characterizes. The one remains irreducible to the other, and yet, the eternal recurrence at issue is less a Platonic form, as I just suggested, than a particular feature of musical, poetic, or metric patterns—closer perhaps to Pythagoras than to Plato. Rhythm does not enter directly into the visual field except in those cases where, for instance, we see the rhythmic sway of trees. For the most part, rhythm belongs to movement and to the auditory domain. One hears a rhythm in the midst of melody, or moves with a rhythm when one dances, and there might be a silent rhythm, but that means that it is punctuated by something noisy, or that it itself punctuated a field of sound. Rhythms take various forms, but once they are established, that is, in order to remain rhythmic, they have to repeat in some regular ways. If we are trying to figure out in what sense rhythm is eternal, then it cannot be that we can discover *this* or *that* rhythm, and can say that this one is eternal and this other one is not. We cannot really give an example without making a mess of what we are trying to say. In any case, we don't really have to, since it seems, at least for Benjamin, that not every rhythm is eternal—only the one that characterizes the rhythm of downfall; so we are left having to understand what that means.

To recapitulate: we are left with a formulation that suggests that the eternity of transience or what Benjamin himself calls "the eternity of downfall" both marks and exceeds the domain of transience and thus the domain of immanence itself. Indeed, the eternal recurrence at play in this formulation is precisely not an immanent dimension of this life, but an entry or interruption of the eternal within the transient. It is *in* transience without being *of* it, and this leads us to ask how one temporal modality (eternity) can enter into and inform another (transience) without ever becoming fully absorbed by the latter. To understand this entry of one temporal modality into another, one has to turn to Benjamin's notion of the messianic. And since it is reformulated several times, it is important to distinguish among the versions he offers, and to determine which one is most pertinent to the question under consideration here.

Indeed, as I hope to show, the hyphen that links the *theological* with the *political* in the title of this fragment names a way that the messianic operates as the flashing up of one time within another or, in this passage, a timelessness within the domain of time. We have to understand how an atemporal mode breaks into another, or how an atemporal mode breaks out from within a temporal one. Such traversals are possible only on the condition that finite and present temporality does not contain the other temporality that runs through it, flashes up within it, or breaks into or out of it. In the "Theological-Political Fragment," to say that any given transient object or life is informed by an eternal recurrence of transience is not to say that that eternal recurrence is transience, will stop at some time, or be finished once and for all. For transience to be informed by the eternal means that it is interrupted or broken up by a temporal order that exceeds its frame, indeed, a temporal order that is not itself transient (and that, strictly speaking, is not a temporal modality, but an atemporal one).

Benjamin seems to be stating precisely this at the outset of the "Theological-Political Fragment": "Erst der Messias selbst vollendet alles historische Geschehen, und zwar in dem Sinne, dass er dessen Beziehung auf das Messianische selbst erst erlöst, vollendet, schafft. Darum kann nichts Historisches von sich aus sich auf Messianisches beziehen wollen"[2]—if the Messiah (provisionally anthropomorphized in this formulation), redeems, completes, and creates the reference to the messianic (not anthropomorphized), and what follows from this is that nothing historical can from within itself (or only with its own resources) refer to the messianic, then even the anthropomorphic version of the Messiah is not historical. And yet, the figure of the Messiah is credited with bringing about this scene of redeeming, completing, and creating, suggesting that this happens in time. At the same time, as it were, this very scene is one in which the historical fails to refer to the messianic. In other words, a historical account of how the Messiah comes into being or what the Messiah does cannot approach the messianic dimension of the Messiah. This formulation afflicts our very capacity to refer to the Messiah as a historically embodied human figure. Indeed, the Messiah or, rather, the messianic is the name for the break in referentiality that occurs when something historical seeks to relate itself to the messianic and necessarily fails—like when we were momentarily looking for an example of eternal rhythm. The historical action of a person as well as the historical understanding of messianic power cannot properly refer to the ahistorical dimension of the messianic—it can only do this through an allegory whose very temporal presuppositions—usually narrative sequence—belie the way the messianic works.

Of course, this does not mean that there is no correspondence between the historical and the messianic, only that it is one for which no allegorical decoding will work. Hence, when Benjamin writes, "the spiritual *restitutio integrum*, which introduced immortality [*Unsterblichkeit*], corresponds [*entspricht*] to a worldly restitution that leads to the eternity of downfall,"[3] this is hardly a one-to-one correspondence that we might expect from traditional allegory. The relation is neither one of mirroring nor of analogy. The problem is immediately apparent, since in what sense can downfall function as restitution? Restitution implies that what has been lost is restored to its rightful place, or that an equivalent compensation makes up for the loss. But in what sense can downfall satisfy either or both possible meanings of restitution? And if it can be neither reparation nor compensation, then how do we interpret its meaning or effect?

The previous translation cuts short this rather complex passage which continues this way: "and the rhythm of this eternally transient worldly existence [*dieses ewig vergehenden*], transient in its totality [actually: "the temporal totality of a passing worldly"], in its spatial but also in its temporal totality, the rhythm of Messianic nature, is happiness."[4] And then the penultimate line: "For nature is Messianic by reason of its eternal and total passing away [*Vergängnis*]."[5]

So the spiritual restitution that introduces immortality (*Unsterblichkeit*) corresponds to a worldly situation in which eternity emerges as a feature of downfall, but this suggests that a passage from the worldly to the eternal has to take place. The idea of immortality presupposes that a mortal human seeks to overcome his or her finite condition; but the eternal (*Ewigkeit*) vacates that anthropocentric presumption. As the immortal becomes the eternal within the realm of transience, some kind of crossing takes place from one domain to another, suggesting that a human-centered temporal perspective (that presumes and struggles against transience) is supplanted by the rhythmic nature of an eternal recurrence of passing away. One temporal perspective interrupts, converts, and follows from another. The sentence in which Benjamin relays this news works by substituting *Ewigkeit* for *Unsterblichkeit*, shifting the perspective from that of human finitude to one that is decidedly not human centered. Something recurs in the sentence: the human-centered temporal perspective shifts into an eternal perspective on recurrent transience, one that requires the abandonment of the anthropocentric perspective itself. And it takes place by substituting one word for another, effecting a translation that refuses the equivalence between the two terms. That such an abandonment may have something to do with happiness in the Benjaminian sense is, of course, most interesting. But first, let us, if we can, be clear about what is meant by *eternal* (presuming that the eternal is something that any of us *can* be clear about).

As clarified earlier, the eternal no longer is posited exclusively in a spiritual domain considered as distinct from the worldly one, but becomes a characteristic of transience or downfall that defines the worldly. At the same time, it would be a mistake to say that the eternal is now *expressed* in some final and readable form within the worldly or worldly terms, since we have already established that nothing in the historical or the worldly can adequately or properly refer to the messianic. So neither the eternal nor the messianic is expressed directly or instantiated in the transient and finite world—it enters in a more oblique way. One might suspect that the messianic is not all of what is meant by the eternal, but for Benjamin, it seems to be the name for "nature in its eternal and total transience." If we conclude that the messianic is nature, and it *includes* the eternal, we have missed the point that the messianic works in and through nature and its transience in a way that remains irreducible to it. The conclusion is not that the messianic belongs to another order, but only that it operates within this one as a constitutive alterity—breaking in, breaking out, flashing up, confounding without collapsing the spheres of the this-worldly and the otherworldly.

This point becomes more important, however, when we ask about the meaning of happiness in this short text, but also as we turn, even briefly, to the meaning of the hyphen that joins the *theological* with the *political*. In my essay "Sacred Life in Benjamin's 'Critique of Violence,'" I sought to consider the following line from the "Fragment": "in happiness all that is earthly seeks its downfall [*im Glück erstrebt alles Irdische seinen Untergang*]."[6] I suggested that downfall does not just mean my downfall or yours, and that downfall is less an event than a recurrence, and so part of transient life, if not precisely what is sacred or eternal in that life. Further, I suggested that this notion of recurrent downfall can help to shed light on what Benjamin in "Critique of Violence" referred to as the "the soul of the living." This remains an enigmatic notion in that 1921 essay, especially when he writes, "violence can be inflicted 'relatively against goods, right, life, and suchlike' but it never absolutely annihilates the soul of the living [*die Seele des Lebendingen*]".[7] How is life distinguished from the soul of the living, and why is it that violence cannot be inflicted against the soul? (Is there no soul-murder in Benjamin? No Schreber?)

One is tempted to understand Benjamin as subscribing to a certain kind of Platonism at this instance, since life, including corporeal life, or "mere life" is itself not invulnerable to destruction. What is indestructible, rather, is "the soul of the living" and even divine violence cannot do away with this. So how do we understand the soul of the living? And is this to be explained by the idea of messianic intensity referenced in that same fragment?

Messianic intensity characterized the so-called inner man and is conditioned, if not intensified, by suffering, understood as misfortune or fate. To suffer from fate is precisely not to be the cause of one's own suffering. Such suffering follows from no moral or causal source, so persists prior, even apart from, individual responsibility, guilt, or moral law. This domain of suffering underscores that not all suffering is brought upon oneself, and delineates the limits of reflexive forms of guilt that assume the self as the cause of its own suffering. Indeed, it is not just that the self does not bring about its own suffering, but that its own suffering is not finally its own. Without cause, yet recurrent, this domain of suffering is described by Benjamin as bearing a rhythm and also as the condition of a certain kind of happiness—with an impersonal power and reach. He writes: "The rhythm of this eternally transient worldly existence, transient in its totality, in its spatial but also its temporal totality, the rhythm of Messianic nature, is happiness."[8] Can we understand happiness as the apprehension of the rhythm of transience, and even consisting in the abandonment of an anthropocentric relation to loss?

One way of understanding this is to understand that what one suffers and loses is part of a recurrent suffering and loss, and that one is paradoxically connected to broader rhythms of loss even in one's own private and most isolating sorrow. So even if what I love is lost, or if I myself will be lost to life, I am yet part of a rhythm in which, it seems, the living undergo a certain downfall. It is interesting that this recurrence of downfall is described through a poetic or musical term, *rhythm*, since that seems to be already an aesthetic formulation of demise. It draws upon strong romantic traditions that posit a musical language of nature (Rousseau, Goethe), but it also suggests a certain affinity with the Nietzschean claim that only as an aesthetic phenomenon is life justified. Although Benjamin is surely less interested in the justification of life, he does suggest that happiness may well be an internal musical dimension of mourning and sorrow, if not its outcome. In what sense can this be true?

Indeed, the rhythmic dimension of suffering becomes the basis of the paradoxical form of happiness with which it is twinned. If the rhythm of the messianic is happiness (or produces it), and the rhythm consists in an apprehension that all is bound to pass away or undergo its downfall, then this rhythm, the rhythm of transience itself, is eternal, connecting the inner life of the person, the person who suffers, with what is eternal, and so vacating the singular perspective of the finite individual. This seems to account for that restricted sense of life that is invoked by the commandment. It is not the opposite of *mere life*, since transience surely characterizes mere life; it is, rather, mere life grasped as the rhythm of transience, and this provides a perspective that is counter to the view that life itself is sinful or must be paid for with death.

There is, then, a kind of correlation between inner life and a suffering that is eternal, that is, unrestricted to the life of this or that person. And although it seems that we are being counseled to adopt this point of view on individual suffering, Benjamin invokes an even larger scale, a greater humility. The embrace of transitoriness implies the loss of the very first-person perspective that would make the embrace; to hear or sense the rhythm of transience is precisely to allow one's own loss, even the loss of one's own finite personhood, to become at once small and iterable. Happiness seems to follow from the vacating of the anthropocentric conceit, the focus on what *I* lose or have lost, or the implications of that first person, even at the moments of extreme loss, repeated by others I do not know (and never lost). The loss of the radical singularity of this first-person *I* becomes one way to apprehend the rhythmic dimension of loss. Happiness, rather, is that rhythmic movement or sound by which each and every living process is washed away, thus linked with one another in their vanishing. One might understand this as a radical break with narcissism, including, most importantly, the negative narcissism of guilt.

In a brief text called "He" (1917), Franz Kafka writes about the judgment of others, the necessity to fight that judgment, but also the limits of winning any such fight. The text is also concerned with life and death, fighting for one's life, although not precisely the life and death struggle we know from Hegel. The short investigation takes place, on and off, through probing the possibilities and the limits of the third person, *he*, representing at a textual level the attempted evacuation of the first person and even the proper name. In a sense, it is a text about the third person, how much can be said in that voice and from that perspective. Kafka writes, "The difference between 'Yes' and 'No' that he says to his contemporaries and those that he should actually say, might be likened to the difference between life and death, and is just as vaguely denied by him." Further, he writes, "the strength to deny [*die Kraft zum Verneinung*], that most natural expression of the perpetually changing, renewing, dying, reviving human fighting organism [*menschlichen Kämpferorganismus*], we possess always, but not the courage [*den Mut aber nicht*], although life is denial [*Verneinen*], and therefore denial affirmation [*also Verneinung Bejahung*]."[9]

The third-person *he* is one about whom Kafka makes some rather firm claims. He follows the above passage with this one: "He does not die along with his dying thoughts. Dying is merely a phenomenon within the inner world [*innerhalb der inneren Welt*] (which remains intact, even if it too should only be an idea), a natural phenomenon [*eine Naturerscheinung*] like any other, neither happy nor sad." Earlier, Kafka adds the following: "Death is to the individual like Saturday evening to the chimney sweep; it washes the dirt from his body [*den Russ vom Leibe*]."[10] This idea that death absolves moral fault can be found early on in the writings of Walter Benjamin.

Paradoxical in Kafka is the idea that death is at once a natural phenomenon and one that takes place within the inner world, so twice within, suggesting that the phenomenal is to be found in this region that might be called by Benjamin "the soul of the living." This phenomenal interior is perhaps precisely the de-personalized zone of death, one that crosses the phenomenal and the nonphenomenal in ways that prove difficult to conceptualize within ready spatial categories. For Kafka, it is a question of dying, and not death; moreover, dying is linked with saying no to the judgments of one's contemporaries, the power of negation (*Verneinung*). At the same time, the third-person *he*, we are clearly told, does not die along with his dying thoughts. *He* escapes the fate of the *I* perhaps, but also marks a certain way of living on through a pronominal shift on the page, entering the problem of writing, even fiction, into the heart of this problem of death. That dying belongs to him, but also to every possible third person, establishing us all as the *he* or *she* about whom others might one day comment, or already have. The point of view of the contested obituary is already there on the page, as part of its narrative presumption and effect.

For Benjamin, a certain happiness and sorrow go along with the rhythms of suffering, set apart from the moral universe of blame and fault. But for Kafka, it seems, it is neither happy nor sad (*weder fröhlich noch traurig*). Indeed, about this third person or, rather, this possibility of becoming a third person for others, Kafka writes, "the current against which he swims is so rapid that in certain absent moods he is sometimes cast into despair by *the blank peace* amid which he splashes, so infinitely far has he been driven back in a moment of surrender."[11] So for Kafka, it seems to portend a despair within a blank peace, blank page, perhaps, without writing, without even the pivot of the third person for the story.

Whereas for Kafka, living or, rather, dying is figured as a rapid current, for Benjamin these modalities are more often than not bound up with storms. In "The Meaning of Time in the Moral Universe" (1921), Benjamin figures forgiveness as a storm that eradicates all traces of guilt (echoes of Kafka's chimney sweep suddenly now swept clean). The bonds of guilt are dissolved, as they are on the eve of Yom Kippur in the Kol Nidre service when promises are relinquished—and the broken ones forgiven and forgotten—in order then to be renewed, and for a general renewal of the individual to take place. The relinquishing of the bonds is a form of this forgiveness in Benjamin. And although it should lead to the reconstitution of those bonds and renewed promises, it becomes an important moment for Benjamin, one that focuses on the divine power to expiate guilt. In that same essay, Benjamin refers, for instance, to "the immeasurable significance of the Last Judgment, of that constantly postponed day which flees so determinedly into the future after the commission of every misdeed." The last judgment, then, does not quite arrive; it is a permanently postponed appointment, and in this way vanquishes the idea of the day in which there is a final reckoning or judgment of guilt.

In this sense, citing Kafka's "The Coming of the Messiah" (a parable extracted from his *Blue Octavo Notebooks*) the Messiah arrives not on the last day (Judgment Day) but on the very last (*allerletzten*) day. That last day is not a day in any calendrical sense, but a day beyond days, a time beyond sequential time. In that same essay on morality and time, Benjamin elaborates on this "final judgment" as one that is indefinitely postponed. Benjamin writes:

> This significance is revealed not in the world of law, where retribution rules, but only in the moral universe, where forgiveness comes out to meet it. In order to struggle against retribution, forgiveness finds its powerful ally in time. For time, in which Ate [moral blindness] pursues the evildoer, is not the lonely calm of fear but the tempestuous storm of forgiveness which precedes the onrush of the Last Judgment and against which she cannot advance. This storm is not only the voice in which the evildoer's cry of terror is drowned; it

is also the hand that obliterates the traces of his misdeeds, even if it must lay waste to the world in the process.[12]

The references here to the drowning of the cries of the evildoers and the hand that lays waste to the world recall this same eternal recurrence of downfall, suggesting that the nonanthropocentric apprehension of transience is what releases the human subject from guilt, self-vilification, and cycles of retribution. It obviously opens up the question of the broader idea of destruction that becomes so central to the idea of divine violence as it is developed in "Critique of Violence," written only a year before. There the enigmatic claim was made that violence can destroy life, rights, and goods, but not "the soul of the living." It would now appear that the soul of the living is precisely the rhythmic recurrence of transience, and the reformulation of eternity as this rhythm. If no violence can be done to the soul of the living, it is precisely because that soul, understood as messianic intensity, is characterized by that rhythmic recurrence of loss—it is the very rhythm of destruction, and so any effort to destroy it is already under its sway.

Messianic intensity is the happiness that follows from this eternal downfall, or is coincident with it, precisely because it constitutes the unshackling of guilt and the release from cycles of debt, recrimination, and revenge. In a sense, we are tracking a specifically Jewish departure from the cycles of Greek tragedy. This particular form of happiness does not imply that we should all be happy that we will pass away or that we will inevitably lose those whom we love most. Neither does it mean that we ought to pursue a politics that mandates the destruction of living beings. Rather, the apprehension of transience is what interrupts cycles of retribution, which would include accusations of guilt and rationales for war. Further, from the perspective of eternal transience, my own life is equal to the life of every other, that is, equally subject to this eternally recurrent dying away.

"The Theological-Political Fragment" begins with a mute citation to Kafka, whose parable, "The Coming of the Messiah" begins with a similar line and cadence.[13] Kafka writes, "The Messiah will come as soon as the most unbridled individualism of faith becomes possible—when there is no one [*niemand*] to destroy this possibility and no one to suffer its destruction; hence the graves will open themselves."[14] Kafka figures a time when there is no human figure on the landscape as the time when the Messiah will come (which is to say that whatever comes, no human will come). This means that the Messiah himself will not be a "one" and that we are asked to imagine a nonanthropocentric understanding of the messianic in terms of a nonhuman time. The deconstitution of the human subject into its "living soul" is precisely the access to the nonanthropocentric basis of his or her happiness, a link with an eternal rhythm that washes away the traces of guilt, and affirms transience as an eternal link among all living beings.

If we then finally turn to the question of the hyphenated link between the theological and the political, we can see that no causal or prescriptive relation is implied. And that what is at stake is a form of destruction that is directed against legal violence (its compulsory ordering of the subject through the inculcation of guilt) in "Critique of Violence." The final line of the "Theological-Political Fragment" opens up the question of nihilism, and yet refuses its facile reduction to a political injunction for humans to destroy institutions at will. Benjamin writes, "To strive after such passing [eternal and total passing away], even for those stages of man that are nature, is the task of world politics, whose method must be called nihilism."[15] In fact, Benjamin does not say that it must be called nihilism, only that it has been called that [*zu heissen hat*], suggesting that his statement is less prescriptive than descriptive. In any case, the final line remains perplexing. "To strive after [*Diese zu erstreben*]" certainly suggests that some historically existing human figure is striving, even when that human remains in its natural stages. This striving, which may or may not be intentional, is apparently equivalent to "the task of world politics," that is, a politics that is not restricted to a given community of nation. If there is to be a world politics that transcends the local or communitarian instances we know, it will be one whose method is nihilism. Here Benjamin identifies this striving of humans and this task of world politics, and further claims that there is a method in this striving. *Method* is a curious term, to be sure, recalling Methodism or scientific method, and difficult to understand as a "method" of nihilism. If, however, we think of this method as a repeated application, then it would seem that Benjamin is giving voice yet again to the problem what recurs eternally.

The task of world politics would be nihilism to the extent that human institutions can be de-constituted (and renewed), that they are grounded neither in natural or divine laws, and so are considered immutable. Indeed, in the place of eternal laws derived from nature or religion, Benjamin proposes an eternity of the destructible, insisting that the transient character of institutions implies that they can be taken apart and overthrown, and that revolution remains a permanent possibility of humanly crafted structures. Human deeds can be forgiven and pass away, and so too can human institutions suffer downfall and pass into history or, indeed, oblivion. It is a world politic at issue here precisely because the worldly is characterized by the rhythm of eternally recurrent downfall. Regimes fall, as they must; hence none of them can claim to be eternal. And yet, an eternal truth seems to imply and to be their very downfall— music to someone's ears, but whose, and in what key? And who will be around to sense it?

Notes

1. See my "Walter Benjamin and the Critique of Violence," in *Parting Ways* (Columbia University Press, 2012).

2. Walter Benjamin, "Theologisch-Politisches Fragment," in *Zur Kritik der Gewalt und andere Aufsätze* (Frankfurt am Main: Suhrkamp, 1965), 95; translated by J. Jephcott as "Theological-Political Fragment," in *Reflections*, ed. Peter Demetz, (New York: Schocken Books, 1978), 312–313.

3. Ibid., 96/313.

4. Ibid.

5. Ibid.

6. Ibid.

7. Walter Benjamin, "Critique of Violence," *Reflections*, trans. Edmund Jephcott (New York: Harcourt, Brace, Jovanovich, 1978), 297–298.

8. Benjamin, "Theologisch-Politisches Fragment," 96; "Theological-Political Fragment," 313.

9. Franz Kafka, "He: Notes from the year 1920," in *The Great Wall of China* (New York: Schocken Books, 1972), 153–161. The German version is available online at http://gutenberg.spiegel.de/buch/franz-kafka-aphorismen-166/3.

10. Ibid., 159.

11. Ibid.; emphasis added.

12. Walter Benjamin, *Selected Writings*, vol. 1, *1913–1926* (Cambridge, MA: Harvard University Press, 1996), 286–287.

13. The parable is an extract from his notebooks, so foregrounded as a self-standing parable by editorial decision.

14. Franz Kafka, "The Coming of the Messiah," in *Parables and Paradoxes* (bi-lingual edition) (New York: Schocken Books, 1961), 81.

15. Benjamin, "Theologisch-Politisches Fragment," 96; "Theological-Political Fragment," 313.

Walter Benjamin and Christian Critical Ethics—A Comment

HILLE HAKER

As enigmatic as it is at times, Walter Benjamin's retrieval of Jewish theological language has perhaps done more for postwar German Christian theology than it could do for itself after the Holocaust, even though, admittedly, only a few theologians marked the Holocaust as a radical rupture of their tradition.[1] My reading of Benjamin engages specifically with two texts: "Critique of Violence" and "Theological-Political Fragment."[2] I will demonstrate how an analysis sensitive to theological concepts may further inform a reading of Benjamin's essays, before turning to Johann Baptist Metz's reinterpretation of Christian theology as a new political theology. By linking the scholarship to this line of the reception history, my goal is to point to some of the topics that should be further discussed in an interdisciplinary conversation between theology and philosophy.

The "Critique of Violence"

One of the most contested texts by Walter Benjamin is his "Critique of Violence" ("Zur Kritik der Gewalt").[3] The text was written in 1921, after World War I and the 1917 Russian Revolution, and during the first years of the parliamentary Weimar Republic. No *Notstandsgesetze* (emergency laws) had yet been issued. Many intellectuals in Germany at the time were particularly intrigued by the Russian Revolution—the abolition of the death penalty, the guarantee of religious freedom and nondiscrimination of ethnic groups, and the beginning of peace negotiations in Eastern Europe during World War I. By 1921, however, all this belonged already to the past; Russia was in the middle of a civil war after the revolution had turned bloody and violent. Benjamin, at the time, was certainly interested in political philosophy and philosophy of law, but even more so in the reflection on a moral philosophy that was both personal and political; and his reflection was deeply influenced by Jewish philosophy. It is this particular ethical interest that has been overlooked in many of the recent interpretations of Benjamin's text, because the debates were too engaged with political philosophy and political theology, echoing Carl Schmitt's criticizing Benjamin for the political theology of Carl Schmitt too far in his political writings; or the debate centered on Benjamin's position on the issue of secularism and postsecularism.[4]

Benjamin understands the critique of violence (*Gewalt*) as the analysis of its relation to law and justice. The critique (*Kritik*)—taking up Kant's term of self-reflective reasoning that discerns the transcendental conditions of a concept—is applied to a reflection on the conditions of justified violence via its relation to law (*Recht*) und justice (*Gerechtigkeit*), or legal and moral justice.[5] Put differently, the question is whether legal or political *Gewalt* is possible as a moral concept, and whether *Gewalt* is legitimate within the realm of justice at all. I will present his argument, emphasizing Benjamin's refusal to justify arbitrary violence with political *Gewalt*. However, since my text is concerned with theology rather than political philosophy, I will comment on one aspect of the text only, namely the relation of mythical and divine violence as the (metaphorical) lens through which the question of the legitimization of political and legal violence is to be seen.[6] More specifically, I will emphasize the function of the rebellion of the group led by Korah against Moses and Aaron, and compare Benjamin's interpretation of this biblical text with a contextual interpretation of the narrative as it may be conceived from a theological perspective.[7] From this reading, I intend to present a clearer understanding of the concept of divine justice that informs Benjamin's critique of political and legal violence.

The term *Gewalt* has at least two distinct meanings in the German language: it is used for *brute force* or *violence*, but also for the *power of force*, for example associated with the power of the law or the state, associated in the English language with *authority*. This *ambiguity*—or even, at times, the equivocation of how the term is used—is exactly what Benjamin maintains throughout the essay.[8] *Gewalt* always requires reasons in order to be justified: individual or collective civil actions require moral justification if they entail violence, while in addition to this justification, state actions or practices must be politically or legally legitimized. Normally, we presuppose that legitimization entails not only the political but also the moral justification; but the history of political philosophy, ethics, and theology, too, is full of theories and even more so, of practices where the politically legitimized law (*Recht*) and morally justified justice (*Gerechtigkeit*) come into conflict. Hence Benjamin's question: can the mere political legitimization also serve as a justification from the moral perspective? Critique is subsequently the way in which this reflection is provided. Benjamin discusses it in three different contexts: *Gewalt* as an act by an individual, the state, or a collective. He affirms the possibility of justification in all three cases, pointing to (individual) self-defense, state laws, and civil resistance, for example by way of a general strike directed against the state. In his argumentation Benjamin contrasts two possible foundations of *Gewalt*, illuminated by two stories of violence: one from Greek mythology, and the other from the Hebrew Bible.[9]

Niobe, having born seven sons and seven daughters, boasts of her fecundity mocking the goddess of fecundity, Lethe, who has given birth to only two children, Apollo and Artemis. She is punished for her act of hubris by Lethe's children, who murder all of her children, while Niobe herself survives. Begging for the relief of her mourning, Zeus (in another recounting it is Artemis) transforms her into a rock, but even as a rock, her tears never run dry.

While being led through the desert to the Promised Land, a Levite group led by Korah challenges the role of Moses. Against Moses's claim to his and Aaron's exclusive sacredness in relation to God, Korah holds that *everyone* is sacred and that God is among all people. In response, Moses, who accuses them that their revolt is not aimed against him and Aaron but in fact against God (because of jealousy that they have not been made leaders), calls for God to resolve the issue. He orders Korah and the other men to bring sacrifices to God and see whether God would receive them. Indeed, God appears before the group; however, he only speaks to Moses and Aaron, ordering them to tell everybody to separate from the rebellious group so that they will be saved. In this conversation with God, Moses and Aaron appeal to God's justice and plead not to destroy innocent lives—and God answers their plea. When Korah's sacrifice is prepared, Moses risks his life and leadership in the ultimate confrontation: if Korah and the others will die a natural death, he tells the community, this may be taken as a sign that Korah is justified to sacrifice to God, and he and Aaron do not have the exclusive authority to represent God. Only upon their unnatural death will it become clear that they have revolted against God. Immediately after this, the earth opens, and Korah, together with his and his follower's families and all of their property, fall down.[10] God, however, orders that the censers Korah and the others used for the sacrifice are kept as a sign of Moses's and Aaron's sacredness.

With respect to the story of Niobe, Benjamin's interpretation is the following: Any concept of violence that is rooted in the arbitrariness of power can be called mythical, resembling Lethe's violence against (and power over) Niobe—hardly a *means* to a (potentially justifiable) end but rather a *mere* or immediate manifestation of power. With her act of hubris, Niobe clearly violates the mythical order of being defined by the gods—challenging a god (in this case: mocking the goddess of fecundity to be less fecund than a human being) threatens this order. Mythical violence reaffirms this order of being but also exposes human beings to arbitrary power, often in the form of violence—what appears as the law, entailing punishments for transgression, is in fact, Benjamin argues, rooted in "the endless pagan chain of guilt and atonement."[11] As a result, we can see that insofar as a political regime applies such arbitrary power, it dominates via violence, rooted in a divine albeit mythical power.[12] Radically distinct from a moral notion of justice, mythical violence is not related to justice; not justice, but the manifestation of power *is* its legitimization.

The interrelation of law and justice is at stake, too, in the biblical story of Korah—although depicted very differently. When read in context, the Korah narrative is part of the postexilic redaction of the Priestly source, showing the traces of several editorial interpretations; it reflects the power struggle between different groups (Aaronites and Levites) over who is to represent God through the presentation of sacrifices.[13] In the Book of Numbers, this struggle is presented from the perspective of the priests who have a particular interest distinguishing between the sacred and the profane for the postexilic community, and arguing for a theocentric religious community.[14] Moses and Aaron are clearly the models for the *just* leadership at this point in the overall story of the Exodus and Israel's goal of reaching the Promised Land: Shortly before the Korah story unfolds (Num. 11), Moses, tired of the angry group, had in fact shared power with a group of leaders who had been installed by God; as the Korah rebellion emerges, God speaks to Moses and Aaron directly, and Moses *negotiates* with God about the fate of Israel, appealing to God's proportional justice (which God approves of).[15] *Justice*, one might say, is as much an attribute of Moses as of God; and justice is at stake in the struggle for leadership; without Moses, the reader knows, Israel will not reach the Promised Land. In the story, God takes Moses's side; therefore, the violence enacted against the Korah rebellion reaffirms God's as much as Moses's leadership, shaped by faith in God, his justice, and the hope for the future. Hence, divine *Gewalt* (a force that may or may not entail violence) serves as a judgment on the legitimacy of leadership via its definition by justice. The interrelation of law and justice (*Recht* and *Gerechtigkeit*) is maintained in the biblical story and contrasted in Benjamin's essay with the relation of mythical law and order and mere power. Interestingly, in the biblical story this relation defines, at the same time, the notion of sacredness.[16]

Benjamin defines divine *Gewalt* as "pure," as opposed to "mere" *Gewalt*. It is pure insofar as it is not manifestation of power but rather, at its core it is aimed at the living. Divine *Gewalt*, Benjamin maintains, is bloodless. Therefore, the link between the depicted divine violence of the Korah story and the ethical concept of justice is crucial. If law and justice are the terms that define the critique of violence, the Korah story has the function of establishing divine *Gewalt as* the (moral) force of justice.[17]

Divine *Gewalt* is in fact a potentially violent (read: forceful!) and judging force, albeit always based on the relation of an action and justice. Benjamin acknowledges the destructive force of the divine judgment in the narrative, as he acknowledges that it is exactly not *always* nonviolence (as the pacifists of his time held) that renders an action just or justified. However, the two lines of the argument—the one on legal violence and force, the other on moral violence and force that is justified, rooted in divine violence and force that is linked to divine *justice*—seem to be tied together too quickly in this case. This difference becomes clear when Benjamin's interpretation of the theological-ethical commandment "Thou shalt not kill" is compared to the legal system of law: Since the moral—and at the same time theological—commandment not to kill serves as an orientation for one's action, Benjamin holds, it functions very differently than a legal norm. The act of killing as such may be considered as the transgression of a law, but as a transgression it can only be justified on the basis of a *moral* judgment. Put differently: the justification of a transgression of a legal or moral prohibition cannot be ruled out in every case. The critique of violence—the discernment of the conditions of the concept's truth— results in the acknowledgment of violence as a kind of last resort to make the exception for the sake of the living: The commandment ("Thou shalt not kill") "exists not as a criterion of [legal] judgment, but as a [moral] guideline for the actions of persons or communities who have to wrestle with it in solitude and, in exceptional cases, to take on themselves the responsibility of ignoring it."[18] Not the law but morality, understood as justice, with its link to agency, decision, and individual—sometimes lonesome—responsibility is the perspective which may demand of an agent to make the exception on behalf of the living; in exceptional cases this may indeed involve the violation of the fifth commandment.

Analyzing the narrative in its context, it remains ambivalent concerning both divine judgment and Moses. Considering the tradition (as a reinterpretation) of the Korah narrative in other biblical texts, divine violence as a "striking judgment" is in fact not the last word. Given the historical time of the postexilic community that has just survived exile—which was precisely interpreted as a divine judgment on Israel's unjust conduct, for example, in the prophetic tradition—Korah's sons' survival (noted later in the Book of Numbers) and the reappearance of Korah in the Book of Psalms proves the ambivalence—or rather the pluralism that has left its traces in the different schools of redaction—within the tradition. Furthermore, Korah's question concerning the sacredness of all members of the community because of God's universal presence among them is later taken up in the biblical debate on the exclusion versus inclusion of the gentiles and the universality of redemption.[19] This reinterpretation of the biblical Korah story concerns the status of sacredness that prompts the rebellion: Even though Moses seems to be perfectly rehabilitated after Korah's destruction, the biblical narrative leaves no doubt (partly due to the different editions which did not necessarily back the priestly claims) that the divine judgment, entailing the destruction of Korah, is not as clear-cut as it may seem: the question of where God is present (in the sacred space, in the profane space, among everyone, or only in the sacred space the priests occupy), which is an urgent question for the postexilic community, is not entirely resolved. Analyzing the narrative structure of the priestly school's theology, the text may well be unmasked as ideological or at least partial and politically interested—because *its* narrative function is clearly to use the divine judgment as a *political* legitimization of the priestly concept of sacredness that was bound to its cultic presentation. The narrative entails a subversive line of this political theology: since God receives Korah's sacrifice anyway, as Benjamin stresses, it reveals the identity struggle *within* the tradition to which Korah becomes one witness who is remembered only later on.[20]

After having addressed justified killing, as in the case of self-defense and political authorities' use of deadly force, including the death penalty, the last context of violence Benjamin examines is civil resistance.[21] The "bloodless violence" of justice that is aimed at the living but never at the soul—"would seem to imply," writes Judith Butler, "that it is not waged against human bodies and human lives,"[22] and in fact it would have the paradoxical structure of a "nonviolent violence."[23] Taking this insight further to the level of resistance against state law, Butler explains that Benjamin argues that in cases of unjust laws, divine violence requires them to be broken. However, the Korah story does not apply to this: if Korah rebels against the political structure of the exilic community

(*Recht*, embodied in Moses's leadership), he and his group are not justified but rather destroyed in the name of justice (*Gerechtigkeit*).

What does this mean for the political critique of violence? In the case wherein (positive) law and (ethical) justice (*Recht und Gerechtigkeit*) fall apart, divine violence, Butler holds, "not only releases one from forms of coerced accountability, a forced or violent form of obligation, but this release is at once an expiation of guilt and an opposition to coercive violence."[24] In other words: civil disobedience, Butler argues with Benjamin, such as expressed in a general strike, may be justified if rooted in justice. If the semantic element of force is emphasized in the German term *Gewalt*, one touches upon the understanding of civil resistance that informed, for example, the civil disobedience of Martin Luther King Jr. and the civil rights movement, which, as in all social movements, at one point itself wrestled with the question of violence. But as was the case in the exceptional violation of the fifth commandment by state authorities, here, too, it may not be decidable by merely looking at the act itself as to whether civil disobedience is in fact just or whether it is motivated just by the desire to replace one rule of law with another. In the Korah rebellion, we have a divine judgment that ends with the downfall of Korah. This is certainly violent and bloody, as well as unforgiving to Korah and the other rebels, but it is not a paradox.[25] In the biblical tradition, however, God's violence against Israel's enemies (from within, as in the story of Korah, or from outside its border of collective identity) remains a difficult concept to grasp, one that is contested and criticized within the tradition—for example, as Abraham wrestles with God concerning the fate of Sodom, as Moses negotiates about the fate of his own community, and as God over and over again corrects his judgments so that they indeed serve the living. Theologically speaking, it is exactly the ambivalence of violence that divine *Gewalt*, too, is confronted with in the overall biblical narrative, thereby rendering the concept of pure *Gewalt* as a concept that only evolves in the history of the Jewish tradition as nonviolent, ultimately even as a *forgiving* justice. In this history, the Jewish conceptualization of the love of one's neighbor, reiterated but also radicalized as the love of one's enemies, as in the Christian gospel tradition, is crucial for the paradoxical understanding of nonviolent violence or force.[26] This reinterpretation of justice as forgiveness transforms the cycle of human injustice and divine violence as atonement (*Sühne*) into a theology of forgiveness. In the Christian tradition, this interpretation of justice as forgiveness sheds light, too, on the theology of the cross, which, after all, is a very different concept than the atonement theology that was taught for centuries as a centerpiece of Christian theology, and which Benjamin roots in the mythical tradition of fate in his essay "Fate and Character."[27]

Benjamin has an interesting footnote to this distinction between justice as retribution (which can be linked to atonement) and forgiveness (here interpreted as expiation)—and for a theological reflection which is, at least ultimately, more interested in the criterion of legal justice via the concept of moral justice, this is of particular interest, because it resonates with the biblical transformation process of the relation between violence and justice:

> In order to struggle against retribution, forgiveness finds its powerful ally in time. For time, in which Ate pursues the evildoer, is not the lonely calm of fear but the tempestuous storm of forgiveness which precedes the onrush of the Last Judgment and against which she cannot advance. This storm is not only the voice in which the evildoer's cry of terror is drowned; it is also the hand that obliterates the traces of his misdeeds, even if it must lay waste to the world in the process. As the purifying hurricane speeds ahead of the thunder and lightning, God's fury roars through history in the storm of forgiveness, in order to sweep away everything that would be consumed forever in the lightning bolts of divine wrath.
>
> What we have expressed here metaphorically must be capable of being formulated clearly and distinctly in conceptual form: the meaning of time in the economy of the moral universe. In this, time not only extinguishes the traces of all misdeeds but also—by virtue of its duration, beyond all remembering or forgetting—helps, in ways that are wholly mysterious, to complete the process of forgiveness, though never of reconciliation.[28]

It has been my intention in this comment to analyze only the motive of mythical versus divine violence, as presented in the "Critique of Violence." The result of this reading is that in the Jewish (and, I would add, also in the Christian) tradition, the critique of violence becomes a central determinant of how to define the concept of justice or, vice versa, the moral concept of justice becomes the criterion for the legitimacy of violence or force. In a theological reading, this question is much more closely linked to the question of morality and responsibility than to the question of political or legal philosophy. Insofar as the theological perspective, rooted in a particular history and tradition, requires justice (*zedeka* is the Hebrew term for the moral-theological concept of justice) to be the criterion of morality and moral norms *and* legality and laws (*mizpah*), it becomes the implicit moral criterion of political violence or force—*Gewalt*, too. And for Benjamin, one could show with respect to other texts that the commitment to *moral agency* at the same time becomes the critique of a spiritualized religious experience that is separated from justice.[29]

The Weak Messianic Power

The "Theological-Political Fragment" is a key text at least for one important strain of thought in Benjamin's early work, namely the difference and interrelation of the order of the profane (political, legal) and the messianic. What makes this text difficult to read is the decontextualization of the conversation it engages with—apart from Ernst Bloch, no other author is mentioned. Yet, they can be brought to the table: Herman Cohen, Franz Rosenzweig, and, of course, Gershom Scholem, all offer important insights into the background. Read from a Jewish-Christian theological perspective, the question Benjamin raises is all too familiar: Can the Kingdom of God be established by human acts or a political order?[30] Or is the time of history so distinct from the messianic time (or the Kingdom of God) that we can only wait for its realization, sometimes associated with the end-time as apocalypse? In contrast to a philosophy of history that is indifferent to the marking of the profane as a category of the "quietest approach of the Kingdom [eine Kategorie, und zwar der zutreffensten eine, seines leisesten Nahens]"[31]—the Jewish (and part of the Christian) tradition defines time as the ever-possible coming or expectation of the Kingdom of God and, relating it back to morality, as the *kairos* of human agency or praxis—as the time of decision.

The "Theological-Political Fragment" is based on several juxtapositions which interrelate dialectically—the hyphen in the title of the fragment, given to it by Adorno, alludes to this dialectical relation that undoes the mere opposition between the two spheres without merging them into one. When read together with "Critique of Violence," we can discern four different spheres that Benjamin analyzes throughout his work: First, the state of nature with its attributes of eternal and total transience—a-historical, and a-moral. Second, myth as a transition sphere between the natural and the political-historical or, as the latter is termed here, the profane—still a-historical and a-moral in its dependence on the arbitrary power of the gods or *fatum*, defining the state of the human as guilt. Third, the profane, which is at the same time the sphere of the political-legal governance as of historical events. As discussed, this sphere is ambivalent not only because of the human beings' "mere life" that relates us to the natural sphere exactly in our transience but also with respect to its own foundations in violence (mythical violence, as one result of the "Critique of Violence," survives in the legal and political order insofar as it is separated from justice, which is the order of morality). Fourth, again going beyond the historical, is the sphere of the theological or messianic.

In the "Theological-Political Fragment," Benjamin is now concerned with the relation of (transient, i.e., historical) happiness and (theological or messianic) redemption.[32] While nature may well be defined through an "eternal and total transience," philosophy of history compares and contrasts nature and history by way of teleology—something echoed not only in the major theories (and theologies) of providence, but also in Kant's question raised in his *Critique of Judgment*, Hegel's concept of the world spirit, or even Marx's concept of a secularized salvation history. Benjamin disputes such a teleology of history, emphasizing not only that teleology would render the particular stages and experiences as mere transition stages in the process (or progress) of history, but also arguing for the strict separation of the spheres of the profane and the theological: therefore, as the political, historical, and profane is juxtaposed to nature (and, we could add, to the mythical) by the capacity to moral agency, likewise the theological is juxtaposed to the political-historical sphere. *Theocracy* is but another term for what is also called the Kingdom of God, and which must therefore be positioned in the theological, not in the political, sphere.[33] The theological, defined more particularly as the messianic, is certainly transcendent and enigmatic, but it inserts a category that cannot be explained by philosophy—and this category is hope, as the hope of the completion of history, or theologically speaking: redemption. The Messiah—as the religious personification of the messianic[34]—redeems, completes, and creates the relation of historical events (*historisches Geschehen*) with the messianic; hence without the Messiah, history cannot relate to the messianic. Without it, this means, neither hope—on which Benjamin insists "for the sake of the hopeless"[35]—nor forgiveness, as the ultimate definition of justice, would be categories applicable to human history. As completion and redemption, the Kingdom of God is the end of the historical *dunamis* (i.e., the end of its force, not its *telos*).

From here, of course, the question arises as to whether and *how* the relation of the messianic to history can be described at all. And it is here that the philosophy of history fails—the relation cannot be explained philosophically. Benjamin chooses a geometrical and physical metaphor, that is, the image of two arrows that influence each other through their opposing *dunamis* or force to describe the relation: the force of direction (the profane) and the force of intensity (the messianic). The profane force of direction is happiness, Benjamin explains, and by its unintended (or rather: unintendable) influence on the messianic it becomes a category of the latter's "quietest coming"—while the "force of messianic intensity" passes through tragedy (*Unglück*).[36] This juxtaposition of happiness and tragedy is certainly difficult to interpret, but at least it defines the messianic precisely not (only) as a force that is *transcendent* to the profane, but also as a force of *immediate* intensity, namely as the immediate intensity of the *heart*. Benjamin emphasizes this rhetorically: the heart signifies the "inner, individual" human being, which is somehow immediately "hit" (if the arrow is still a correct image) in its human tragedy and suffering by the messianic intensity. *Being hit*, however, is not the term Benjamin uses; rather, he speaks of the messianic force "passing through" the individual's suffering. This image could well be read as a counterimage to the divine judgment of the Korah narrative, and indeed, a possible theological reading would interpret this "passing through" not as judgment as in the Korah story but rather as a recognition of and solidarity with the unhappiness and suffering of the individual. This is exactly Metz's interpretation (as I will demonstrate shortly): God's presence with the suffering, experienced as immediate intensity, must be echoed in the human striving to transform unhappiness—through compassion, solidarity, and justice.[37] In the "Theological-Political Fragment," suffering is a dimension of the profane, that is, of the historical life of the individual; hence, the aim to transform unhappiness into happiness is a profane goal—yet, *in* their suffering, the individual person is somehow touched by the Messianic force.[38] Rather than being a judgment, the messianic, directed at the completion and redemption of transient life exactly *without* reference to eternity, cannot be conflated with the "profane"; and yet, it leaves its mark in the "heart" of the individual, in their unhappiness and suffering.[39]

For Benjamin, taking up Aristotle's definition of the universal object of human striving—that is, happiness, human agency, articulated as striving for happiness—indeed defines the profane order. While it is not entirely clear to me why this striving toward happiness is at the same time a striving toward one's downfall (*Untergang* is much more dramatic a term than the "end," and normally not used in the context of individual life), it can only mean that humanity's downfall must coincide with happiness, rather than seeking happiness *in* one's downfall.[40]

In summary, we can see how Benjamin experiments with a nonteleological philosophy of history that at the same time informs political theory, without giving up on the claim to happiness and hope. Restricting the political to the telos of happiness excludes any political-theological interpretation of redemption that blends the two spheres together. This is in line with the "Critique of Violence." The theological, however, does not disappear as a category for the profane; rather, it keeps the expectation of redemption and completion of history alive without conflating it with the teleological striving of human beings. Furthermore, in connecting the messianic to the *suffering* individuals, it rejects any theology that justifies suffering in the name of a greater good. Interpreted in this way, both the priestly theology and Korah's claim to *own* God's presence in history or the political sphere can be criticized in the name of messianic theology.

In "On the Concept of History," Benjamin returns to the topic of happiness. The text's perspective, however, has changed dramatically: Rather than looking at the prospective striving of the individual, happiness is now found retrospectively: "only in the air we have breathed, among people we could have talked to, women who could have given themselves to us."[41] Thus, happiness is the *promise* of opportunity, a potential, but seen only from the historical perspective of the "future of the past," and exactly not as the "future of the present": happiness is a memory, entailed in the past's dreams of the future. And yet, this potentiality and opportunity is "the weak messianic power" of every generation; from the historical perspective, it is this future of the past, the past's unfulfilled momentum (or longing) of happiness that puts a *claim*, as much as an *endowment* onto the present.

At the root of this relation between the present and the past lies the indissoluble connection between happiness and redemption. The language of downfall is not taken up again; instead, here the Day of Judgment, also depicted as the day of justice, is now also the day of another kind of completion or completed, ended time: it is the day in which time collapses as sequence: "only a redeemed mankind is granted the fullness of its past—which is to say, only for a redeemed mankind has its past become citable in all its moments."[42] Therefore, what is linked to the "eternal downfall" in the "Theological-Political Fragment" is linked to redemption as a *total* retrieval of the past in the theses in "On the Concept of History." This is important because history (or rather: historiography) tends to forget those parts of history which may counter their own narratives— historical materialism therefore needs to attend to and retrieve the opportunities and dreams of the past that were betrayed, in order to render them productive again in our own striving and action. From here, the intensity of the messianic is redefined as the messianic power of each generation, to be retrieved as the past's unfulfilled longing for happiness. Because the messianic power is weak,[43] the retrieval is possible only in "moments," in "flashes," in "a moment of danger," and always at risk of disappearing unrecognized. "Fanning the spark of hope in the past" is therefore not a theological enterprise but a historical one—it is located within the sphere of the profane, even though it is held alive by the theological concepts of hope and redemption.[44] The theological dimension of history and historiography is neither a logical or causal necessity nor does it rest in a theology of providence. In a secularized world in which logic and causality reign, this transcendent messianic force passing through the suffering of the individual, is certainly so strange a concept that it is mainly hiding from the secular discourse. Nevertheless, without the theological concepts of hope and redemption, the "remembrance" of the past's missed opportunities of happiness as well as its tragedies and suffering—which is identified as the task of historical materialism—will be impossible; instead, the historical dreams and wounds will be forever lost to those who have no intention to remember them because they are a stain on their victory. "The only historian capable of fanning the spark of hope in the past is the one who is firmly convinced that *even the dead* will not be safe from the enemy if he is victorious. And this enemy has never ceased to be victorious." And: "Whoever has emerged victorious participates to this day in the triumphal procession in which current rulers step over those who are lying prostrate."[45]

After World War II and the revelation of crimes against humanity were slowly revealed, sentences like these could only be read with horror. But, on the one hand, for decades philosophy was unaffected by the urgency with which Benjamin insisted on the theological dimension of concepts of justice or hope; furthermore, he also discerned the limit of secular philosophy when it comes to moral (political) action and historical materialism. On the other hand, Christian theology was also not interested in Benjamin's original reading of the Jewish tradition and continued as if the Shoah did not affect theology itself.

In the next section, I will therefore turn to one big exception in Catholic theology, Johann Baptist Metz who, a few decades after the end of World War II—at a time when normality seemed to have almost returned in the German society—found himself struggling with what the historical experience of his generation meant for Christian theology. This theology, I hold, took up themes that provided an alternative to Schmitt's political theology long before it was newly addressed by our contemporary philosophical thinkers.[46]

The "New Political Theology" of Johann Baptist Metz

In his programmatic book *Faith in History and Society* (1977), Johann Baptist Metz explicitly calls for a new starting point for Christian theology as a theology after Auschwitz.[47] Up to this point, or so it seemed, nothing had radically changed in German academic Christian and Catholic theology. As was the case in German culture in general, the Nazi generation kept silent for decades, until finally, in the late 1960s, the postwar generation demanded to know what had happened, where their fathers and mothers stood, what had happened in their own lives, their social context, and their cities. As so many others, Metz was drafted at the end of the war at the age of sixteen. Due to sheer luck, he survived a deadly bomb attack as the only person of more than a hundred young people in his division.[48] Deeply influenced by this experience, in the late 1960s he began to emancipate himself from the traditional theology he had learned from one of the most influential Catholic theologians of the twentieth century, Karl Rahner, who himself sought to reform Catholic theology. In *Faith in History and Society*, Metz explicitly refers to Walter Benjamin's works (much more than to Adorno or other members of the Frankfurt Institute of Social Research).[49] He proposed a so-called new political theology—new in its explicit opposition to Schmitt's political theology—a political *theology* that reconsiders its Jewish roots over against the traditional, predominant interpretation of Christianity stemming from the tradition of Greek philosophy, and a *political* theology insofar as it situates religious practices and religious reasoning in the given historical time and sociopolitical context of late twentieth century and early twenty-first century's globalized world. In fact, the new political theology could at least in part be read as a comment on the writings of Benjamin, a reading that carefully avoids transforming Benjamin himself into a theologian but rather tries to take seriously the challenges Benjamin poses for any theology—although even more so for Christian theology.

As a political theology, Metz's theology seeks to break with the individualistic, inward, and spiritual-experiential tradition of what he calls "bourgeois Christianity." In the reinterpretation of Catholic theology as political theology, Metz draws upon concepts central to Benjamin; rather than offering a close analysis of Benjamin's texts, however, they are a kind of a jump-start toward looking at his own tradition differently. As for many readers at the time, Benjamin's intense writing style resonated with the sense of an ongoing crisis in the postwar German culture. Certainly, any reminder of the importance of historical memory, and more so Benjamin's sense of urgency, could also be held against a theology that did not seem to care about its recent past. Benjamin's remembrance of a theological tradition that seemed to have been dismissed almost completely or which was considered as mere prehistory to Graeco-Roman Christianity, initiated a new Christian theology, or gave it a new language by way of *estrangement*,[50] enabling Metz to see more clearly what, in the Christian tradition as much as in the Jewish tradition, is at stake when a theology predominantly shaped by Greek philosophy returns to its Jewish roots.[51]

All of the central concepts Metz uses in his theology can be read as influenced by Benjamin, yet reinterpreted or retranslated back into Christian theology, from where they, too, may reflect on Benjamin's own interpretation: the return to a theological understanding of *time* as "limited time" (*befristete Zeit*), and the theological perception of *history* as "apocalyptic" in a specific sense echoes the image of Benjamin's "Angel of History": apocalypse means revelation—laying open; Metz interprets this biblical tradition not as the "end-time" but rather as a time of crisis. What is revealed in the Jewish and Christian sensitivity of (and for) time, is the history of suffering; theology, then, is defined as the *interruption of this continuity* (the shortest definition of theology, Metz writes, is "interruption").[52] Commitment to the Christian faith is bound to the Jewish concept of memory as remembrance (*Eingedenken*), with a primacy placed upon the remembrance of those who suffered (or suffer) and are forgotten in history (including the present). Narrative reasoning and the narrative tradition—tightly linked to the storytelling that commits itself to teaching, studying, and learning the tradition, but also to the concept of remembrance as actualization—are juxtaposed to hermeneutical theories that aim at preserving the past as static order of events.[53] To see history and historical experiences theologically, namely as limited time and a time of crisis, is as theological in its apocalyptic element as it is moral in its connection to the kairos of decision. In fact, crisis is the time of decision and judgment, which in Jewish-Christian theology is linked, at least partly, to apocalyptic judgment as the ultimate justice (although the two religions differ in their identification or rejection of Jesus Christ [the Greek term for the Anointed] as Messiah [the Hebrew term for the Anointed]).[54] In both traditions, however, hope is the central concept marking the expectation of the fulfillment (or completion) of the Kingdom of God. Metz realizes that Benjamin's concept of time and history as crisis, expectation, decision, and hope can indeed be transferred back into Christian theology, putting an end as well to a naïve theological history of salvation as well as contrasting it to the evolutionary concept of an endless perfection or historical progress. Both concepts forget those who have suffered and died— and this is not only, Metz claims, historically irresponsible after Auschwitz but also theologically untenable, at least for a theology maintaining that God is to be conceived as a loving and a just God. Over against salvation or evolutionary history, Christianity claims a specific sensitivity for time, which in Metz's words is translated into "dangerous memory" as resistance against forgetfulness of the necessary solidarity with those who suffer or, put differently, resistance against forgetfulness of those who are the victims of history, and the sin against the very idea of the human and humanity.[55] Since the turn of the century, Metz has added another term to his theological vocabulary: compassion now functions as a political-ethical concept that is rooted in the framework of political theology, countering the often apolitical application of Christian love or mercy in current theologies.[56]

Metz's theology marks a radical turn within Christian and Catholic theology, because it renders any Christian theology impossible that does not embrace its Jewishness, namely the Jewishness of Jesus and his first followers, and the Jewishness of almost all central biblical concepts. Christianity's Jewishness turns out to be its own forgotten other side—and this insight, as trivial as it is historically or even from the perspective of social psychology, cannot be ignored after Auschwitz. But—and this marks the historical precariousness of Metz's insistence on breaking with traditional theology—it still raises the question of *how* Christianity can embrace its own Jewishness *after* the Holocaust? Can there even *be* a Christian theology after this date? Auschwitz is the abyss that separates the two religions, and yet the recognition of Auschwitz is the presupposition for any Christian theology to continue reasoning about God. Theological reasoning cannot, Metz holds, evade theodicy, but theodicy is exactly what has become impossible. For the recognition of the active responsibility of so many Germans (if collective guilt is to be avoided) renders it *morally* impossible—as if it had ever been possible—to transfer the accountability for the genocide to God. And *theologically* speaking, after Auschwitz, theodicy also cannot be discussed abstractly or taught as scholastic theodicy anymore. Theodicy cannot justify violence or suffering: reference to a divine force, that is, violence, as we have seen, may all too easily represent one's own ideology and affiliation with mythical violence. Rather, it raises the desperate question for those who, like Metz, hold on to a transcendent and just God, how theology is still possible: How is it possible at all to speak of the God of liberation, justice, and redemption in view of any murder, or any suffering? Theology, therefore, is first and foremost a question, and a questioning, not a statement; but as long as it is a question that is addressed to the God of the tradition, it cannot be transformed quickly into a statement or reasoning *about* God—as an address *to* God, Metz holds, it is prayer. Hence, theology insists that when it speaks *of* God (*theo-logein*), it must not render invisible or inaudible the question addressed *to* God that initiated theology's reflection in the first place.

When comparing Benjamin's wrestling with the political order or the order of the profane—which he confronts in both its mythical and its messianic elements—to Metz's wrestling with theology, one realizes that both thinkers are concerned with the question of violence. Rather than limiting justice to a political-philosophical concept, they provide an *ethical critique* (transcending, at the same time, the Kantian concept): pointing to the trope of messianic completion in forgiveness and redemption, and the total presence of the past on the day of judgment, their common interest is the political-ethical moment, that is, the kairos of action in the moment of danger. While Benjamin comes to this conclusion through his analyses of the profane, for Metz, who identifies the implications of theological-ethical justice *for* and *in* the historical-political arena, the starting point is the *specific* theological commitment to the "dangerous memory" of Jesus and the political-ethical implications of Jewish-Christian theology. It is the commitment to this particular "apocalyptic" rupturing and political-ethical dimension of faith (and not, contra Schleiermacher or William James, psychologized, private religious experience) that defines the "new political theology" within Catholic theology. It is a theology that first and foremost attends to those who suffer, that seeks compassion, solidarity, and justice with them and especially with all of those who are the victims of unjustified violence. However, it is also a faith that remembers God's promise of the future in the past. In Christianity this hope is separated from any notion of space as in the notion of the Promised Land; instead, it is transformed into the temporal category of the Kingdom of God, and *as* temporal category, it "undoes" (completes, ends) the sequence of time that we call history.[57] Finally, I maintain—going perhaps further than Metz but not Benjamin—divine justice is ultimately to be interpreted as forgiveness, and not as retributive judgment.[58]

The reception of Benjamin in Metz's theology is therefore not an attempt to transform Benjamin's writings into theology but rather an attempt to explore the common ground between a philosophy that acknowledges a force that cannot be entirely translated into philosophy and a theology that takes serious the political dimension of its own tradition, calling for the ethical primacy of those who suffer and the consequential priorities of actions. As I have stated, theology is more than the reasoning *of* or *about* God—it is also reasoning and struggling *with* God. Metz insists on the importance of theology's performative speech act, namely prayer—as a speech act addressing God, even though it may only be the "silent scream," horrified by the experience of God's absence.[59]

Seen from the perspective of the tradition of Christian religion, faith is therefore not a private, psychic, spiritual, or experiential affair that can be separated from the specific memory of God: rather, faith *is* remembrance—not as apolitical, ahistorical, or amoral imagination of the past but rather as an ethical, "dangerous remembrance", aimed at transforming practices and structures of violence:[60] responsibility, solidarity, compassion, and justice—these terms belong to the Jewish-Christian theological-ethical inventory long before they lose their religious connotation. *Within* the theological tradition, however, it is not only human beings who are called upon to be responsible, solidary, compassionate, or engaged in a struggle for liberation and justice—all these attributes originate, at the same time, in the God of Israel and, in the Christian tradition, are incarnated in Jesus Christ, the son of human and son of God. Christian theology there-fore makes two claims on the witnesses of faith: to practice their faith as "dangerous remembrance", and to give reasons to anybody of what their hope is grounded in: "But treat the Messiah as holy, as Lord in your hearts; while remaining always ready to give a reasoned answer to anyone who asks you to explain the hope you have in you" (1 Pet. 3:15). And yet, in view of suffering, Metz holds, any utterance of hope may be possible only negatively, as a form of lament, protest, or outcry—addressing God with the question of what has become of the promise, and what the future of this promise will be, and thereby linking this particular theology to those elements of the tradition (the prophets, Psalms, Jesus's outcry in his own experience of passion) that similarly show a loss of confidence in God. If lament and hopelessness are not to be the last words—or, put dif-ferently, if there is to be a *reason* for hope—then turning to the tradition by attending and remembering the past *also* through the lens of the hopes of past generations may indeed offer new perspectives: for within the tra-dition, every lament is countered by a prayer of hope and joy, and every destruction and downfall countered by a new beginning. Remembering the past's hopes and dreams, then, means not only to resist both the for-getting of suffering *but also* to respond to the "claim" of the past: it means to believe in the weak messianic power with which *every* generation is endowed.

This perspective of resistance against forgetting—expressed in the re-membrance of the history of suffering that makes a claim to the actual solidarity with those who suffer today, *together* with the theological insis-tence on the possibility of justice and hope on behalf of those who have no hope—is central to my own reading of Benjamin. The ethical claim, it seems to me, is indisputable; the theological claim, however, depends on one's perspective on time: theological justice not only transcends the force of any legal system but it also transcends the secular philosophical under-standing of time: for justice in this theological sense can only be com-pleted when (not if) it is done to *all* victims of *all* times. Acknowledging that this insistence on justice will lead exactly to the question of theodicy or God's (as *divine*) justice, I hold, connects a theology that is informed by Metz to Benjamin's work, which acknowledges exactly this: any philosophy of history that is engaged with the question of justice will ultimately lead to the question of theology, or at least to a theo-philosophy—that is, a philosophy of history that does not dismiss its own theological other—it leads to a theology of hope and redemption as the completion of time. At the same time, however, the difference between Metz's interest in reinterpreting theology and Benjamin's interest in the secularized culture, the philosophy of modernity and its entanglement with a suppressed theology, on the one hand, and the concern about and critique of a new "mythical naturalization" that Benjamin contrasts with the theological and moral claims of Judaism, on the other, cannot and shall not be denied.[61] Metz, certainly in contrast to Benjamin, remains committed to his faith. This separation must be respected on both sides when the concepts Benjamin wrests away from the tradition in which they originated, transforming them into fragments of an almost lost tradition, are translated back into their original semantic field, theology.[62]

The challenge, then, is to understand theology not as triumphant philosophy of history but in the fragmented form of historical time that we cannot transcend, while still, on behalf of those who have no hope, testifying for the hope of redemption "at the end of time." This is the direction that, much in line with Metz, the American Catholic theologian David Tracy has long proposed as the task ahead—not coincidently referring to Walter Benjamin as a major source for this endeavor. For Christian *ethics*, however, the way forward is to further develop its ethics in the realm of Benjamin's (and, I should add, Adorno and Horkheimer's) critical theory, spelling out its political and moral implications for a critical Christian ethics.

Conclusion: Elements of a Critical Christian Ethics

Although this is far too brief of a sketch of the wrestling with the possibilities of a new dialogue between philosophy and theology, I am interested in further spelling out what I want to call a critical Christian ethics, situated in the tradition of the new political theology of Metz. Benjamin reflects on several central concepts of ethics, and he offers a critical hermeneutical perspective for a critical Christian ethics. Here, I have commented on three texts only, because most authors in this volume discuss them as the central starting point for Benjamin's theological reflections.[63] The specific point of departure that I took, from within Catholic theology, namely Metz's new political theology, was meant to create the space for a new philosophical and theological conversation, engaging the *theological* perspective that as such differs from the recent philosophical interest in political theology.

Benjamin's "Critique of Violence," a critique via the relation of law and justice, and his philosophy of history in relation to the concept of Messianism, both reveal an understanding of justice that goes far beyond the common concepts of contemporary political theory, because it brings together the political, moral, and theological reasoning. In contrast to what Judith Butler has called "ethical violence," which in her understanding is involved in every moral judgment, Benjamin argues for a different kind of ethical violence, now understood as *justified Gewalt*: this is the normative, orienting *force* of morality, rooted in justice, which indeed may, in cases of "last resort," involve violence. In my understanding, a critical Christian ethics can indeed follow Benjamin in his route of reasoning that led him to the reflection of political action, especially the possibilities of a struggle against injustice. On the basis of the conceptual analysis (the Kantian understanding of critique), the critical *ethics* I am interested in will turn to the historical, contemporary sites of political injustice; critiquing these will at the same time remind us—the moral agents—that it is exactly our moral self-respect that is at stake when we believe we can ignore injustice. In the analysis of these conflicts, *critical* ethics will proceed via *negative critique*, revealing acts, practices, or structures of violence insofar as they are the "mere" expression of power and, hence, injustice.[64] In this endeavor, philosophical and theological ethics can support each other.

Christian ethics will depart, however, from both its philosophical and its Jewish counterpart with respect to the understanding of theology: Christian theology claims that the Messiah is not a fictitious metaphor, and he (or she?) is not a "figure" of the future: *Christos* is not always "coming," because he has come already. Christianity claims that God has indeed taken her place in history, albeit certainly not in the sacred spaces the churches have provided for her; rather, and first and foremost, Christianity claims, God lives in everyone who suffers and is declared superfluous, waste of the earth.[65] In my understanding, critical Christian ethics must therefore start there, at the sites of waste of past and present history, acting very much like Benjamin's *Lumpensammler* (collector of waste). As *ethics*, critical Christian ethics will therefore attend to the catastrophes of the past (and the present), in praxis-oriented acts of remembrance; it will attend to anybody who has suffered or is suffering from the acts, practices, or structures of violence. In turning the attention to the "wasted lives," moral agents will strive to respond to the claim that any suffering individual lays upon them, with compassion, solidarity, and critique of injustice. As critical *Christian* ethics, however, it will at the same time remember the apocalyptic, eye-opening dimension of faith. Acknowledging the urgency of action, it will not have any false illusions about the opportunities—but it will not despair either. Rather, reconnecting with the biblical tradition, it will give the reason *why* it testifies to its hope that justice can and indeed will be done to the victims of history: echoing Benjamin's conviction, it will state that we have (to have) hope on behalf of those who have no hope, and that it is *this* hope in view of hopelessness, that is brought forward to God. This critical Christian ethics cannot afford to engage in a vision of a triumphant "return of religion" in a postsecular political order or, even worse and against every intention Benjamin had, it has neither time nor reasons to partake in the political-theological legitimization of the existing one.

Notes

1. In this article, I constrain my perspective to Catholic theology, and within this tradition, to my reception of Benjamin in light of the Catholic theologian Johann Baptist Metz.

2. It seems to me that the reception history within Christian theology has been mostly ignored in Benjamin scholarship, and my comments are meant to shed some preliminary light on how Benjamin can be read, and in fact has been read, from a Christian-Catholic perspective. It may come as a surprise to those who identify Christian theology either with the psychological religious experience of nineteenth-century Protestant theology or with the normative moral theology of the Roman Catholic Church that Catholic theology has developed a new political theology, which can at least in part be read as a response to Benjamin.

3. Walter Benjamin, "Critique of Violence," in *Selected Writings*, 4 vols., ed. Michael W. Jennings et al. (Cambridge, MA: Harvard University Press, 1996–2003), 1:236–252. "Zur Kritik der Gewalt," in *Gesammelte Schriften*, vol. 2.1, ed. Rolf Tiedemann and Herman Schweppenhäuser (Frankfurt am Main: Suhrkamp, 1977), 179–203.

4. One can certainly argue that engaging questions of political theory and philosophy of law also concerns questions of moral philosophy. I argue, however, that one may in fact reverse the question and confront political philosophy with the question of ethics and morality more fundamentally.

5. The essay begins with the introduction of these two terms: "The task of a critique of violence can be summarized as that of expounding its relation to law and justice" (*Selected Writings*, 1:236).

6. Judith Butler has closely analyzed Benjamin's text to argue with it for a Jewish ethics of justice that calls for a nonviolent resistance against state power that is exercised in the name of the law. However, I wonder whether Benjamin argues indeed for a strategy of resistance in the name of justice, or whether the

juxtaposition of legal and moral justice ("'Recht' und 'Gerechtigkeit'") points beyond the political sphere altogether. See Judith Butler, *Parting Ways: Jewishness and the Critique of Zionism* (New York: Columbia University Press, 2012).

7. My reading cannot replace a thorough biblical exegesis, but this is not the focus of my comment that is strictly related to Benjamin's essay. The biblical text stems from Num. 16:1–40.

8. I translate *Gewalt* as violence unless the ambiguity is at stake, in which case, I will use the German term.

9. In a closer reading of the text, one would need to distinguish the different forms of violence/force Benjamin discusses—but here, I am only concerned with the distinction of the mythical and divine violence/force and therefore ignore the overall complexity of the essay. However, highlighting the two stories, I will show that Benjamin's texts can never be skimmed through; rather, they require the closest possible study of the metaphors, allusions, quotations, and ideas he presents in his typical condensed style. Reading Benjamin, then, means to unpack or unfold the images in a philosophical analysis—a practice that Benjamin often demonstrated, imitating the medieval emblematic style that is also an important element of his study of the seventeenth-century German *Trauerspiel*. For a recent interpretation of "Critique of Violence" and, in particular, the Niobe narrative, see Butler, *Parting Ways*.

10. The text does not say that God actively kills Korah and his group. Rather, it says that the earth opens and they are "swallowed alive" and "perish."

11. Walter Benjamin, "Fate and Character," in *Selected Writings*, 1:203.

12. The relation between the Greek gods and fate is complex insofar as it is not clear whether the gods, too, are subjected to it or whether *fatum* is in fact dependent on a god's will. Therefore, it is not even clear whether Niobe's fate is the result of Lethe's arbitrary power or fate that originates in the necessity of the *fatum*. But since Zeus (or Artemis) shows pity to Niobe before turning her into a rock, he at least seems to have the power to change *fatum*. And yet, with the "rebel" Niobe, morality is shown in its infantility (*Infantilität*): she is another "moral hero, still dumb, not yet of age" (ibid., 1:203) Hence, what Benjamin states about Greek tragedy, similarly holds true for Niobe: "It was not in law but in tragedy that the head of genius lifted itself for the first time from the mist of guilt, for in tragedy demonic fate is breached. But not by having the endless pagan chain of guilt and atonement superseded by the purity of man who has expiated his sins, who is reconciled with the pure god. Rather, in tragedy pagan man becomes aware that he is better than his god, but the realization robs him of speech, remains unspoken" (ibid.).

13. The presentation of sacrifices marks the presenting person as sacred, which is further interpreted as being just. The concept of sacredness in the Priestly school is complex and has been explored in multiple works. For a general overview, see Peter Weimar, *Studien Zur Priesterschrift* (Tübingen: Mohr Siebeck, 2008); Ernst Zenger, *Einleitung in das Alte Testament*, 7th ed. (Stuttgart: Kohlhammer, 2008).

14. Note that the Korah story is told in the context of the disbelief that Israel will ever reach the Promised Land; and even though Moses and Aaron (the representatives of the Priestly source) will be legitimized in this story, later on in Numbers, God decides that they will not enter the Promised Land. It is this context of expectation and doubting on Israel's part, and divine leadership on the way to the Promised Land that is the context of the Korah revolt. Only in studying this context thoroughly, can the tradition be retrieved and, ultimately, redeemed. And, I would add, it is doubtful that the Korah story belongs to the common knowledge of our secularized culture today. Therefore, it is theology's task (though certainly not exclusively theology's) to actively remember this tradition through study, and to keep the question of the relation between law and justice alive.

15. This, of course, is reminiscent of Abraham's negotiation with God about the fate of Sodom in Gen. 18:22–33.

16. Therefore, the "sacredness of life" that Benjamin engages with after this passage is not linked to *mere* life but to moral agency or morality. What is at stake in the reflection on violence/force, and its critique through the reflection on the interrelation of law and justice, is exactly the concept of morality. Sacredness is the capacity to be a moral agent or, in the religious terms of the Bible, to be just. Translated back into the text, this means that not theology but morality becomes the criterion of legitimate violence; only insofar as justice itself is *ultimately* linked to a theological concept, is the theological element to be maintained. This is the topic of the next part of my contribution.

17. Benjamin's interpretation is uncritical of the biblical story insofar as it does not reflect the status of the narrative itself in the identity formation of Israel after the exile. The missing link between the text and the interpretation is perhaps the effect of the status quo of exegesis in the 1920s: while the Priestly source had been identified as one of the main four sources of the Pentateuch, it was not exactly clear what precisely it consisted of. I therefore only present a narrative analysis of the text as it stands, and not as it would be examined after applying what has been called the historical-critical exegesis: a form- or literary criticism, i.e., the exegetic method that discerns the genre (form), different sources (edition history) and tensions in the text structure (literary critique) as necessary elements of the overall interpretation. While Benjamin never studied the tradition exegetically but rather used theological terms as a function of his essays (probably he was pointed to the Korah story through H. Cohen's interpretation), it is precisely a critical reading of the narrative itself that renders it instructive as well for the theological reasoning on justice, law, and violence, as for the critique of violence in Benjamin's essay. Contra Benjamin, divine judgment in the story is not so distinct from the mythical punishment of Niobe as his reading wants to suggest: neither is the violence bloodless nor is the destruction of Korah's group aimed at the living in a nonutilitarian way—the "rebels" are, rather, sacrificed for the overall end

of reaching the Promised Land. Benjamin's argument, resting on the connection between violence and justice, overlooks this narrative perspective, or Priestly ideology.

18. Benjamin, "Critique of Violence," in *Selected Writings*, 1:250.

19. This debate also sheds further light on Butler's argumentation in *Parting Ways*. Although I would hold that she underestimates the distinction between legal and moral justice in Benjamin's text, I think that it is the Jewish tradition of wrestling with God's justice and redemption that supports her overall thesis: Jewish ethics does not limit justice and solidarity to exclusive members of the human community.

20. Hence, the text entails a double critique: a critique of the Korah group insofar as it is merely interested in its own power over against Moses, and a subversive critique of the Priestly school who restricts God's presence to a particular sphere. The first critique concerns the relation of political power and justice, which Benjamin is interested in here; the second critique, however, may be linked to the "sacredness" of the human person over against the sacredness of a particular cultic sphere, to which Benjamin only alludes in his essay. Situated in this biblical context, the wrestling with sacredness does not at all support Agamben's thesis of the homo sacer as reduced to "bare life"; cf. Giorgio Agamben, *Homo Sacer: Sovereign Power and Bare Life* (Stanford, CA: Stanford University Press, 1998).

21. In the *Metaphysics of Morals*, Kant explicitly ruled out that such acts could ever be justified. However, during Benjamin's time, civil resistance was in fact discussed as an important strategy of political action. Modern states, in contrast, grant social groups a right to *Gewalt* (force, authorized itself by the law)—as the political demonstration against the state laws. The general strike, however, takes this right to another level, questioning the whole structure of the state governance. From here, it is not far-fetched to correlate Benjamin's reflections with Michel Foucault's studies on governmentality and resistance; see Michel Foucault, *Security, Territory, Population: Lectures at the Collège de France, 1977–1978* (Basingstoke, NY: Palgrave Macmillan, 2007).

22. Butler, *Parting Ways*, 80.

23. The paradox disappears, however, when the ambiguity of the term *Gewalt* is considered.

24. Butler, *Parting Ways*, 82.

25. Astrid Deuber-Mankowsky (in this volume) touches on a sensitive matter when she claims that Cohen's and Benjamin's Jewish God is the forgiving God while Christians have often juxtaposed the vengeful God of the Hebrew Bible with the forgiving God of the Gospel. The Korah story, however, is certainly not a good proof for this otherwise correct claim, at least as far as the Jewish concept of forgiveness is concerned. What is missing in either the Jewish or the Christian claim is the plurality and the struggle between different theological concepts that takes place within the biblical texts and throughout the tradition (this is the reason why Christianity is a possible interpretation of Judaism and

the reason why Christianity's own Jewishness cannot be ignored). See also Butler, *Parting Ways*, chap. 3, 69–98.

26. Benjamin does not take up this thought; instead, he explores the possibilities of nonviolent conflict resolution in personal relations: "Gewaltlose Einigung findet sich überall, wo die Kultur des Herzens den Menschen reine Mitttel der Übereinkunft an die Hand gegeben hat . . . Herzenshöflichkeit, Neigung, Friedensliebe, Vertrauen" ("Kritik der Gewalt," in *Gesammelte Schriften*, 2.1:191); the English translation reads: "Nonviolent agreement is possible wherever a civilized outlook allows the use of unalloyed means of agreement . . . courtesy, sympathy, peaceableness, trust" (*Selected Writings*, 1:244). This translation, more than the original text with its explicit allusions to ethical and not just civil virtues, conceals the *ethical* nature of these means of conflict resolution. In the political sphere, Benjamin points to the long history of diplomacy as an example.

27. It is impossible here to elaborate on the theology—or, rather, theologies of atonement (*Sühne*), forgiveness as expiation (*Entsühnung*), and reconciliation (*Versöhnung*) as three possible interpretations of divine justice—but I would argue that only the first can correctly be called divine violence while the other two rather connote *Gewalt* as force. Butler, who draws on this text, too, in her interpretation in *Parting Ways*, refers to the paradox of "nonviolent violence". But she ignores the theological transformation process to which the biblical texts testify. Note, for example, the relation of the Korah narrative to the story of Isaac's binding where exactly the same thing, namely human life, is negotiated in relation to the sacrifice. In that text, the paradoxical nature of "bloodless violence/force" is far more evident than in the Korah story—and even there, it cannot be completely reconciled with the loving God. The comparison therefore reveals the specific function of the Korah story in "Critique of Violence," namely to demonstrate that the act of violence itself does not reveal its legitimacy.

28. Walter Benjamin, "The Meaning of Time in the Moral Universe," in *Selected Writings*, 1:286–287. Read against the discourse on justice and forgiveness mentioned earlier, this connection between the alliance of forgiveness and time becomes a crucial point, connecting, too, forgiveness to the messianic, which I discuss later in this essay.

29. In this respect, Sigrid Weigel's interpretation of Benjamin's essay on Goethe's *Elective Affinities* in this volume is instructive.

30. From a Christian ethical perspective, it would be interesting to interpret Benjamin's essay on the German *Trauerspiel*, as the plays are tightly connected to the (Protestant) Christian theology of the seventeenth century and the ongoing wrestling with Reformation theologies in Europe. To my knowledge, however, this essay has not raised much interest in theological scholarship.

31. "Theologisch-Politisches Fragment," in *Gesammelte Schriften*, 2.1:204; "Theological-Political Fragment," in *Selected Writings* 3:306. The quote reads in the English translation: "The profane, therefore, although not itself a category

of this Kingdom, is a decisive category of its quietest approach." Subsequent excerpts are from *Selected Writings*.

32. For more on the experience of transience and transient experience, see Annika Thiem's essay in this volume.

33. Hence, Benjamin radically criticizes Schmitt's legitimizing dictum that political power entails a theological dimension. This critique, however, can only be understood if the separation of the profane and the messianic in "Theological-Political Fragment" is taken seriously.

34. The Messiah is in fact, in most traditional lines of this idea, a human figure; besides Judaism and Christianity, this figure can also be found in Islam as well as beyond the monotheistic religions, in Hinduism—sometimes connected to the idea of a kingdom, sometimes to the prophets, or to the priests. An alternative term for the Messiah is "son of man," that is, human. In contrast to the figure, however, the Jewish/Christian idea of the messianic (justice, redemption, salvation) is in fact connected to the divine, insofar as it is God who anoints the Messiah (Hebrew for Anointed, as *Christos* is the Greek term for it), who will bring justice to the world.

35. Walter Benjamin, "Goethe's *Elective Affinities*," in *Selected Writings*, 1:356. With this sentence, the essay closes: "Only for the sake of the hopeless ones have we been given hope.".

36. "Theological-Political Fragment," in *Selected Writings* 3:306. The whole sentence reads: "Whereas, admittedly, the immediate Messianic intensity of the heart, of the inner man in isolation, passes through misfortune, as suffering."

37. Hence, faith is not so much linked to a spiritual-religious experience or even a (naïve) belief in the supernatural but rather to testimony and witnessing of suffering in acts of compassion, solidarity, and engagement for justice.

38. *Unglück* is the linguistic opposite of *Glück*, which is concealed in the English translation of "tragedy" which can only translate the semantic dimension of *Unglück*.

39. The Jewish tradition knows the "happy completion" of life without any reference to the afterlife; in this line of thought, happiness and death are only contradictory terms insofar as life is *not* completed in old age.

40. I admit that no interpretation of this passage has convinced me yet—the downfall can only be a category of apocalypse as the end-time, or redemption. For a thorough interpretation Rosenzweig must be brought into the conversation, which is beyond the scope of this paper.

41. Walter Benjamin, "On the Concept of History," in *Selected Writings*, 4:389.

42. Ibid., 339.

43. The translation of this power into poetic language can be found in the concept of correspondence and Proust's *memoire involuntaire* in the essay on Baudelaire.

44. Benjamin, "On the Concept of History," in *Selected Writings*, 4:391.

45. Ibid.

46. It is beyond the scope of this article to critically engage with the new emergence of political theology within philosophy, such as in the works of Hent de Vries, John Caputo, Giorgio Agamben, Alain Badiou, Slavoj Žižek, Simon Critchley, and others. Quite strikingly, however, the term *theology* is separated from what I would call faith as commitment, testimony, or witnessing. It is this dimension I find most interesting from a theological-ethical perspective, because it refuses to disconnect theology from (political) practice.

47. Johann Baptist Metz, *Glaube in Geschichte und Gesellschaft: Studien zu einer Praktischen Fundamentaltheologie* (Mainz: Gruenewald, 1977). Later, in *Memoria Passionis: Ein provozierendes Gedächtnis in pluralistischer Gesellschaft*, 4th ed. (Freiburg: Herder, 2011), Metz writes:

In meiner Biographie signalisiert Auschwitz einen Schrecken jenseits aller vertrauten Theologie, einen Schrecken, der jede situationsfreie Rede von Gott leer und blind erscheinen lässt. Gibt es denn, so fragte ich mich, einen Gott, den man mit dem Rücken zu einer solchen Katastrophe anbeten kann? Und kann Theologie, die diesen Namen verdient, ungerührt nach einer solchen Katastrophe einfach weiterreden, von Gott und von den Menschen weiterreden, als ob angesichts einer solchen Katastrophe nicht die unterstellte Unschuld unserer menschlichen Worte zu überprüfen wäre? Durch solche Fragen sollte Auschwitz nicht etwa zu einem "negativen Mythos" stilisiert werden, der diese Katstrophe ja wieder unserer theologischen und historischen Verantwortung entzogen hätte. Es ging primär um die beunruhigende Frage: Warum sieht man der Theologie diese Katastrophe—wie überhaupt die Leidensgeschichte der Menschen—so wenig oder überhaupt nicht an?

In my biography Auschwitz signals a horror beyond any known theology; a horror that considers any decontextualized speech of God empty and blind. Is there a God, I asked myself, to whom one can pray, with the back turned to such a catastrophe? And can a theology that deserves this name continue to speak untouched after such a catastrophe, continue to speak of God and of Man as if in the face of such a catastrophe the assumed innocence of our words is in no need to be reexamined? With these questions, Auschwitz was not to be stylized as a "negative myth" that would have detracted this catastrophe again from our theological and historical responsibility. Primarily, it concerned the question: Why does one so little or not at all recognize this catastrophe—as the human history of suffering as such—in theology? (Translation mine)

48. See Metz, *Memoria Passionis*, 93–94.

49. Cf. Metz, *Glaube in Geschichte und Gesellschaft*.

50. This estrangement effect (*Verfremdungseffekt*) is the main method Brecht used in his dramas—but it can also be described as Kafka's poetic style. What is *estrangement* in Brecht, is *disfiguration* in Kafka's characters, and this is of utmost importance to Benjamin because it is exactly through such estrangements and

disfigurations that truth is revealed. Benjamin's own method of fragmentation and reassembling of historical, philosophical, and literary sources, together with the reinterpretation of the theological tropes, enables theologians to read their own tradition in a new way. From this perspective, it would be rather absurd to read Benjamin as a theologian—but the opposite, namely to ignore his claims to and on theology, would also be wrong. See Michael Jennings's critique of a specific religious reading of Benjamin in this volume.

51. In this way, Metz's theology sent also a clear message to his colleagues to critically deal with Christian theology's anti-Judaism throughout its history.

52. For a theology of interruption indebted to Metz, see Lieven Bouven, *God Interrupts History: Theology in a Time of Upheaval* (New York, London: Continuum, 2007).

53. The term *actualization* is echoed in Gadamer's hermeneutics of application that, too, speaks of the practical implication of understanding juxtaposed to a psychological understanding of an other, be it a text or a person. Where he ultimately sees a necessary ontology that guarantees the unity and reality of understanding, Benjamin and Metz insist on a more specifically historical, but fragmented understanding that can only be represented discontinuously (in "flashes"). Metz, in contrast to Benjamin's concept of messianism, understands the theology related to this hermeneutics as apocalyptic—theology in the historical time of (constant) crisis, with its eye-opening connotation to revelation. In the prophetic tradition, both concepts, messianism and apocalypticism, are tightly connected—what separates Judaism and Christianity is the specific Christian personification of Jesus Christ as Messiah, that is, as incarnated son of God—clearly, this causes the well-known theological problems the Gospels, Paul, and early Christianity wrestled with (cf. Jacob Taubes's essays in this volume and in his other works, as well as Hille Haker, Andres Torres Queiruga, and Marie-Theres Wacker, eds., *The Return of Apocalypticism, Concilium* no. 3 (2014). For Metz, as for Benjamin, however, this wrestling with messianism or, in the Christian understanding, with the *parousia* (the expectation of the return of the Messiah) or the present eschatology of the Kingdom of God is to be taken seriously at any time. As I have shown earlier, this is not only alluding to a philo-theology of history that can only be explained metaphorically in images but, moreover, to a theo-philosophy of hope that cannot be founded philosophically. It is beyond the scope of this essay to analyze Benjamin's reading of Kafka, particularly the relation between judgment and hope (or hopelessness), which I still find most significant in this respect.

54. While both Jewish and Christian traditions entail extremely violent images of the Day of Judgment, it is the Jewish concept of justice depicted in my reading of the "Critique of Violence" that ultimately also determines the Christian understanding of judgment. In this respect, the forgiveness that Jesus expresses at the minute of his violent death is the criterion of how exactly justice and judgment must be understood in Christian ethics. A very deep and difficult

debate on forgiveness after the Holocaust centers on exactly this relation of justice and forgiveness—especially among some Jewish thinkers including Vladimir Jankelevitch, Jacques Derrida, and Emmanuel Levinas. As their conversation partner stemming from the Christian tradition, Paul Ricœur took up this debate only late in his life. All these authors discuss the question of justice and forgiveness in view of the Shoah. Metz seems to be very cautious not to disconnect justice from forgiveness—but also vice versa: not to disconnect forgiveness from justice. See below for a further comment.

55. This theological naming of *sins* against humanity returns in the secular terminology as *crimes* against humanity in the International Criminal Court:

> Auschwitz hat die metaphysische Schamgrenze zwischen Mensch und Mensch tief abgesenkt. So etwas überstehen nur die Vergesslichen. Oder die, die schon erfolgreich vergessen haben, dass sie etwas vergessen haben. Aber auch sie bleiben nicht ungeschoren. Man kann auch auf den Namen des Menschen nicht beliebig sündigen. Nicht nur der einzelne Mensch, auch die Idee des Menschen und der Menschheit ist zutiefst verletzbar. (Metz, *Glaube in Geschichte und Gesellschaft*, 6).

> Auschwitz has lowered the metaphysical threshold of shame between man and man to a low point. Only those who forget survive this. Or those who already were successful to forget that they forgot something. However, even they will not remain unaffected. It is not possible to sin against the name of Man for convenience. Not only is the individual human being deeply violable, the idea of the human is violable, too. (Translation mine)

56. See Hille Haker, "'Compassion als Weltprogramm des Christentums'— Eine ethische Auseinandersetzung mit Johann Baptist Metz," *Concilium*, no. 4 (2001): 436–450; Johann Baptist Metz, "Compassion. Zu einem Weltprogramm des Christentums im Zeitalter des Pluralismus der Religionen und Kulturen," in *Compassion: Weltprogramm des Christentums. Soziale Verantwortung lernen*, ed. Johann Baptist Metz, Lothar Kuld, and Adolf Weisbrod (Freiburg im Breisgau: Herder, 2000).

57. The retrieval of the biblical land in modern Zionism—and its literal interpretation and claims on the land of Palestine in the late nineteenth and early twentieth centuries—is apparently avoided in the theological imagery of Benjamin, but it is a topic that determined the political Jewish discourse of his time. Therefore, it would be wrong to juxtapose the Promised Land and the Kingdom of God as Jewish versus Christian theology—the Kingdom of God is a Jewish thought as much as it is Christian, and it has in fact a long history in Judaism—although, again, with different interpretations. Obviously, the formation of the Jewish political and religious identity changed dramatically after the Shoah, and it changed again after 1967; today, any critique of the state of Israel is somehow portrayed as a betrayal of the Jewish claim to land (or rather: Land), and this not only from a non-Jewish perspective but also from

within the Jewish tradition as the scandal surrounding Judith Butler's Adorno award in Germany in 2012 has made sufficiently clear. But how can a state legitimize its violence (in both senses of violence and force) when it cannot even tolerate the critical deliberation of its policies? As Butler has shown in her *Parting Ways*, Benjamin's essay "Critique of Violence" may well be read as a response to such an immunization of the political against the questions of justice. In the context of my interpretation, the transformation of a spatial term (Promised Land) into a temporal term (Kingdom of God) is crucial for the universalization of the theological claims linked to the messianic or redemption. Only as universally inclusive concepts can they be separated from theological colonialization. This may also explain why I interpret the Korah narrative as the emergence of a new theology of justice—but only in its "infantility."

58. It should be clear that the theological concepts of hope and forgiveness lose their innocence when *Christian* theology points to this consequence of the shared heritage between Judaism and Christianity. Therefore it is crucial to repeat that any theology is at the same time reasoning about God *and* address to God. In this way, the question of divine justice as forgiveness can also be addressed as a question: can there be (divine) forgiveness for deeds that exceed any imagination? And exceeds this excessive forgiveness not in the same way our imagination of justice as excessive violence does?

59. Metz calls these speech acts "mystical," rendering the only possible theological language after Auschwitz "mystical" in the sense of a language of suffering, crisis, contestation and radical danger, a "language of lament and accusation" ("Sprache der Klage und der Anklage"), or a "language of outcry" (Metz, *Memoria Passionis*, 24; translation mine).

60. Yerushalmi has explained the Hebrew term *zakor* as a form of practical reasoning that is rooted in experience and practical wisdom as much as in a specific memory of history. Hence, the German word Benjamin uses, *Eingedenken*, keeps the link to *Denken* (thinking, reasoning) better than the more common term *Erinnern*. The English equivalent for *Eingedenken* would be more precisely "thinking in or with memory." See Yosef Hayim Yerushalmi, *Zakhor: Jewish History and Jewish Memory* (Seattle and London: University of Washington Press, 1982).

61. Read in this light—and taking Sigrid Weigel's interpretation further— secularization or the secular modernity suffers from a double forgetfulness: first, it ignores its relation with religion, in particular with the Christian (Protestant) tradition, as Weber has shown in his study on the relation of Protestantism and Capitalism; second, it ignores its relation to the mythical, namely *the a-religious*, *amoral*, and *ahistorical* violence or force of the gods which are identified with the "mere" power or order of being. The naturalization thesis as a "return of the myth within modernity" that Benjamin works on in numerous texts was, of course, further explored in the *Dialectic of Enlightenment* by Adorno and Horkheimer. See Sigrid Weigel, *Walter Benjamin: Die Kreatur, Das Heilige, Die Bilder* (Frankfurt am Main: Campus, 2008).

62. Annika Thiem (in this volume) argues that a metaphorical language that Benjamin often employs cannot, at the same time, be theological; but this might be a rushed statement when the metaphorical biblical language is considered: It would be interesting in this respect to explore the necessary metaphorical language of religion, and the function of the metaphor in general (see Paul Ricoeur: *La metaphor vive* (Paris: Editions du Seuil, 1975), translated as *The Rule of Metaphor: The Creation of Meaning in Language* (London: Routledge, 2004). What separates Metz from Benjamin, however, is the primacy of the performative Christian speech act, addressing God as person, in prayer, and addressing Jesus, the son of hu/man, as brother. If religious language is less concerned with universal statements of truth (*about* God or the divine)—and more with the explorations and interpretations of personal, collective, historical experiences brought forward, addressed *to* God in lament, protest, or outcry as well as in expressions of joy, hope, and gratefulness—its poetic, and hence metaphorical, dimension becomes in fact a necessary element of theological language: religious language has always been exactly this. Therefore, the metaphorical use of theological language cannot serve as the dividing line between theological and a-theological rhetoric; it is rather related to the question of self-commitment, or faith as a category of one's practical, moral identity. As a result, what (potentially) divides philosophy and theology is their distinct position regarding one's practical, moral, and religious identity, and precisely not a supposedly categorically different condition of reasoning.

63. What I have not shown and could not show at this point is the fact that one could analyze many more texts in order to spell out how deeply Benjamin's philosophy is invested in the questions, the concepts, and the tropes of theology. It goes without saying that this does not make Benjamin a crypto-theologian; neither did the literary estrangement and constructive distortion of the Jewish tradition, to the point of rendering its core truths visible *in and through* the distortion, make Kafka a Jewish theologian.

64. I am not suggesting that determination of what counts as injustice, domination, or violence as "mere" power is an easy task; part of this difficulty is explained in Benjamin's essay, which I have not even started to touch upon. Furthermore, it is the reason why I believe that what I conceive as critical ethics is situated in the ongoing *tradition* of critical theory, starting with the so-called early Frankfurt school.

65. Cf. Zygmunt Bauman, *Wasted Lives: Modernity and Its Outcast* (Cambridge: Polity Press, 2003).

Acknowledgments

We first had the idea for this collection of essays while sharing a meal together at a conference in Bangalore, India. It would be a couple of years until we were able to see this dream come to fruition, but the many wonderful conversations along the way made it more than worth the while.

Our thanks are due to the many people who helped bring this book to the light of day with their advice and encouragement. Specifically, we would like to thank Werner Hamacher, Samuel Weber, Eric Santner, Andrew Benjamin, and Eric Jacobson, among others, for their early encouragement of the project. Thanks are deservingly due as well to Chiara Libonati and Nicoletta Bettucchi at Neri Pozza publishers and Elettra Stimilli and the people at Königshausen und Neumann for their helpful and prompt assistance in numerous ways.

Heartfelt thanks also go to Adam Kotsko, Ryan Wines, and Kaspar Bulling for their excellent translations of the Agamben and Taubes essays.

We extend our gratitude to Jeff Campbell, Jacob Torbeck, and Jeffrey Tripp for their assistance with the texts of the volume and for providing much-needed editorial assistance with the manuscript in various phases of its production.

Our thanks are also due to Tom Lay at Fordham University Press and John Caputo, the present series editor, for being willing to see this project to its completion.

Giorgio Agamben's essay was first published in Italy as an introduction to Walter Benjamin's *Charles Baudelaire: Un poeta lirico nell'età del capitalismo avanzato*, ed. Giorgio Agamben, Barbara Chitussi e Clemens, and Carl Härle (Milan: Neri Pozza Editore, 2012).

The two texts written by Taubes have been published in German in *Der Preis des Messianismus: Briefe von Jacob Taubes an Gershom Scholem und andere Materialen*, ed. Elettra Stimilli (Würzburg: Königshausen und Neumann, 2006); we thank the publisher for granting us permission to publish the English translations.

Contributors

Giorgio Agamben is an influential contemporary Italian philosopher and political theorist whose works have been translated into numerous languages.

Judith Butler is Maxine Elliot Professor of Comparative Literature and Critical Theory at the University of California at Berkeley. She is the author of *The Psychic Life of Power* (1997), *Antigone's Claim* (2000), *Giving an Account of Oneself* (2005), *Parting Ways: Jewishness and the Critique of Zionism* (2012), and *Senses of the Subject* (2015). She works in the fields of feminist and queer theory, European philosophy, social theory, and ethics.

Howard Caygill is professor of modern european philosophy in the Centre for Research in Modern European Philosophy at Kingston University, London. He was previously Professor of Cultural History at Goldsmiths College, London. His books include *Art of Judgement* (1989), *Walter Benjamin: The Colour of Experience* (1997), and *On Resistance: A Philosophy of Defiance* (2013).

Astrid Deuber-Mankowsky is professor of media studies and gender studies at the Ruhr-University Bochum, Germany. She has published extensively on topics in feminist theory, representation and mediality, media theory, and philosophy as well as religion and modernism. Her book *Der frühe Walter Benjamin und Hermann Cohen: Jüdische Werte, Kritische Philosophie, vergängliche Erfahrung* (2000) was awarded the Humboldt University prize for best dissertation. English translations of her writings include *Lara Croft: Cyber Heroine* (2005). Her recent book is entitled *Praktiken der Illusion: Kant, Nietzsche, Cohen, Benjamin bis Donna J. Haraway* (2007).

Colby Dickinson is assistant professor of theology at Loyola University, Chicago. He is the author of *Agamben and Theology* (2011), *Between the Canon and the Messiah: The Structure of Faith in Contemporary Continental Thought* (2013), *The Spiritual and Creative Failures of Representation: On Poetry, Theology and the Potential of the Human Being* (2015) and, with Adam Kotsko, *Agamben's Coming Philosophy: Finding a New Use for Theology* (2015). He is also the editor of *The Postmodern "Saints" of France: Refiguring "the Holy" in Contemporary French Philosophy* (2013) and *The Shaping of Tradition: Context and Normativity* (2013).

Howard Eiland is co-author, with Michael W. Jennings, of *Walter Benjamin: A Critical Life* (2014). He is coeditor of volumes 2–4 of *Walter Benjamin: Selected Writings*, and has also contributed to the translation of several Benjamin texts, including *The Arcades Project, Berlin Childhood around 1900, On Hashish*, and *Early Writings 1910–1917*.

Peter Fenves is the Joan and Serepta Harrison Professor of German, Comparative Literary Studies, and Jewish Studies at Northwestern University. He is the author of several books, most recently *Late Kant: Towards Another Law of the Earth* (2003) and *The Messianic Reduction: Walter Benjamin and the Shape of Time* (2011).

Eli Friedlander is professor of philosophy at Tel Aviv University. Among his publications are *Signs of Sense: Reading Wittgenstein's Tractatus* (2001), *J.J. Rousseau: An Afterlife of Words* (2005) *Walter Benjamin: A Philosophical Portrait* (2011) and *Expressions of Judgment: An Essay on Kant's Aesthetics* (2015). His current research is devoted to Walter Benjamin's *Arcades Project*.

Hille Haker holds the Richard McCormick S. J. Endowed Chair of Catholic Moral Theology at Loyola University Chicago. She has published extensively on issues of moral identity, literature and ethics, bioethics, feminist ethics, and social ethics. Her books include *Moralische Identität: Literarische Lebensgeschichten als Medium ethischer Reflexion* (1999), *Ethik der genetischen Frühdiagnostik* (2002), *Hauptsache gesund* (2011), and several coedited books including *The Ethics of Genetics in Human Procreation* (2000), *Ethik-Geschlecht-Wissenschaften* (2006), *Medical Ethics in Health Care Chaplaincy* (2009), and *Religiöser Pluralismus in der Klinikseelsorge*

(2014). She is a former member of the Frankfurt Institute of Social Research and currently works on a book on recognition and responsibility.

Michael Jennings, Class of 1900 Professor of Modern Languages in the Department of German at Princeton University, is the author of *Dialectical Images: Walter Benjamin's Theory of Literary Criticism* (1987) and, with Howard Eiland, *Walter Benjamin: A Critical Life* (2014). He also serves as the general editor of the standard English-language edition of Benjamin's works, *Walter Benjamin: Selected Writings* and the editor of *The Writer of Modern Life: Essays on Charles Baudelaire* (2007); with Brigid Doherty and Thomas Levin, *The Work of Art in the Age of Its Technological Reproducibility and Other Writings on Media* (2008); and *One Way Street* (2015).

Stéphane Symons is assistant professor at the Institute of Philosophy at Katholieke Universiteit Leuven, Belgium. His main research interests are Weimar thought and twentieth-century French philosophy. He is the author of *Walter Benjamin: Presence of Mind, Failure to Comprehend* (2013), the editor of *The Marriage of Aesthetics and Ethics* (2015), and together with Willem Styfhals, the co-editor of *Theological Genealogies: Reflections on Secularization in Twentieth Century German Thought* (forthcoming).

Jacob Taubes (1923–87) was a rabbi, philosopher, and Jewish scholar. He was the author of many celebrated insights into both political theology and the philosophy of religion, with certain of his works being recently translated, as well as heavily lauded. He is the author of *The Political Theology of Paul*; *Occidental Eschatology*; *To Carl Schmitt: Letters and Reflections*; and *From Cult to Culture: Fragments Towards a Critique of Historical Reason*.

Annika Thiem is associate professor of philosophy at Villanova University. She is completing a book manuscript on the contributions of the German-Jewish thinkers Hermann Cohen and Walter Benjamin to critical engagements with theological and religious discourse in the early twentieth century. She is the author of *Unbecoming Subjects: Judith Butler, Moral Philosophy, and Critical Responsibility* (2009) and of numerous articles in political theology, feminist and queer theory.

Sigrid Weigel is the former director of *Zentrum für Literatur- und Kulturforschung* in Berlin (1999–2015). She has published on Heine, Warburg, Freud, Benjamin, Scholem, Arendt, and Bachmann, and on cultural history, image theory, memory, secularization, genealogy, and the cultural history of sciences. She has also edited the works of Aby Warburg and Susan

Taubes. Her recent publications include *"Escape to Life." German Intellectuals in New York: A Compendium on Exile after 1933* (2012), *Walter Benjamin: Images, the Creaturely, and the Holy* (2013), and *Grammatologie der Bilder* (2015).

Index

Benjamin, Walter (*continued*)
143nn61–62, 182, 185, 187, 219, 239; *Berlin Childhood around 1900*, 113, 134n2, 249n4, 320; "Blanqui," 154; "Books by the Mentally Ill," 150; "Capitalism as Religion," 13, 46n15, 147, 149, 153, 255, 262, 268n7, 273; *Charles Baudelaire: A Poet of the Age of Advanced Capitalism*, 12, 81, 91n12, 92n32, 95, 103–106, 109nn32–34, 217–230, 317; *Concept of Criticism in German Romanticism*, 122, 255; "Convolute N: On the Theory of Knowledge, Theory of Progress," 37, 94, 106n2, 137n20; "Critique of Violence," 7, 16n40, 44n4, 88–89, 138n2, 140n39, 142n56, 158, 231, 235, 238, 242, 253–265, 273, 278–279, 283–284, 286, 293–294, 296, 305, 307n9, 310n27, 313n54, 315n57; "Dialogue on the Religiosity of the Present," 114, 117–118; "Diary, Pentecost 1911," 134n1; "Eduard Fuchs, Collector and Historian," 96, 219; "Experience and Poverty," 49n39, 96; "Fate and Character," 142n56, 293; "First Sketches," 142n59, 143n61; "Franz Kafka: On the Tenth Anniversary of his Death," 82, 140n39, 142n56, 257; "The Free School Community," 135n5; "Goethe's *Elective Affinities*," 41, 54n69, 75–90, 132, 248, 310n29, 311n35; "Ibizan Sequence," 236; "The Life of Students," 62–63, 69, 118, 141n49; "Materials for the Exposé of 1935," 142n59; "The Meaning of Time in the Moral Universe," 282, 310n28; "Metaphysics of Youth," 64, 122, 136n16; "Modernity as Hell," 9, 16n42; "Moral Education," 136n12; "On Language as Such and on the Language of Man," 232, 249n8; "On Painting, or Signs and Marks," 251n16; "On Perception," 25, 29, 51n49; "On the Concept of History," 2, 7, 21, 43n1, 44n2, 52n53, 93–94, 106, 126, 137n21, 139n36, 140n43,

169, 179–208, 222, 267, 274, 297; "On the Program of the Coming Philosophy," 23–25, 29, 31, 33–34, 36–38, 45n11, 51n49, 108n19, 130, 242, 251n12; *One-Way Street*, 89, 150, 153, 157, 161, 321; *Origin of German Tragic Drama*, 9, 16n42, 36, 46n15, 52n51, 53, 53n60, 54n65, 105, 137n21, 142n56, 146, 149–150, 153, 161, 182, 194, 238, 240, 246, 252n17, 307n9, 310n30; "Outline of the Psychophysical Problem," 108n21; "Religious Attitudes of New Youth," 65, 67, 70; "Socrates," 142n58; "Surrealism: The Last Snapshot of the Intelligentsia," 109n31; "The Task of the Translator," 94, 137n20, 233; "Theological-Political Fragment," 8–9, 23, 38–40, 44n4, 54n63, 56–57, 69–70, 73n33, 81–83, 94, 122–123, 137n24, 167, 186, 231, 255, 264, 266, 272–274, 276, 278, 283–284, 286, 294–297, 311n3; "Theses on the Philosophy of History" (*see* Benjamin, Walter: "On the Concept of History"); "To the Planetarium," 89, 150, 153, 162n21; "Two Poems by Friedrich Hölderlin," 137n18
Bergson, Henri, 57, 89, 121–122, 136n16, 163n30
Berl, Emmanuel, 107n15
Blanqui, Auguste, 9, 104–105, 154–157, 205
Bloch, Ernst, 73n33, 94, 142n57, 145, 165–167, 170, 174–175, 176n1, 207, 214n80, 255, 268n14, 294
Blochmann, Elisabeth, 60
Blücher, Heinrich, 94
Blumenberg, Hans, 46n15
Blumenthal (Belmore), Herbert, 137n19, 218
Blumhardt, Christoph, 168
Blumhardt, Johann, 168
Bohr, Niels, 145, 158
Bolz, Norbert, 179, 196–197, 201, 208, 209n13, 210n26
book of life, 84–85, 129
Bornhausen, Karl, 176n12

Bouven, Lieven, 313n52
Brahe, Tycho, 151
Brecht, Bertolt, 12, 44n5, 95, 107n7, 186, 220, 312n50
Breton, Stanislas, 2
Breuer, Isaac, 208n1
Brod, Max, 157
Bruno, Jean, 217–218
Buber, Martin, 3, 134n3, 135n8, 136nn11, 13, 15, 169, 172–178
Buck-Morss, Susan, 4, 16n42, 22, 43n1, 44nn5, 7, 52n51, 107n10
Bulling, Kaspar, 208, 317
Burckhardt, Jacob, 206
Butler, Judith, 2, 6, 8, 12–13, 253–267, 270nn38, 44, 291–292, 305, 306n6, 309n19, 310n27, 315n57, 319

Calvinism, 170–171, 262
Cancik, Hubert, 177n19
capitalism, 13, 96, 104–105, 147–148, 229, 254–256, 262–265, 268n8, 273, 315n61
Caputo, John, 2, 312n46, 317
Cascardi, Anthony J., 46n15
Cassirer, Ernst, 92n33
Caygill, Howard, 11, 43n1, 48n27, 50n40, 51nn49–50, 52n51, 319
Clark, T. J., 107n7
Cohen, Hermann, 13, 22, 25–29, 34, 38, 42n1, 45n11, 46n16, 47nn19,21, 48n29, 53n62, 73n18, 129–132, 141nn46,48,50, 142n56, 143n65, 241–242, 254, 256–257, 260–262, 268nn6–7, 273, 294, 308n17, 309n25, 321
Cohen, Margaret, 16n44, 52n51
Copernicus, 151, 163n23, 204
Corngold, Stanley, 54n69, 142n57
Coulanges, Fustel de, 202–203, 205, 213n71
Cowan, Bainard, 54n65
Critchley, Simon, 17n53, 312n46

Deleuze, Gilles, 213n66
demiurge, 145, 152, 166, 174
Derrida, Jacques, 2, 8, 266, 314n56
Descartes, René, 240

Deubner-Mankowsky, Astrid, 12–13, 22, 25, 43n1, 45n11, 46n14, 47n19, 48n29, 51n49, 53nn58,62, 55n69, 272–273, 309n25, 319–320
Devil, 131, 159–160, 164
Dilthey, Wilhelm, 89, 203, 205
divine violence, 7–8, 12, 138n32, 231, 234–235, 240, 242–248, 250n12, 251n15, 253, 255, 257–259, 264, 266, 273, 279, 283, 287, 290–293, 307n9, 310n27
Dobbs-Weinstein, Idit, 45n10
dualism, 68, 118, 125, 131, 136n13

Eagleton, Terry, 44n5
Eddington, Arthur Stanley, 11, 145–146, 154–161, 162n3, 163n30
Eiland, Howard, 5, 11, 15n18, 44n6, 109n32, 136n15, 320
Einstein, Albert, 145, 154, 156–158
eschatology, 8, 11, 15n18, 38, 54n66, 63, 95–96, 98, 125, 129, 138n26, 205, 313
Espagne, Michel, 109n32, 225
existence (*Dasein*), 31–32, 35, 41, 50n43, 52n54, 53n57, 55n71, 59–60, 63, 250n12, 257

fascism, 11, 51n50, 97, 198, 201, 203, 206–207
Fenves, Peter, 6, 8–10, 43n1, 48n27, 51n49, 74n36, 134, 320
Finkelstein, Louis, 171
Fiorato, Pierfrancesco, 43n1, 47n19
Fittko, Lisa, 217
Foucault, Michel, 97, 309n21
Fourier, Charles, 94
France, Anatole, 258
Frank, Jakob, 164
Freud, Sigmund, 80–83, 88–89, 91nn11–13,19, 92n33, 143n61, 321
Friedlander, Eli, 7, 12–13, 14n13, 43n1, 48n27, 320
Fritsch, Matthias, 6, 14n6
Fromm, Erich, 219

Galilei, Galileo, 204
Gasché, Rodolphe, 48n27
Gehrmann, Carl, 150

George, Stefan, 53n58, 54n69, 197
Gernet, Louis, 140n40
Giacometti, Alberto, 224, 229
Gibbs, Robert, 43n1
Gifford, Adam (Lord), 145
Gnosticism, 11, 39, 102, 123, 138n32,
    145–154, 159, 161, 162n10, 173–175
Goebel, Eckart, 91n19
Goethe, Johann Wolfgang von, 41,
    54n69, 77, 84, 86–87, 135n6, 194,
    198, 234, 279
Goldberg, Oskar, 99, 108n16, 134n3
Goldstein, Moritz, 134nn3–4
Gordon, Peter E., 10
guilt (*Schuld*), 13, 88, 128, 146–147, 149,
    152, 243–245, 248n2, 249n9,
    253–254, 256–262, 265–266,
    272–273, 279–280, 282–284, 289,
    292, 294, 301, 307n12
Gundolf, Friedrich, 86, 132, 198,
    212n57
Gutkind, Erich, 134n3
Guyer, Paul, 47n23, 48n30

Ha'am, Ahad, 134n3, 135n7
Habermas, Jürgen, 12, 42n1
Haker, Hille, 13, 313n53, 314n56, 320
Hamacher, Werner, 14n11, 42, 44n4,
    46nn14–15, 54n63, 71n1, 268n7, 317
Handelman, Susan, 43n1, 48n27
Hansen, Miriam, 97, 107nn8,12
Hanssen, Beatrice, 4, 14n7, 16n42
happiness (Glück), 23, 25, 39–42, 46n14,
    53n62, 54n68, 70, 82–83, 104, 127,
    186–188, 191, 209n16, 254, 265–267,
    272, 277–281, 283–284, 295–298,
    311nn38–39
Harnack, Adolf von, 98, 102, 173–174
Hegel, Georg W. F., 35, 50n40, 71n3,
    100, 138n32, 168, 183, 192, 204–205,
    267, 280, 295
Heidegger, Martin, 59–62, 64–65, 67, 71,
    73n18, 136n16, 139n37, 181–182,
    190, 194–195, 198
Heissenbüttel, Helmut, 107n7
Henry, Michel, 2
Hering, Christoph, 52n51
Hiller, Kurt, 99, 108n20

Hobbes, Thomas, 204
Hofmannsthal, Hugo von, 78
Hölderlin, Friedrich, 132, 168, 224
holy, 7, 10, 68–70, 113, 119, 136n10, 165,
    251, 303. *See also* sacred
Holz, Hans Heinz, 205
Honneth, Axel, 21, 42n1
Horkheimer, Max, 1, 4, 14n13, 95,
    213n64, 219–221, 304, 315n61
Huizinga, Johan, 206
hunchbacked dwarf, 3–4, 106n1, 183
Husserl, Edmund, 70, 72n5, 74n36

Jacobson, Eric, 16n44, 21–22, 43n1,
    45n10, 317
James, William, 57, 302
Jankelevitch, Vladimir, 313n54
Jay, Martin, 45n12, 51n50, 53n58
Jennings, Michael W., 5, 8, 10–12, 15n18,
    106n6, 108n24, 109nn30, 32, 34,
    136n15, 313n50, 321
Jesus Christ, 62, 71n3, 103, 120, 125,
    138n32, 171, 174, 300–303,
    313nn53–54, 316n62
Joachim of Fiore, 138n32, 166
Jonas, Hans, 145, 147, 162n10
Josephus, 170–171
Judgment Day, 140n43, 188–189, 191,
    213n64, 282, 293, 300, 302, 313n54
Jung, Carl, 198, 219

Kafka, Franz, 11, 128, 146, 154–155,
    157–158, 160–161, 280–283
Kant, Immanuel, 24, 26–35, 37–38,
    43n1, 46n16, 47nn19,21,23,
    49nn35–36, 50n40, 66, 76, 78–79,
    89, 18, 131, 151–152, 183, 241–242,
    287, 295, 309n21
Karo, Joseph, 164
Kaufmann, David, 45n9
Kautsky, Karl, 184
Keller, Gottfried, 196, 206
Kepler, Johannes, 151, 158
Kierkegaard, Søren, 57, 65–67, 118, 129,
    135n9
Kingdom of God, 62, 126, 130, 192, 265,
    294–295, 300, 302, 310n31, 313n53,
    314n57

Perspectives in Continental Philosophy

John D. Caputo, series editor

Karl Jaspers, *The Question of German Guilt.* Introduction by Joseph W. Koterski, S.J.

Jean-Luc Marion, *The Idol and Distance: Five Studies.* Translated with an introduction by Thomas A. Carlson.

Jeffrey Dudiak, *The Intrigue of Ethics: A Reading of the Idea of Discourse in the Thought of Emmanuel Levinas.*

Robyn Horner, *Rethinking God as Gift: Marion, Derrida, and the Limits of Phenomenology.*

Mark Dooley, *The Politics of Exodus: Søren Kierkegaard's Ethics of Responsibility.*

Merold Westphal, *Overcoming Onto-Theology: Toward a Postmodern Christian Faith.*

Edith Wyschogrod, Jean-Joseph Goux, and Eric Boynton, eds., *The Enigma of Gift and Sacrifice.*

Stanislas Breton, *The Word and the Cross.* Translated with an introduction by Jacquelyn Porter.

Jean-Luc Marion, *Prolegomena to Charity.* Translated by Stephen E. Lewis.

Peter H. Spader, *Scheler's Ethical Personalism: Its Logic, Development, and Promise.*

Jean-Louis Chrétien, *The Unforgettable and the Unhoped For.* Translated by Jeffrey Bloechl.

Don Cupitt, *Is Nothing Sacred? The Non-Realist Philosophy of Religion: Selected Essays.*

Jean-Luc Marion, *In Excess: Studies of Saturated Phenomena.* Translated by Robyn Horner and Vincent Berraud.

Phillip Goodchild, *Rethinking Philosophy of Religion: Approaches from Continental Philosophy.*

William J. Richardson, S.J., *Heidegger: Through Phenomenology to Thought.*

Jeffrey Andrew Barash, *Martin Heidegger and the Problem of Historical Meaning.*

Jean-Louis Chrétien, *Hand to Hand: Listening to the Work of Art.* Translated by Stephen E. Lewis.

Jean-Louis Chrétien, *The Call and the Response.* Translated with an introduction by Anne Davenport.

D. C. Schindler, *Han Urs von Balthasar and the Dramatic Structure of Truth: A Philosophical Investigation.*

Julian Wolfreys, ed., *Thinking Difference: Critics in Conversation.*

Allen Scult, *Being Jewish/Reading Heidegger: An Ontological Encounter.*

Richard Kearney, *Debates in Continental Philosophy: Conversations with Contemporary Thinkers.*

Jennifer Anna Gosetti-Ferencei, *Heidegger, Hölderlin, and the Subject of Poetic Language: Toward a New Poetics of Dasein.*

Jolita Pons, *Stealing a Gift: Kierkegaard's Pseudonyms and the Bible.*

Jean-Yves Lacoste, *Experience and the Absolute: Disputed Questions on the Humanity of Man.* Translated by Mark Raftery-Skehan.

Charles P. Bigger, *Between* Chora *and the Good: Metaphor's Metaphysical Neighborhood.*

Dominique Janicaud, *Phenomenology "Wide Open": After the French Debate.* Translated by Charles N. Cabral.

Ian Leask and Eoin Cassidy, eds., *Givenness and God: Questions of Jean-Luc Marion.*

Jacques Derrida, *Sovereignties in Question: The Poetics of Paul Celan.* Edited by Thomas Dutoit and Outi Pasanen.

William Desmond, *Is There a Sabbath for Thought? Between Religion and Philosophy.*

Bruce Ellis Benson and Norman Wirzba, eds., *The Phenomenology of Prayer.*

S. Clark Buckner and Matthew Statler, eds., *Styles of Piety: Practicing Philosophy after the Death of God.*

Kevin Hart and Barbara Wall, eds., *The Experience of God: A Postmodern Response.*

John Panteleimon Manoussakis, *After God: Richard Kearney and the Religious Turn in Continental Philosophy.*

John Martis, *Philippe Lacoue-Labarthe: Representation and the Loss of the Subject.*

Jean-Luc Nancy, *The Ground of the Image.*

Edith Wyschogrod, *Crossover Queries: Dwelling with Negatives, Embodying Philosophy's Others.*

Gerald Bruns, *On the Anarchy of Poetry and Philosophy: A Guide for the Unruly.*

Brian Treanor, *Aspects of Alterity: Levinas, Marcel, and the Contemporary Debate.*

Simon Morgan Wortham, *Counter-Institutions: Jacques Derrida and the Question of the University.*

Leonard Lawlor, *The Implications of Immanence: Toward a New Concept of Life.*

Clayton Crockett, *Interstices of the Sublime: Theology and Psychoanalytic Theory.*

Bettina Bergo, Joseph Cohen, and Raphael Zagury-Orly, eds., *Judeities: Questions for Jacques Derrida.* Translated by Bettina Bergo and Michael B. Smith.

Jean-Luc Marion, *On the Ego and on God: Further Cartesian Questions.* Translated by Christina M. Gschwandtner.

Jean-Luc Nancy, *Philosophical Chronicles.* Translated by Franson Manjali.

Jean-Luc Nancy, *Dis-Enclosure: The Deconstruction of Christianity.* Translated by Bettina Bergo, Gabriel Malenfant, and Michael B. Smith.

Andrea Hurst, *Derrida Vis-à-vis Lacan: Interweaving Deconstruction and Psychoanalysis.*

Jean-Luc Nancy, *Noli me tangere: On the Raising of the Body.* Translated by Sarah Clift, Pascale-Anne Brault, and Michael Naas.

Jacques Derrida, *The Animal That Therefore I Am.* Edited by Marie-Louise Mallet, translated by David Wills.

Jean-Luc Marion, *The Visible and the Revealed.* Translated by Christina M. Gschwandtner and others.

Michel Henry, *Material Phenomenology.* Translated by Scott Davidson.

Jean-Luc Nancy, *Corpus*. Translated by Richard A. Rand.

Joshua Kates, *Fielding Derrida*.

Michael Naas, *Derrida From Now On*.

Shannon Sullivan and Dennis J. Schmidt, eds., *Difficulties of Ethical Life*.

Catherine Malabou, *What Should We Do with Our Brain?* Translated by
Sebastian Rand, Introduction by Marc Jeannerod.

Claude Romano, *Event and World*. Translated by Shane Mackinlay.

Vanessa Lemm, *Nietzsche's Animal Philosophy: Culture, Politics, and the Animality
of the Human Being*.

B. Keith Putt, ed., *Gazing Through a Prism Darkly: Reflections on Merold
Westphal's Hermeneutical Epistemology*.

Eric Boynton and Martin Kavka, eds., *Saintly Influence: Edith Wyschogrod and
the Possibilities of Philosophy of Religion*.

Shane Mackinlay, *Interpreting Excess: Jean-Luc Marion, Saturated Phenomena,
and Hermeneutics*.

Kevin Hart and Michael A. Signer, eds., *The Exorbitant: Emmanuel Levinas
Between Jews and Christians*.

Bruce Ellis Benson and Norman Wirzba, eds., *Words of Life: New Theological
Turns in French Phenomenology*.

William Robert, *Trials: Of Antigone and Jesus*.

Brian Treanor and Henry Isaac Venema, eds., *A Passion for the Possible:
Thinking with Paul Ricoeur*.

Kas Saghafi, *Apparitions—Of Derrida's Other*.

Nick Mansfield, *The God Who Deconstructs Himself: Sovereignty and Subjectivity
Between Freud, Bataille, and Derrida*.

Don Ihde, *Heidegger's Technologies: Postphenomenological Perspectives*.

Suzi Adams, *Castoriadis's Ontology: Being and Creation*.

Richard Kearney and Kascha Semonovitch, eds., *Phenomenologies of the
Stranger: Between Hostility and Hospitality*.

Michael Naas, *Miracle and Machine: Jacques Derrida and the Two Sources of
Religion, Science, and the Media*.

Alena Alexandrova, Ignaas Devisch, Laurens ten Kate, and Aukje van Rooden,
Re-treating Religion: Deconstructing Christianity with Jean-Luc Nancy.
Preamble by Jean-Luc Nancy.

Emmanuel Falque, *The Metamorphosis of Finitude: An Essay on Birth and
Resurrection*. Translated by George Hughes.

Scott M. Campbell, *The Early Heidegger's Philosophy of Life: Facticity, Being, and
Language*.

Françoise Dastur, *How Are We to Confront Death? An Introduction to Philosophy*.
Translated by Robert Vallier. Foreword by David Farrell Krell.

Christina M. Gschwandtner, *Postmodern Apologetics? Arguments for God in
Contemporary Philosophy*.

Ben Morgan, *On Becoming God: Late Medieval Mysticism and the Modern
Western Self*.

Neal DeRoo, *Futurity in Phenomenology: Promise and Method in Husserl, Levinas, and Derrida.*

Sarah LaChance Adams and Caroline R. Lundquist, eds., *Coming to Life: Philosophies of Pregnancy, Childbirth, and Mothering.*

Thomas Claviez, ed., *The Conditions of Hospitality: Ethics, Politics, and Aesthetics on the Threshold of the Possible.*

Roland Faber and Jeremy Fackenthal, eds., *Theopoetic Folds: Philosophizing Multifariousness.*

Jean-Luc Marion, *The Essential Writings.* Edited by Kevin Hart.

Adam S. Miller, *Speculative Grace: Bruno Latour and Object-Oriented Theology.* Foreword by Levi R. Bryant.

Jean-Luc Nancy, *Corpus II: Writings on Sexuality.*

David Nowell Smith, *Sounding/Silence: Martin Heidegger at the Limits of Poetics.*

Gregory C. Stallings, Manuel Asensi, and Carl Good, eds., *Material Spirit: Religion and Literature Intranscendent.*

Claude Romano, *Event and Time.* Translated by Stephen E. Lewis.

Frank Chouraqui, *Ambiguity and the Absolute: Nietzsche and Merleau-Ponty on the Question of Truth.*

Noëlle Vahanian, *The Rebellious No: Variations on a Secular Theology of Language.*

Michael Naas, *The End of the World and Other Teachable Moments: Jacques Derrida's Final Seminar.*

Jean-Louis Chrétien, *Under the Gaze of the Bible.* Translated by John Marson Dunaway.

Edward Baring and Peter E. Gordon, eds., *The Trace of God: Derrida and Religion.*

Vanessa Lemm, ed., *Nietzsche and the Becoming of Life.*

Aaron T. Looney, *Vladimir Jankélévitch: The Time of Forgiveness.*

Richard Kearney and Brian Treanor, eds., *Carnal Hermeneutics.*

Tarek R. Dika and W. Chris Hackett, *Quiet Powers of the Possible: Interviews in Contemporary French Phenomenology.* Foreword by Richard Kearney.

Jeremy Biles and Kent L. Brintnall, eds., *Negative Ecstasies: Georges Bataille and the Study of Religion.*

Claude Romano, *There Is: The Event and the Finitude of Appearing.* Translated by Michael B. Smith.

William S. Allen, *Aesthetics of Negativity: Blanchot, Adorno, and Autonomy.*

Don Ihde, *Husserl's Missing Technologies.*

Colby Dickinson and Stéphane Symons, eds., *Walter Benjamin and Theology.*